Fundamentals of Dependable Computing

for Software Engineers

Chapman & Hall/CRC Innovations in Software Engineering and Software Development

Series Editor
Richard LeBlanc
Chair, Department of Computer Science and Software Engineering, Seattle University

AIMS AND SCOPE

This series covers all aspects of software engineering and software development. Books in the series will be innovative reference books, research monographs, and textbooks at the undergraduate and graduate level. Coverage will include traditional subject matter, cutting-edge research, and current industry practice, such as agile software development methods and service-oriented architectures. We also welcome proposals for books that capture the latest results on the domains and conditions in which practices are most effective.

PUBLISHED TITLES

Software Development: An Open Source Approach
Allen Tucker, Ralph Morelli, and Chamindra de Silva

Building Enterprise Systems with ODP: An Introduction to Open Distributed Processing
Peter F. Linington, Zoran Milosevic, Akira Tanaka, and Antonio Vallecillo

Software Engineering: The Current Practice
Václav Rajlich

Fundamentals of Dependable Computing for Software Engineers
John Knight

CHAPMAN & HALL/CRC INNOVATIONS IN
SOFTWARE ENGINEERING AND SOFTWARE DEVELOPMENT

Fundamentals of Dependable Computing
for Software Engineers

John Knight

With Foreword by Brian Randell

 CRC Press
Taylor & Francis Group
Boca Raton   London   New York

CRC Press is an imprint of the
Taylor & Francis Group an **informa** business
A CHAPMAN & HALL BOOK

CRC Press
Taylor & Francis Group
6000 Broken Sound Parkway NW, Suite 300
Boca Raton, FL 33487-2742

© 2012 by Taylor & Francis Group, LLC
CRC Press is an imprint of Taylor & Francis Group, an Informa business

No claim to original U.S. Government works

Printed in the United States of America on acid-free paper
Version Date: 20111129

International Standard Book Number: 978-1-4398-6255-1 (Paperback)

Table of Contents

Foreword

As computer systems have permeated ever more aspects of daily and communal life, so individuals', organizations' and society's dependency on the satisfactory functioning of these systems has become ever greater. This dependency can take many forms. It can arise, for example, from (i) the cost to a manufacturer of recalling a mass-market product of inadequate reliability, (ii) the dangers to life and limb from unsafe actions that are caused by, or fail to be prevented by, a computer system, or (iii) the reputational or financial consequence of failure to protect highly-confidential information.

Computer systems can be employed in many different situations and can fail in many different ways. A system will be judged to be dependable if its failures are neither too frequent, nor too severe. Quite what constitutes failure, and acceptable levels of failure frequency and failure severity, will vary according to the situation and circumstances. And different stakeholders, such as users, operators and system owners may judge these differently.

Just as computer systems can fail in many different ways, so there are many different possible causes of computer system failure, i.e. faults, of various different types. In particular there are hardware operational faults due to component ageing, residual software (and hardware) design faults, and deliberate (or perhaps just accidental) acts by users that trigger little-known vulnerabilities. Moreover, faults in one system may well be the result of failures in some other system, i.e. (i) another system that it is interacting with, (ii) a component sub-system, or (iii) a system that created or modified it. Issues of system boundaries and their careful identification are therefore crucial. Indeed, one cannot expect to achieve high system dependability in systems where the engineers involved do not have a detailed understanding of system boundaries and specifications.

Achieving, and — equally importantly — being able to justify claims of, adequate system dependability from ever more sophisticated computer-based systems is thus a continuing challenge. Unmastered complexity breeds confusion and confusion breeds undependability. Hence as John Knight, the author of this book, rightly emphasizes, the importance of clear concepts and carefully-defined terminology. The concepts and terminology that he describes, and uses carefully throughout this book, are appropriate for all types of system, e.g. (i) a "programmable" washing machine, (ii) a mobile phone incorporating a sophisticated operating system, (iii) a distributed database system supporting the work of a large software design team, and (iv) a global banking system comprising large numbers of computers, networks and banking personnel.

Conceptually, the dependability issues arising in all these different types of system, and from the various types of fault, are in fact very similar — how and to what extent can one: (i) avoid introducing faults into a system, (ii) find and remove faults that nevertheless exist in the system, (iii) provide acceptable service despite any remaining faults, and (iv) estimate the effectiveness of these various measures. This similarity may however be masked by the use of differing terminology by the different technical communities involved. However terminological differences matter little if there is a common understanding of an adequate set of basic concepts, applying to all types of system, all types of system failure, and all the different possible causes of system failure.

One of the biggest fundamental causes of failure in computer-based systems is their complexity, much of which will for good technical reasons reside in the software. Thus many of the challenges facing those responsible for a computer system's dependability concern software, and hence software engineering. Hence a major strength of this book is the systematic way in which it identifies and discusses the many contributions that good software engineering can make to the task of achieving overall system dependability and the various challenges involved in ensuring that the software itself is adequately dependable.

This book takes full advantage of the extensive work that has been undertaken over many years on the creation of a rich set of system dependability concepts. John Knight makes excellent use of these concepts in producing a very well-argued and comprehensive account, aimed squarely at software engineers, of the variety of dependability issues they are likely to find in real systems and of the strategies that they should use to address these issues. Appropriately qualified students who study this book thoroughly, and computer professionals seeking a greater understanding of the various dependability-related problems that they have encountered already in their careers, should gain much from this book. I therefore take great pleasure in enthusiastically recommending it to both classes of reader.

Brian Randell
Newcastle University
31 July 2011

Preface

We depend on computer systems for much of what we do, and our dependence is greater than most of us realize. Without computers working correctly, our lives would be changed dramatically and mostly for the worse. The spectrum of services that computers help to provide is very diverse and includes banking, education, transportation, energy production, telecommunications, health care, defense, farming, manufacturing, business operations, and entertainment. A passenger railway system, for example, might be prevented from providing service because of a computer problem just as service might be prevented by a loss of power, damage to the track or rolling stock, seriously inclement weather, or lack of a crew.

This book is about computer system dependability, more specifically, those aspects of the subject that are important to the software engineer. The material is suitable for a senior undergraduate course or a first-year graduate course in computer science or computer engineering. The material is also suitable for self study, and the practicing engineer can tackle the subject matter directly.

The book has a single pedagogical goal:

To present software and computer engineers with a comprehensive dependability engineering process in which the reasons for and the interrelationships between the various parts are clear and justified.

Many techniques are introduced, although not in great depth. The book does not cover any specific techniques in depth *except* the process. The intent is to summarize the important topics in sufficient depth that the reader can understand their form and role and have the background to pursue these topics if they wish. With the process clear, the reader will be able to study specific topics in depth and determine the extent to which they apply to his or her engineering activities.

To meet the book's goal, four major items of material are covered:

- Sufficient information about the systems engineering aspects of dependability that the software engineer can (a) understand fully why the software is being asked to do what it is being asked to do and (b) understand why the software is being made to operate on the particular platform specified by the system designers.

- A definitional and conceptual framework within which the engineer can reason and make decisions about software and that software's dependability.

- A comprehensive approach to achieving software dependability.
- A bibliography of the most relevant literature.

Why read this book?

Why should a student or a practicing engineer study this material? There is plenty of technology to study, so how does this fit in? The answers to these questions can be found in the title. The dependability of computer systems is as important as the functionality of the systems, perhaps even more important. Less functionality than expected or planned is often tolerable. But a system that fails at an unacceptable rate is usually intolerable. Unless we take action to prevent them, failures will occur, and, if they occur at a rate that is unacceptable, the associated systems might have to be taken out of service. Practicing engineers and students of engineering (engineers in training) need to master the essential elements of computer system dependability so as to help them to make appropriate engineering decisions. Arguably, studying this material is essential.

The things that you will learn from this book are concerned with the actions needed to reduce the probability of failures to an acceptable level, if that is possible. Specifically, you will learn:

- Why dependability matters.
- What it means for a system to be dependable.
- How to build a dependable system.
- How to assess whether a system is adequately dependable.

In order to be able to master this material, the following background is assumed:

- Experience with high-level language programming in a language like C, C++, C#, or Java.
- A basic knowledge of computer organization including the operation of processors, memories, disk storage systems, and basic communication facilities.
- Exposure to elementary probability theory.
- A working knowledge of discrete mathematics, including propositional calculus, predicate calculus, basic functions, and set theory.
- An understanding of the basic principles of operating systems, including processor management, memory management, peripheral management, and the operation of user interfaces.
- A good knowledge of the principles of software engineering, including requirements analysis, specification, design, testing, documentation and software development processes.

The emphasis in this book is on the software engineering elements of the problem. Thus, the intent is to help software engineers meet the challenge of constructing software systems that are sufficiently dependable, and within budget and time constraints.

How to use this book

Computing system dependability should be part of any degree program in computer science or computer engineering. A course on the fundamental elements of the topic should be the minimum, with more elaborate optional courses in topics such as formal methods, mathematical modeling, dependable computing architecture, and advanced software engineering building on the fundamentals as determined by the goals of the degree program.

This book can form the basis of a one-semester introductory course, and the bulk of the material can be covered in one semester. The material should be presented in the same order as in this book, because later material depends critically on earlier material. The overall development that students should see and with which they should become familiar is:

- What dependability is and why dependability is important.

- The substantial but essential conceptual and definitional structure of the subject.

- The computing platforms upon which critical applications operate and how these platforms affect software.

- The difficulties that arise in software engineering that lead to software failures.

- The mathematically based techniques that can improve the quality of software dramatically and that are becoming available even for large software systems.

For a practicing engineer, the book can be treated as a reference. Topics can be studied in any order provided that for each topic of interest the reader is familiar with the preceding material. My experience in discussing dependability with engineers in industry is that they tend to lack adequate backgrounds in much of the material covered. Starting at the beginning to make sure of things like the definitional structure of the field is generally worthwhile.

The organization of this book

This book is organized into 12 chapters, and the reader is encouraged to work through the chapters in order. Each chapter develops the material from the previous chapters and relies upon their content. Chapter 1 introduces the topic and motivates the study of dependability. The terminology of dependability is presented in Chapter 2, and Chapter 3 introduces the different fault types and the approaches to dealing with faults.

Chapter 4 discusses how to identify the faults to which a system is subject, and Chapter 5 examines the four basic mechanisms for dealing with faults, *avoidance*, *removal*, *tolerance*, and *forecasting*, along with a discussion of dealing with Byzantine faults. Chapter 6 summarizes the issues with degradation faults, a type of fault that arises only in hardware, and Chapter 7 surveys the general issues surrounding software dependability. Chapter 8 and Chapter 9 discuss important topics in software fault avoidance.

Chapter 10 is about software fault elimination, and Chapter 11 is about software fault tolerance. Finally, Chapter 12 examines dependability assessment.

Those to whom I am grateful

I am pleased to have this opportunity to thank many people who were influential in the creation of this book. Brian Randell from the University of Newcastle upon Tyne, who kindly wrote the Foreword, taught me an immense amount over many years in many ways about many things. Premkumar Devanbu of the University of California, Davis, started me down the path of assembling this material when he asked me to present a summary lecture on dependability at the 2001 International Conference on Software Engineering. And Dieter Rombach of the University of Kaiserlauten got me started on organizing this material when he asked me to help with a distance learning class on dependability.

The origins of the detailed material in this book are classes that I have taught at the University of Virginia. I am deeply indebted to the dozens of students who attended those classes, put up with my lecture style, asked me thought-provoking questions, and taught me an immense amount. Thanks to all of you; you know who you are.

I benefited greatly from reviews of the manuscript by M. Anthony Aiello, Tom Anderson, Josh Dehlinger, Michael Holloway, Rich LeBlanc, and Brian Randell. Their combined comments were truly transformative. I also benefited greatly from numerous discussions with Patrick Graydon.

None of this would have happened without the help of many people at the publisher, Taylor & Francis. In particular, I thank Alan Apt and Randi Cohen.

Finally, I owe an immense debt of gratitude to my family — my children, Richard, Abby, and Katie, and my wife Virginia — for the lost weekends and evenings that I have spent writing this book.

Further information

Slides based on the material in this textbook and solutions to exercises are available to instructors at institutes of higher education. Details and further information about this textbook are provided at the following address:

```
http://www.dependablecomputing.com/fundamentals.html
```

John Knight
Charlottesville, Virginia

CHAPTER 1

Introduction

> *The dependability of a system is the ability to avoid service failures*
> *that are more frequent and more severe than is acceptable.*
>
> *Algirdas Avižienis, Jean-Claude Laprie,*
> *Brian Randell, and Carl Landwehr*

1.1 The Elements of Dependability

1.1.1 A Cautionary Tale

Imagine that you are an expert in *making chains*, and that you are working on a project to suspend a box containing delicate porcelain high above ground. If the chain, the box, the hook that attaches the chain to the box, or the hook that attaches the chain to the ceiling breaks, the box will fall and hit the ground. Clearly, serious damage to the porcelain will probably result. Everybody involved with the porcelain (the owner of the porcelain, the expert in boxes, the expert in hooks, you, etc.) would like to prevent that.

You are a well-educated chain engineer with a degree from a prestigious academic institution. You have had classes in all sorts of chain-engineering techniques, and so you expect to proceed using the education you have. But, before work starts on the project, you become anxious about the following concern:

Concern 1: If chain failure could cause a lot of damage, everything possible has to be done to prevent failure. Porcelain is delicate and expensive. You wonder whether you know all the available techniques that could prevent damage.

FIGURE 1.1 Delicate porcelain in the museum at the Meissen porcelain factory in Meissen, Germany.

If the porcelain is mass produced, the owner might not care if the chain breaks. At least, in that case, the owner might not want to pay for you and other experts to engineer the chain, the box, and the hooks really well. If the box contains antique Meissen porcelain, such as the porcelain shown in Figure 1.1, the owner would want very high levels of assurance that the chain, the box, and the hooks will not break except under the most dire circumstances. Unfortunately, the owner tells you that the porcelain to be suspended is indeed a rare and expensive piece.

As you start to work on the project, you determine quickly that you need to know *exactly* how strong the chain has to be. Suppose the chain you built was not strong enough, what would happen? These thoughts raise a second concern:

Concern 2: Defining the necessary strength of the chain is crucial so that you have a target for the engineering you will undertake on the chain. You cannot make that determination yourself because the definition is really set by the systems engineer in charge of the suspended-box project.

You ask the porcelain's owner how strong the chain needs to be. The owner of the porcelain just says that the chain has to be "unbreakable". You ask the other engineers working with you. None of them understands the question well enough to be able to give you a complete answer. The engineers tell you:

> *"Use the International Standards Organization chain standard
> for boxes that hold expensive porcelain high above ground."*

But that standard focuses on chain documentation, color, and the shape of the links. Would following the standard ensure that the chain you make will be strong enough?

In order to get this dilemma sorted out, you realize that you need to be able to communicate effectively with others so as to get an engineering answer to your questions. A third concern begins to bother you:

Concern 3: An accurate and complete set of definitions of terms is necessary so that you can communicate reliably with other engineers. You do not have such a set of definitions.

With a set of terms, you will be able to communicate with other chain engineers, metallurgists, experts in box and hook structures, inspectors from the Federal Porcelain Administration (the FPA), physicists who can model potential and kinetic energy, porcelain engineers, and the owner of the porcelain.

As an expert in chains, you know that a chain is only as strong as its weakest link, and this obvious but important fact guides your work with the chain. To protect the porcelain, you search for defects in the chain, focusing your attention on a search for the weakest link. Suddenly, a fourth concern occurs to you:

Concern 4: You need a comprehensive technology that will allow you to find *all* the links in the chain that are not strong enough, and you must have a mechanism for dealing with *all* of the weak links, *not* just the weakest link and *not* just the obvious weak links.

You wonder whether you could estimate how strong the chain is and find ways to strengthen it. You suspect that there are several techniques for dealing with links in the chain that might break, but you did not take the course *"Dealing With Weak Links in a Chain"* when you were in college.

Thinking about the problem of weak links, you decide that you might ensure that the chain is manufactured carefully, and you might examine and test the chain. If you miss a weak link, you think that you might install a second chain in parallel with the first just in case the first chain breaks, you might place a cushion under the box of porcelain to protect the porcelain if the chain breaks, or you might wrap the porcelain carefully to protect it from shock. Other experts would examine the box and the hooks.

Somewhat in a state of shock, a fifth and final concern occurs to you:

Concern 5: You need to know just how effective all the techniques for dealing with weak links in the chain will be. Even if you deal with a weak link in a sensible way, you might not have eliminated the problem.

Because you are a well-educated chain engineer, you proceed using the education you have and you mostly ignore the concerns that have occurred to you. The

chain and all the other elements of the system are built, and the porcelain is suspended in the box. The owner of the porcelain is delighted.

And then there is an enormous crash as the porcelain breaks into thousands of
pieces. The chain broke. One link in the chain was not strong enough.

You wake up and realize that all this was just a nightmare. You remember you
are not a chain engineer. Phew! You are a *software* engineer. But you remain in a
cold sweat, because you realize that the porcelain could have been the computer system you are working on and the "crash" might have been caused by *your* software
— a really frightening thought.

1.1.2 Why Dependability?

From this story you should get some idea of what we can be faced with in engineering a computer system that has to be dependable. The reason we need dependability
of anything, including computer systems, is because the *consequences of failure* are
high. We need precise definitions of how dependable our computer systems have to
be. We cannot make these systems perfect. We need definitions of terms so that all
stakeholders can communicate properly.

In order to get dependability, we are faced with a wide range of engineering
issues that must be addressed systematically and comprehensively. If we miss something — anything (a weak link in the chain) — the system might fail, and nobody
will care how good the rest of the system was. We have to know just how good our
systems have to be so that we can adopt appropriate engineering techniques. And so
on.

This book is about *dependability* of computer systems, and the "cautionary tale"
of Section 1.1.1 basically lays out this entire book. The way in which we achieve
dependability is through a rigorous series of engineering steps with which many
engineers are unfamiliar. Having a strong academic background does not necessarily
qualify one for addressing the issue of dependability. This book brings together the
fundamentals of dependability for software engineers, hence the name. By studying
the fundamentals, the software engineer can make decisions about appropriate engineering for any specific system. Importantly, the software engineer can also determine when the available technology or the planned technology for a given system is
not adequate to meet the dependability goals.

Examining the computer systems upon which we depend and engineering these
systems to provide an acceptable level of service are important. Most people have
experienced the frustration of their desktop or laptop computer "locking up", their
hard drive failing with no recent backup, or their computer coming to a halt when
the power fails. These examples are of familiar systems and incidents that we would
like to prevent, because they cause us inconvenience, often considerable inconvenience. But there are many major systems where failures are much more than an
inconvenience, and we look at some examples in Section 1.4.

As in the cautionary tale where the chain engineer was "a well-educated chain engineer with a degree from a prestigious academic institution", most software and computer engineers are well educated in the main issues that they face in their professions. Typically, however, the major issues of dependability are unfamiliar to computer and software engineers.

1.2 The Role of the Software Engineer

Why should a software engineer be concerned about dependability in the depth that the subject is covered in this book? Surely software engineers just write software? There are four important reasons why software is closely involved with everything to do with system dependability:

- **Software should perform the required function.**
  If software performs something other than the required function, then a system failure could ensue with possibly serious consequences. No matter how well implemented a software system is, that system has to meet the requirements. Determining the requirements for software is difficult and usually not within the realm of expertise of other engineering disciplines. The software engineer has to help the entire engineering team with this task.

- **Software should perform the required function** *correctly.*
  If software performs the required function incorrectly, then, again, a system failure could ensue with possibly serious consequences. The software engineer has to choose implementation techniques that will increase the chances that the software implementation will be correct.

- **The software might have to operate on a target platform whose design was influenced by the system's dependability goals.**
  Target platforms often include elements that are not necessary for basic functionality in order to meet dependability goals for the platform itself. Many systems use replicated processors, disks, communications facilities, and so on in order to be able to avoid certain types of fault. Software engineers need to be aware of why the target was designed the way it was. The target platform design is very likely to affect the software design, and software is usually involved in the operation of these replicated resources.

- **Software often needs to take action when a hardware component fails.**
  Software usually contributes significantly to the engineering that provides overall system dependability and to the management of the system following some types of failure. Many things can be done to help avoid or recover from system failures if sufficient care is taken in system design. In almost all cases, software is at the heart of these mechanisms, and so software requirements actually derive

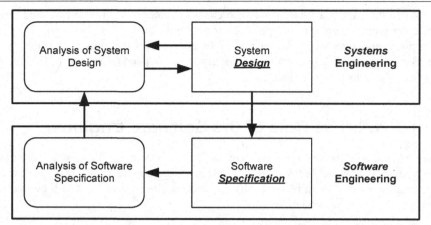

FIGURE 1.2 The interaction between systems and software engineering. System designers develop and analyze their design, and from that determine what the software has to do. When analyzing the software specification, software engineers might need to influence the system design and thereby the software specification because of practical concerns for the software raised by the specification.

from the need to meet certain dependability goals. A simple example is to monitor the input coming from system operators and to inhibit response to inappropriate or erroneous commands. This type of dependability enhancement imposes a requirement that the software has to meet.

These four reasons are a manifestation of the interaction between systems engineering and software engineering. The interaction is illustrated in Figure 1.2. Systems engineers are responsible for the system design, and they use a variety of analyses to model the dependability of their designs. These analyses include fault tree analysis (FTA), Failure Modes Effects and Criticality Analysis (FMECA), and Hazard and Operability Analysis (HazOp). Eventually a system design is created, and the software *specification* derives from that system *design*.

The interaction is not just in the direction from systems engineers to software engineers. A software system is a complex entity that has characteristics and limitations of its own. As a result, information from software engineers needs to be made available to and discussed with systems engineers if the entire system is to perform as desired. Changes to the design of a system might be needed to accommodate software limitations.

Clearly, software is an important component of the systems with which we are concerned. The software engineer has to be prepared to build software that often goes well beyond that needed for primary functionality. The software engineer is far more capable of creating software that meets its objectives if he or she understands something of the systems engineering context and the systems engineer's tools and techniques. In some cases, those techniques can be adapted usefully and easily to support software engineering.

Two important factors in understanding the role of the software engineer in dependability are the following:

- The software in systems that need high levels of dependability has become involved in far more of the systems' functionality than was the case in the past.

- Software defects have become common causal factors in failures. We have to engineer software carefully if that software is to provide the level of service that modern systems require.

The second of these factors is related, at least in part, to the first. But the crucial point is that the software engineer now plays a much more central role in systems dependability than was the case in the past. As a result, the software engineer needs to understand why the system is asking the software to undertake functionality that is sometimes non-obvious, why the target platform is what it is, and how to achieve the high levels of software dependability that are required.

1.3 Our Dependence on Computers

Whether we like it or not, we depend on computer systems for much of what we do. Without them, our lives would be changed dramatically and mostly for the worse. The spectrum of services that they help to provide is very diverse and includes:

Banking and financial services. Computers keep track of bank accounts, transmit money between banks, even between banks in different countries, provide financial services such as ATMs and credit cards, operate markets and exchanges, and engage in financial transactions on behalf of their owners.

Transportation. Commercial aircraft employ extensive computer systems on-board, and the air-traffic-control system employs computers in a variety of ways. Cars depend on computers for engine management, anti-lock brakes, traction control, and in-car entertainment systems. Passenger rail systems rely on computers for a variety of services, including, in the most sophisticated system, actually operating the train.

Energy production. Computers help control energy production equipment such as electrical generators, help control gas and oil pipelines, manage electrical transmission lines, and control energy systems when demand changes because of weather.

Telecommunications. All of the telecommunications systems that we use, from traditional wired telephone service in our homes to mobile service using smart telephones and iPads, are really just elaborate distributed computing systems.

Health care. Many health care services depend upon computers, including the various forms of imagery, and devices such as drug-infusion pumps, surgical robots, and radiation therapy machines. Information systems play a central role in health care also in areas such as patient records, drug inventories, and facility planning.

Defense. Defense employs extensive computer systems in command and control, in weapons management, within complex systems such as aircraft, ships, and missiles, and in supply-chain management.

Manufacturing. Manufacturing operations rely on computers for robotic production lines, supply-chain management, resource and personnel management, scheduling, inventory management, financial and accounting activities, and parts scheduling.

Business operations. Businesses rely on computers for inventory management, accounting, advertising, customer services, billing, and point-of-sale services.

Entertainment. By definition, computer games use computers. But multi-player games communicate via computer networks, and movies are beginning to be created and presented digitally.

In some cases we receive service without realizing that computers are at the heart of providing that service. Most people are unaware, for example, of how many computers are embedded in appliances in their homes and in their cars. There are computers in thermostats, kitchen appliances, televisions, and so on. These computers do not look like the ones we see on our desks at work, but they are powerful computers nonetheless. These computers are called *embedded* because they are integrated within other equipment. Every such computer has a processor, main memory, and I/O devices. Some are connected to a network, and some have peripherals such as specialized displays and keyboards that allow them to communicate with humans.

Just as with home appliances and cars, most people are unaware of how many computers and networks are involved in authorizing a credit card purchase or processing a check for payment. Even an action as simple as using a credit card at a service station to purchase gasoline requires the actions of dozens of computers and several private networks. The gasoline pump contains a computer that is connected to a private data network which communicates with the bank that issued the credit card. That bank's computers then check for the possibility of fraudulent use and check the card holder's account. Finally, if the transaction does not appear fraudulent and the card holder has the necessary credit, the transaction is authorized and a message to that effect is sent back to the gasoline pump. And all of this is done in a few seconds.

The credit card and check processing systems are examples of national networked infrastructure systems. Another important national infrastructure in the United States. is the freight-rail system, a technology much older than cars and much more complex. Normally all we see are locomotives and freight cars, and we usually notice them only when we are stopped at a railway crossing. But the movement of freight by rail with modern levels of efficiency and performance would not be possible without a wide range of computers helping to track payloads, operate locomotives, schedule train operation, and optimize overall system performance. Much of this activity relies upon track-side equipment that regularly reports the location of individual freight cars to centralized databases. Importantly, computers help to watch over the system to ensure safe operation.

A careful examination reveals that the computer systems underlying the provision of modern services span a wide spectrum of system characteristics. Some services depend on wide-area networks, some on local-area networks, some on embedded computers, some on large databases, and some on complex combinations of many characteristics.

1.4 Some Regrettable Failures

Before proceeding, it is worth looking at some examples of significant failures that have occurred and in which a computer was one of the (usually many) factors involved in causing the failure. In general, examining failures so as to learn from them and to help prevent similar failures in the future is important. Investigating accidents is a difficult challenge and the subject of study in its own right [73].

1.4.1 The Ariane V

The Ariane V is one of a range of launch vehicles developed by the European Space Agency (ESA). The maiden flight of the Ariane V, known as flight 501, took place on June 4, 1996 at the ESA launch site in Kourou, French Guiana. The vehicle rose from the launch pad and, about 40 seconds later, veered off course, broke apart, and exploded. The reason the vehicle veered off course was that the engines were gimbled to extreme positions, and this caused the vehicle to pitch over. This unplanned pitch over led to excessive aerodynamic loads that caused the self-destruct mechanism to operate as it was designed to do.

An investigation was started immediately by an inquiry board assembled by ESA and composed of international experts. The report of the board was published on July 19, 1996. The report describes many background details of the launch site and the launch vehicle, the steps in the inquiry, and detailed conclusions [89].

Many factors were involved in the accident, but one of the most important factors involved the software in part of the vehicle's Flight Control System called the Inertial Reference System (IRS). The IRS supplies velocities and angles from which calculations are undertaken that set the various control surfaces. The goal is to keep the vehicle on the planned trajectory.

Just prior to the end of the short flight, a software component that is used for alignment while the vehicle is on the ground prior to launch was still executing. This was not necessary but not viewed as a problem. That particular module was written originally for the Ariane IV, and the module was used on the Ariane V because the required functionality was similar. The module calculated a value related to the horizontal velocity component, but the value to be calculated was higher than the values that occur on the Ariane IV. Unfortunately, the higher value was not representable in the available precision, and that resulted in an exception being raised.

The software was written in Ada, and neither an explicit guard on the value nor a local exception handler was provided to deal with this situation. The exception was propagated according to the Ada exception-handling semantics, and this caused execution of significant amounts of the software to be terminated. The deflection of the engines that caused the vehicle to pitch over just prior to the abrupt end of the maiden flight occurred because test bit patterns were sent to the engine control actuators rather than correct values.

1.4.2 Korean Air Flight 801

On August 6, 1997 at about 1:42 am Guam local time, Korean Air flight 801, a Boeing 747-300, crashed into Nimitz Hill, Guam while attempting a non-precision approach to runway 6L at A.B. Won Guam International Airport. Of the 254 persons on board, 237 of whom were passengers, only 23 passengers and 3 flight attendants survived. The National Transportation Safety Board (NTSB) investigated the accident and classified the crash as a controlled-flight-into-terrain accident [101].

Korean Air flight 801 crashed during its final approach while operating under instrument flight rules (IFR). At the time of the accident, the runway glideslope was out of service, meaning that pilots were not to rely on the glideslope signal when landing at Guam. When the glideslope is unavailable, a non-precision or localizer-only instrument-landing-system (ILS) approach is still possible. In lieu of a glideslope, pilots make a series of intermediate descents using a series of step-down altitude fixes.

Post-accident analysis of radar data indicated that flight 801 began a premature descent on its non-precision approach and violated the 2,000 feet step-down clearance, i.e., the clearance to descend below 2,000 feet. The aircraft proceeded on a steady descent, violating the 1,440 feet step-down clearance before impacting terrain approximately 3.3 nautical miles short of the runway threshold. The NTSB concluded that "the captain lost awareness of flight 801's position on the [ILS] localizer-only approach to runway 6L at Guam International Airport and improperly descended below the intermediate approach altitudes ... which was causal to the accident."

During its investigation, the NTSB found that the ground-based Minimum Safe Altitude Warning System (MSAW) had been inhibited. MSAW is a software system that monitors radar data, and, using a map of the local terrain, alerts air-traffic controllers to aircraft that might be flying too low. MSAW is just one of many defenses against CFIT accidents, but it is an important defense. In Guam at the time of this accident, controllers had been disturbed by false alarms from MSAW, and so MSAW coverage had been disabled intentionally in a circle centered on the airport and with a radius of 54 nautical miles. MSAW's coverage was a circle of radius 55 nautical miles, and so, at the time of the Korean Air 801 crash, MSAW's actual coverage was a ring of width one nautical mile that was entirely over the Pacific ocean.

1.4.3 The Mars Climate Orbiter

The Mars Climate Orbiter (MCO) was a spacecraft designed to orbit Mars and conduct studies of the Martian weather. The spacecraft had a secondary role as a communications relay for the Mars Polar Lander (see Section 1.4.4).

According to the report of the mishap investigation board [94], the MCO was lost on September 23, 1999 as the spacecraft engaged in Mars Orbit Insertion. At that time, the spacecraft was 170 kilometers lower than planned because of minor errors that accumulated during the cruise phase. The spacecraft was lost because of unplanned interaction with the Martian atmosphere.

The source of the minor errors was a series of trajectory corrections in which the calculation of part of the trajectory model was not in metric units. Thus, part of the software was written assuming that the data represented measurements in metric units and part was written assuming that the data represented measurements in Imperial units. Both software parts worked correctly, but the misunderstanding of the data led to errors in calculated values. The cumulative effect led to the difference between the actual and planned altitudes and the subsequent loss of the spacecraft.

1.4.4 The Mars Polar Lander

The Mars Polar Lander (MPL) was a spacecraft designed to land on Mars and which was planned to arrive at Mars several months after the Mars Climate Orbiter. The MPL mission goal was to study the geology and weather at the landing site in the south polar region of Mars.

The spacecraft arrived at Mars on December 3, 1999. Atmospheric entry, descent, and landing were to take place without telemetry to Earth, and so the first communication expected from the spacecraft would occur after landing. That communication never arrived, and nothing has been heard from the spacecraft subsequently.

According to the report of the Special Review Board [118], the exact cause of the failure could not be determined. The most probable cause that was identified was premature shutdown of the descent engine. Magnetic sensors on the landing legs were designed to detect surface contact. However, these sensors also generated a signal when the legs were deployed from their stowed position prior to the final descent to the surface. The spacecraft's software should have ignored this signal, but apparently the software interpreted the signal as surface contact and shut down the descent engine. Since leg deployment occurred at an altitude of 40 meters, the lander would have fallen to the surface and not survived.

1.4.5 Other Important Incidents

A very unfortunate example of how a seemingly benign system can be far more dependent on its computer systems than is obvious occurred in October 1992 with the dispatching system used by the ambulance service in London, England. A manual dispatch system was replaced with a computerized system that was not able to meet the operational needs of the dispatch staff in various ways. Delays in dispatching ambulances to emergencies might have been responsible for several deaths before the computerized system was shut down, although this has not been proven [47].

The Therac 25 was a medical radiation therapy machine manufactured by Atomic Energy of Canada Limited (AECL). The device was installed in numerous hospitals in the United States. Between June 1985 and January 1987, six patients received massive overdoses of radiation while being treated for various medical conditions using the Therac 25. Software requirements and implementation were causal factors in the accidents. A comprehensive analysis of the failures of the Therac 25 has been reported by Leveson and Turner [88].

Finally, an incident that was potentially serious but, fortunately, did not lead to disaster was the launch failure of the Space Shuttle during the first launch attempt in 1981 [49]. The launch was due to take place on Friday, April 10. The Shuttle has two flight-control systems, the primary system and the backup system, each with its own software. During the countdown, these two systems are required to synchronize. Synchronization includes ensuring that they agree on the total number of 40-millisecond, real-time frames that have passed since the initialization of the primary system at the beginning of the countdown. During the first launch attempt, they failed to synchronize because the primary system had counted one more frame than the backup system. At the time, the problem appeared to be in the backup system, because the problem came to light when the backup system was initialized shortly before launch. Efforts to correct the situation focused on the backup system, but the fault was actually in the primary system. The Friday launch had to be canceled, and the launch was finally completed successfully on the afternoon of Sunday, April 12.

1.4.6 How to Think about Failures

In reading about failures (these and others), do not jump to conclusions about either the causes or the best way to prevent future recurrences. There is never a single "cause" and there are always many lessons to be learned. Also, keep in mind that failures occur despite careful engineering by many dedicated engineers. What failures illustrate is the extreme difficulty we face in building dependable systems and how serious the effects can be when something goes wrong.

Finally, when our engineering techniques are insufficient, the system of interest will experience a failure, and sometimes an accident will ensue. As part of our engineering process, we need to learn from failures so that we can prevent their recurrence to the extent possible. When we read about a system failure in which a computer system was one of the causal factors, it is tempting to think that the lesson to be learned is to eliminate the identified defect. This is a serious mistake, because it misses the fundamental question of why the defect occurred in the first place.

As an example, consider the loss of the Mars Climate Orbiter spacecraft [94]. The lessons learned certainly include being careful with measurement units. This was identified as a causal factor, and so obviously care has to be taken with units on future missions. But the reason the units were wrong is a more fundamental process problem. What documents were missing or prepared incorrectly? What process steps should have been taken to check for consistency of both units and other system parameters? And, finally, what management errors occurred that allowed this situation to arise?

1.5 Consequences of Failure

The term that is usually used to describe all of the damages that follow failure is the *consequences of failure*, and that is the phrase that we will use from now on. The consequences of failure for the systems that we build are important to us as engineers, because our goal is to reduce losses as much as possible. We have to choose the right engineering approaches to use for any given system, and the choices we make are heavily influenced by the potential consequences of failure.

In this section, we examine the different consequences of failure that can occur. In particular, we examine the non-obvious consequences of failure and the consequences of failure for systems that seem to have essentially none. We will discuss exactly what we mean by a "system" later. At this point, remember the intuitive notions of a system, of a system of systems, and of a system connected to and influencing other systems. Such notions are needed to ensure that we consider all the possible consequences of failure.

1.5.1 Non-Obvious Consequences of Failure

For the examples in the previous section, the damage done was fairly clear. In each case, the losses were significant and came from various sources. A little reflection, however, reveals that the losses might go well beyond the obvious. In the Ariane V case, for example, the obvious loss was sophisticated and expensive equipment: the launch vehicle and payload. There was a subsequent loss of service from the payload that was not delivered to orbit.

What is not obvious are the losses incurred from:

- The environmental damage from the explosion that had to be cleaned up.
- The cost of the investigation of the incident and the subsequent redesign of the system to avoid the problem.

- The delays in subsequent launches.
- The increased insurance rates for similar launch vehicles.
- The loss of jobs at the various companies and organizations involved in the development of the launch vehicle.
- The damage to the careers of the scientists expecting data from the scientific instruments within the payloads.
- The loss of reputation by the European Space Agency.

In practice, there were probably other losses, perhaps many.

1.5.2 Unexpected Costs of Failure

For some systems, the cost of failure seems insignificant. In practice, these *trivial* systems can have significant consequences of failure. In other systems, the consequences of failure seem limited to minor inconvenience. But for these *non-critical* systems, the consequences of failure are not with the systems themselves but with the systems to which they are related. Finally, for *security* applications, the consequences of failure are hard to determine but are usually vastly higher than might be expected at first glance.

We examine each of these system types in turn. As we do so, be sure to note that, for any particular system, the consequences of failure will most likely be a combination of all of the different ideas we are discussing. For example, a text-message system operating on a smart phone might seem trivial, but, if the system is used to alert a population to a weather emergency, failure of the system would leave the population unprotected. Security is also an issue because of the potential for abuse either through malicious alerts or denial-of-service attacks.

Trivial applications. Sometimes, the consequences of failure seem to be minimal but, in fact, they are not. Consider, for example, a computer game that proves to be defective. Such a failure does not seem important until one considers the fact that millions of copies might be sold. If the game is defective, and the defect affects a large fraction of the users, the cost to patch or replace the game could be huge. The loss of reputation for the manufacturer of the game might be important too.

If the game is an on-line, multi-user game, then the potential cost of failure is higher. Many such games operate world wide, and so large numbers of servers provide the shared service to large numbers of users and an extensive communications network connects everybody together.

Access to the game requires a monthly subscription, and the revenue generated thereby is substantial. Supporting such a community of users requires: (1) that the client software work correctly, (2) that the server software work correctly, and (3) that the communications mechanism work correctly. Downtime, slow response, or defective functionality could lead to a large reduction in revenue for the owners of the game.

Non-critical applications. Some computer systems do not provide services that are immediately critical yet their consequences of failure can be serious because of their impact on systems that do provide critical services. This indirection is easily missed when considering the consequences of failure, yet the indirection is usually a multiplier of the consequences of failure. This multiplier effect occurs because one non-critical application might be used to support multiple critical applications.

As an example, consider a compiler. Compiler writers are concerned about the accuracy of the compiler's translation, but their attention tends to be focused more on the performance of the generated code. A defect in a compiler used for a safety-critical application could lead to a failure of the safety-critical application even though the application software at the source-code level was defect free. And, clearly, this scenario could be repeated on an arbitrary number of different safety-critical applications.

Security applications. In July and August of 2001, the Code Red worm spread throughout large sections of the Internet [143]. Hundreds of thousands of hosts were infected in just a few days. The worm did not carry a malicious payload so infected computers were not damaged, although the worm effected a local denial of service attack on the infected machines. The infection had to be removed, and this worldwide cleanup activity alone is estimated to have cost at least $2,000,000,000.

Many modern information systems process critical data, and unauthorized access to that data can have costs that are essentially unbounded. Far worse than the Code Red worm are attacks in which valuable private information is taken and exploited in some way. Between July 2005 and mid-January 2007, approximately 45.6 million credit card and other personal records were stolen from the TJX Companies [30]. The degree to which this data has been exploited is unknown, but the potential loss is obviously large.

Both the Code Red worm and the attack on the TJX Companies were the result of defects in the software systems operating on the computers involved. Neither was the result of a failure of security technology per se.

1.5.3 Categories of Consequences

Although we all have a general understanding that failure of computer systems might lead to significant losses, the damage that a failure might cause needs to be understood in order to determine how much effort needs to be put into engineering the system.

The various categories of the consequences of failure include:

- Human injury or loss of life.

- Damage to the environment.
- Damage to or loss of equipment.
- Damage to or loss of data.
- Financial loss by theft.
- Financial loss through production of useless or defective products.
- Financial loss through reduced capacity for production or service.
- Loss of business reputation.
- Loss of customer base.
- Loss of jobs.

All of the items in this list are important, but they become less familiar and therefore less obvious as one proceeds down the list. This change is actually an important point. One of the activities in which we must engage is to determine as many of the consequences of failure as possible for the systems that we build. Things like "loss of reputation" are a serious concern yet rarely come to mind when considering the development of a computer system.

1.5.4 Determining the Consequences of Failure

As we saw Section 1.5.2, just because a computer is providing entertainment does not mean that dependability can be ignored. The complexity of determining the cost of failure for any given system means that this determination must be carried out carefully as part of a systematic dependability process. Adding up the costs of failure and seeing the high price allows us to consider expending resources during development in order to engineer systems that have the requisite low probability of failure.

There is no established process for determining the consequences of failure. In general, a systematic approach begins with a listing of categories such as the one in Section 1.5.3. Typically, one then proceeds informally but rigorously to examine the proposed system's effects in each category and documents these effects.

There is no need to compute a single cost figure for a system, and, in fact, assessing cost in monetary terms for consequences such as human injury is problematic at best. Thus, a complete statement about the consequences of failure for a system will usually be broken down into a set of different and incompatible measures including (a) the prospect of loss of life or injury, (b) the forms and extents of possible environmental damages, (c) the prospect of loss of information that has value, (d) services that might be lost, (e) various delays that might occur in associated activities, and (f) financial losses. This list (or an extended or localized version) can be used as a checklist for driving an assessment of consequences of failure.

1.6 The Need for Dependability

We need computer systems to be dependable because we depend upon them! But what do we really need? There are several different properties that might be important in different circumstances. We introduce some of them here and discuss them in depth in Chapter 2.

An obvious requirement for many systems is *safety*. In essence, we require that the systems we build will not cause harm. We want to be sure, for example, that medical devices upon which we depend operate safely and do not cause us injury. Injury, however, can occur because of action or because of *lack* of action, and so making such devices safe is far from simple.

Many systems cannot cause harm and so safety is not a requirement for them. A computer game console, for example, has little need for safety except for the most basic things such as protecting the user from high voltages, sharp edges, and toxic materials. The computer system itself cannot do very much to cause harm, and so, as developers of computer systems, we do not have to be concerned with safety in game consoles.

Another obvious requirement that arises frequently is for *security*. Information has value and so ensuring that information is used properly is important. The customers of a bank, for example, expect their financial records to be treated as private information. Trusted banking officials may view the information as can the owners of the information. But that information is held in a database that is shared by all of the bank's customers, and so security involves ensuring that each customer can access all of his or her own information *and no more*.

A less obvious dependability requirement is *availability*. Some systems provide service that we do not use especially frequently but which we expect to be "always there" when we want to use the service. The telephone system is an example. When we pick up a telephone handset, we expect to hear a dial tone (switched on by a computer). In practice, occasional brief outages would not be a serious problem, because they are unlikely to coincide with our occasional use. So, for many systems, continuous, uninterrupted service is not especially important as long as outages are brief and infrequent.

In examining these requirements, what we see is a collection of very different characteristics that we might want computer systems to have, all of which are related in some way to our intuitive notion of dependability. Intuitively, we tend to think of these characteristics as being very similar. As part of an informal conversation, one might state: "computer systems need to be reliable" or "computer systems need to work properly" but such informality does not help us in engineering. For now, our intuitive notions of these concepts will suffice, but in Chapter 2, we will examine these various terms carefully.

1.7 Systems and Their Dependability Requirements

Many computer applications have obvious consequences of failure. However, as we saw in Section 1.5.2, other applications do not seem to have any significant consequences of failure, although it turns out that they do. In yet others, the detailed consequences of failure are hard to determine, but all the consequences have to be determined if we are to be able to engineer for their reduction.

In this section we look at several systems to see what dependability they require. We also look at some examples of systems from the perspective of their interaction and the consequent impact that this interaction has on the consequences of failure. The primary illustrative example comes from commercial aircraft, and we examine an aircraft system, the production of aircraft systems, and the management of controlled airspace.

1.7.1 Critical Systems

Avionics

The avionics (*avi*ation electr*onics*) in commercial aircraft are complex computer systems that provide considerable support for the crew, help to maintain safe flight, and improve the overall comfort of passengers. This is not a small task, and several distinct computers and a lot of software are involved. Aircraft engines have their own computer systems that provide extensive monitoring, control, and safety services.

In military aircraft, avionics make things happen that are otherwise impossible. Many military aircraft literally cannot be flown without computer support, because actions need to be taken at sub-second rates, rates that humans cannot achieve. Such aircraft have a property known as *relaxed static stability,* meaning that their stability in flight is intentionally reduced to provide other benefits. Stability is restored by rapid manipulation of the aircraft's control surfaces by a computer system.

Commercial and military avionics have different dependability requirements. The overwhelming goal in passenger aircraft is safe and economical flight. Military aircraft, on the other hand, frequently have to be designed with compromises so as to improve their effectiveness in areas such as speed and maneuverability. The damages caused by failure are very different between commercial and military aircraft also. If there is an accident, loss of the aircraft is highly likely in both cases, but death and injury are much more likely in passenger aircraft. Military pilots have ejection seats, but passengers on commercial aircraft do not.

Thus, the consequences of failure of avionics systems are considerable and reasonably obvious, although they differ between aircraft types. When engineering a computer system that is to become part of an avionics suite, we know we need to be careful. But the engineering approaches used in the two domains will differ considerably because of the differences in the operating environments and the consequences of failure.

Ships

Ships share many similarities with aircraft and employ sophisticated computer systems for many of the same reasons. On-board ships, computers are responsible for navigation, guidance, communication, engine control, load stability analysis, and sophisticated displays such as weather maps. In modern ships, all of these services are tied together with one or more shipboard networks that also support various more recognizable services such as e-mail.

An important difference between ships and aircraft is that stopping a ship is usually acceptable if something fails in the ship's computer system. Provided a ship is not in danger of capsizing or coming into contact with rocks, the ship can stop and failed computer systems can be repaired. Stopping an aircraft is not even possible unless the aircraft is actually on the ground, and engineering of computer systems must take this into account.

An important example of the role of computers on ships and the consequences of failure occurred on September 21, 1997 [153]. The U.S.S. Yorktown, a Navy cruiser, was disabled for more than two hours off the coast of Virginia when a critical system failed after an operator entered a zero into a data field. This zero led to a divide-by-zero exception that disabled a lot of the software, including critical control functions.

Spacecraft

Spacecraft are complex combinations of computers, scientific instruments, communications equipment, power generation devices and associated management, and propulsion systems. Those that leave the vicinity of the Earth and Moon present two intriguing dependability challenges. The first is longevity. No matter where the spacecraft is going, getting there will take a long time, usually several years. That means that the on-board computing systems must be able to operate unattended and with no hardware maintenance for that period of time. The second challenge is the communications time. Many spacecraft operate at distances from the Earth that preclude interactive operation with an Earth-bound operator. Thus, in many ways, spacecraft have to be autonomous. In particular, they must be able to protect themselves and make decisions while doing so with no external intervention.

Medical Devices

In the medical arena, devices such as pacemakers and defibrillators, drug infusion pumps, radiotherapy machines, ventilators, and monitoring equipment are all built around computer systems. Pacemakers and defibrillators (they are often combined into a single device) are best thought of as being sophisticated computers with a few additional components. Pacemaking involves sampling patient parameters for every heartbeat and making a decision about whether the heart needs to be stimulated.

Pacemakers are an example of the type of system where our intuition suggests, correctly, that safety is the most important aspect of dependability with which we need to be concerned. But safety can be affected by both action and inaction. A pacemaker that stimulates the heart when it should not is very likely going to cause harm. But if the device were to detect some sort of defect in its own operation, merely stopping would not be a safe thing to do. Obviously, the patient needs the pacemaker and so stopping might lead to patient injury or death. Engineering such systems so that they operate safely is a significant challenge, and that engineering has to be done so as to maximize battery life.

Critical Infrastructures

The freight-rail system mentioned earlier is one of many critical infrastructure systems upon which we all depend and which themselves depend heavily on complex computer systems. Many other critical infrastructure systems are in the list of services included at the beginning of this chapter. The computer systems therein do not seem at first sight to have the same potential for serious damage as a result of failure as do systems such as passenger aircraft, medical devices, or spacecraft.

In practice, this is quite wrong. The banking system has to protect our money and make it available as needed. However, were the computing systems within the banking system to fail in some general way, the result would be much more than a minor inconvenience to citizens; an international economic crisis would result. Similarly, failure of the computers within the energy production, transport, or telecommunications industries would have a major impact as service became unavailable.

1.7.2 Systems That Help Build Systems

In areas such as aviation, one tends to think only of the product in operation, an aircraft in flight. But there are two other major and non-obvious areas of computer system engineering for which dependability is important, product design and product manufacturing.

Product design includes many forms of computerized analysis, and if that analysis is not completed correctly, the dependability of the resulting product, safety of an aircraft for example, might be jeopardized. Thus, the development of computer systems that will be involved in the *design* of other artifacts must consider the needs of the target systems as well as the system being developed. A computer system that performs structural analysis on the fuselage and wings of an aircraft is just as important as the avionics system that will fly the aircraft.

During manufacturing of virtually all products, many computers are involved in robotic assembly operations, managing inventories, routing of parts, examining parts for defects, and managing the myriad of data associated with production. Again, using commercial aircraft as an example, if something such as a robotic welder or the subsequent weld examination system were defective, the safety of the resulting aircraft might be jeopardized.

Often neglected because software takes the spotlight, *data* is a critical item in many systems. For example, in terms of managing data during manufacturing, it is interesting to note that a modern passenger aircraft has more than 100 miles of wire in hundreds of separate wiring harnesses, each of which has to be installed correctly. Labeling alone is a major data management problem. Any mistakes in the data that is used to manufacture, label, locate, or test wiring in an aircraft could obviously lead to serious production delays or failures during operation.

Thus, again we see that computers which do not have obvious high consequences of failure can often be involved with manufacturing such that their failure can lead to defective products. This is far more common than most people realize, and the surprising result is that the consequences of failure of many manufacturing systems are high, although initially this observation is counterintuitive.

1.7.3 Systems That Interact with Other Systems

Air-traffic control is another area in which computer systems play an important role in aviation. These computers are very different from avionics systems yet no less important. Air-traffic-control systems employ radars and other sources of information to present controllers with an accurate picture of the status of the airspace. With this information, controllers are able to make decisions about appropriate aircraft movements that they then communicate to the crews of the aircraft.

The dependability requirements of air-traffic control are primarily in four areas: (1) the data provided by the system to controllers must be accurate; (2) the data must be available essentially all the time; (3) computations that drive displays and other information sources must be accurate; and (4) there must be comprehensive security.

Interactions between systems that are in fact critical do not have to be as complex as something like the air-traffic-control system. For example, pacemakers do not operate in isolation. They have numerous adjustable parameters that physicians set to optimize operation for each patient. This adjustment is carried out by a device called a "programmer" that is itself just a computer system. Pacemakers also capture patient information during operation, and that data can be downloaded for examination by physicians. Both parameter setting and patient data analysis are critical activities, and the associated computer system, the programmer, has to be understood to have significant consequences of failure and correspondingly high dependability requirements.

The important conclusions to draw from these various examples are: (1) that the need for dependability does not lie solely in glamorous, high visibility systems, and (2) the specific dependability requirements that systems present vary widely. The need for adequate dependability is present in practically any system that we build.

1.8 Where Do We Go from Here?

For almost all applications of interest, dependability is not something that can be added to an existing design. Certainly the dependability of a system can probably be improved by making suitable changes to the design, but being able to transform a system developed with just functionality in mind into one that meets significant dependability goals is highly unlikely. Without taking specific steps during the entire development process, systems end up with dependability characteristics that are ad hoc at best.

This limitation appears to present us with a significant dilemma. Does this limitation apply to everything, including the components that we use to build systems? In other words, are we at an impasse? If we can only build dependable systems from dependable components and only build dependable components from smaller dependable components, and so on, then we are indeed facing a serious challenge.

Fortunately, the answer to the question is "no". Building dependable systems relies in part upon our discovering how to meet *system* dependability goals using much less dependable *components* [18, 19, 37]. This concept goes back to the earliest days of computing [6, 144]. The pioneers of computing were able to build computers that could operate for useful periods of time using vacuum tubes (the Colossi, for example [113]), components that were notoriously unreliable.

The path that we will follow is a systematic and thorough treatment of the problem of dependability. As we follow that path, keep the following in mind:

> *The attention paid during system development has to be*
> *thorough and orderly. Point solutions are not sufficient.*

For example, knowing that a system requires backup power because the usual power source is "unreliable" is helpful, but far from complete. Having a backup power source seems like a good idea. But, how reliable is the backup power source? How quickly must the backup power source become available if the primary source fails? For how long can the backup power source operate? Can the backup power source supply all of the equipment? What about the myriad other issues such as the possibility of hardware or software failure?

If attention is not paid to *all* of the potential sources of difficulty, the resulting system will not have the dependability that is required. Being sure that attention has been paid to potential sources of difficulty to the extent possible is our goal.

The subject of dependability of computer systems is complex and detailed. Dependability has to be dealt with in a methodical and scientific way. The path we will follow from here is a comprehensive and systematic one. The path mirrors the technology that we need to apply to computer system development. In particular, we will seek general approaches and learn to both recognize and *avoid* point solutions.

Finally, keep in mind that the engineering we undertake to provide the dependability we seek in our computer systems is not without cost. The cost of careful engineering can be considerable. But the cost of failure is usually far higher.

1.9 Organization of This Book

Dependability and our study of it in this book is much like engineering the chain suspending the box of porcelain. The various analogies are shown in Table 1.1. The service that a computer system provides corresponds to the porcelain and all of the things that have to work correctly in the computer system correspond to the box, the chain, and the hooks.

Porcelain Example	Computer System
Antique porcelain	Application service provided by computer system
Wooden box	Part of target computer system
Chain and hooks	Other parts of target computer system
Weakest link in chain	Part of computer system most likely to fail
Smashed porcelain	Failure of computer service

TABLE 1.1. Analogies between expensive porcelain and critical computer systems.

Our study of dependability begins in Chapter 2 with a careful look at terminology. Without a precise definition of terms, we will not be able to establish the goal that we have when setting out to design and implement a dependable computer system nor will we be able to discuss the detailed engineering activities we need to undertake.

Links in a chain can fail in various ways. A link could crack, bend, stretch, wear out, melt, be made of the wrong material, be manufactured with the wrong shape, and so on. To make our chain strong enough, we need to know how links can fail, and, once we know that, we can engineer the links to be strong enough and search for links that might be defective. In doing so, we *must* remember our insight about the weakest link. There would be no point in expending effort to make one of the links extremely strong if another link were not strong enough.

With the terminology in hand from Chapter 2, our study of dependability moves on in Chapter 3 to examine faults in computer systems, the different fault types, and the four approaches at our disposal to deal with faults. The four approaches to dealing with individual faults or sometimes entire classes of faults are: *avoidance, removal, tolerance* and *forecasting*.

In Chapter 4, we tackle the problem of identifying all of the faults to which a system is subject. Only by knowing what faults might arise can we have any hope of dealing with them. If we miss a fault to which a system is subject, the potentially serious effects are obvious. Going back to our porcelain analogy, missing a fault, or worse, an entire class of faults is like missing a weak link in the chain.

In Chapter 5, we examine the four basic mechanisms for dealing with faults. Our preference is to avoid faults but, if that is not possible, we would like to remove the ones we introduce. Sometimes, faults survive avoidance and elimination, and so if we cannot avoid or remove faults, our next option is to try to tolerate their effects at run time. Finally, there are sometimes faults that remain untreated because either (a) we have no technology that allows us to deal with the faults, (b) the cost of dealing with them is prohibitive, or (c) we fail to identify them. In order to determine whether the associated system will provide acceptable service, we have to forecast the effects of those faults.

Chapter 6 summarizes the issues with degradation faults, a type of fault that arises only in hardware. In Chapter 7 we turn to the general issues surrounding software dependability. Chapter 8 and Chapter 9 discuss important topics in software fault avoidance. Chapter 10 is about software fault elimination, and Chapter 11 is about software fault tolerance. Finally, in Chapter 12 we examine dependability assessment.

Key points in this chapter:

+ Dependability is a complex subject that has to be addressed systematically.
+ Software has to be dependable and provide support for hardware dependability.
+ Software specifications derive from system design.
+ The specifications for software are often influenced by the need to support the dependability of the target system.
+ Many types of system need to be dependable, not just obviously safety-critical systems.
+ The consequences of failure of systems can be considerable.
+ Consequences of failure often arise in areas beyond the scope of the system's functionality, such as repair costs, loss of reputation, and lost jobs.

Exercises

1. Read the report of the Ariane V explosion and prepare a one-page summary of what happened [89]. Using your summary, explain the accident to a colleague.

2. Read the report of the Therac 25 accidents by Leveson and Turner and prepare a one-page summary of what happened [88]. Using your summary, explain the accident to a colleague.

3. Read the report of the loss of the Mars Climate Orbiter and prepare a one-page summary of what happened [94]. Using your summary, explain the accident to a colleague.

4. The Ariane V software was written in Ada, and the semantics of Ada exception handling were a causal factor in the failure. Acquire a copy of the Ada Language Reference manual and read about the semantics of exception handling in Ada [4]. Pay particular attention to the way in which exceptions are propagated in Ada. Under what circumstances could a large Ada program be completely terminated if an exception were raised during execution of a low-level function?

5. The computer network upon which the U.S. Federal Reserve Bank relies for electronic funds transfer is called Fedwire. Search for details of how Fedwire works and try to determine: (a) how Fedwire transfers funds for its member banks, (b) roughly how much money is transferred each day by Fedwire, and (c) roughly how many fund transfers are provided by Fedwire each day.

6. Search for details of the functionality and design of an implantable pacemaker. What are the consequences of failure of the pacemaker that you have identified?

7. Consider the consequences of failure of a large-area, multi-player game such as Final Fantasy. Itemize separately, the consequences of failure resulting from (a) a defect in the graphics system that affects the appearance of game elements, (b) a defect in the client code that causes a user's computer to crash, (c) a server defect that causes loss of game state for large numbers of players, and (d) a network defect that causes game availability to be limited in the United States on several weekday evenings.

8. Lots of costs arise from security attacks. Viewing a major Internet worm attack such as that of Code Red [143] as a system failure, itemize as a series of bullets the consequences of failure associated with the attack.

9. Amazon is a company that depends on computers and communications entirely for its business operations. Itemize, as a bulleted list, the consequences of failure for Amazon of the company's web-based customer ordering system (i.e., the online system by which customers examine the Amazon selection of products and place orders), where failure means that the company could not operate at all for outages lasting (a) one minute, (b) one hour, (c) one day, and (d) one week.

10. Again for Amazon, determine the consequences of failure of the company's warehouse inventory management system (i.e., the system that is used to facilitate collection and dispatch of ordered items) for outages lasting (a) one minute, (b) one hour, (c) one day, and (d) one week.

11. Without reading ahead, develop your own definition of *safety*. In doing so, think carefully about how your definition would work in a rigorous engineering context.

12. Details of new vehicle wiring harnesses (including lengths, wire type, color, insulation type, labeling, terminator, binding, etc.) are supplied as a data file by an automobile manufacturer to the supplier who builds the harness. Itemize in a bulleted list the consequences of failure of the software that controls the manufacturing of wiring harnesses at the supplier's plant. Organize your list around the different types of software failure that might occur, including (a) failures caused by a functional defect in the software implementation, (b) failures caused by a defect in the specification of the data file, and (c) failures caused by mistakes made by the operators of the system using the software.

13. The computing system for a medical radiation therapy machine consists of a single, real-time application program that operates on a Unix platform. The application program interacts with the operator, turns the radiation beam on and off, aims the beam to the correct location in the treatment field, and sets the beam intensity. Making any assumptions that you wish to about the computing system, hypothesize examples of (a) a software requirement that derives from the system design, (b) a requirement of the application software that derives from the need to cope with the failure of system components, and (c) an aspect of the target hardware upon which the application runs that is affected by the need for hardware dependability.

CHAPTER 2

Dependability Requirements

Learning objectives of this chapter are to understand:

- The basic terminology of dependability.
- The overall importance of dependability requirements and how to state them.
- The relationship between systems and software dependability.
- The principle of *As Low As is Reasonably Practicable*.

2.1 Why We Need Dependability Requirements

The computer systems with which we are concerned provide a service, and, as we have seen, failure of that service can have a variety of serious consequences. When considering the development of a new system, the fundamental engineering that we undertake is determined considerably by the need to avoid failure.

Setting out to build a system that "does not fail" is not sufficient. We cannot do that. No matter what we do, the hardware with which we build computer systems has a finite life, and we cannot predict precisely when any given system will fail. Without such a prediction, we cannot avoid the effects of hardware failure. One might think that we could avoid the problem by using more hardware, but no matter how much hardware we use, failure at some unpredictable point is inevitable. And much or all of the hardware could be destroyed at the same time by a serious external trauma.

What is needed for any given system is a precise statement of what level of dependability is adequate for that system. In this chapter we examine the problem of defining *dependability requirements*. Intuitively, the dependability requirements for a system state properties such as the required fraction of time the system has to be operational, the degree of protection that the system must afford against catastrophic consequences, and so on. The dependability requirements are different from the requirements that define functionality. For most systems of interest here, we need both sets of requirements.

We begin by discussing the terminology that we need, and then we look at the problem of defining dependability. A key aspect of that problem is the distinction between *system* dependability and *software* dependability. These are closely related but not the same, and we look at the distinction in Section 2.4 and Section 2.8.

2.2 The Evolution of Dependability Concepts

The various important attributes of dependability have evolved over time as computers have evolved and been used in more diverse applications. In the 1940s, the concern was just to develop computers that would keep running long enough to complete some desired application. This led to the modern notion of computer-system *reliability*. Applications such as structural analysis of physical systems where large numbers of calculations have to be completed for the analysis to be useful require reliability. Computer failure just before the entire set of calculations is finished leads to all the results being lost.

The 1960s saw the advent of interactive applications in which users sought service directly from a computer. Examples include:

- Record-keeping systems such as hospital patient-data systems and airline-reservation systems.

- Digital telephone exchanges.

In record-keeping systems, users interrogate the computer system for information based on a key, often a name. In a modern telephone system, users initiate computer service by picking up the handset. Such systems do not have to provide continuous service for long periods; brief outages are acceptable even in telephone systems.

These interactive applications led to the modern notion of computer-system *availability*. A brief failure between enquiries might not even be noticed unless a new enquiry was initiated. If one were and the system were unavailable, the user would not be inconvenienced much by a brief delay. The actual period of continuous service required in such systems is often quite short, and for that period what is required, of course, is reliability.

In the 1970s, computers were introduced into the control mechanisms of systems such as those that control large amounts of energy (chemical, kinetic, and nuclear). Clearly, great care had to be paid to ensuring that the controlled energy was not released inadvertently, and this led to the modern notion of *safety*.

Finally, in the 1990s the use of computers in networked information systems raised a variety of concerns about the use and protection of information. Frequently, the information, financial records and health records, for example, is critical in one way or another. Information such as this must be accurate and only available to designated individuals. These issues have led to the modern notion of computer-system *security*.

An important phrase that we do not need to define at this point (but we will later) is *fault tolerance*. Sometimes fault tolerance is stated as a requirement for a system to be built or as a property of an existing system. Fault tolerance is neither a system requirement nor a system property, because fault tolerance is a mechanism for achieving dependability, not an attribute of dependability. Requiring that a system be fault tolerant would not tell us anything useful about the system's overall dependability performance, nor would such a requirement provide a useful goal for developers unless the specific faults of interest were specified in detail.

For many systems requiring high dependability, the *public interest* must be protected. The public has a right to expect that systems with high consequences of failure will be engineered with appropriate care. With that expectation comes the further expectation that catastrophic failures will be rare. Failures do occur; aircraft crash, power systems and telephone systems fail, and so on. But the goal is always to make the rate of failure as low as possible, and especially for serious failures, quite literally, to keep the failure rate below that which society finds acceptable. For example, society abhors aircraft accidents, yet aircraft accidents occur. Fortunately, the rate is very low indeed, and infrequent accidents have not stopped people from flying.

Notice that in discussing the public interest, we have not used technical terms but intuitive ones, because, understandably, that is how members of the public tend to think about system dependability As engineers, we have to work with precise and testable notions of dependability, but such complexity is wholly inappropriate in communicating with members of the public.

The subjectivity of the public interest is well illustrated by the difference in the public's acceptance of automobile accidents and of aircraft accidents. Table 2.1

	2002	2003	2004	2005	2006	2007	2008	2009
Motor Vehicles	43,005	42,884	42,836	43,510	42,708	41,249	37,423	33,808
Commercial Aircraft	0	19	11	18	47	0	0	45

TABLE 2.1. Deaths per year in the United States for all types of motor vehicles including related pedestrian fatalities [99], and for commercial aircraft operated by U.S. carriers [100].

shows the number of fatalities that occurred in the United States which resulted from aircraft accidents and automobile accidents for several years. Fatal commercial aircraft accidents would be weekly events if as many people were killed in such accidents as are killed in automobile accidents. No matter how useful air travel was, public acceptance of air travel would almost certainly disappear under such circumstances.

2.3 The Role of Terminology

A complete and accurate terminology is essential if we are to be able to communicate about dependability. Precise notions of the terms that we use help communication between customers, domain experts, systems engineers, software engineers, engineers in other disciplines, and managers.

Terminology is generally useful, but terminology becomes crucial when defining the dependability requirements for a system. We must be able to set those requirements so that those building the system know what their goals are. Developers also have to show that the engineering of their system meets the dependability requirements. Both engineering a system to be adequately dependable for a given application context and showing that this dependability level has been met are difficult challenges.

The obvious place to look for definitions is a dictionary. Unfortunately, a typical office dictionary does not help us in a complex engineering field such as computer system dependability. Here, for example, are three definitions taken from Webster's dictionary [115]:

Dependable: capable of being depended on: RELIABLE

Reliable: that may be relied on: DEPENDABLE in achievement

Rely: 1) to depend confidently; 2) to put trust in

As you can see, the definitions are circular and imprecise.

The next place that one might look is the collection of standards that various organizations have developed. Typically, these standards are developed by volunteers under the jurisdiction of a professional body such as the Institute of Electrical and Electronics Engineers (IEEE). While such standards are useful, they have several limitations:

- They are not anonymously peer reviewed. Although volunteers examine standards carefully, the standards are not examined thoroughly and anonymously by experts who have established expertise in the area.

- They tend to proliferate. For example, the IEEE presently has 53 active standards in the area of software that are either drafts or approved standards.

- They tend to separate related topics and thereby do not provide a comprehensive technical picture.

- They tend to be incomplete. As a result of the development process, standards often miss subtle items that should have been included. Incompleteness often shows up when users of the standard raise questions that the standard fails to answer.

In this book, we will use a different source for our terminology. Working over a period of more than 25 years, a group of dedicated scientists has produced a comprehensive taxonomy for the dependability field [13]. This taxonomy provides us with precise definitions of all the terms we need in a single integrated set. During development of the taxonomy, the various versions have been subjected to anonymous peer review on multiple occasions. We will use this taxonomy throughout this book. Whenever the term *taxonomy* is used, this taxonomy is meant.

2.4 What Is a System?

We run into trouble with imprecision the moment we try to speak of anything to do with dependability. Up to now, we have not had to face up to the need for precision, but the need arises with the most fundamental notion that we have to discuss, the word *system*.

What do we mean by a *system*? When speaking informally, the meaning of the word depends on who you are and where you stand. For example, software engineers usually mean the software system they are building, computer engineers usually mean the hardware system they are building, systems engineers usually mean the deliverable composite entity that they are building, component designers such as engineers building disk drives usually mean the component they are building, and so on.

Making things more difficult is the fact that some systems are described as subsystems of another system, and some systems are described as components that are part of the structure of another system. Unless we have a precise notion of the word "system", there is a serious danger that we will be misunderstood when we use the word. Even in circumstances where we have a good idea of what we are talking about when we use the word, the edges of the "system" are often blurred. For example, in considering an information system providing financial data to a user, is the user part of the information system? Similarly, is the backup copy of the data part of the system?

We need to use the word *system* frequently, and we need to apply the word in different ways. We have to be careful, and so we turn to the taxonomy [13] for help. Here are the taxonomy's definitions of *system* and *system boundary*:

System: A system is an entity that interacts with other entities, i.e., other systems, including hardware, software, humans, and the physical world with its natural phenomena. These other systems are the environment of the given system.

System boundary: The system boundary is the common frontier between the system and its environment.

So a *system* is an entity of interest and those entities with which that system interacts are the system's *environment*. These definitions provide us with a clear framework:

> *Systems are composed of systems,*
> *that are composed of systems,*
> *that are composed of systems,*
> *and so on.*

This view immediately deals with the problems raised by the informal notions of sub-systems and components. Both are just systems that happen to be parts of other systems. The view also provides us with a clear distinction between a system of interest and the environment in which the system of interest operates. That environment is just another system. Finally, the common frontier shared by the system of interest and the environment is the boundary of the system of interest.

Provided that we are clear about *exactly* to which of perhaps many systems we are referring, we have a clear identification of the system of interest to us. This system is the *subject* system. Those systems with which the subject system interacts constitute the subject system's environment. Frequently the environment is a single system within which one considers the subject system to be embedded.

A computer system that is embedded in some other equipment is a common case that helps to illustrate these terms. Consider, for example, a computer that is being used to control a microwave oven. The computer reads input from the user via a keyboard and from sensors, generates a display, and controls the electrical devices. There are several different systems and environments that we need to recognize:

- The computer software is a system that operates within the environment that is the computer hardware system including connections to peripherals.

- The computer hardware (with functionality defined by the software system) is a system that operates within the environment that is the oven's sensors, actuators, and electrical devices.

- The microwave oven is a system that operates within the environment that is the kitchen and the various items in the kitchen, including people.

Because embedded computers are so common, we will refer to the system within which the computer system is embedded as the *application* system. In this example, the application system for the computer system is the microwave oven.

In addition to the subject system and the environment system(s), a third system is important in our study of dependability, the *judgment* system. In practice, systems fail, and determining that a system has failed is part of one mechanism for achieving

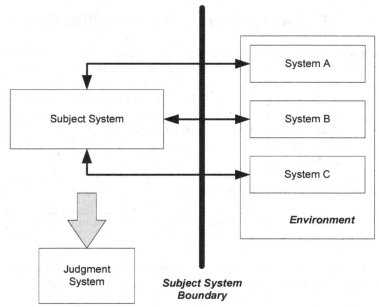

FIGURE 2.1 The relationship between systems of interest. The system at the focus of discussion is usually the *subject* system. This system has an explicit *boundary*. The subject system interacts with one or more other systems that constitute the *environment*. Finally, a *judgment* system determines things like failure states in the subject system.

dependability, i.e., fault tolerance. The difficulty is that, unless we have some way of determining that a system has failed, we will not be able to respond to the failure. The judgment system is the mechanism whereby a determination is made about whether the subject system has failed.

Since the notion of a system is recursive, i.e., environment for one subject system is the subject system for another subject system, etc., there will likely be several judgment systems at different levels of the recursion. This hierarchy is totally appropriate, because determination of failure is needed typically at more than one level.

In summary, then, we have three basic types of system with which we have to be concerned in any discussion: the *subject* system, the *environment* system(s) with which the subject system interacts, and the *judgment* system that attempts to determine whether the subject system has failed at any point in time. An example is shown in Figure 2.1.

In the remainder of this book, we will use these definitions, but, where no confusion will result, the subject system (the system being referenced) will be referred to just as "the system". Further, provided no confusion will result, we will use the terms sub-system and component so as to remain closer to the more familiar usage of these terms.

2.5 Requirements and Specification

Before proceeding with the specific terminology of dependability, we need to establish precise definitions of *requirements* and *specification* for computer systems.
These terms are often confused, because they are closely related. Where they are not
confused, many people have different definitions of them. Those different definitions work well in the circumstances of a particular system where all of the engineers involved can discuss their local understandings of terms, but in this book we
need to have agreed definitions of all the concepts discussed, especially terms such
as these that are fundamental.

We will start with the following definitions of these terms as a basis upon which
to build the extensive set of definitions about dependability that we need:

Requirements: The requirements for a computer system define the problem that the computer system has to solve.

Specification: The specification for a computer system defines the solution
that the computer system has to implement to solve the problem.

We have an intuitive notion of what is meant by dependability requirements
(Section 2.1). The definition of requirements here includes both the *functional* and
dependability requirements. The dependability requirements are part of the problem
to be solved. If the functional requirements are met by a system and the dependability requirements are not met, then the problem has not been solved.

Unfortunately, we are not done with defining the notion of requirements. The
problem we now face is the difference between the problem that the computer has to
solve and our *understanding* (and therefore our *documentation*) of that problem. The
documentation of the problem to be solved might not be the same as the problem to
be solved. If somehow we can engineer a perfect solution to the problem as documented, we might still have a solution that does not solve the actual problem that the
computer has to solve.

At this point, you might feel that this is an esoteric issue that we can ignore. But
the issue is real and serious, and we have to be on our guard. Documenting the problem to be solved is tricky and error-prone.

In order to be precise in discussing requirements, we need to have separate terms
for the problem to be solved and our documentation of that problem:

Abstract Requirements: The *abstract* requirements for a computer system
define the problem that the computer system has to solve.

Documented Requirements: The *documented* requirements for a computer system document the problem that the computer system has to solve.

Thus, the definition of requirements on the previous page was of the abstract requirements. In the remainder of this book, unless otherwise stated, *requirements* means *documented requirements*.

What about our definition of specification? Do we have to deal with specification in a similar way? We do, and that leads quickly to the notions of an *abstract specification* and a *documented specification*. As with requirements, in the remainder of this book, unless otherwise stated, *specification* means *documented specification*.

Finally, the use of "problem" and "solution" is confusing because one engineer's solution is usually another engineer's problem. Although the specification for a computer system is characterized as a solution, those who have to build the computer system consider the specification to be a problem statement. This difference in view is understandable and reasonable, but the difference comes from their perspective as implementors. Our concern is with computer *system* dependability, and so we need to take a more general view.

2.6 Failure

2.6.1 The Notion of Service Failure

The notion of *failure* is what we want to avoid. Intuitively we know that we are seeking to build systems that do not fail. The notion of failure seems simple enough, and we all have a good idea of what failure means. Nevertheless, as we shall see repeatedly during our journey through terminology, the intuitive meanings we have for many concepts are not precise enough for our purposes.

Failure is a complex topic and is perhaps the most important definition. Without a precise notion of failure, we cannot have precise definitions of anything else. Even worse is the fact that, without a precise definition of failure, we cannot have appropriate engineering targets. If we do not know *precisely* what we mean for a system to fail, we cannot engineer to limit failures to acceptable levels.

We acquire the necessary precision by observing that a system has failed when a service failure occurs. Turning to the taxonomy [13], we find these definitions:

Correct service. Correct service is delivered when the service implements the system function.

Service failure. A service failure, often abbreviated here to failure, is an event that occurs when the delivered service deviates from correct service.

Critical to deciding whether a system has failed is the notion of the *system function*. The taxonomy's definition of system function is:

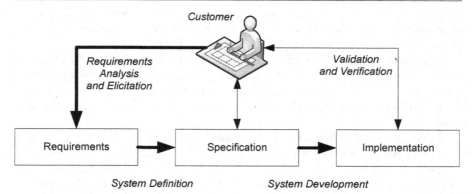

FIGURE 2.2 Requirements are acquired from the customer and define the problem to be solved. The specification defines the solution designed to meet the requirements. The implementation is the operational version of the solution derived from the specification.

System function. The function of a system is what the system is intended to do. System function is described by the system's specification.

Here, the taxonomy is referring to the *abstract* specification. The taxonomy goes on to explain:

> *A service fails either because it does not comply with the functional specification, or because this specification did not adequately describe the system function.*

Here, the taxonomy is referring to the *documented* specification.

The taxonomy does not distinguish between the case where the documented requirements differ from the abstract requirements and the case where the documented specification differs from the abstract specification. In both cases, the documented specification will be incorrect and hence can be a source of service failure. Here, we do make this distinction, because the technology of requirements and of specification are different and both are within the sphere of interest of the software and computer engineer.

2.6.2 Sources of Service Failure

In general, creating a system involves preparation of the requirements, the specification, and the implementation. These three stages are shown in Figure 2.2.

There are three possible situations that might lead to a service failure:

- The requirements for the system document the abstract requirements *incorrectly*. The specification of the system was *a correct solution to the problem stated in the requirements.* The implementation of the specification was *a correct refinement of the specification.*

- The requirements for the system document the abstract requirements *correctly.* The specification of the system was *an incorrect solution to the problem stated in the requirements.* The implementation of the specification was *a correct refinement of the specification.*

- The requirements for the system document the abstract requirements *correctly.* The specification of the system was *a correct solution to the problem stated in the requirements.* The implementation of the specification was *an incorrect refinement of the specification.*

Of course, in practice, a specific system might suffer from any combination of these three sources of service failure.

In examining what happened after a failure, we might realize that there was some element of functionality that was required but not documented, i.e., not communicated to the computer-system developers, and therefore not implemented. This possibility demands that we make every effort to document the *abstract* requirements thoroughly. The *documented* requirements are what go forward.

Why a system failed does not matter to the users of a system.

The problem might be in the requirements, the specification, or the implementation, i.e., the three situations listed above, but what matters is that the system did fail.

As an example of the sources of service failure, consider a simple, single-player computer game. The requirements for the game, defined by game designers, describe the overall functionality and goals of the game. However, there is a requirement that the game be capable of restarting after a power failure. In terms of developing requirements, most of the attention of the game developers will be focused on functional characteristics of the game. Indeed, as long as the host computers being used by players do not fail, nothing will be noticed. The need to retain the game state in non-volatile storage might not be included in the *documented* requirements but certainly *is* a part of the *abstract* requirements. Following a power failure when a partially completed game cannot be resumed, the system has experienced a service failure. The failure arises from the first of the sources of service failure listed above.

Requirements derive from the goal of solving a problem in an application domain, and so much of the responsibility for getting the requirements correct lies beyond the scope of computer system development in general and software engineering in particular. Getting the requirements right is a responsibility that lies mostly with domain experts, i.e., engineers who understand and have experience with the greater context within which the computer operates. The software engineer is not an expert in the application domain, and so he or she cannot be expected always to notice requirements defects and understand their significance, i.e., the software engineer cannot be given the total responsibility of finding defects in requirements.

To understand this point, all that most computer or software engineers have to do is to try to write (or for that matter even just read and really understand) the requirements for a sophisticated system such as an automatic landing system for an aircraft or an automatic, implantable heart defibrillator. Such systems are beyond the scope of what can properly be expected from the expertise of even the most expert software engineer.

This assignment of responsibility does not mean that software engineers, both practitioners and researchers, are not involved in requirements elicitation and analysis. When working with requirements, software practitioners must note anything that appears to be a defect. Software engineers can comment about, question, model, and analyze requirements. Similarly, software researchers have examined these problems and continue to do so in order to develop technical approaches that can assist in developing complete and accurate requirements. Software engineers can also make sure that the domain experts understand the capabilities and limitations of computing systems.

2.6.3 A Practical View of Requirements and Specification

In an ideal situation, the documented requirements would record the abstract requirements properly, i.e., be complete and accurate, before system development began. Nevertheless, experience with building systems reveals that in practice:

- Requirements often change during the development of a subject system.

- Some requirements or details of requirements might be unknown when development of a subject system begins.

- Development engineers with different levels of domain knowledge for the subject system will need differing levels of detail in the documented requirements and documentation of requirements might not match the needs.

- Resource limitations might preclude various forms of analysis of requirements and specifications.

And so on.

Practical issues such as these affect the way that systems are built. The goal should always be to determine requirements completely and precisely, but this might not be possible in practice. This limitation does not mean that engineers should not strive to meet the goal. The limitation does mean that the possibility of system failure occurring because of defective requirements must always be kept in mind.

2.6.4 Viewpoints of Service Failure

A service failure can take a variety of forms and have a variety of effects. Each form has to be addressed with different techniques. The taxonomy organizes the characteristics of service failures using four *viewpoints*: (1) failure domain, (2) detectability, (3) consistency of failure, and (4) consequences of failure on the environment.

Failure Domains

Clearly, if a system delivers the wrong results, the system has failed. Equally important in many cases, however, is the late delivery of results. In real-time systems, a result often only has value until a particular deadline. After the deadline, the result is no longer useful.

Control systems and weather forecasting systems are two examples of systems where the value of the results essentially disappears after a certain period of time. A control system that fails to update actuators on a prescribed schedule will lose control even if the correct actuator settings are computed eventually. And what would be the value of finding out about today's weather tomorrow?

Finally, failures can be either constant or intermittent. In practice, for a system to fail in a "clean" way, e.g., by providing service and then halting, would be rather unusual. Far more common are intermittent failures and failures that become progressively worse over time.

Failure Detectability

A system failing and the users of the system knowing that the system has failed are two different things. In order to know that a system has failed, there has to be some sort of detection mechanism, i.e., a judgment system. The users observing a lack of output is one detection mechanism. Another might involve checking software that operates in parallel with the application. The need to detect failure arises because we might choose to take some sort of specific action when the system fails, and we need to get a failure indication in order to initiate whatever action is to be taken. As a minimum, those depending on the system for service need to know that the system has failed in some way other than not receiving service.

The idea of failure detectability leads to two important ideas:

False positive. A failure is indicated when a failure has *not* occurred.

A *false positive* will lead us to take action to cope with a failure when no failure has occurred. This action could lead to an actual failure, and so avoiding false positives in building judgment systems is important.

False negative. A failure is *not* indicated when a failure has occurred.

A *false negative* will lead us to fail to act to cope with a failure when we should act. The result is obviously both potentially catastrophic and undesirable. Again, avoiding false negatives in building judgment systems is important.

Failure Consistency

In many systems, when part of the subject system fails (a sub-system or component) several other parts need to take some action. Consider a multi-player, on-line game, for example, in which several server computers are providing real-time game service and several database computers are providing game and player information. If one of the database computers fails, perhaps critical player information becomes unavailable, and all of the server computers have to switch to a backup.

This would be acceptable provided the database computer failed completely. But suppose that the failure did not stop the computer from processing. Instead, suppose that the failure led to corrupt data being provided to the servers. This situation would be bad enough, but if different servers actually got *different* data about the *same* player, the potential exists for a more serious situation. The players whose information was corrupted would find that their interaction with other players would depend on which server was performing the interaction. Subsequent updates to the backup database would be inconsistent, and the game would degenerate into chaos.

A failure in which different users (people or computers) have different, i.e., inconsistent, views of a failure is referred to as a *Byzantine* failure. Such events are notoriously difficult to both analyze and prevent.

Consequences of Failure

The important idea of the consequences of failure was introduced in Chapter 1. Clearly different service failures have different consequences, and so we need to determine the consequences of failure for each service failure that might occur.

Some service failures might have such minimal consequences that we can choose to allow them to happen, e.g., an obvious and non-confusing typographical error in a display. For a system with many displays, each involving a lot of text and where the text changes frequently, the cost of checking the text carefully might be more than that of the negligible "failure" associated with an erroneous display. Other failures, such as those we saw in Chapter 1, might be so serious that we choose to apply tremendous effort to try to avoid them.

2.6.5 Informing the User about Failure

Many crucial computer systems operate in monitoring or standby mode most of the time. The protection system for a nuclear reactor, for example, monitors the reactor constantly, but only acts if circumstances warrant. A more familiar example is an anti-lock braking system on a car. The system is only needed if the vehicle skids, and so most of the time the system is merely monitoring. Such monitoring systems provide immense value to the users of the associated application.

An important characteristic of systems of this type is that there is usually a reasonable strategy to follow if the monitoring system fails during normal operation. The danger comes if a monitoring system fails *silently*, i.e., the users of the application are unaware of the failure. For example:

- In the case of a nuclear reactor, the failure of the protection system is benign provided the failure does not occur during an emergency. The reactor operators can initiate a planned shutdown or switch to a different monitoring mechanism. However, normal operation without the protection system and with the operators *unaware* of the lack of protection would be dangerous.

- In the case of a car's anti-lock braking system, if the system fails when braking is not needed, the driver could either stop carefully or proceed with caution. Driving a car normally with a failed anti-lock braking system and with the driver *unaware* of the failure would be dangerous.

Since monitoring systems do not provide any active service during normal operation, the failure of a monitoring system might go unnoticed unless explicit provision is made to signal the failure to the user of the system. Signaling failure is a critical point in defining the dependability of a system that intervenes only under unusual circumstances. We are presented with two choices:

- Require that the monitoring system's functionality be extremely dependable. If the system is engineered to meet those requirements, then the system will be available for service when needed with very high probability.

- Require that the monitoring system's functionality be moderately dependable, but require that the mechanism by which the system detects and signals its *own* failure be extremely dependable.

The first of these two options seems preferable, but that option is expensive. This option might even be unachievable, because the associated engineering might be infeasible. Thus, the second option has to be seriously considered, and this option is often chosen. Detecting failure with high probability is usually much easier than preventing failure.

2.7 Dependability and Its Attributes

With a clear picture of the notion of failure, we can now proceed to look carefully at what we are seeking from the systems we build, *dependability*. The following definition comes from the taxonomy:

Dependability: The dependability of a system is the ability to avoid service failures that are more frequent and more severe than is acceptable.

Note the following four points in this definition:

Dependability is about avoiding service failures. Although apparently obvious, this observation immediately gives us a clear direction for the engineering of a system. Provided the rate of severe service failures of a system is below a threshold deemed to be acceptable, the system will be considered "dependable". Thus, as we will discuss in depth in Chapter 3, dependability is about attempting to determine *all* the ways that a service failure might come about and engineering the system to keep the rate of service failure to an acceptable level.

The dependability of a system is subjective. Subjectivity arises from the use of the word "acceptable". This situation seems to be quite contrary to our goal of precision and accuracy in terminology.
Actually:

> *Subjectivity is inevitable, because we*
> *cannot build systems that never fail.*

If we could build systems that never fail, i.e., perfection, all we would need to do is state that the system (whatever it is) must never fail. Since we cannot do that, we have to set a bound on the failures we are prepared to accept. So the subjective element of this definition is requiring us to decide *just how close to perfection we have to come*.
How does one determine when "service failures are more frequent and more severe than is *acceptable*"? As we saw in Section 2.2, an acceptable failure rate for any given system is determined by factors such as acceptance by society and business interests. The number of fatalities in car accidents is far higher than the number of fatalities in aircraft accidents, and this situation is accepted by society (see Table 2.1 on page 29).
For any given system, the system's stakeholders (owner, customer, users, regulators, etc.) must identify the necessary dependability requirements, and, to the extent possible, developers must design so as to achieve them. The stakeholders have to assess the consequences of failure of the system, and make a judgment about how frequently they are prepared to be subject to such consequences.
Perhaps strangely, the definition of dependability for a given system comes down then to being what the users and those affected by the system say it is.

Dependability of a system is defined in an operating context. A system can only be expected to operate as desired in an operating context for which the system was designed. Service failures are likely to occur if the context is different from that which was planned. For example, a computer system designed to operate at room temperature is highly likely to fail at an unacceptable rate if operated in a harsh, high temperature environment.

Dependability is defined as an average. The definition includes the word "frequency", and so the determination of whether a system is dependable according to the definition requires that we state a means by which the frequency will be determined. For example, if, after a protracted period of safe operation of commercial aircraft, two aircraft accidents occur in the same week, that does not mean that somehow commercial aircraft are no longer dependable.

The foundation for the dependability requirements of any system is the following set of six attributes, all of which come from the taxonomy:

Reliability:	Continuity of correct service
Availability:	Readiness for correct service
Safety:	Absence of catastrophic consequences on the user(s) and the environment
Integrity:	Absence of improper system alterations
Confidentiality:	Absence of unauthorized disclosure of information
Maintainability:	Ability to undergo modifications and repairs

These attributes provide a framework for defining the rates and types of service failures that are relevant to any given system. The framework allows us to take the basic definition of dependability and instantiate the definition properly for any given system to reflect the dependability requirements desired for that system.

For reliability, availability, and safety, we need to use definitions based on probability so that we have a feasible engineering target. The conceptual notions defined by the taxonomy are not meant to do that.

We will examine each of these attributes in turn, and then we will see how they can be combined and their parameters set in practice to provide a comprehensive dependability requirements statement for any given system.

2.7.1 Reliability

The definition of reliability is:

Reliability: $R(t)$ = probability that the system will operate correctly in a specified operating environment up until time t.

Reliability is the probability that a system will operate as required for a period of time of length t. Since reliability is a probability, for any given value of t the system might fail before t time units have passed, and the system might continue to operate correctly after t time units have passed. For any given system, our concern is to be sure that the system does not fail during the planned mission time more often than is acceptable. Thus, in defining a reliability function that we need from a system, we have to decide what the acceptable rate of mission failure is and determine the associated probability accordingly.

The parameter t is important because t is related to the timeframe of interest, i.e., the mission time. For example, the computerized avionics system on an aircraft might be required to operate continuously for an entire flight with high probability. In this case, the typical mission time might be ten hours and the required probability of operating for ten hours might be 0.999999. For a planetary spacecraft, the mission time might be months or years and the required probability of operating for these mission times might be 0.999.

Measuring Reliability

As a probability, the reliability of a population of systems can be estimated using standard statistical techniques. If provision of service is required repeatedly for a single system, then that single system's reliability can be estimated also. In both cases, the times when failures occur are recorded, and an estimate of the reliability calculated, assuming that the underlying distribution is uniform. A confidence interval can be computed also that provides an interval within which the reliability is known to lie with a certain confidence.

2.7.2 Availability

The definition of availability is:

Availability: $A(t) =$ probability that the system will be operational
at time t.

Availability is the probability that the system will be ready for service at time t. Availability says nothing about whether the system will remain available for any period of time after t. Availability is the notion that we want for systems where outages are acceptable. Importantly, note that:

*Availability brings the concept of **repair** into the discussion. A system might fail, be repaired, and thereby become operational again. The notion of availability allows repair to be included in dependability requirements.*

At this point we have said nothing about how frequent outages will be, how long they will be, the state the system will be in when service returns, who will repair the system, and so on.

Why would one want availability when we have just defined reliability? Why not just require that systems be reliable? Surely, a system that is highly reliable is better than one that is highly available.

The reason to consider availability is that an availability requirement is easier to meet than a reliability requirement. Brief outages, even brief outages of less than a second, provide the opportunity for repair. So systems can be built that meet high availability requirements by including within their designs the ability to detect failed components and the ability to replace them *without* having to maintain service. This behavior is quite different from reliability, where continuous service is required.

System	Availability	Approx. Total Downtime/Year
General web site	0.99	5,000 minutes
Retail web site	0.999	500 minutes
Enterprise server	0.9999	50 minutes
Telephone system	0.99999	5 minutes
Telephone switch	0.999999	30 seconds

TABLE 2.2. Planned availability for several domains.

Table 2.2 shows examples of hypothetical but realistic availabilities for a variety of systems in various domains and what the availabilities mean in terms of the approximate outage times per year.

Complexities of Availability

Availability is more complicated than it appears because of the possibility of repair. To be useful, we need to define how the probability will be stated and how compliance will be determined. To see the difficulty, consider two different systems that have the same stated availability requirement of 0.99 with no further explanation. Suppose that the following outages were observed over a 1,000 hour period:

System A: nine one hour outages

System B: one eleven-hour outage

Have these systems met their availability requirements? One's immediate reaction is that system A has and that system B has not. Actually, we do not know, because nothing is stated about how availability was to be assessed. The requirement is for a certain rate, but the duration over which the rate is estimated from the observations of operation must be included in the requirement or there is no way to obtain an estimate. System A above might not meet the stated availability requirement if the system were to fail for a protracted time during the next period of operation. Similarly, system B might meet its availability requirement if that system operated without failure over a long period following the eleven-hour outage.

But if we measure the systems over a period of days, they will appear to have completely different levels of availability. If the measurement time is short, we might measure levels of availability that are far from the average seen over long periods of time.

In order to have a meaningful and practical statement of availability we need to add to the basic probability the period of time over which that probability has to be achieved. We will refer to this as the *performance time*. In the example, the observed failures occurred in a 1,000-hour period, but the performance time might have been 100, 1,000, 10,000 hours or something else completely.

Mean Time To Repair

Now consider two different systems that have the following observed outage rates:

> *System A: a single one-minute outage per day*

> *System B: one six-hour outage per year*

Over a one-year period, both systems have the same availability, 0.9999. But suppose systems A and B were different airline reservation systems that were accessed by travel agents needing to work with passenger flight records. For system A, a one-minute outage, even if such outages occurred once per day, would be annoying but little more than a minor inconvenience. Most users would never see the outages, and, on average, a user would see an outage of only 30 seconds.

The outages experienced by system B, however, could be serious. Complete loss of access for six hours, even if the outage occurred only once per year, would lead to a significant loss of business for the airline, a loss of business for travel agents, and a loss of reputation for both.

So now we see a third important parameter that we have to specify if our goal is a practical notion of availability, *Mean Time To Repair* (MTTR). Here is the definition:

Mean Time To Repair (**MTTR**): Mean Time To Repair is the expected time to repair once the system has failed if the system is repairable.

Since MTTR is an expected value, there is no notion of prediction that the value will be met by any particular device. On average, however, a large collection of devices operating under identical conditions will average this value of time to repair. The shorter the time taken to repair a system, the more likely it is that outages will not interfere with acceptable operation.

Two other important expected values are closely related to MTTR[1]:

Mean Time To Failure (MTTF): Mean Time To Failure is the expected value of the time to failure of the device type after being placed into service and assuming no repair.

Mean Time Between Failures (MTBF): Mean Time Between Failures is the expected value of the time to failure of the device type assuming that the device is repairable.

Thus, the MTTF is the average time to failure with no repair, and the MTBF is the average time between failures where a device is repaired after each failure.

Maximum Time To Repair

Unfortunately, things get more complicated when we try to define the availability we need from a system when we include *Mean Time To Repair*. Since MTTR is an expected value, there is nothing that bounds the actual repair time that a system will experience. If a system has a required MTTR of one minute and a single repair takes fifty nine minutes, has the system violated its dependability requirement? Again, we do not know, because we do not know the performance period. If that period included 59 other repairs, each of which took only one second, then the answer is "no", the system has not violated its dependability requirement. In that case, 60 repairs took 59 minutes and 59 seconds, making the MTTR just less than a minute.

So specifying MTTR will not protect us from long repair downtimes. Repair is an engineering activity and so we can engineer systems for repair times that meet requirements also. For systems for which availability and MTTR are important, the requirement is often not the mean time to repair but the *Maximum Time To Repair* (also MTTR, although we will avoid that use of the acronym) that has to be met with a certain probability. Thus, the repair requirement might be stated as:

Maximum time to repair not to exceed a time T with probability q.

The Parameters of Availability

Finally, we can see that availability is a complicated concept. Rather than a single probability, in practice, availability is a four-tuple: $\{A, p, T, q\}$ where A is the probability that the system will be available, p is the period of performance over which this probability must be met, T is the maximum repair time, and q is the probability by which that maximum must be met.

---

1. The definitions given here are the more common definitions. There are a number of variations and extensions that are beyond the scope of what we can consider here.

As should be clear from the definitions, a system can be highly available yet unreliable. For example, a system that fails on average once per hour but which restarts automatically in ten milliseconds has an availability of 0.9999972, a figure that one would consider to be highly available. If the system also had a reliability requirement of 0.999 for an operation time of 10 hours, then the system would be unreliable.

Measuring Availability

Provided all four parameters are stated, availability for a single system or a population can be estimated using standard statistical techniques just as reliability can. The only difference is that more data has to be collected, because there are two different estimates involved, A and T.

2.7.3 Failure per Demand

Closely related to availability is the notion of *failure per demand*. For the type of monitoring systems introduced in Section 2.6.5, complete functionality is not required continuously, only when certain circumstances arise. In such systems, the monitoring function might be required to be operating with a certain probability for time periods that are defined by the preventive maintenance interval. The response function for events of interest is only needed on demand, and that functionality might be required to operate correctly with a certain probability per demand. Recall from Section 2.6.5 that highly reliable monitoring might be replaced with highly reliable error detection of the monitoring system.

As an example, consider a fire-alarm system for a large building. The details might be:

- Reliability of the alarm system for a period of 24 hours: 0.999.

- Reliability of the failure detection mechanism of the alarm system for a period of 24 hours: 0.999999.

- Probability of correct operation of the alarm mechanism per demand: 0.999999.

2.7.4 Safety

Safety is a complex and important topic that can only be discussed superficially in this book. The safety of any particular system has to be approached carefully and systematically, and safety must be included at the earliest stages of a system's development. Failures that lead to catastrophic consequences are usually subtle, involving combinations of circumstances that were unexpected.

The construction of a safety-critical system should not be undertaken without the necessary preparation and experience. There are several textbooks available on system safety (for example, the text by Bahr [14] and the text by Leveson [84]), and the

System Safety Society holds annual conferences dedicated to the various aspects of safety [138].

Safety as an Absolute

In considering the various attributes of dependability, safety stands out as a rather special case, because safety deals with the most serious consequences of failure. In a very real sense, that characterizes what a safety-critical system is: a safety-critical system is a system whose consequences of failure are extremely serious. Thus, for example, systems whose failure can injure or kill people, cause significant pollution, or cause extensive physical damage are generally thought of as safety critical.

The taxonomy states that safety is the absence of catastrophic consequences on the user(s) or the environment. Since the consequences of failure are extraordinary, our goal is the total absence of failures. Thus, when we are seeking a safe system, we are seeking perfection.

We are now facing quite a dilemma. How are we going to be sure we have achieved safety if we think of safety as an absolute? If we build something controlled by a computer, failures occur for a myriad of reasons, often because of events that we did not anticipate. For example, how can we be sure that the hardware or software will never fail?

Public Perception of Safety

In practice, we have to accept some catastrophic consequences. Many millions of people fly on commercial aircraft each year, and, unfortunately, there are occasional accidents. Are commercial aircraft "safe"? We could make them safe by keeping them stationary on the ground, but they would not be very useful if we did. When you hear the phrase "your safety is our biggest concern" from an airline representative, keep in mind that, if safety were the airline's biggest concern, the airline would keep its aircraft grounded. In practice, what is meant is that safety is the airline's biggest concern given that the airline will operate a set of scheduled flights using a variety of aircraft to a variety of destinations in a variety of weather conditions while still maintaining the economic viability of the airline.

So, in practice, our goal with safety has to be tempered by reality. We can make systems safe by never using them, but that is not really what we want. In practice, a certain number of accidents with any given system has to be accepted, and society has to define what makes an accident rate acceptable. And, as we saw in Table 2.1, society is not consistent in establishing such definitions. The number of people killed each year in scheduled airline flights is low, but there is no public statement about how many aircraft crashes are too many. The fact that people continue to fly with the current accident rates indicates that society finds this accident rate acceptable. This notion is a special case for safety of the more general discussion about the meaning of "acceptable" in the definition of dependability at the beginning of Section 2.7.

Safety and Risk

Acceptance of some service failures means that, in practice, safety does not have to be absolute in order for the resulting systems to be acceptable to the public. The practical mechanism that is used is to require systems to subject the public to a total risk that is less than a prescribed threshold. In this case, the definition of risk is:

> **Risk**: Risk is the expected loss per unit time that will be experienced by using a system.

We can express this mathematically and thereby work with the concept as follows:

$$risk = \sum_i \text{pr}(failure_i) \times \text{loss}(failure_i)$$

where *i* ranges over all possible failures and the probabilities of failure are per unit time.

This leads us to a workable definition of safety:

> **Safety**: Expected loss per unit time is less than a prescribed threshold.

To estimate the risk to which the users of a system will be subject, we need to attempt to elaborate all of the failures, estimate the probability of each, and estimate the loss associated with each. Once we have estimated the risk, we can determine whether the estimate is below a subjective threshold set by community discussion.

In practice, estimating the necessary probabilities accurately is rarely possible, making risk estimation problematic. The probabilities are for new systems, so in most cases they cannot be estimated directly from operational experience. In addition, many probabilities of interest cannot be estimated accurately, because no suitable models exist. For example, the probability of human error in complex operational situations is impossible to model accurately, because the probability is affected considerably by the specific circumstances and the specific individual.

For passenger aircraft, the threshold has been set by the Federal Aviation Administration based on experience with accidents over many years. The threshold corresponds roughly to a requirement that the probability of a catastrophic loss of a passenger aircraft due to an engineering failure has to be less that 10^{-9} per flight hour. Acts of terrorism are not included in this particular number.

Safety by Proactive Functions

In order to reach levels of risk that are acceptable, a wide spectrum of techniques is needed within a system to prevent catastrophic failure to the extent possible even if failure is inevitable. The simplest and most familiar way in which this idea manifests itself is what is referred to as *fail-safe operation*. The intuitive notion here is that if a service failure which might have catastrophic consequences is about to happen, then an action that replaces that failure with one that is not catastrophic would be desirable. The common idea for achieving this is just to turn a system off.

Turning a system off to avoid danger is a nice thought, but that approach is naive to the point of being itself dangerous. Ideally, safety engineering requires that all of the various possible catastrophic failures be enumerated and functionality developed to minimize the likely damage from a failure. This functionality is sometimes complex and usually proactive in the sense that the functionality acts before a service failure occurs.

As an example, consider the operation of a protection system in a nuclear power plant. The monitoring system's role is to monitor the plant and to shut the plant down automatically if there is any prospect of a serious plant failure. The shutdown system acts automatically and takes what is usually a long series of steps to effect the plant shutdown. In this case, safety is achieved by proactive functionality.

2.7.5 Confidentiality

The definition of confidentiality is:

Confidentiality: The absence of unauthorized disclosure of information.

There is a lot of information stored in computers, communicated between them, and displayed on various devices. Much of that information is meant to be available only to particular individuals. The notion of confidentiality is that only those who are authorized to see information can actually do so.

As with safety, confidentiality as defined in the taxonomy is an absolute. Confidentiality is the "absence of unauthorized disclosure of information". In practice, confidentiality cannot be addressed properly unless we enhance this definition quite a bit. If we try to work with just this definition, there are several ways in which we can fail:

- If an individual has physical access to a computer and knows the appropriate password, ensuring that the individual does not look at information for which he or she does not have authorization will be difficult. Even if the data were encrypted, we can imagine a scenario in which the individual had the tools needed to decrypt the data. A little collusion between malicious individuals can make this problem much worse.

- Using a process of elimination, data items can sometimes be inferred even though the data is not exposed explicitly. By examining data that is available, perhaps from multiple sources, an adversary can either determine facts that should be private or reduce the number of possible values to a disturbingly small number.

The way in which we have to enhance the definition of confidentiality in order to permit proper statements of dependability requirements is to be precise in what we mean. We need to add a series of assumptions that document the scope of our concern. These assumptions are determined by the inherent value of the data and the environment in which the data is stored and used, specifically:

- We have to determine the **consequences of failure** of confidentiality. Inventory records for a retail store are not meant to be available publicly, but a flaw that exposed the information would not be especially serious. Exposing credit card account numbers, by contrast, could be serious because of the possibility of financial and identity theft.

- We have to determine the **population** from whom the information has to be restricted. Those who have access as part of their normal actions either to critical information, the computers upon which the information is stored, or even the buildings in which the computers are housed are sometimes referred to as *insiders*. Inappropriate access by insiders is referred to as the *insider threat*. The insider threat is known to be one of the most difficult to combat. Confidentiality is vastly harder to achieve if insider access has to be dealt with.

- We have to determine the acceptability of any **restrictions** that have to be applied to achieve confidentiality. Most people appreciate the need for security items such as passwords but are not good at following rules such as changing passwords regularly. Imposing rules that people will not follow in order to achieve confidentiality is not going to work.

So in specifying confidentiality, we have to document the consequences of failure, the population whose access needs to be restricted, and the limits that have to be imposed on technical solutions. With those additional considerations, we can define what we need adequately.

2.7.6 Integrity

The definition of integrity is:

Integrity: The absence of improper system alterations.

Much like confidentiality, this definition is absolute and has to be enhanced before we can use the term in a statement of dependability requirements. The enhancements are identical to those needed for confidentiality, the difference between the two lying in the distinction between reading information and changing that information. We will not discuss integrity further.

2.7.7 Maintainability

The definition of maintainability is:

Maintainability: The ability to undergo repairs and modifications.

The issue of maintainability arises primarily in circumstances where we need to include details of repair and modification in defining dependability. The two major concerns are the feasibility of repair and, for systems that can be repaired, the distribution of repair times.

In practice, we cannot discuss repair unless we know a lot about the failure that necessitated the repair. In particular, we need to know:

- The extent of the damage to the system that accompanies a system failure. Without a precise statement of damage, repair could require resources bounded only by a complete system replacement.

- The extent of the damage outside the system that accompanies a system failure. If a system failure leads to data corruption or physical changes in the operating environment such as printing, altered switch settings, or incorrect setting of actuators, then repair will include the need to address all the changes in the environment that accompanied the failure. Again, the time and cost could be unbounded. In some cases, the damage cannot be repaired. If failure of a system includes printing, for example, we almost certainly cannot erase the printed material from the paper.

Thus, merely stating that a system can be repaired in some general sense is insufficient. If we are going to specify maintainability as part of a dependability requirements statement, we have to document which failures have to be repaired and we have to document the damage that will accompany such failures.

Many, many software failures occur as a result of upgrades, i.e., when the software is being modified, including changes that occur as part of maintaining a system. No matter how carefully prepared and tested, experience has shown that introducing a software upgrade into an operating computer system has a disturbingly high probability of leading to system failure. Knowing this, engineers routinely make provision to remove (or back out) an upgrade if necessary.

2.7.8 A Word about Security

Security does not appear on the list of dependability attributes, yet terms that are obviously security related do. The reason that security does not appear as an individual term is because security is inherently a composite. We cannot define what being a "secure" system will mean, because concerns in the security area are quite diverse. Some systems are concerned with unauthorized access to information, some with denial-of-service attacks, and so on.

Security is best defined in terms of integrity, confidentiality, and availability. Where a system requires a notion of security, the stakeholders need to determine what the threat model is, what the consequences of failure are, and from those determine the role of integrity, confidentiality, and availability.

2.7.9 The Notion of Trust

The terms "trust" and "trustworthy" appear frequently in discussions about computing systems. Do we need definitions of these terms? The answer is "yes", because the notion of trust actually complements the notion of dependability in an important way.

In many cases, one system depends on another. By "depends", we mean that the dependability of one system depends upon that of another. If system A depends upon system B, then a failure of system B affects system A. So, the dependability of system A depends upon the dependability of system B. This dependence might be total, i.e., system A fails whenever system B fails, or zero, i.e., system A does not fail whenever system B fails, or anywhere in between.

The taxonomy defines *dependence* as follows:

Dependence. The dependence of system A on system B represents the extent to which system A's dependability is (or would be) affected by that of system B.

Closely tied to the notion of dependence is the notion of trust. The taxonomy defines *trust* as follows:

Trust. Trust is accepted dependence.

Thus, we have come to the point where the acceptability of an achieved level of dependability has a precise meaning. Assuming that failure of system A will have serious consequences for system B, system B is *trusted* by system A if system A accepts the dependability of system B.

These definitions of dependence and trust are useful for *any* two systems. A special case of particular interest arises for a system that provides service to human users in some way. Setting levels of dependability for critical systems was seen as a matter of public interest in Section 2.2 and in Section 2.7.4. In the limit, the level that is set is a statement that the users of the subject critical system *trust* that system.

2.8 Systems, Software, and Dependability

2.8.1 Computers Are neither Unsafe nor Insecure

In general, there is no such thing as a safe computer or a secure computer. These notions apply to a computer system operating in an *environment* (another system, see Section 2.3). A computer system that is isolated, i.e., not connected to any other entity, cannot do any harm and so cannot be "unsafe". In order for safety to be a consideration, a computer has to be operating as part of a larger system (the environment) for which damage is possible. Making appropriate provision for computer failure by some other means within the larger system would mean that there might be no damage if the computer system failed.

The same considerations apply to security. A computer system by itself cannot be insecure. In order for security to be a consideration, a computer has to be dealing with information that has some specific value, providing an application that uses that data, and operating in an environment where there are adversaries who would like to either access or change the information.

A useful computer system is just a *component* of an application system (more generally an environment system, see page 30), albeit an important one, that enables some aspects of the application system's functionality and helps to implement the application system's dependability properties. But the computer itself does not have and must not be considered to have the dependability properties associated with the application system. This distinction is hard to accept and non-obvious, but the distinction is crucial and has significant implications in terms of both the definitions of dependability requirements and our responsibilities as computer or software engineers.

Although safety and security are not properties of computers directly, there is a lot that we can do to facilitate these properties at the application system level. For example, buffers that are subject to overrun are a major cause of security vulnerabilities. Searching for such buffers in software is an important aspect of *verification* but elimination of buffers subject to overrun does not make software "secure". Such elimination just means that an important class of software faults has been eliminated.

2.8.2 Why Application System Dependability?

The reason that we as computer and software engineers have to understand the detailed concepts and definitions of application system dependability in some depth is that application system dependability relies on computers and their software to a large extent. Specifically:

- Much of the proactive functionality needed in modern application systems to provide acceptably dependable operation is implemented digitally.

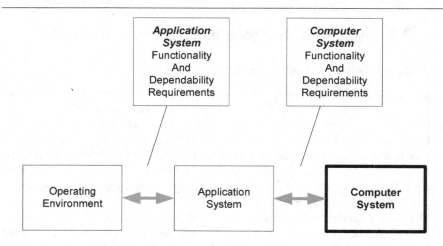

FIGURE 2.3 The relationship between the requirements for the application system and those of the computer system. The computer system requirements amount to a *contract* between the system engineers and the computer and software engineers.

- Defects in the computer systems that we build could result in an application system failure.

As an example, consider once again the implementation of shutdown systems in a nuclear reactor. This implementation is digital for the most part, and so the development of the critical safety functionality falls to the software engineer. This reliance on software means that the software engineers, computer engineers, systems engineers, and application engineers have to work together closely in order to make sure that everything that needs to be done is done.

The distinction between the application system and the associated computer system does not mean that software or computer engineers cannot treat application system failures, such as accidents, as anything other than something to be avoided if at all possible. *All* engineers must do everything practicable to prevent application system failures. And when an accident occurs, *all* engineers need to determine how best to prevent such accidents in the future.

2.8.3 Application System Dependability and Computers

Computer System Dependability as a Contract

The relationship between the requirements for an application system and those of the computer system is shown in Figure 2.3. The application system has to meet the requirements that are determined by that system's environment. Safety and security dependability requirements, for example, will be defined by the role of the application system in its environment.

The computer system's requirements are determined by the design of the application system. If the design of the application system includes actions that the computer system has to perform, then this aspect of the application system's design will translate into functionality and associated dependability requirements for the computer system.

Establishing the requirements for both the application system and the computer system is a matter of negotiation. That is why the two large arrows in Figure 2.3 are bidirectional. The need for negotiation derives from the fact that either of the sets of requirements might not be implementable. For example, the engineers responsible for the design of the application system might require a level of dependability from the computer system that is either unachievable (such as perfection) or that is unreasonably expensive to achieve. In that case, the software and computer engineers have to inform the application engineers of the issue, and then the application engineers have to redesign the system so as to impose reasonable dependability requirements on the computer system.

The large bold arrow on the right of Figure 2.3 is identified as a *contract*. The relationship between the application engineers and the computer and software engineers is best thought of as a contract because that best summarizes the situation. Essentially, the contract means:

> **Application engineers**: *If the computer system (both hardware and software) meets the functional and dependability requirements derived from the application system design, then, provided the remainder of system development is completed correctly, the application system will meet its functional and dependability requirements.*

> **Computer and software engineers**: *Our engineering target is to meet the functional and dependability requirements supplied by the systems engineers.*

In practice, this contract might be in several parts, because the application system requires multiple functions from the computer system. Similarly, there might be multiple contracts, because there might be multiple computer systems. Finally, the other large arrow in the figure is also a contract. This arrow represents a contract between the environment in which the application system operates and the application system itself.

A Simple Example

As an example, consider the role of a computer system in a (hypothetical) shutdown system for a nuclear plant (the application system). The role of the computer system in the functionality of the application system is to monitor a set of critical system state variables such as temperatures, pressures, radiation levels, flow rates, equipment functionality, and operator actions, and to shut the plant down if a condition arises that is determined to be dangerous. These requirements are supplied to the computer and software engineers purely as logic statements. There is no room for interpretation or judgment on the part of those engineers. The data channels to be monitored, the rate of monitoring, the definition of the states in which the plant is to be shut down, and how the shutdown is to be effected are all prescribed.

Importantly, the dependability of the monitoring system's computer system has to be specified also. The notions of reliability and availability are meaningful for computer functionality, and that is what will be stated for the computer system dependability of the shutdown system. We might find typical requirements to be something such as:

Reliability of monitoring function. The shutdown system is expected to be monitoring the plant continuously, but we cannot document a reliability requirement with the time parameter set to infinity. Failures of the monitoring system that lead to the system being non-operational must be expected. The approach we might use is to define the period required in a reliability statement as a daily rate. Safe operation might be possible without interruption if loss of the monitoring system were less than a minute provided the operators knew about the lack of monitoring and were informed about the system's return to service after repair. We might find a reliability requirement such as this:

pr(monitoring system operates correctly for 24 hours) > 0.9999

Maximum time to repair: sixty seconds

pr(maximum time to repair > sixty seconds) < 0.0001

Probability of failure per demand. If the shutdown system is called upon to act, then shutdown has to be completed successfully with very high probability:

pr(correct operation of shutdown mechanism per demand) > 0.999999

Probability of failure of judgment system. The mechanism that determines whether the monitoring system is operating correctly must be ultra reliable:

pr(failure of monitoring system detected and signalled) > 0.9999999

Combining the necessary functionality and the necessary dependability of the computer system creates the contract between the application system engineers and the computer and software engineers.

2.9 Defining Dependability Requirements

Recall from the beginning of Section 2.7 that the definition of dependability is:

Dependability: The dependability of a system is the ability to avoid service failures that are more frequent and more severe than is acceptable.

This definition is not system specific and is subjective. Recall that what we need to do in developing the dependability requirements for a particular application is to document the frequency and severity of the service failures that will be *acceptable* for that system. In practice, this is done by stating the details of service failures that are expected and then setting bounds on failures in the form of probabilities.

The dependability requirements for systems in practice are combinations of the attributes discussed in the previous section, usually with an emphasis on one of them. The various parameters have to be defined in such a way that:

- The system dependability will meet the needs of the stakeholders.
- The system can be constructed in a cost-effective manner given the dependability requirements.
- The system design allows the values of the various parameters that were set during development to be predicted so that developers can make engineering choices.
- The selected parameters can be assessed during operation so that stakeholders can tell whether the engineering choices are meeting the system goals.

Stating clearly, precisely, and completely what the dependability requirements are for a computer system before starting to build the system is essential. These requirements dictate the engineering techniques that will be used in the creation of the system to a much larger extent than the required functionality. In practice, therefore, we have to examine:

- The operating context.
- The consequences of failure.
- The needs of the users.
- The expectation that society has for the system.
- The demands of regulators if the system is to operate in a regulated environment.

Table 2.3 shows the major areas of the dependability requirements for several safety-critical computer applications. For example, in telecommunications, availability is critical, although reliability is not. Loss of a telephone system for a small fraction of a second is unlikely to be a major problem for users. Maintainability is also important because maintainability is needed to support availability. Finally, both integrity and confidentiality are important because the data (which might be digitized voice) is private.

The dependability of weapons systems is dominated completely by safety, although, obviously, some availability is expected. Weapon system safety is conveniently thought of in most cases as an absence of undesired energy release. Achiev-

Telecommunications		A			I	C	M
Passenger rail		A	S				
Weapons			S	I	C		
Nuclear power		A	S				
Bank ATM network		A			I	C	
Aircraft autopilot	R		S				
Home thermostat	R		S				
Computer game	R						
Drug infusion pump		A	S	I			

TABLE 2.3. Dependability requirements for a variety of application domains where R = Reliability, A = Availability, S = Safety, I = Integrity, C = Confidentiality, and M = Maintainability.

ing this apparently simple goal means that measures have to be taken to guard against undesired energy release during manufacture, transport, storage, dispatch, transit to the target, and decommissioning.

2.9.1 A First Example, an Automobile Cruise Control

As a simple example of defining dependability requirements, consider a computerized cruise control for a passenger car. This is an entirely hypothetical example, of course, and so the probabilities and performance parameters are typical and not from any specific system.

A cruise control is likely to be used for extended periods when driving on a major highway, and so the user will be interested in continuous operation. A service failure in which the cruise control disengages and the car slows down is not too serious, mostly inconvenient. But if such inconveniences occur too frequently, there are likely to be complaints from drivers, and so the dependability requirements have to state a rate that is going to avoid such complaints.

Looking a little further, we note that maintaining speed within a fairly narrow range is important, because the driver will probably rely on the cruise control to avoid speeding. Thus, an excessive deviation from the planned speed would be a service failure. Combining this requirement with the requirement for continuous operation leads us to stating a reliability requirement for the device:

Reliability: pr(|vehicle_speed − set_speed| < 5 m.p.h. for 60 minutes) > 0.999

What this statement says is that the probability that the cruise control will keep the car's speed within five miles per hour of the desired speed and do that for one hour has to be greater than 0.999.

There are important safety issues that arise with a cruise control. First, the cruise control must not engage unless the driver requests that the system operate. Second, the cruise control must not remain engaged if the driver presses the brake pedal or clutch pedal. Third, the cruise control must not cause the vehicle to accelerate rapidly to an excessive speed that might lead to an accident.

These three states that should be avoided are called *hazards*, and we will discuss the notion of hazard in more detail in Chapter 3. Identification of all of the hazards that a system faces is important, and there might be other hazards that we have not listed for the cruise control. For now, we will just use these three as examples. We can conveniently define the safety requirement for the cruise control as follows:

Safety: pr(hazard arises < 0.000001 per hour)

If we associate a value with the loss that might result from one of these hazards arising, we can multiply the value by this probability to obtain the associated risk. There is little advantage to doing so, however. If an accident results from a malfunction of the cruise control, human life would be endangered, and so the loss is best thought of as catastrophic.

With the reliability and safety requirements defined, developers can begin the process of designing the cruise control. As they do so, they will have to analyze their design, and predict what the dependability probabilities actually are. By comparing these predictions with the dependability requirements, developers can determine whether they have a design that will be adequate.

2.9.2 A Second Example, a Pacemaker

A heart pacemaker is a sophisticated and immensely useful device. Some pacemakers stimulate two of the heart's chambers and some three chambers. Many pacemakers are combined with defibrillators. All modern pacemakers can be configured to suit the patient's needs using an external "programmer" and a through-the-skin communications mechanism. Some pacemakers attempt to adjust their performance based on the patient's activity as measured by accelerometers. Finally, all modern pacemakers collect data about the patient for analysis by a physician. Although the major characteristics of a pacemaker discussed in this example are realistic, this example is completely hypothetical. Real pacemakers and defibrillators are much more complex than the device described here.

Despite its sophisticated functionality, a pacemaker is basically a computer with some special peripherals. When a heartbeat is expected, the computer reads information about the heart from sensors and makes a decision about whether the heart requires a stimulating pulse. If the heart beats on its own, the pacemaker takes no action. If the heart does not beat as expected, the pacemaker generates the necessary stimulation. To extend battery life, pacemakers typically turn themselves off between heartbeats. A simplified version of the required processing is shown in Figure 2.4.

A pacemaker is an example of the type of monitoring system that was discussed in Section 2.6.5. If the device fails completely and becomes inert, the patient might survive, although in that case, the device would not be available if needed. If the

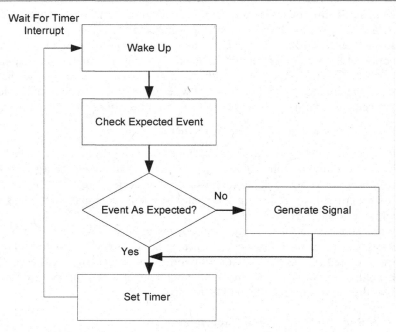

FIGURE 2.4 Basic processing of a heart pacemaker. A pacemaker requires battery life to be as long as possible, so the device shuts down most circuitry between heartbeats.

patient knew that the device had failed, then he or she could seek immediate medical advice. If the device failed actively and started generating stimulation when not needed, serious harm to the patient could result and quickly.

A pacemaker is also an example of a system with *inertia*. Failure of a pacemaker for a small fraction of a second is unlikely to be noticed. Failure for a few seconds might be noticed, but the effect is unlikely to be serious. The consequences of failure become really serious if the pacemaker fails for several minutes during a time when the patient needs help from the device.

This notion of inertia occurs in many systems that interact with real-world entities (such as a person), and inertia can be very valuable when engineers are concerned with dependability. The reason is that inertia allows brief periodic failures. Thus many situations that appear to require reliability in fact require availability, and availability is much easier to provide than reliability.

The dependability requirements for a pacemaker are quite complex. One might think, initially, that all one has to do is make the pacemaker reliable. Similarly, since a pacemaker is a device that operates inside a human patient, one might also think that the only requirement is safety. Certainly, reliability and safety enter into the analysis, but an informal statement about just one attribute is far from an adequate analysis of the dependability requirements.

The definition of the pacemaker's dependability requirements can be structured by identifying the critical elements of functionality that have to be provided. For each, we can define the associated dependability requirements and tailor them to the specific needs of that element of functionality. There are two elements of functionality:

- **Heart Pacing.**
  The provision of necessary pacing stimuli is the crucial activity that is needed for the patient. The patient could be injured in many ways by inappropriate actions, and so the fundamental dependability requirement is safety. As with the cruise-control example, the cost of failure is injury or death, and there is no advantage to going beyond defining the maximum acceptable probability of a hazard arising. So we could define this dependability requirement for the pacemaker as:

Safety: pr(hazard arises < 0.00000001 per hour)

- **Patient Data Recording.**
  Patient data recording is the second element of functionality. Long-term data recording (tens of minutes) is not necessary for correct pacing action. The dependability requirement for this functionality is availability, and the actual probability required need not be high.

The pacemaker system depends upon four major sub-systems. These sub-systems do not appear in the statement of the system-level dependability, but each has its own dependability requirement that derives from the system-level requirement. In other words, each of the sub-systems has to achieve a certain level of dependability in order for the system to meet its safety requirement. The difference between the system dependability requirements and the sub-system requirements is important.

For purposes of illustration, the dependability requirements of the four major sub-systems are as follows:

- **Timing.**
  The timing function turns the device on when a heartbeat is expected and off again once the heartbeat has happened. Timing must happen correctly, although brief outages in which the timing system deals with its own failure would be acceptable because of the system's inertia. We conclude that the basic dependability requirement for the timing system is availability. The quantification of this requirement depends on the degree to which a patient could withstand the system being unavailable, and this is a medical decision. Typically, one would expect values such as an availability of 0.999999 with a maximum tolerable outage time of one second and no more than 10 seconds of accumulated outage per month.

- **Sensing And Pulse Decision.**

  The action taken on any given pulse is determined by a fairly complicated algorithm that bases the decision on sensed data, archived data, and patient-specific parameters. The calculation of the necessary pulse details must be done correctly with high probability. An incorrect pulse could be fatal, literally. So the dependability requirement is that the computation be carried out correctly for each heartbeat. This is not an obviously continuous calculation since the result has to be tailored to the circumstances of each heartbeat. The calculation is brief, periodic, and critical, but the calculation takes place within a framework that is managing the sequencing and the manipulation of the critical data elements. The dependability requirement is availability with a high probability. Once again, a typical probability value might be 0.999999.

- **Parameter Setting.**

  Setting operational parameters is a crucial activity since the operational parameters affect the therapy that the patient receives in many ways. Waveforms, times, energy levels, and so on can be set, and any flaw in this could be severely detrimental. Setting parameters occurs rarely, however, and so the dependability requirement that is needed is a low probability of failure per demand. An example value might be that the failure of the parameter setting system has to be less than 0.9999 per demand.

- **Component Failure Diagnosis.**

  Because of its patient monitoring and support characteristics, component failure detection is critical for a pacemaker. No external access is possible to test components during operation, and so the device must undertake all the testing itself. The testing element of functionality is important, because of the need to protect the patient if at all possible if there is an internal failure. With this in mind, the dependability requirement for the failure diagnosis subsystem is availability. Again, thanks to inertia, the diagnosis system can be unavailable for brief periods. Typically, an availability of 0.999999 might be required with a maximum tolerable outage time of one second and no more than five seconds of accumulated outage per month.

For a pacemaker, these are the areas that need to be addressed first in composing the dependability requirements. Real pacemakers have other sub-systems and components that provide additional functionality, and, in practice, all of these additional elements have to be included in the overall dependability requirements.

2.10 As Low As is Reasonably Practicable ALARP

2.10.1 The Need for ALARP

While developing dependability requirements, the difficulty of meeting them must be kept in mind. Requiring a small probability of failure might seem the right thing to do when considering the consequences of failure, but the result might be a goal that is unachievable, either technically or economically.

Developing a system for which the consequences of failure are high presents the following three difficult engineering dilemmas:

1. *Can the system be built to meet the probabilities that have been specified?*

2. *Can the actual probabilities that the system achieves be measured?*

3. *If more resources were expended on developing the system, then the rate of failure might be reduced. That being the case, should the developers expend all possible resources on developing the system?*

The first dilemma is concerned with how effective our engineering techniques are. Whether we can meet the requisite probabilities depends on many factors in the engineering process. The second dilemma is concerned with assessment, and we will discuss that in Chapter 12. In practice, for the first and second dilemmas, probabilities are difficult both to meet and to demonstrate. As we see in Chapter 12, assessment is often virtually impossible, because the associated probabilities are so small.

The third dilemma is a complex and difficult judgment we have to address. If the developers do not expend all possible resources on developing the system, will they be doing a disservice to the system's stakeholders? If a failure occurs and significant losses were incurred, would the developers be liable for the losses if they did not use every possible technique to avoid the failure?

As an example, consider the use of formal verification in the development of software (see Chapter 7). That formal verification permits important dependability conclusions to be drawn about software is well known, yet formal verification is sometimes considered an exotic and expensive technique. Should formal verification always be used "just in case"?

These dilemmas arise in all fields of engineering, and the problems are usually dealt with by modeling the effects of development techniques. Structural engineers and architects can predict the strength of a building based on the design of the building, the materials used, the building techniques used, rates of corrosion, and so on. With such models, the effect of changes in parameters such as the strength of materials can often be predicted. Structures can thus be engineered to be as strong as required.

In computer engineering in general and in software engineering in particular, such modeling is difficult for a variety of reasons:

- Mistakes in design (design faults, see Chapter 3) dominate failures of computer systems and they are notoriously difficult to model.

- Computer systems tend to be much more complex than other engineered systems.

- Computer systems are usually immersed in complex environments that create stimuli which are difficult to model.

- Computer systems are the components that bring together the various non-computer components of engineered systems.

That modeling is difficult does not mean that we cannot undertake modeling. What the difficulty means is that we have to be careful with our expectations and conclusions. This situation has led to the ALARP concept.

2.10.2 The ALARP Concept

Without the benefit of accurate predictive models, computer engineers have to deal with these difficult dilemmas in a more general way. Part of that generalization is economics, and, at least indirectly, that is the concept of *As Low As is Reasonably Practicable* (ALARP) [60, 117].

The idea underlying ALARP is that the risk associated with a system that has high consequences of failure shall be reduced to a point where further reductions would not be commensurate with the cost of achieving those reduction, i.e., there is *gross disproportion* between the costs and benefits. The ALARP concept, therefore, immediately helps to address the third of the three dilemmas that we face.

Using the formal methods example above, the cost of applying formal methods to a complex application might be several person years of effort. Yet, the experience for that type of application might have shown that the benefit of formal methods is minimal in that particular case. Thus, the cost would be high and the benefit perhaps negligible, and so *there is gross disproportion between the costs and benefits*.

For a typical system that has multiple possible failures each with different consequences, ALARP is applied separately for each of the possible failures. For failures with higher consequences, more resources can be invested in reducing the probability of failure and hence the risk. For failures with lower consequences of failure, fewer resources can be justified. Some failures with trivial consequences of failure can be ignored. All failures might still occur, and what ALARP has done is to provide a reasonable stopping criterion for the effort expended to deal with each type of failure.

The notion of gross disproportion between the costs and benefits also helps with the other two dilemmas. If we have poor models for probabilities and hence poor

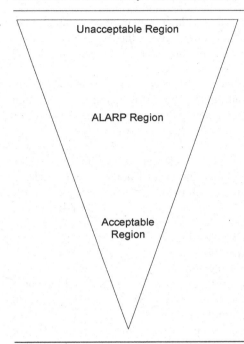

Unacceptable Region

ALARP Region

Acceptable
Region

FIGURE 2.5 Risk partitions in ALARP. The top region is for risks that are unacceptable and for which measures must be taken to mitigate the risk. The cost in this region is expected to be high. The middle region is the ALARP region within which risk is reduced to the extent that the cost is commensurate with the value. Finally, the bottom region is for risks that are considered acceptable.

risk estimates, we can accept a high degree of imprecision if the decision rests on an assessment of the cost being *grossly disproportionate* to the expected reduction in risk. The fact that there is a large (i.e., gross) difference means we will likely make the correct choice even with relatively poor data.

By appealing to human judgment, we can extend the utility of cost being grossly disproportionate to benefit to situations where we have essentially no models. Even if we have no useful models of risk, we can utilize the experience of experts. Although available quantification might not be adequate, expert judgment based on experience with similar systems often allows experts to decide on questions such as: "Is the cost of this technique grossly disproportionate to the expected reduction in risk?"

2.10.3 ALARP Carrot Diagrams

ALARP is sometimes explained using what are referred to as "carrot" diagrams [150]. An example is shown in Figure 2.5. The role of the diagram is to display the risks associated with each possible failure with the highest at the top and in decreasing order of severity. The risks are then partitioned into three ranges: *unacceptable*, *ALARP*, and *acceptable*. The risks in the unacceptable range are so significant that they must be reduced. The system cannot be deployed with these

risks present. Reducing these risks is achieved by either system or operational modifications, and the result should be that the risk is reduced to the ALARP range.

The risks in the acceptable range are insignificant and so the cost of reducing
them would exceed the value.

The risks in the ALARP range are subject to reduction provided the cost is considered reasonable. In the end, the risks in this range should be reduced to a point
where the level of risk is considered acceptable by the system's stakeholders, and
further reduction would, by definition, have a cost that was grossly disproportionate
to the reduction in risk achieved.

The ALARP partitioning concept is useful and reasonable. The important thing
is to apply risk reduction to any risk for which the cost of doing so is considered
acceptable. If, after risk reduction, risks remain in the unacceptable range, then the
system is considered unsuitable for deployment. For risks in the ALARP range,
losses are expected, but the risks have been reduced, by definition, to As Low As
Reasonably Practicable, and the resulting risk level is acceptable to the stakeholders.
This partitioning helps guide the economics of risk reduction. Whether the risk is
acceptable after applying ALARP is then a question for society to answer.

ALARP arose and is used primarily in the United Kingdom (U.K.) where
ALARP is applied broadly across a range of industries. ALARP derives from an
important piece of legislation, the Health and Safety at Work etc. Act 1974 [59].
Outside the U.K., engineering practice tends to be based on the use of prescriptive
standards (see Section 12.3) and a cultural expectation of engineers using good engineering practice.

Key points in this chapter:

- When building a computer system that has to be dependable, we need a
  well-defined and testable target for the dependability needed.
- The dependability target that we have to reach is often determined by
  the public's informal notion of sufficiently dependable. The public's
  notion of sufficiently dependable varies considerably between domains.
- In order to be able to define dependability requirements, we need a precise terminology that we can use in the various statements that have to
  be made.
- Terminology has been defined to a large extent in a taxonomy that is in
  the archival literature and so available to all.
- By themselves, computer systems are neither unsafe nor insecure. Computer systems need to provide service to a larger application system of
  which the computer system is just a part and where this larger system is
  providing a service in order for there to be a meaningful notion of safety
  and security.
- A mechanism for managing the activities involved in risk reduction is
  required. A pragmatic approach is to use the ALARP principle — reduction of risk to a point that is as low as reasonably practicable.

Exercises

1. Develop an example of a system that could be considered adequately *safe* but not highly *available*.

2. Develop an example of a system that could be considered highly *available* but not highly *reliable*.

3. Develop an example of a system that could be considered highly *reliable* but not adequately *safe*.

4. A system is often referred to as *fail safe* if the system maintains safety after a component failure even though the system does not continue to provide service. Many people assume that a fail-safe state can be achieved by having a system suspend all functionality. This is almost always incorrect; some minimal functionality is always required. Give two examples of systems in which this is not correct and for each explain what the minimal functionality needs to be.

5. Explain in your own words why *fault tolerance* is not a system characteristic.

6. Carefully and precisely document the dependability requirements that might be used for a typical *pacemaker* based on the material in Section 2.9.2. Consider all the elements that have to be defined, the content of the specification, the format of the document, and the details of the content.

7. Assuming that Google is prepared to accept no more than a cumulative downtime of 100 minutes per year for a specific data center, carefully and precisely state this requirement in a form that will meet Google's *intent*.

8. Assuming 35,000 people are killed in fatal car accidents each year in the United States, estimate the *risk* associated with road transport. (Note this question requires you to make a number of computational assumptions such as the "value" of a human life).

9. In your own words, explain why a computer system cannot be thought of as either "safe" or unsafe".

10. The taxonomy of definitions by Laprie et al. revised the definition of the critical term *dependability* from the *old* to the *new*:

    Old: *Dependability is the ability to deliver service that can justifiably be trusted.*

    New: *The dependability of a system is the ability to avoid service failures that are more frequent and more severe than is acceptable.*

    Why do you think that the developers of the taxonomy felt the necessity to make the change from the old to the new? (Hint: the answer lies in the subjectivity in the definitions).

11. The radiation therapy machine described in Chapter 1, Exercise 13 is used to treat cancer patients with a constant source of radiation for a ten-minute period. Stopping therapy before ten minutes has passed is dangerous for the patient. The treatment team specified a reliability for ten minutes of continuous operation of 0.999. Observation of the machine shows that failures interrupted treatment on two occasions, and, in the same time period, there were 2,329 successful treatments. Did the machine meet the reliability goal?

12. An information system is required to have an availability of 0.999 or better and a maximum duration for a single outage of 40 minutes in each 30-day operating period.

   (a) If a 30-day period begins with the system unavailable for a period of 30 minutes, during which day of that period will its availability exceed 0.999?

   (b) If a second outage occurs during that same 30-day period, what is the longest outage that can occur and the system still meet its availability goal?

   (c) If the system is unavailable for a period of 90 seconds each day during a 30-day period, what would its observed availability be?

13. The manufacturer of the computerized dispatching system (the 911 system) being considered for Gotham City's ambulance service claimed that the system availability is 0.99999. The mayor decided that this level of availability was excellent and had the system installed. Lengthy outages have occurred since installation, leading to ambulances not being dispatched when needed. The manufacturer claims that the system is meeting its dependability requirement and has been absolved of blame. How can this be the case?

14. A freight rail system that transports toxic gases for specialized manufacturing is subject to two major types of failure: (a) catastrophic failure in which toxic gases are released and damage the local environment; and (b) major failure in which the train damages the track and other equipment but no toxic gas is released. The cost of a failure of type (a) is determined to be $15,000,000 and the cost of a failure of type (b) is $825,000. If the probability per train trip of a failure of type (a) is determined to be 0.0000039 and the probability per train trip of a failure of type (b) is determined to be 0.0000861, what is the risk per trip?

15. A technology company makes an information system for pharmacists. The system provides inventory control of prescription drugs, electronic drug ordering from manufacturers, insurance company billing, and patient prescription records. The system uses several client computers for pharmacists' access and a small server that is connected to the Internet. The system supports retail pharmacy operation and is used by pharmacy staff constantly. For the application software in the client computers, identify the subject system, the system border, and the environment systems. (This is a brief overview — make assumptions if you need to.)

16. *WahooMart* is a (hypothetical) retail company that operates thousands of retail stores. The company has a world-wide computer network that automatically manages store inventories, financial accounting, retail point-of-sale terminals, interaction with suppliers, scheduling of deliveries to retail stores, and scheduling of all train and truck movements. All records of sales, payments, store inventories, train and truck locations, and orders sent to suppliers are maintained in a central database located in Charlottesville, VA.

All sales are recorded and transmitted immediately from retail stores to the main database site. Overnight processing analyzes the inventory of all stores and generates orders for suppliers to keep inventories at the correct level. Orders to suppliers are transmitted once per day. Separate applications monitor the transport system and schedule trucks and trains, and monitor for transport problems.

Develop requirements statements for the dependability of: (a) the central database, (b) the network and telecommunications system supporting the point-of-sales network, (c) the transport management system, and (d) the inventory-management and order-generation system.

17. A simple anti-lock braking system (ABS) for an automobile uses the following design:

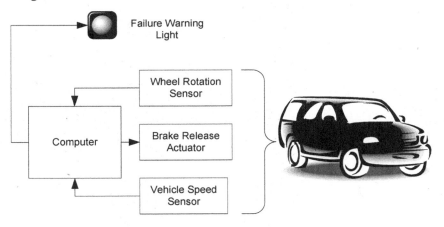

Each wheel incorporates a sensor to detect wheel rotation and an actuator to release the brake on that wheel. A computer is used to monitor wheel rotation and vehicle speed. If a wheel is not rotating but the vehicle is moving, then the wheel is skidding and so the actuator is used to release the brake for a very brief time, typically about 50 milliseconds. The system cycles at a rate of about 20 Hz. The system performs numerous self checks on the hardware whenever the brakes are not being used. If a self check fails, the system is disabled (but normal mechanical braking remains operational) and a light is illuminated to inform the driver of the system's non-operational status. Failure of the system is not considered dangerous provided the failure does not occur during braking and provided the driver's warning light is illuminated and remains illuminated.

Carefully and precisely document the dependability requirements for the system. Consider all the elements that have to be defined, the content of the specification, the format of the document, and the details of the content.

18. The developers of the automobile ABS system in Exercise 17 have determined that the probability of failure per demand could be reduced by 5% if the ABS computer system used a more powerful processor at a cost of $600 per car. Laboratory testing, modeling, and field experience have shown that the probability of failure per demand of the *current* system is approximately 0.000001. At that rate, failures are unlikely during the entire life of a car. In fact, failures are seen at a rate of roughly one failure during the combined lives of 100 cars with only one in ten failures leading to an accident.

Construct an ALARP argument to allow a decision to be made about whether to replace the processor.

CHAPTER 3

Errors, Faults, and Hazards

Learning objectives of this chapter are to understand:

- The distinction between hazard, error, and fault.
- The basic approaches to fault treatment.
- The difference between degradation, design, and Byzantine faults, and which types affect software.
- The concept and importance of anticipating faults.
- The dependability engineering process using hazards, errors, and faults, and what can be done to prevent failures.

3.1 Errors

In the last chapter, we saw that our goal is to avoid service failures. But before considering the engineering techniques that can be used to build computer systems that meet defined dependability requirements, we need to look carefully at the notion of failure again. In essence, before we can deal with failures, we need to answer the question:

Why do failures occur?

We need a general answer to this question, not one that is associated with a specific class of failures or a specific type of system. If we had an answer, that answer would provide the starting point for the engineering necessary to build dependable computer systems.

The answer to this critical question is simple, elegant, and powerful, and the answer provides precisely the starting point we need. The answer to the question is in two parts. A failure occurs when:

- The system is in an **erroneous state.**

- Part of that erroneous state is included in the system's **external state.**

where we have the following definition from the taxonomy:

Erroneous state. An erroneous state, often abbreviated to just **error**, is a system state that could lead to a service failure.

Intuitively, an error is a system state that is not intended and that is one step (or state change) away from a service failure. The elegance and power of this answer to our question lies in its generality and the fact that the answer is based on the notion of system state. We cannot, in general, prevent the error from including part of the external state, and so our basic engineering goal is to avoid errors.

As examples of errors, consider the following situations:

- A payroll system in which a calculation has been made using an incorrect entry from one of the tax tables. The system state contains a value that is wrong, and, if that value is used for output, the system will have failed.

- The same payroll system in which the calculation of a certain salary value was performed using an expression in which multiplication rather than division had been used by mistake in the software. Again, the system state contains a value that is wrong, and, if the value is used for output, the system will have failed.

- An aircraft navigation system in which the data received from the altitude sensor is incorrect because of a break in the cable supplying the data. Further processing by the avionics system using this faulty altitude value, in the autopilot, for example, would probably lead to failure very quickly.

"Error" is a common word in conversation where error is often used as a synonym for *mistake*. In discussing dependability, error is a state, not an action. Before going on, make sure that you have put your intuitive definition of error to one side and that you use the definition here when thinking about dependability.

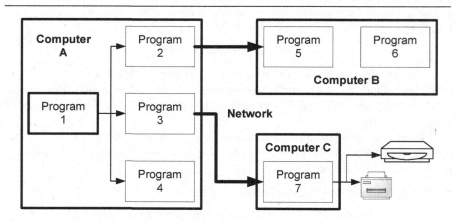

FIGURE 3.1 Software defect in a distributed system.

In order to begin the process of engineering dependable systems, we need to look closely at the notion of error, determine how to find all the errors associated with a system, and then determine how errors arise. Fundamentally, achieving dependability comes down to the following process:

- Identify all of the possible erroneous states into which a system could move.

- Ensure that either those states cannot be reached or, if they can, the negative effects are known and every effort has been taken to reduce those effects.

Needless to say, this is a difficult challenge, but this process is a useful way to think about what we have to achieve.

3.2 The Complexity of Erroneous States

In computer systems, erroneous states can be very complex. A bug in a program can cause some piece of data to be incorrect, and that data can be used in subsequent calculations so that more (perhaps a lot more) data becomes incorrect. Some of that data can be transmitted to peripherals and other computers, thereby extending the erroneous state to a lot of equipment. All of this can happen quickly and result in a major corruption of the system state.

As an example, consider the system shown in Figure 3.1. In the system shown, three computers are connected over a network, and one computer has a disk and printer connected. Suppose that, because of a software defect, Program 1 generates an erroneous state element that is then sent to programs 2 and 3, and that they then send erroneous data to programs 5 and 7. Finally, program 7 writes erroneous data to

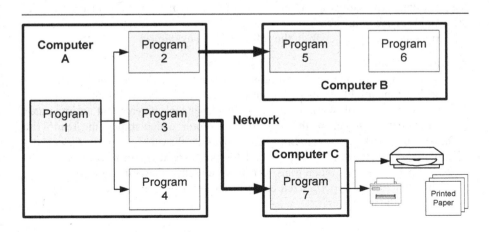

FIGURE 3.2 Extensively damaged state in a distributed system from a single bug.

the disk and prints some part of that data. The result is the extensive erroneous state, the grey components, shown in Figure 3.2.

In this example, a failure actually has occurred, because the printed material is part of the external state. Users will have access to the printed material, and so the system is no longer providing the desired service. Whether the users act on the printed material or not does not matter; the system has experienced a service failure.

3.3 Faults and Dependability

3.3.1 Definition of Fault

The reason that the systems we build are not perfectly dependable is the existence of *faults*. The definition of fault from the taxonomy is:

Fault. A fault is the adjudged or hypothesized cause of an error.

The first thing to note in this definition is the use of the word *cause*. When we say "A is a cause of B" what we mean is that A happened and as a result B happened. This notion is the logical notion of implication. Note that the converse does not follow. In other words, the fact that B has happened does not mean that A has happened. In our context here, this means that there could be more than one fault capable of causing a given error.

A fault causing an error seems like a simple notion. If we have an error, surely this means that we can find the fault which caused the error and do something about the fault. In practice, two other words in the definition, *adjudged* and *hypothesized*, are important. The words are there to inform us that there might not be a clearly identifiable cause of an error.

This issue is easy to see from the following two examples:

- **Hardware fault.**
  Suppose that a computer system fails because the hard drive in the system stops working. One might say that the fault is the failed disk drive. But the majority of the disk drive is still working correctly. A closer look reveals that an integrated circuit in the mechanism that controls the motor which moves the read/write head is not working. So one might then conclude that the fault is the failed integrated circuit. But the majority of the integrated circuit is still working correctly. A closer look reveals that a transistor in the integrated circuit is not working. So is the adjudged or hypothesized cause of the error the disk drive, the integrated circuit, or the transistor?

- **Software fault.**

Consider a program designed to calculate the tangent of an angle specified in degrees. The software is part of the navigation system for an aircraft. During flight, the crew of the aircraft discovers that the navigation system fails when the aircraft heading is exactly due North. Investigation by software engineers reveals that the problem lies with the tangent software, because the tangent is not defined for 90° and that computation was needed when the heading was due North. One way to fix this problem is to treat 90° as a special case in the tangent software so that the software behaves in an appropriate manner. A second way to fix the problem is to make sure that the software which calls the tangent software never makes the call with the angle set to 90°. So is the adjudged or hypothesized cause of the error the tangent software or the calling software?

As should be clear from these examples, the reason for the difficulty in identifying the fault responsible for a given error is the need to take a systems view of both the notion of error and fault. Recall from the discussion of the term "system" in Section 2.3 (page 30) that a subject system operates within an environment system. The notion of error, no matter how extensive, is associated with the environment system, and the notion of fault is associated with a subject system operating within the environment system. Thus, in the first example above, the error is in the computer system regarded as the environment system for the disk drive. From that perspective, the disk drive is the subject system, and the failed disk drive is the fault.

In a sense, the motto of dependability is "no faults, no problem". But we do have a problem because in real systems:

Faults do occur.

And those faults lead to errors.

And those errors lead to service failures.

More importantly, though, we must keep the definition of service failure from Section 2.6 in mind. Here is the definition again:

Service failure. Correct service is delivered when the service implements the system function. A service failure, often abbreviated here to failure, is an event that occurs when the delivered service deviates from correct service.

Recall that this definition includes the notion of abstract vs. documented requirements. A system that does something other than the intended system function has failed even if the system does the wrong thing correctly. The abstract requirements define the problem to be solved, i.e., the intended function. If the documented requirements and hence the resulting system differ from the abstract requirements, then the differences are likely to lead to service failures. Thus, differences between the abstract requirements and the documented requirements are *faults*.

3.3.2 Identifying Faults

In order to be able to build dependable systems, we have to gain an understanding of faults and how to deal with them.

Our understanding of faults must be complete and thorough,
because our treatment of faults must be complete and thorough.

Failing to identify a possible fault in a system and failing to deal with that fault while we are designing the system leave the possibility of failure.

In practice, identifying all of the faults to which a system is subject might not be possible. As we shall see in the Chapter 4, the process of identifying fault types is neither formal nor exact, and determining completeness is, at least in part, a matter of experience. Sometimes something gets missed, and sometimes that leads to incidents, accidents, and other forms of loss.

Also in practice, we might choose not to bother to deal with one or more faults that we identify as being possible in a system, because the cost of dealing with the fault is excessive. The cost might require too much equipment or too much analysis, or dealing with the fault might lead to an operating environment that is too restrictive.

3.3.3 Types of Fault

Faults come in three basic types: *degradation, design,* and *Byzantine.* The distinction between fault types is of *crucial* importance. We will use the various fault types extensively in developing our approach to dependability engineering.

Briefly, a *degradation* fault is a fault that arises because something breaks; a *design* fault is a fault in the basic design of a system; and a *Byzantine* fault is a fault for which the effects are seen differently by different elements of the system. These three fault types are discussed in depth in Section 3.5, Section 3.6, and Section 3.7.

Each of these fault types is fundamentally different from the other two, and different techniques are needed to deal with each type. Understanding the characteristics of the three fault types and the differences between them is important. The differences allow us to begin the process of systematically dealing with faults.

Dealing with faults means we have to understand their characteristics, know how to determine the faults about which we need to be concerned in a given system, and know how we will deal with those faults.

3.3.4 Achieving Dependability

We have made a lot of progress toward our goal of being able to develop dependable systems. We have a precise terminology that allows us to document dependability requirements. We know that errors can lead to service failures and therefore that we have to try to prevent them. And, we know that faults are the cause of erroneous states. With this framework in hand, our task becomes one of identifying the faults to which a system is subject and then developing ways of dealing with those faults. This is not a simple task, but now we have a path forward.

3.4 The Manifestation of Faults

A fault in a system is a defective component within the system. If the component is not actively involved in providing service, then the component's presence, whether faulty or not, is not important. The component cannot affect the state and so the component will not cause an error. This leads to four important definitions:

Active fault:	A fault is active if it causes an error.
Dormant fault:	A fault is dormant if it does not cause an error.
Permanent fault:	A fault is permanent if it is present and remains present.
Transient fault:	A fault is transient if it is present but does not remain present.

The distinction between an *active* and a *dormant* fault lies in the effect of the fault on the state. A fault associated with a component, including a software component, need not be of immediate concern provided the component is not being used. Many faults can be present in software, for example, but have no effect if the execution path of the software does not include them.

The distinction between a *permanent* and a *transient* fault lies in how we have to deal with the fault. An active transient fault might affect the system state in a way that does not cause a failure, and so designers can exploit the transient nature of the fault.

All of these concepts apply to software. Although software usually fails only on certain inputs, there is a natural tendency to assume that the same software will always fail when given the same input. This is not the case. The reason is that there are numerous sources of non-determinacy in the operation of software, for example:

- The software might use uninitialized variables, in which case its behavior will depend upon whatever values happened to be in the memory location used for the variables.

- The software might be concurrent, in which case the scheduling of the individual threads, tasks, or processes will be different on different executions.

- The software might depend upon hardware- or operating-system-specific information such as timer values, response rates, and sizes of data structures for making decisions.

The idea that the same software might not always fail on the same input led Jim Gray to coin the term *Heisenbug* (after the physicist Werner Heisenberg, who discovered the Uncertainty Principle) for the associated software faults. For faults that always lead to errors, he coined the term *Bohrbug* (after the physicist Neils Bohr, who developed the planetary model of the atom) [51]. The practical importance and ways to exploit Heisenbugs are discussed in Section 11.5.

3.5 Degradation Faults

A degradation fault occurs when a component (or maybe more than one) within a system fails. That component used to work but no longer does. The way to think of this is that the component within the system has failed but the system itself has experienced a fault. If we do things right, the system itself will not fail because we can intercede and make sure that the effects of the failed component do not lead to outputs from the system that constitute system failure.

A simple example of a degradation fault can be seen with an incandescent light bulb. When a light bulb is new, the bulb (usually) works, but, as time passes, the filament weakens and eventually breaks. There are many familiar degradation faults in computing systems, including failures of hard disks, power supplies, monitors, keyboards, etc. In each case, the device was working but then failed. Degradation faults are sometimes referred to as *wearout faults* or *random faults*.

3.5.1 Degradation Fault Probabilities — The "Bathtub" Curve

A set of components that all seem to be identical will all have different lifetimes. However, if the lifetimes of the members of the set are measured and the mean computed, we will find an average lifetime that is a function of the materials used, the manufacturing process used, the operating environment, the design of the device, and random events.

If the lifetimes of the individual members of the set are measured and the distribution of lifetimes is plotted, the resulting distribution has a well-known shape known as the *bathtub curve* (see Figure 3.3). The bathtub curve tells us that there are two periods of time when the members of a collection of identical devices tend to fail: shortly after they are put into service and after a long period of service. The former failures are referred to as *infant-mortality failures* and the latter as *end-of-life failures*. Failures occur throughout the measurement period but there are two obvious peaks.

Engineers use these two peaks to their advantage in two ways. First, since infant mortality is bound to occur, devices can be put into service by the manufacturer for a period of time at the manufacturer's facility before delivery. During this period of time, the vast majority of infant mortalities occur. By putting devices into service for a prescribed amount of time before delivery, the manufacturer ensures that the majority of customers will not experience an early failure.

The second use of the bathtub curve is to estimate the MTTF or MTBF of the device. Customers can use this number to determine whether the device will operate for adequate service periods in their application.

In the case of some electronic devices, the failure rate is so low that meaningful population statistics are hard to obtain. Modern integrated circuits, for example, have extraordinary lifetimes if they are operated under conditions of low humidity, low vibration, constant operating temperature (i.e., low thermal stress), and low operating temperature.

3.5.2 An Example of Degradation Faults — Hard Disks

One of the least dependable components of modern systems is the hard disk. Despite this relative lack of dependability, hard disks provide remarkable service. Although the loss of a disk in one of our personal computers is serious for us, having to deal with the prospect of hard-disk failures is very different for operators of large information systems. Such information systems often include storage sub-systems that involve thousands of individual disk units, and on any given day several disks might fail and need to be replaced.

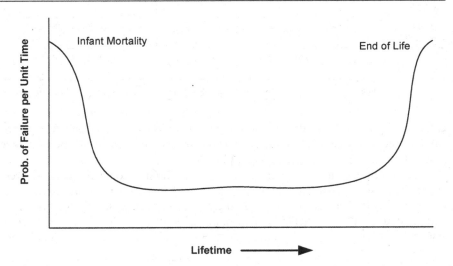

FIGURE 3.3 The bathtub curve showing the variation in failure rate of hardware components over time.

Types of Failure

For disks, there are two important failure effects with which we have to be concerned:

- An unrecoverable data error in which a read operation fails to return data identical to that which was written.

- Loss of service from the device in which read and write operations do not complete.

These two types of failure effects[1] can arise with a wide variety of failures within the device, and many of the underlying failures can be intermittent, with complex behavior patterns. These effects lead to difficulty in deciding whether a disk has actually failed. A total lack of response from a disk is fairly clear, but a disk that has to retry read operations and thereby experiences a slight performance loss might: (a) be about to fail permanently, (b) have already lost data that has not been requested, or (c) be suffering from a temporary mechanical flaw.

Rates of Failure

Table 3.1 shows published estimates of failure rates for a number of disks from sev-

Disk	Capacity (GBytes)	Unrecoverable Data Errors	Stated Dependability Statistic
Seagate Atlas® 10K V SAS	Up to 300	Less than 1 per 10^{15}	MTTF 1,400,000 hrs
Toshiba MK8009GAH	80	Less than 1 per 10^{13}	Product life of 20,000 hours on, ~5 years use
Hitachi Deskstar E7K1000	Up to 1,000	Less than 1 per 10^{15}	Target MTTF 1,200,000 hrs

TABLE 3.1. Estimates of disk dependability parameters for typical products from several manufacturers.

eral manufacturers. These data are only generally indicative of what can be expected from devices like these. A helpful analysis of the complex issue of the performance of desktop machines has been prepared by Cole [29].

Actual failure data of commercial disk drives is hard to come by. Manufacturers are reluctant to publish data about failure rates of their products, and researchers rarely have sufficient samples to study the necessary probability distributions with sufficient accuracy. Another important point about disks is the variety of circumstances in which they operate. Among other things, disks in different personal com-

---

1. Actually, what we are discussing here is the semantics of failure. This will be discussed in Section 3.8.

puters are subject to different rates of use (idle versus operating), different types and severities of mechanical shock, different rates of power cycling (on or off for long periods versus frequent switching), and different temperature and humidity conditions (in a car, near a heating vent, blocked or partially blocked internal fan ducts). With such variety, estimates of rates of failure are of marginal use since they provide little predictive value for any specific disk in operation.

For the use of disks in large information systems, an important study by Schroeder and Gibson [129] provides data from 100,000 disks from four different manufacturers. The observed MTTF for the disks in the study was approximately 1,200,000 hours. But the focus of the work was to look deeper than the simple MTTF, and the detailed results show how many other factors need to be included in models of large numbers of disks in large information systems.

A second important study was carried out by Pinheiro et al. [106]. In that study, more than 100,000 disks from different manufacturers used in the Google File System were monitored. Various disk models were included in the study and the disks were of different ages, because the disk system in the experiment was being maintained and enhanced during the period of study. The results are extensive and detailed, and to a large extent unique because of the large sample size. Some of the results reported include strong correlations between some of the disks' self-diagnosis data (Self-Monitoring Analysis and Reporting Technology (SMART)) and subsequent failure. Other important results include observation of a lower-than-expected correlation between failure rates and disk temperatures and utilization rates.

Other Concerns About Disks

Further important issues about disks were raised by Gray and van Ingen [52]. In a study of the performance of commodity hardware when a very large amount of data is moved (two petabytes, approximately 10^{15} bytes), they observed a variety of system failures that were more significant than the notion of unrecoverable errors in the disk itself. The point is not that unrecoverable errors in the disk are unimportant; they are. The point is that there are other sources of unrecoverable error, such as the cables, the bus, and even the processor and memory, that make the actual rate higher. In addition, unrecoverable errors are not the only source of failure. Gray and van Ingen observed failures of controllers and system reboots.

Other Types of Device

Disks are a good example of the challenge we face when working with computer systems. Many of the issues we have discussed have analogies in other computer-system components. With that in mind, we need to pay attention to two critical points when engineering systems that have to meet specific dependability goals:

- The role of software in coping with degradation faults in all computer systems is much more elaborate than one might expect. Software at many levels, from the firmware in the disk controller to the operating system, is often called upon to contribute to the goal of dealing with degradation faults.

- Any effort to estimate the actual dependability of computer systems cannot depend upon simple performance statistics. The actual performance of devices in real application environments is complex and frequently counter-intuitive.

3.6 Design Faults

A design fault is literally a defect in the design of something. An example is a wiring error in a piece of equipment. If a switch is wired backwards, the switch and therefore the equipment of which the switch is part will never work as intended. Nothing changes during the lifetime of the equipment. The switch did not work correctly following manufacture, and the switch will not work correctly at any point during the equipment's operational lifetime. Unless the switch is repaired, the users of the equipment will have to have a work around for the defective switch whenever they need to use it.

There is no bathtub curve associated with design faults because a device that is subject to a design fault is broken from the outset. This does not mean that the device will not be manufactured or used. Some design faults are unknown at the time of manufacture and end up being present in operational equipment. Design faults do not necessarily manifest themselves in a way that permits their detection during routine testing. This is in complete contrast with degradation faults, where failures will occur over time.

An important thing to note at this point is the following:

All software faults are design faults.

This statement usually raises eyebrows and motivates questions such as "Well, what about coding errors?" The problem here is that we are forced to use the word "design" in two different ways — the design phase of the software lifecycle and the type of fault to which software is subject.

The software development lifecycle is shown in Figure 3.4. The lifecycle includes a phase called software "design", and software engineers consider things like improper use of information hiding and poor choices of abstractions to be defects in the software's design. Software engineers might not consider defects that are revealed by erroneous outputs from a test case to be defects in the design of their software, because they think of design as one of several specific phases in the software lifecycle. But from the perspective of dependability, *all* software defects are design faults. We have to be careful to keep in mind that design in the software lifecycle is not the meaning of design in the context of dependability.

Design faults make developing dependable systems challenging. They are faults, and they have to be dealt with. Except for the intentional introduction of a fault to promote malicious interests, design faults are not introduced maliciously. The system's developers will build the system's software and undertake all the other design activities using techniques that are meant to produce the "right" product. Where there are defects in a product's design, in part the defects are the result of unfortunate oversights in the development process.

Determining the design faults to which a system is subject is difficult. To see how significant the problem is, consider the issue of determining the faults in a large software system. Any phase of the software lifecycle could have introduced faults into the software. What are the effects of those faults? The faults could remain dormant for extended periods, because the software component with which they are associated might not be on the execution path. When a fault manifests itself, the software might do anything, including crashing, hanging, generating the wrong output, and generating the correct output but too late. And any of these faults could be Heisenbugs and so even their manifestation would not be certain.

3.7 Byzantine Faults

3.7.1 The Concept

Byzantine faults are faults with completely unpredictable behavior [83]. One might think that the effects of all faults are unpredictable in many ways, and this is cer-

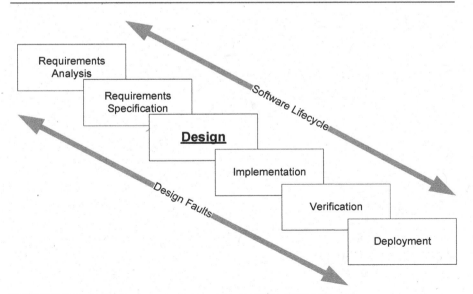

FIGURE 3.4 Design faults can occur at any point in the software lifecycle.

tainly true. Rather surprisingly, we all tend to limit the unpredictability that we expect from faults in a way that caused the existence of Byzantine faults to be missed by scientists for a long time.

The primary place where we expected predictability is in the effects of a fault when manifested. The problem is that the expectation that all "observers" of a fault will see the same thing, though reasonable, is wrong. Sometimes this expectation is not the case, and then different parts of a system perceive a fault differently.

The basis of this inconsistency in observation is usually a degradation fault. So, in principle, Byzantine faults are not different. In practice, the inconsistency in observation that characterizes Byzantine faults is so important and the treatment of the inconsistency so different, that we are well served by splitting Byzantine faults off as a special case and discussing them separately.

3.7.2 An Example Byzantine Fault

Byzantine faults were first brought to the attention of the scientific community in the development of clock synchronization algorithms. Synchronizing clocks is a vital element of building distributed systems. That the different computers have a view of time that differs by less than a bounded amount is important. If clocks drift at a rate that is less than some threshold, then a set of machines can have clocks that differ from each other by no more than a specific bound if they are synchronized at appropriate intervals.

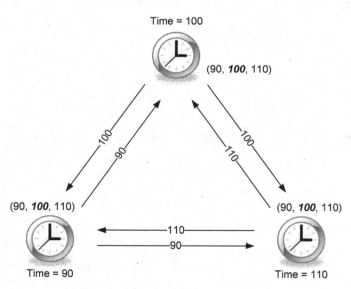

FIGURE 3.5 Clock synchronization by mid-value selection.

Suppose that we want to synchronize three clocks. An algorithm that we might use is *mid-value selection*. Each clock sends its current value to the other two, and all three clocks sort the three values they have (their own and the two they received from the other two clocks). By choosing the middle value of the three and setting their times to these values, all three clocks can synchronize to the same value. This process is shown in Figure 3.5.

Now suppose that one clock is faulty and this clock has a time that is very different from the other two. What we would like to happen is for the mid-value selection algorithm to work for us and make sure that the two non-faulty clocks get the same value. This is shown in Figure 3.6. One of the clocks has drifted well outside the expected range; the clock's value is 60. Yet both of the other clocks synchronize their values correctly as desired.

Now suppose that one of the clocks has a Byzantine fault. By definition, this means that different observers will see its failure differently. This is illustrated in Figure 3.7. The observers are the two non-faulty clocks, and what they see are different times (90 and 105). The result is that the two good clocks now fail to synchronize.

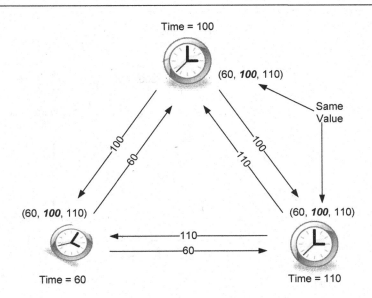

FIGURE 3.6 Clock synchronization by mid-value selection with drifting clock.

3.7.3 Nuances of Byzantine Faults

The idea of a Byzantine fault seems bizarre (or at least Byzantine), and one might be tempted to think that they either do not arise or are rare. Unfortunately, they do arise and cannot be regarded as rare [38].

One might also be tempted to think that the problem lies in the mid-value select algorithm, and that if we could find a different algorithm, all would be well. Again, unfortunately (or fortunately depending upon how you look at the issue) Shostack et. al showed that there is *no* algorithm that will work [83].

The causes of Byzantine faults are many, and looking at some known causes is instructive if only to get an appreciation of just how subtle they are. Most Byzantine faults arise in data transmission between system components. The causes include:

- Voltages and clocks operating at marginal levels.

- Faulty connectors or other mechanical elements of transmission paths.

- Electrical noise.

- Other forms of radiation such as cosmic rays.

Some Byzantine faults arise within digital electronics as a result of voltages that lie between logic 1 and logic 0 [38]. Where circuits are operated with imprecise voltages, the logic outputs can vary between logic 0 and logic 1, and a single output that is supplied to different parts of the circuit can end up being different at the different destinations.

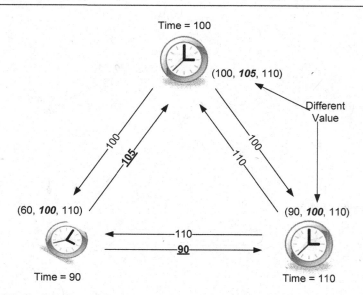

FIGURE 3.7 Clock synchronization failure with a clock experiencing a Byzantine fault.

3.8 Component Failure Semantics

We are not quite finished with the notion of a fault even though we have looked at the three basic fault types. The problem we now need to deal with is to understand what happens to a component when that component fails. More specifically, we need to know what the component's interfaces will look like and the extent of the damage to which the fault leads. The interface that the component presents after failure and the damage outside the component are referred to as the *component failure semantics*.

3.8.1 Disk Drive Example

To understand the need for a precise statement of component failure semantics, consider what happens to a disk drive when the drive fails. Disk failures typically result in the disk contents being unreadable, at least partially. Other than loss of data, the failure of a disk drive rarely has much of an effect. Thus, the failure semantics of a disk drive are usually restricted to a loss of data. For purposes of analysis, assuming that all of the stored data is lost is probably best, although that might not always be the case.

Suppose however, that we had to worry about failing disk drives that do not lose data but instead started supplying data that was corrupted in some way. The data supplied on a read request would not be that which was requested by the operating system but was, instead, something that was the wrong information (from a different file, for example) or was random but reasonable looking data. Such a situation would be catastrophic because the data would be supplied to the application, and the application might act on the data without realizing that the data was not that which was needed.

When a disk crashes and all the data is lost, we generally think of this as being catastrophic, and, if there is no backup, the disk crash probably is catastrophic. But the fact that we cannot get any data tells us immediately that the disk has failed. With that knowledge, we can be sure that applications will not operate with corrupt data, a situation that would more than likely be much worse than a total loss of data. Knowing how a component will fail allows us to protect systems from the effects of the component failure. If we do not know, then there is a good chance that we could do nothing to protect the rest of the computer system from the component failure.

Just as with a component's interface, knowing the extent of the damage that might result from a component failure is important. In the case of a disk drive, for example, there is little likelihood that the disk will affect data stored on a different device. Violent mechanical failure of a disk drive in which nearby components are damaged physically is also unlikely. So the damage to the state that results from a disk failure is limited to the disk's own contents.

3.8.2 Achieving Predictable Failure Semantics

When examining components in order to determine what faults might arise, we have to determine not just what the faults are but also the component failure semantics. This determination is sufficiently important that components are frequently designed to have well-defined failure semantics. Achieving well-defined failure semantics might just involve careful selection of design techniques or include explicit additions to the design that help to define the failure semantics. Parity in memory is an example of an explicit addition. By including a parity bit, a single bit error in the data can be detected. Thus, for a failure of a memory component in which a single bit is lost, the failure semantics are made detectable and thereby actionable by the provision of a parity mechanism.

In the case of a disk drive, error detecting codes are added extensively in data storage and transmission to allow corrupt data to be detected. The types of failure to which the disk is subject help to define the types of codes. In some cases, disks suffer burst errors and in others random bits are lost. Different codes are added to allow the detection of each of the different anticipated types of failure. Without such codes, data could become corrupted and the failure semantics would be arbitrary. With the error codes present, a disk's failure semantics can be made precise and properly signaled, raising an interrupt, for example.

3.8.3 Software Failure Semantics

Unfortunately, the well-defined and predictable damage that we achieve with disk drives and most other hardware components is usually not possible for software components. As we saw in Section 3.2, when a software component fails, propagation of the immediate erroneous state is possible, and the erroneous state could be acted upon so as to damage the state extensively outside of the failed software component. By passing elements of an erroneous state to other programs and devices, a failed software component can cause damage that is essentially arbitrary.

We noted in Section 3.8.2 that the creation of manageable failure semantics for a disk drive requires the addition of explicit mechanisms, often including error-detecting codes, to help ensure that the failure semantics are predictable. Could we do the same thing for software? The answer to this question is both "yes" and "no". Including checks in software to ascertain whether the results being produced are as they should be is certainly possible. The problem is that such checks are far too weak to allow them to be trusted under all circumstances. Unlike disks, where essentially all types of failure to which the disk is subject can be both predicted and checked for, software is so complex that there is no hope of doing as well with software as we can with disks and similar devices. We will examine software error detection in detail in Chapter 11 as part of our discussion of fault tolerance.

3.9 Fundamental Principle of Dependability

As we saw in Section 3.3, faults are the central problem in dependability. Thus, in order to improve the dependability of computing systems, we have to get the right requirements and then deal with faults in the system as constructed. If we can make the improvement in dependability sufficient that the resulting system meets its dependability requirement, then we achieved our most important goal.

Requirements engineering is the process of determining and documenting the requirements for a system. Requirements engineering is a major part of computer system development and the subject of textbooks, at least one journal, and a conference series. We do not discuss requirements engineering further, because the topic is complex and discussed widely elsewhere.

There are four approaches to dealing with faults:

- **Avoidance** - **Section 3.9.1**
- **Elimination** - **Section 3.9.2**
- **Tolerance** - **Section 3.9.3**
- **Forecasting** - **Section 3.9.4**

If we were able to predict *all* of the faults that can occur in systems and combine the results with these four approaches in various ways, we could produce an engineering roadmap that will allow us to either meet the dependability requirements for a given system or show that the dependability requirements were sufficiently extreme that they were unachievable with the available engineering. This idea is central to our study of dependable systems, and so I refer to the idea as the *Fundamental Principle of Dependability*[2]:

Fundamental Principle Of Dependability: If all of the faults to which a system is subject are determined, and the effects of each potential fault are mitigated adequately, then the system will meet its dependability requirements.

This principle provides a focus and a goal for our engineering. In all that we do, the role of our activities can be assessed and compared with other possible activities by appealing to this principle. The principle combines the two major issues we face:

- We need to have a high level of assurance that the documented specification is a solution to the problem defined by the abstract requirements, i.e., that faults in the documented specification (and by implication the documented requirements) have been dealt with appropriately.

---

2. I have introduced this term in this text, and so the term is not in common use. Focusing our attention on the central issue that we face is helpful, and the link between our study of terminology and our study of computer system dependability engineering is essential.

- We need to have a high level of assurance that the system as implemented is a refinement of the solution as stated in the documented specification, i.e., that the faults in the system as built have been dealt with appropriately.

In this section, we examine each of the four approaches to dealing with faults so as understand what is involved in each one. In later chapters, we explore the various techniques available for effecting each approach.

3.9.1 Fault Avoidance

Fault avoidance means, quite literally, avoiding faults. If we can build systems in which faults are absent and cannot arise, we need to do nothing more. From a software perspective, fault avoidance is our first and best approach to dealing with faults, because the alternatives are not guaranteed to work and can have substantial cost. Fault avoidance must *always* be the approach that we attempt first.

Degradation fault avoidance might seem like an unachievable goal, but it is not. There are many techniques that allow the rate of degradation faults to be reduced to a level at which they occur so infrequently in practice that they can be ignored. For design faults, analysis and synthesis techniques exist that allow us to create designs in some circumstances and know that there are no design faults. Finally, architectural techniques exist that allow us to limit and sometimes eliminate the possibility of Byzantine faults.

All of the techniques that can help us to achieve fault avoidance have limited capability, applicability, and performance, and so we cannot use them exclusively. But remembering the possibility of fault avoidance and seeking out ways to avoid faults in any development are important.

3.9.2 Fault Elimination

If we cannot avoid faults, then the next best thing is to eliminate them from the system in which they are located before the system is put into use. Although not as desirable as fault avoidance, fault elimination is still highly beneficial.

A simple example of degradation fault elimination is the treatment of infant mortality. By operating hardware entities before shipment, manufacturers are looking for those entities that would normally fail early in the field.

A simple example of design fault elimination is software testing. By testing a piece of software, developers are looking for faults in the software so that they can be removed before the software is deployed.

3.9.3 Fault Tolerance

If we can neither avoid nor eliminate faults, then faults will be present in systems during operational use. They might be degradation faults that arise during operation or design faults. If a fault does not manifest itself, i.e., the fault is dormant, then the fault has no effect. Fault tolerance is an approach that is used in systems for which either: (a) degradation faults are expected to occur at a rate that would cause an unacceptable rate of service failure or (b) complete avoidance or elimination of design faults was not possible and design faults were expected to remain in a system.

3.9.4 Fault Forecasting

Finally, if we cannot deal with a fault by avoidance, elimination, or tolerance, we have to admit that untreated faults will be present during operation, and we must try to forecast the effects of the fault. By doing so we are able to predict the effect of the fault on the system and thereby make a decision about whether the system will meet its dependability requirements.

3.10 Anticipated Faults

The fundamental principle of dependability tells us that one thing we have to do in order to meet our dependability requirements is to determine all of the faults to which a system is subject. This goal is easily stated but hard to do, and the goal leads to the notion of *anticipated faults*.

An anticipated fault is one that we have identified as being in the set to which a system is subject. We know that the fault might arise, and so we have anticipated the fault.

If our techniques for determining the faults to which a system is subject were perfect, we would be done. But these techniques are not perfect. The result is that some faults will not be anticipated. Because they are unanticipated, such faults will not be handled in any type of predictable way, and so their effect on the system of interest is unknown.

Unanticipated faults are the cause of most but not all system failures. There are two reasons why they are not responsible for all system failures:

- Some system failures result from anticipated faults that were not dealt with in any way. Their effects and probability of occurrence were examined using fault forecasting, and the system designers decided that no treatment was warranted.

- Some system failures result from failures of fault tolerance mechanisms designed to cope with the effects of anticipated faults.

In summary, our goal is to eliminate unanticipated faults and to make sure that all anticipated faults are dealt with adequately. In order to reach this goal, we need a systematic way of identifying and therefore anticipating faults. The approach we will follow to perform this identification is to first identify the hazards to which the system is subject and then identify the faults that could lead to those hazards.

3.11 Hazards

3.11.1 The Hazard Concept

A *hazard* is a system state. The notion of hazard arises primarily in the field of safety. Informally, a hazard is a system state that could lead to catastrophic consequences, i.e., a system state that could lead to a violation of safe operation.

The word "hazard" has various meanings in everyday speech, and hazard is another example of why careful attention to definitions is so important. Here is the definition from the taxonomy:

Hazardous state. A hazardous state, often abbreviated **hazard**, is a system state that could lead to an unplanned loss of life, loss of property, release of energy, or release of dangerous materials.

Closely related to the notion of hazard is the notion of an *accident*:

Accident. An accident is a loss event.

An accident results when a system is in a hazardous state and a change in the operating environment occurs that leads to a loss event.

A system being in a hazardous state does not necessarily mean that an accident will result. The system could stay in a hazardous state for an arbitrary length of time, and, provided there is no change in the environment that leads to a loss, there will be no accident. Similarly, a system could enter and exit a hazardous state many times without an accident occurring. Clearly, however, we cannot rely on systems in hazardous states remaining accident free.

Some examples of hazards and accidents are the following:

- **An elevator shaft with a door open but with no elevator car present.**
  For an accident to occur, an environmental circumstance has to arise, e.g., a person walks through the open door unaware of the state.

- **A gate at a railway crossing that fails up.**
  If a vehicle crosses the track as a train approaches because the driver believes, incorrectly, that proceeding is safe, a collision is likely to occur.

- **A failed automobile anti-lock braking system (ABS) that does not alert the driver to the lack of anti-lock braking capability.**
  The car could skid and crash if the driver applies the brakes on a slippery surface expecting that the ABS would act to facilitate proper braking.

- **A failed nuclear reactor shutdown system that does not alert the reactor operators to the lack of monitoring capability.**
  With the shutdown system non-operational, the operators should shut down the reactor immediately. Not doing so is not dangerous in and of itself, but, if an automatic shutdown becomes necessary, the shutdown will not occur and the result could be catastrophic.

- **Crucial information such as credit-card or social-security numbers stored in a publicly accessible file.**
  The confidentiality and integrity of the data would not necessarily be compromised if information were available to unauthorized users. But should the availability of the data become known to individuals with malicious intent, the result could be catastrophic.

Note that all of the hazards in this list are likely to arise because of defects in computer systems. Instances of all of them have occurred at various times. Hazards, therefore, have a significant impact on all phases of the software lifecycle.

A system can enter a hazardous state for two reasons:

The system design includes states that are hazardous. In this case, the cause is incomplete analysis by the system's original designers. An example of such a design is a toy with a separable part that could choke a child.

The failure of some component causes the system to enter a hazardous state. In this case, the cause is the component failure. An example of such a failure is the loss of brake hydraulic fluid in a car.

These two reasons are equally important. The first is concerned with the basic design of a system, and the second with states that might arise because of the manifestation of faults. This book is concerned mainly with the latter.

3.11.2 Hazard Identification

In developing systems for which safety is an important dependability requirement, hazards are the states we have to avoid. Provided all the hazards have been identified, by avoiding them, we can be sure that there will be no catastrophic consequences of system operation. In order to arrange for a specific system to avoid hazards, we need to know what hazards can arise. Only then can we seek ways of eliminating them as possible states. The process of identifying and assessing hazards is *hazard identification*.

Hazard identification and the subsequent analysis of the hazards is a complex and sophisticated process that is conducted primarily by engineers in the associated application domain. In domains such as nuclear power engineering, the determination of what constitutes a hazard is based on a wide variety of inputs. A lot of undesirable states can arise but determining those that are hazards requires analysis by a

Pacemaker/Defibrillator Hazards		
Hazards Associated With Heart Pacing	**Hazards Associated With Heart Defibrillation**	**Hazards Associated With Equipment Management**
o Heart stimulated when **not** needed o Heart **not** stimulated when needed o Stimulation pulse has **wrong** waveform o Stimulation pulse generated at **wrong** time	o Heart shocked when **not** needed o Heart **not** shocked when needed o Shock pulse has **wrong** waveform o Shock pulse generated at **wrong** time	o Failed component **not** diagnosed o Healthy component diagnosed as failed o Incorrect battery management o Incorrect power component conditioning

FIGURE 3.8 Some of the hazards associated with a pacemaker/defibrillator.

range of experts. Many industries have developed standards to guide the hazard-analysis process, for example, the nuclear power industry [7].

Our interest is in computer systems, and, in many cases, the computer systems that we build will be responsible for the prevention of hazards. We, as software engineers, have to be aware of hazard identification and analysis, because the results of the analysis will frequently appear in the computer system's requirements. However, primary responsibility for hazard analysis does not lie with the computer or software engineer.

As an example of what is involved in hazard identification, consider a hypothetical implantable combined pacemaker and defibrillator. The only significant accident with which the designers of such a device have to be concerned is patient injury. Clearly, for a device like this, injury could lead to death.

The hazards for a combined pacemaker and defibrillator break down conveniently into three categories, as shown in Figure 3.8 — those associated with heart pacing, those associated with heart defibrillation, and those associated with equipment management. In each category, there are four hazards of which we have to take note. The first two categories are concerned with fairly obvious treatment failures. The third category concerns equipment management and is concerned with the possibility of things like a detached lead going unnoticed or the backup analog pacing circuit becoming unavailable and this situation not being detected.

3.11.3 Hazards and Faults

Note carefully that a hazard is an error, i.e., erroneous state. Recall that a fault is the adjudged cause of an error, and this provides the link between faults and hazards. In order to avoid a hazard, we need to identify the faults that might cause the hazard and make sure that each fault has been suitably treated. In Chapter 4, we will examine ways of identifying the faults that might cause a given hazard. Combining this process of fault identification with hazard analysis, we finally have a comprehensive way of identifying the faults to which a system is subject.

Although the notion of hazard is most commonly used in the field of safety, we can exploit the notion generally to help define a systematic approach to dependability engineering. We will treat the notion of hazard as any state that we would like to avoid rather than just those with catastrophic consequences. As we shall see in Section 4.2 on page 104, treating the state in which a component has failed as a hazard is useful even if that state could not lead to an accident in the sense of Section 3.11.1. The component might be a computer system or part of one.

3.12 Engineering Dependable Systems

We can now bring together all the various ideas we have explored in this chapter and create an overall process for engineering dependable systems. For any system, there are two sets of requirements: the *functional* requirements and the *dependability* requirements, and these two sets of requirements are used to guide the system design process. Both are needed because the system has to supply the required functionality *and* do so with the required dependability.

From the fundamental principle of dependability, we know that our engineering task is to anticipate the faults to which a system is subject and to deal with each in a manner that ensures that the system meets its dependability goal to the extent possible.

Hazards are states that we want to avoid, and we will anticipate all the faults to which a system is subject by identifying all of the hazards that might arise and then determining the faults that could lead to each hazard.

Next, for each fault that we have identified, i.e., anticipated, we will determine a suitable approach to dealing with that fault using one of the four available techniques: avoidance, elimination, tolerance, or forecasting.

Finally, we will assess the dependability of the resulting system as best we can, and, if the assessment indicates the possibility of not meeting the dependability requirements, we will cycle through the process again, beginning with a system redesign.

This leads us to a dependability engineering process that is illustrated in Figure 3.9. The overall flow of engineering activities is:

- Define the system's functional requirements.

- Define the system's dependability requirements.

- Determine the hazards to which the system is subject based on the functional requirements.

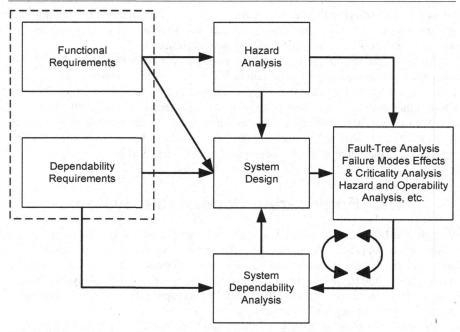

FIGURE 3.9 The dependability engineering process.

- Design the system to meet both the functional and the dependability requirements.

- For each hazard, determine the faults that could lead to that hazard. This analysis is based on a variety of different information, but the goal is to obtain the complete list of anticipated faults.

- For each anticipated fault, determine a means of dealing with the fault. Each fault will be dealt with by avoidance, elimination, tolerance, or forecasting.

- Assess the resulting system to determine whether the system's dependability goals will be met. If the dependability requirements will not be met, then the system has to be redesigned and the assessment process repeated.

The assessment step might lead to multiple iterations of the process if the system design does not necessarily lead to the dependability requirements being met. For example, if the dependability assessment shows that the rate of hardware failure will lead to service failures from the complete system that are beyond the rate defined to be acceptable, the hardware will have to be redesigned and the assessment repeated.

Our discussion in this section is a high-level overview intended to act as something of a road map. Dependability engineering of a modern software-intensive system is a complicated process that expands on this road map considerably. However, underneath the detail, the principles are the same.

Key points in this chapter:

+ Error is an abbreviation for erroneous state, a state in which a service failure is possible.
+ Erroneous states can be complex, involving a large fraction of a computer system's state.
+ There are three major types of fault: degradation, design, and Byzantine. Software faults are always design faults.
+ Our goal is to identify the faults to which a system of interest is subject and to design the system to deal with all of the faults we have identified.
+ Faults can be avoided, eliminated, tolerated, or forecast.

Exercises

1. Carefully and succinctly explain why a mistake in the implementation source code of a piece of software is referred to as a *design* fault rather than an implementation fault.

2. Explain the difference between a *hazard* and an *accident* and illustrate your answer using examples from a system with which you are familiar.

3. For the ABS system described in Exercise 17 in Chapter 2:

    (a) Determine the set of hazards that can arise.

    (b) Identify the *degradation* faults that need to be anticipated.

    (c) Identify the *design* faults that need to be anticipated.

4. For each degradation fault you identified in Exercise 3(b), determine whether software functionality might be used to help deal with the fault when the fault is manifested. For those where this is the case, state informally what you think the software might be required to do.

5. Consider the pharmacy information system described in Exercise 15 in Chapter 2.

    (a) List the dependability attribute or attributes that need to considered for this system and for each explain why each attribute is important.

    (b) For one of the attributes listed in part (a), carefully define a possible requirement statement for that dependability attribute for this system.

6. Identify three *major* hazards that the pharmacy information system faces.

7. In August 2005, a serious incident occurred aboard a Boeing 777 flying over Australia. The official report of the incident is available from the Australian Transport Safety Bureau [11].

    (a) For the B777 incident, document the failed component combinations that were deemed safe for flight.

    (b) For the B777 incident, clearly the aircraft was in a hazardous state. What where the characteristics of the state that made the state hazardous?

    (c) For the B777 incident, how and when did the hazardous state arise?

8. For one of the hazards that you identified in Exercise 6, indicate *how* you would go about calculating the associated *cost of failure* in dollars.

9. A robotic surgery system is a machine tool designed for use in an operating room to assist surgeons in joint-replacement surgery. The system operates by

cutting bone to a specific shape that accepts a joint-replacement implant. The system is illustrated in the following figure:

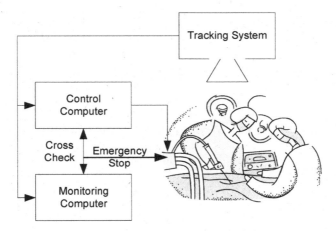

The system is much more precise than human surgeons and the benefits to the patient of robotic surgery are tremendous. Needless to say, the cutting process is complex and computer controlled. The cutting tool moves in an elaborate pattern to shape the bone. The location of the patient and all the robot equipment is determined precisely by a 3D tracking system.

Obviously the concern that the robot's developers have is the possibility of the robot cutting something that it should not, for example, if the software calculated the wrong direction or distance for the cut. In an effort to prevent this, the cutting edge of the tool is monitored by a *second* computer system that computes the tool's planned track separately. The primary computer and the tracking computer have to agree in order for the robot to proceed.

For the robotic surgery system:

(a) Identify the hazards to which you think the system is subject.

(b) Identify the degradation faults to which you think the system's cutting head might be subject.

(c) Identify possible Byzantine faults that might occur in the system.

CHAPTER 4

Dependability Analysis

Learning objectives of this chapter are to understand:

- The technology of fault tree analysis.
- The technology of failure modes, effects, and criticality analysis.
- The technology of hazard and operability analysis.
- The technologies that can be used to determine the faults to which a system is subject.
- The consequences for a system of critical-component failures.
- The requirements for a system related to component failures.

4.1 Anticipating Faults

The concept of *anticipated faults* was introduced in Section 3.10. Anticipating faults is important because, in almost all circumstances, provided we know that a certain fault is present or might arise, we can do something to at least mitigate the ensuing effects of the fault. Much of the time, we can mask the effects. For example, knowing that a disk might fail leads us to take a variety of measures to deal with such failures. We might back up the disk regularly or incrementally, or we might operate two disks in parallel with identical content in what is referred to as a *mirrored-disk* configuration. Similarly, knowing that software might fail leads us to try to discover as many of the faults in the software as possible by testing or using some other form of analysis. We will discuss how to cope with faults in a comprehensive, systematic way in later chapters.

The faults that we do *not* know about, the *unanticipated faults*, are the ones that tend to cause failures. Not knowing about a fault means that we will not employ any techniques to cope with the effects of the fault, and, of course, those effects could be extensive. Imagine (or perhaps remember) a situation in which you were unaware that a disk could fail, but the disk did fail. Most likely, you lost all your data. Had you known about the possibility of the fault, things would be very different. This point seems rather obvious, but ignoring the point has resulted in a lot of unexpected and sometimes disastrous system failures.

Importantly, this simple observation is one of the keys to making dependability into a systematic engineering activity rather than an ad hoc practice. The reason for this transition is that it forces engineers to seek ways of identifying, i.e., anticipating, the faults to which their systems are subject.

In practice many engineers follow an engineering path that is based entirely on their experience. They know that disks fail, that power fails, that software fails, and so on, and so they make provision for these situations. The ensuing system failures then almost always are from other, previously unidentified faults. This leads to statements after failures of the form: "Oh, I did not think of that."

Seeking out faults to which a system is subject is a *crucial* step, and the more successful that step is, the fewer the number of unexpected failures the system will experience. The criticality of this step leads to the following observations:

The identification of faults has to be as comprehensive and systematic as possible. Never rely on personal experience or ad hoc methods alone for the identification of faults.

Given this observation, our next engineering step is to try to identify all the faults that might manifest themselves in a system along with details of their effects. To do so, a variety of analysis techniques have been developed of which we can only cover the most important in this chapter. Specifically, we will discuss Fault Tree Analysis (usually abbreviated FTA), Failure Modes, Effects, and Criticality Analysis (usually abbreviated FMECA), and Hazard and Operability Analysis (usually abbreviated HazOp).

4.2 Generalizing the Notion of Hazard

As discussed in Section 3.11.3, we are going to use the notion of hazard in a broad way. The concept is used most commonly in dealing with safety. Safety makes reference explicitly to serious consequences of failure, and so does "hazard" as defined in Chapter 3. However, using the notion of hazard to refer to any state that we want to avoid is convenient. This is quite satisfactory, because all we are really doing is deciding what will be considered "serious" consequences of failure, and that is subjective.

As an example, consider a system that displays flight information at an airport. This is an important information system, but, if the display fails so that it can no longer provide service, the failure is unlikely to lead to a loss of life or equipment, or cause environmental damage. But to the system's stakeholders, including the flying public, such a failure is serious, and the owners of the system will want to avoid this.

A convenient way to proceed is to use the notion of a hazard even in this case, and, in fact, to do so universally. We can then exploit the techniques for dependability analysis that arose initially in the field of safety-critical systems to help meet the goals of any system with well-defined dependability requirements. We will examine these techniques in the rest of this chapter.

4.3 Fault Tree Analysis

Fault tree analysis is a technique for determining the events that can lead to a hazard. The technique was developed in 1962 by Bell Laboratories in order to analyze the systems associated with the Minuteman missile program [43].

The name, fault tree analysis, is somewhat misleading. The analysis results in a structure called a fault tree yet, in practice, the structure need not be a tree and the nodes are not faults, they are events. Nevertheless, the term is in common use, and so we will use it. Be careful to keep a proper understanding of the term "fault" when discussing, building, or analyzing fault trees.

Fault tree analysis is a backward search technique. The starting point in performing the analysis is the hazard of interest, and the goal is to determine all of the events that could lead to that state. The events are then used to identify the faults that could cause them in a manner that is as comprehensive as possible. Getting a comprehensive set of faults for a system is extremely difficult, and documenting them in a fault tree is a sophisticated and complex process. We will restrict our discussion of fault tree analysis to an elementary level, because a comprehensive treatment of the topic is beyond the scope of the book.

4.3.1 Basic Concept of a Fault Tree

Informally, a fault tree is a structure that is used to help answer the question:

How can a given hazard arise?

The answer to this question is a collection of events, specifically, the events that would cause the system to enter a hazardous state if they arose.

In well-engineered systems, hazards do not usually arise because of just a single event, even with our extended notion of hazard. In such systems, hazards arise because several events occur, none of which would cause the hazard alone. In fact, many accidents occur because of complex and rare combinations of events where the combination was unexpected, not the specific events. By contrast, in poorly engineered systems, hazards can arise when one event, perhaps one of several, occurs.

4.3.2 Basic and Compound Events

Fault trees help us to document all the events that can lead to a hazard. To do so, we need the notions of *basic* and *compound* events. A basic event is something that happens to a system which we can treat as an indivisible action, and a compound event is a logical combination of basic events. The important difference is determined by whether we need to refine an event in order to identify possible events that are associated with faults in subcomponents.

Notice here that the issue is whether we *need* to refine a specific event. We always *can* refine an event, because we can always examine the internal design of a system component. Failure of the component itself is sometimes sufficient, but on other occasions we need to examine the component's design. Once we are convinced that we have sufficient detail to cover all the faults of interest, the events we have identified can be considered basic.

As an example of a basic event, consider a disk drive. In preparing a fault tree for a system that incorporates a disk drive, we will have an event labeled: "Disk drive fails." If the disk drive is built with proper failure semantics, then the interface that the disk presents on failure will always be the same and will be properly defined. The interface might be that the disk no longer responds to read or write requests and is essentially inert. If this behavior is adequate for our purposes, then the failure of the disk drive can be treated as a basic event.

However, we might be interested in what goes wrong with the disk itself, in which case we need to look at its design. This level of interest is only likely to occur at the device's manufacturer. Events that might occur in a disk include failure of the drive motor, failure of the head movement mechanism, failure of the head itself, various failures of the drive electronics, and failure of the disk surface. If we need to deal with faults that might lead to these events, then clearly we need to analyze the design of the disk drive, and the event "Disk drive fails" cannot be treated as basic. Note that for our purposes as computer engineers or software engineers, the internal workings of a disk drive are not relevant to our activities, and so failure of a disk drive is a basic event.

The combinations of basic events to form compound events are documented using logical expressions. These expressions are built in various ways using logical operators, most commonly logical **and** and logical **or**. This formalizes statements such as:

- Compound event H will arise if basic event I **or** basic event J occurs.

- Compound event E will arise if compound event F **and** basic event G occur.

- The hazard will arise if event C **and** event D occur.

- The hazard will arise if event A **or** event B occurs.

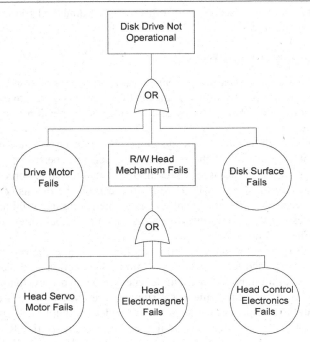

FIGURE 4.1 A fault tree fragment for a disk-drive failure.

A simple example fault tree fragment for the disk drive example above is shown in Figure 4.1. The hazard is the state in which the disk has failed, and this state is presented in the node at the top of the tree. Three separate events might cause this hazard: (1) the drive motor fails, (2) the disk read/write head mechanism fails, and (3) the disk surface fails. The fact that any one of these three events could lead to the hazard means that they are combined with a logical **or**, shown in the diagram using the usual symbol for inclusive **or**.

For purposes of this example, we assume that two of the three events in the second level in Figure 4.1 are basic and illustrated as circles. We need to elaborate the third node until the leaves of the fault tree are basic events. In the example, one extra level of refinement is shown for the event of the read/write head mechanism failing, and the resulting events are assumed to be basic.

Various standards have been developed for documenting fault trees. Some of these standards use a textual representation, some a graphic notation, and some both. Some place the root of the tree at the top of the structure and some to the side. A common standard is IEC 61025 [65]. In this standard, the logical operators are represented as logic gates, compound events as labeled rectangles, and basic events as labeled circles. Where a fault tree will not fit on a single page (as is usually the case) or where analysis is best served with multiple interconnected trees, triangles are used to indicate the links.

4.3.3 Inspection of Fault Trees

Fault trees provide a compact and elegant representation of important system information. That they are largely informal means that there is no way to establish completeness or correctness properties by analytic means. Inspection is essentially the only alternative.

Inspection of fault trees has to be systematic and thorough. Since fault trees are descriptions of systems, all of the relevant engineering expertise has to be represented in the inspection process. This requirement means that experts in the design of every subsystem must be involved so as to ascertain the details of every event, including the precise form of the event, the associated component failure semantics, the completeness of the failure event descriptions, the probabilities of the various events (if available), and so on.

Although they are informal, inspections of fault trees must be rigorous. Some of the techniques developed for software inspections (see Section 10.2) can be adapted to the inspection of fault trees. For example, checklists can be developed, the inspection process can include the same basic steps as are used in software inspection, such as preparation, inspection, and rework, a reader can be used to guide the systematic elaboration of the structure, and innovations such as Active Reviews can be adopted.

4.3.4 Probabilistic Fault Tree Analysis

Although a fault tree is an essential tool in the determination of the faults to which a system is subject, fault trees as we have discussed them so far have no quantitative role. If the fault tree for a system is developed carefully, there is a good chance that most of the faults to which the system is subject will have been identified. If the fault tree is inspected carefully by knowledgeable inspectors, the chances that the fault determination is complete are increased.

This is a desirable situation, but it leads to two intriguing questions:

- Are some faults more critical than others, and, if so, could the faults to which we should pay attention first be identified?

- Could the probability of occurrence of the hazard be estimated from the fault tree?

Both of these questions require quantitative analysis. The obvious way to answer the first question is to look for the faults most likely to cause the hazard. Faults that might cause events that lead to the hazard with high probability should be examined first.

The answer to the second question is related. If probabilities of occurrence can be determined for basic events, then various forms of.quantitative analysis are possible. For basic events that are statistically independent, the most elementary form of quantitative analysis is to add the probabilities of basic events that are inputs to an **or** gate and to multiply the probabilities of basic events that are inputs to an **and** gate. This allows the calculation of probabilities for the associated compound events, and this analysis can be continued up the fault tree until a probability estimate for the hazard is obtained. Where dependability requirements are stated quantitatively, e.g., R(ten hours) > 0.999999, then the quantitative goal can be restated in terms of the probabilities of the associated hazards, and the system's probability of entering those hazards can be estimated from the fault tree.

4.3.5 Software and Fault Trees

Software Failure Events

Events corresponding to failures of software components will appear in fault trees. The failure of a software component is an event that needs to be included in the determination of the faults to which a system is subject. Since the primary purpose of a fault tree is to document the events that can lead to a hazard, inclusion of events relating to software is essential.

Figure 4.3 (page 112) shows the design for the airport information display system example introduced in Section 4.2, and Figure 4.4 (page 114) shows part of the system's fault tree. In the fault tree, there is a compound event labeled "Data Computer System Fails". If that compound event were elaborated in detail, software failures in the data computer would be very likely to occur as basic events.

Such nodes point out clearly how significant software failures will be for the system being analyzed. If the hazard can be brought about by a software failure, then this will be clear in the fault tree. With insight about how the system is affected by software failures, specific dependability requirements can be set for software.

Software and Interlocks

Software is one of the most complex if not *the* most complex component in many crucial systems, and software is a common cause of failure. An approach that can help to protect systems from software failure is to examine the fault tree for each hazard and to make sure that software failure by itself cannot lead to the hazard. The basic structure that this implies is an *interlock*. An interlock is a design in which an alternate technology is used for a system component that stops the system from transitioning to a hazardous state irrespective of what the software does. The hazard can only occur if both the software *and* the alternate technology fail. Thus, in the fault tree, the software failure event and the failure of the alternate technology event will be inputs to an **and** gate in the tree for which the hazard is the root. Since both events are required for the hazard to occur, the probability of the hazard occurring is considerably reduced.

As an example of an interlock, consider the hazard that arises if the door of a microwave oven is opened with the microwave generator operating. A software check for this would be a normal approach, but an electro-mechanical interlock is a common addition. The interlock would consist of a mechanical switch in the door connected in series with the power to the microwave generator. Only if both the interlock and the software failed could the hazard arise. The fault tree fragment corresponding to this element of a hypothetical system is shown in Figure 4.2.

Such structures provide a very effective means for protecting users of systems from software failures. Relying completely upon software is undesirable, because software is so difficult to get right. An interlock is a special case of a design that includes *defense in depth* (see Section 4.3.7).

Software and Probabilities

Probabilistic analysis is an important but secondary purpose of a fault tree. Even with the most basic form of probabilistic analysis described in Section 4.3.4, the occurrence of software failure events is problematic. The problem arises because software faults are design faults, and there are no simple probabilistic models of software failure. In practice, probabilistic analysis of fault trees for systems that include software typically uses one of three approaches:

Assume the probability of software failure is zero. This approach limits the analysis to the non-software components of the system. The software failure events are documented in the fault tree so that their effects can be examined, but the probabilistic analysis of the system ignores them.

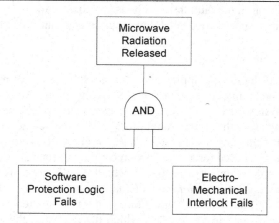

FIGURE 4.2 Fault tree fragment for interlock on microwave oven door.

Assume the probability of software failure is one. This approach is realistic but pessimistic. In practice, almost all real software systems do fail at some point, and so assuming that the probability of software failure is one is entirely reasonable. However, software that is developed carefully and considered suitable for use in systems that have to be dependable will not fail every time that it is used. Thus, making this assumption will provide unrealistically pessimistic probabilities at the system level.

Separate the analysis of the software. Since the quantitative analysis of software failures is so difficult, a reasonable approach is to separate it from analysis of other parts of the system. Quantitative analysis of the platform upon which software will run and the system within which it operates can be conducted quite successfully, and the resulting hazard probabilities stated as *conditional* upon the proper operation of the software.

4.3.6 An Example Fault Tree

Returning to the airport flight information display example introduced in Section 4.2, a hypothetical architecture for such a system is shown in Figure 4.3. In this architecture, two large displays are used for "Arrival" and "Departure" flight information. These displays are driven by a local, client-display computer. At a central location, two application servers, each formed from four single computers, provide the system's main functionality, and a database server that is replicated supplies the various items of data. An operator's console is provided at the central location for operators to control the system, and both the database servers and the application servers are connected to a wide-area network from which the flight data is supplied by the various airlines.

There are various hazards that might arise, but the most obvious one is:

The display is blank.

The display is merely an output device, and the actual data displayed is produced by a sophisticated computer system. We can see how the notion of a fault tree operates by asking how the hazard could arise, i.e., by trying to answer the question:

How could the display go blank?

For convenience, we will refer to the display going blank as $hazard_1$, but note that there are other hazards for which we would have to develop fault trees in practice. The most important additional hazard is the display of erroneous information. We will refer to this hazard as $hazard_2$. Arguably, $hazard_2$ is more important than $hazard_1$, the loss of the display, because at least in the case of $hazard_1$ we will know that the system has failed. With $hazard_2$, subtle errors in the display might easily go unnoticed and lead to a lot of difficulty.

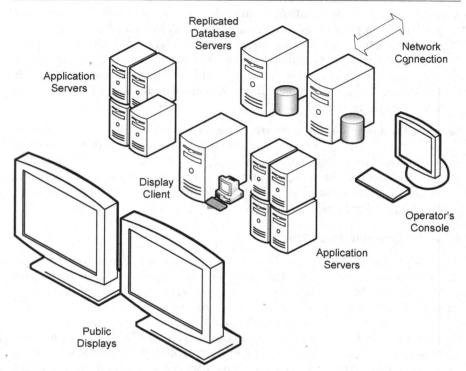

FIGURE 4.3 Hypothetical structure of an airport flight-information display.

The display device fails.
The data computer system fails.
The link between the computer system and the display fails.
The operators disable the display.

TABLE 4.1. Events that could cause *hazard₁*.

The answers to the question about *hazard₁* might include those shown in Table 4.1. We might be wrong, but this list seems to be exhaustive. This conclusion reminds us of another important point about determining the events in a fault tree, namely, that this determination is largely *informal*. Recall that there is no generally applicable algorithmic technique that can be used to identify the events that can cause a hazard. The process requires insight about a system and experience. Also, although the syntax and types in a fault tree can be checked mechanically, there is no algorithmic approach to verifying the contents of a fault tree either, and so the standard technique is to conduct human inspections.

A partial fault tree for the airport information system is shown in Figure 4.4. $Hazard_1$ is at the root of the tree, and the four events that could cause the hazard are shown as nodes on the level below the root of the tree. Any one of the events could cause the hazard by itself, and so the graph structure shows the associated logical expression with the graphic for an **or** gate.

The four events we have identified are compound events. We cannot associate any specific fault with any of them, and so we have to refine each by identifying the events that could lead to each of them.

Here, we will only develop the leftmost event in the fault tree, "The Display Device Fails". The events that could cause this event are shown in Table 4.2 and in the third row of Figure 4.4.

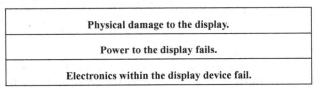

| Physical damage to the display. |
| Power to the display fails. |
| Electronics within the display device fail. |

TABLE 4.2. Events that could cause the compound event "The Display Device Fails".

To complete the fault tree for this example, we would apply the same process we have just followed to each of these compound events and thereby document the logical structure of these compound events until we have only basic events as leaf nodes. Again, for purposes of illustration, we will look at a single event.

The second compound event, "Power fails to the display" is more complex than it looks. For this example, we assume that there is a supplementary, backup power source. A fairly complete elaboration of this subtree is shown in the lower left of Figure 4.4. In this elaboration, the power to the display might fail if both the primary source of power fails and the backup power source fails. In the fault tree, this is indicated with an **and** gate.

The size of real fault trees requires that they usually cover several pages of documentation. Even for what seem to be simple systems, the refinement of compound events down to the basic events that we need can be very time consuming and can lead to large subtrees. They have been omitted for convenience in this example.

4.3.7 Defense in Depth

An important notion in dependability engineering is *defense in depth*. The basic idea is to have more than one barrier between normal operation and the hazardous states. By having more than one barrier, perfect operation of a single barrier is not required. If there are several barriers, hazards will be avoided if at least one barrier holds.

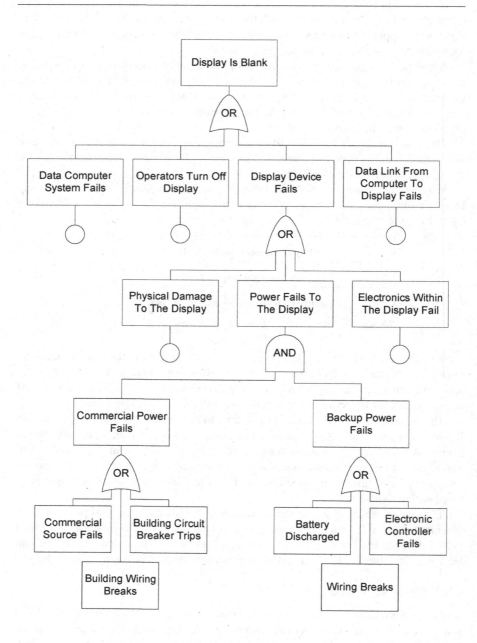

FIGURE 4.4 Fault tree fragment for airport information display.

Each barrier might be imperfect, but their combination is probably more likely to be effective than any single barrier. Defense in depth is the generalization of the concept of an interlock introduced in Section 4.3.5. As we noted with interlocks, defense in depth is important to software engineers, because a system designed using defense in depth can reduce the importance of software in achieving system dependability.

The intuition behind defense in depth is sometimes explained with what is referred to as the *swiss cheese system* model. The model is shown in Figure 4.5. If each barrier is thought of as being like a slice of swiss cheese with the holes representing faults, then defense in depth is like having a pile of swiss cheese slices. Provided the holes in the cheese slices do not line up, then there is no way to get through the stack of slices.

Intuition is helpful, but we need to have a rigorous understanding of defense in depth if we are going to be able to build real systems using the idea. We gain part of that understanding with a fault tree, as shown in Figure 4.6. The essence of defense in depth is the logic **and** whose output is connected to the hazard. The hazard cannot arise unless *all* of the events connected to the input of the logic **and** occur, where each of the events corresponds to failure of one of the barriers.

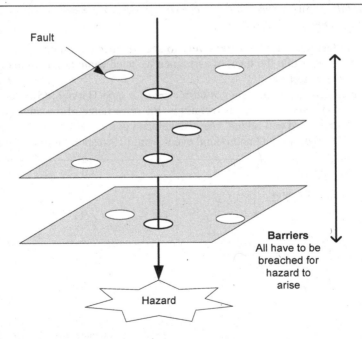

FIGURE 4.5 Swiss cheese model of defense in depth.

The swiss-cheese model is helpful, but the underlying approach of defense in depth is more complicated than it looks. The model and the associated fault tree fragment are only valid if two critical conditions hold:

- The faults in the barriers are not correlated. Clearly, a system could be built in which several barriers were present but one or more faults were common.

- The failure of a barrier does not cause a failure of or functional change to one or more other barriers. The worst possible situation is that a failure within one barrier somehow disables the others, thereby removing all protection.

4.3.8 Other Applications of Fault Trees

Software Fault Trees

The fault tree concept can be used to explore the logic structure of software. Suppose that we consider a particular output from software to be especially undesirable. Using the microwave-oven door as an example again (Section 4.3.5), even with an interlock the software should not turn on the microwave generator with the door open.

The issue is to answer the question:

Could the software turn on the microwave generator when not required, i.e., could the undesirable output occur?

We can test the software extensively to see whether the output ever arises, but we might discover that the level of assurance we need cannot be obtained with reasonable levels of testing.

An alternative approach suggested by Leveson and Harvey [85] is called *Software Fault Tree Analysis*. In this technique, the occurrence of the undesired output is treated as a hazard and a fault tree is developed corresponding to the logic of the program. The highest-level compound event would correspond to the condition that

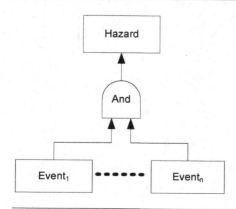

FIGURE 4.6 Fault tree model of defense in depth.

caused the output to be generated. That event would then be broken down into its constituent events, until the basic events corresponding to the original statements are reached.

System fault trees and *software* fault trees are different from each other, and the difference is important. The former is a technique used to analyze system designs so as to elaborate the events and event combinations that could lead to a hazard. Along with several other techniques, fault tree analysis is carried out before a system is built in order to predict whether the system dependability requirements will be met. Software fault tree analysis is a software verification technique that can be applied after software is built to determine the software states that might lead to an undesirable output.

Attack Trees

Attack trees have been proposed by Schneier [125] as a means of analyzing systems to determine how security attacks might be perpetrated. The idea is the same as a fault tree, with a successful attack being the hazard and actions taken by an attacker as the events. Attack trees provide a lot of insight into how an attacker might succeed just as fault trees provide a lot of insight into how a system might fail.

4.4 Failure Modes, Effects, and Criticality Analysis

4.4.1 FMECA Concept

Failure Modes, Effects, and Criticality Analysis (FMECA) is a technique that helps to answer the question:

What are the consequences that would result from the failure of a component within a system?

FMECA is a forward analysis technique, and the name of the technique sums up the approach quite well:

- Determine the *failure modes* for the various systems components.

- Determine the *effects* of these component failures on the system as a whole.

- Assess the *criticality* of the failures in the operating context of the system.

Using FMECA, a lot can be learned about the specific causes and effects of component failures, and insight can be gained about how important the various component failures would be. FMECA can be used as part of designing a system to evaluate the design. Thus, the design can be enhanced if the analysis shows that the effects of a component failure would be unacceptable.

An important by-product of this process is to focus attention on the need for complete and accurate failure semantics for all the components of the system. If a component failure will not cause a lot of harm, no special attention needs to be paid to that component. In particular, if the failure of a component leads to a benign loss of service by a system, then there might be no need to address that possible failure further.

The FMECA process begins with an elaboration of all the components of interest. For each component, all of the failures to which the component is subject are identified. Applying FMECA requires engineers to determine the different ways in which a component might fail. For example, a switch might fail with its contacts shorted together so that the switch is permanently "on". The switch might also fail with its contacts never touching so that the switch is permanently "off". Finally, the switch might fail by having its contacts "bounce" in such a way that it rapidly changes from "on" to "off" before settling in a single state.

Once the failures of the components are identified, the failure semantics can be carefully elaborated and then the effects of each failure are determined. These effects begin with the effects on connected components and continue with the effects on components connected to those components, and so on.

The effects of the failure end up being a detailed statement about the state of the system following the failure, and thus they define the erroneous state. The importance of the criticality step of FMECA is to identify the component failures with the most serious effects. This is the point at which a decision can be made about each failure to determine whether additional design effort is required.

FMECA details are usually recorded in tabular form, and different organizations use different forms. The forms typically list the components of interest, the various failure modes (failure semantics) for each component, the effects of the failure locally in terms of the local functionality that is lost, the effects on the complete system, and the criticality of these effects.

FMECA and fault tree analysis are complementary in many senses. Fault tree analysis provides a systematic way to explore the design of a system to ascertain the events that can lead to a hazard. In practice, fault trees are often developed with events tied to failure semantics, but this is somewhat awkward because the basic fault tree structure is not ideal for this representation. Fault trees for a set of hazards might contain the same event more than once since the same event is often involved in multiple hazards. Once a fault tree has been used to identify the hazards that can result from a basic event corresponding to the failure of a component, FMECA applied to the component can be used to reveal all of the details associated with that component.

Several organizations have developed standards for both conducting and documenting the results of FMECA [124, 12, 36, 66, 21, 123], and standardized FMECA is required in a number of application domains such as military weapons systems, spacecraft and launch vehicles, and parts of the automobile industry.

4.5 Hazard and Operability Analysis

4.5.1 The Concept of HazOp

Hazard and Operability Analysis, HazOP, was developed initially by the chemical engineering industry in the 1970s as a means of improving the dependability of chemical processes. HazOp is a powerful technique for seeking out process weaknesses that might lead to failures, and the technique has been applied to processes in other fields of engineering and to entities other than industrial processes. HazOp is immediately applicable to computer systems and even to software systems.

The goal of the technique is to present the developers of a system with a series of safety "what if" questions about the system of the form:

"What if <this event occurred>?"

The questions are constructed algorithmically using an approach that forms questions by combining question components from lists. Some questions end up being meaningless, but this is a small price to pay for the coverage that is possible with an algorithmic mechanism. By presenting system designers with questions of this form, the designers are challenged to think through events in a systematic way that they might not have explored otherwise. Developers would be expected to have taken care of all such circumstances in the system's design, and so the response to the questions is expected to be something like:

*"<This set of steps> would be taken, and the plant would
<react in the following way>."*

If the developers did not take care of the issue raised by the question, then a change in the system design could be effected.

The structure of the questions is a form of perturbation analysis. The "<this event occurred>" part of the question is formed by taking a system parameter and hypothesizing a question. In a chemical reactor, for example, a reactant might have to be maintained at a particular temperature and pressure in order for the reaction to run smoothly. Typical questions of interest for such a system would include:

*"What if the temperature in tank A
(a) rose above the maximum allowable value?"
(b) fell below the minimum allowable value?"
(c) rose faster than the maximum allowable rate?"
"What if the pressure in tank B fell below the minimum threshold?"*

Any of these events could have serious consequences, and determining the consequences is important. The great advantage of HazOp is that it provides an algorithmic (i.e., systematic and methodical) approach to forming (but obviously not answering) these questions.

The algorithmic approach to forming the questions is based on: (a) a list of system components that is derived from a model of the system of interest and (b) a list of domain-specific words. There is a valid expectation that the coverage of unusual events would be more thorough than if the questions were posed in an ad hoc manner. The quality of the coverage can be increased by careful word selection.

4.5.2 The Basic HazOp Process

The basic HazOp process begins with the development of a *flow model* of the system of interest. For chemical reactors, the system is the plant and the flow is of all the reactants. The items flowing in the flow model are referred to as *entities*, and they are typically tied to both the actual flowing substance, the plant location, and perhaps time. For example, in a chemical plant flow model, a substance such as nitric acid might be flowing between tanks A and B according to some sort of schedule. Entities of interest might include "nitric acid flowing out of tank A as the main plant reaction is initiated".

The what-if questions are derived from two lists of words, the *attribute* list and the *guide words*. The attribute list is the list of attributes associated with all the various entities. The guide words are adjectives that describe states of interest associated with the entity attributes. For the nitric acid entity described above, the attributes might be "temperature", "pressure", and "flow rate". The guide words might include "high", "low", and "absent".

The what-if questions are formed by taking each attribute, applying each guide word, and keeping the question if the question makes sense. Thus, there will usually be a lot of questions because of the number of combinations of attributes and guide words. But many of the questions will not make sense and so can be eliminated. Note, however, that this approach gives us reasonable confidence that the important questions have been formed. The combinatorial approach ensures that all combinations appear in the list even if some are meaningless.

4.5.3 HazOp and Computer Systems

HazOp and Software Requirements

Why should the computer engineer and the software engineer be concerned about HazOp analysis for a system such as a chemical plant? The answer lies in the software requirements for the chemical plant's computer system. The software requirements derive in large measure from the need to react to undesirable situations. If any of these situations arises in practice, the software might be the way in which a hazard is avoided. Not knowing about one of these situations could be very serious, so the requirements must document all of them if possible. The completeness of the software requirements can be aided considerably by a systematic HazOp analysis.

Important aspects of HazOp are (a) that HazOp can be applied to a variety of different entities and (b) HazOp's application tends to cross disciplines and so multiple forms of engineering expertise will become involved. To practice HazOp success-fully requires that the overall management approach be systematic and detailed. Computer and software engineers need to understand that their requirements might come from any of the other disciplines involved, and these engineers might have to interact with engineers using a variety of domain-specific terminologies.

Applying HazOp to Computer Systems

As you might expect, we can apply HazOp to computer systems just as we can to things like chemical plants. For example, consider a computer network. The flow model is the set of network nodes and their interconnections, and the flow is the net-work traffic. For software, the system is the software itself, and the flow might be data being manipulated during execution. For other types of system, a similar model is usually easy to develop.

For a computer network, the entities would include network packets or messages depending on the level of the flow model. The attribute list might include all aspects of network activity such as load, throughput, queue lengths, delays, and latencies. Guide words might include "high", "low", "absent", and "delayed".

HazOp has been applied to computer systems with great efficacy. For computer systems, the flow model would be based on information. A great deal has been writ-ten about HazOp in a wide variety of circumstances. An important reference that includes a discussion of the application on HazOp to software is *System Safety: HAZOP and Software HAZOP*, by Redmill et. al [116]. HazOp standards have also been developed [67].

Key points in this chapter:

- Anticipated faults are the classes of faults that we expect to occur. Since they are anticipated, we can make provision for them. The faults that we do not anticipate will have effects for which most likely no provision has been made.
- Fault tree analysis can help us to the anticipate faults that could lead to each hazard.
- Developing fault trees is largely informal, and inspection is the primary technique available to help ensure completeness and accuracy.
- Including software in fault trees is problematic.
- The substantial effectiveness of defense in depth can be seen and ana-lyzed using a system fault tree.
- Failure Modes, Effects, and Criticality Analysis (FMECA) is a technique for assessing the effects of certain types of failures.
- Hazard and Operability Analysis (HazOp) is a technique for systemati-cally refining the requirements of a complex system.

Exercises

1. Generally, having the input to the top element of a fault tree come from an **and** gate is considered desirable. Explain why this is the case.

2. Suppose you have been hired by the Bell Computer Corporation to help deal with the least dependable component of a laptop computer, the hard disk drive. In order to improve the dependability of the disk drive systems used in laptops, the goals are to analyze the current designs to see where the likely causes of failure are and to consider ideas like mirrored and solid-state disk designs. What is the most significant *hazard* associated with the disk that a laptop faces?

3. For the hazard identified in Exercise 2, draw the top three levels of the associated (hypothetical) fault tree.

4. List the nodes in the fault tree in Exercise 3 that would *not* be present with a disk-drive replacement based on compact-flash technology.

5. Suppose the current laptop disk in Bell Computer Corporation laptops were replaced with a *mirrored* disk (two drives operating in parallel with identical data). Using the fault tree from Exercise 3, estimate how effective mirroring the disk would be at increasing the MTTF of the disk system.

6. What is the most significant *hazard* associated with the pharmacy information system described in Exercise 15 in Chapter 2?

7. For the hazard identified in Exercise 6, draw the top three levels of the associated (hypothetical) fault tree.

8. For the most significant *hazard* associated with the robotic surgery system described in Exercise 9 in Chapter 3, draw the top three levels of the associated (hypothetical) fault tree.

9. Develop an inspection technique for fault trees that would allow you to have increased confidence that the fault tree was accurate and complete. Carefully consider the engineering disciplines that should be involved, the checklists that might be used, and the inspection process that might be followed.

10. The failures of the Therac 25 might have been prevented if the system were designed to include defense in depth. Examine the details of the Therac 25 system and explain how defense in depth was present in earlier Therac designs but eliminated in the Therac 25.

11. If you were to adapt HazOp for use with software, to which phase of software development might you apply it?

12. If you were to adapt HazOp for use with software, what attributes and guide words would you use?

CHAPTER 5　　　　*Dealing with Faults*

Learning objectives of this chapter are to understand:

- The concepts and roles of fault avoidance, fault elimination, fault tolerance, and fault forecasting.
- How to avoid the introduction of faults into a system.
- What can be done to eliminate the faults in a system.
- What can be done to tolerate the faults that remain in a system during operation.
- What can be done to forecast the effects of the faults that remain in a system during operation.

5.1 Faults and Their Treatment

Once we have done the best we can to determine the faults to which a system might be subject, we have to do something about what we found. Recall that there are four approaches to dealing with faults: *avoidance, elimination, tolerance,* and *forecasting.* As shown in Figure 5.1, with avoidance we are trying to stop faults from entering the system during development, with elimination we are trying to remove those that manage to enter the system during development, with tolerance we are trying to keep the system operating despite the presence of faults, and with forecasting we are trying to assess the effects of faults that remain in a system and will not be tolerated. In any system under development, each fault that is identified by means such as fault tree analysis *has* to be dealt with by one of these means.

The preference is always to use the four approaches in the order listed above. We must start by trying to avoid faults. Only if we cannot avoid them should we try to eliminate them. Only if we cannot eliminate them should we try to tolerate them. And finally, if we cannot tolerate them, then we have to resort to trying to forecast them.

Software faults are our biggest concern, and so we will focus on them. This concern means, of course, that we will focus on design faults. Despite this focus, as software engineers we have to be familiar with degradation faults, and so we will discuss them as necessary. In addition, we need to be familiar with Byzantine faults, and they are discussed at the end of this chapter in Section 5.7.

5.2 Fault Avoidance

Fault avoidance means building a system in which a particular fault or class of faults does not arise. This idea is powerful but somewhat counter-intuitive. If we could avoid *all* faults, we could be confident that our system would meet its dependability goals. Even if we could avoid only *some* faults, our task would be simplified, and we could focus our attention on those faults that could not be avoided. But how can we actually avoid faults?

5.2.1 Degradation Faults

For degradation faults, fault avoidance is not possible in an absolute sense. In the end, essentially any device built with any technology has a non-zero probability of failure per unit time. In other words, if you wait long enough, any device will fail.

In some cases, however, we can proceed as if degradation faults have been avoided, provided the rate of manifestation of the fault is known to be sufficiently small. This idea is especially important if the dependability requirements for a system do not require long periods of operation. If reliability is the concern and the dependability requirement is for hundreds of hours of continuous operation, then proceeding with an assumption that degradation faults have been avoided is quite reasonable if the device is known to have a Mean Time To Failure (MTTF) of sev-

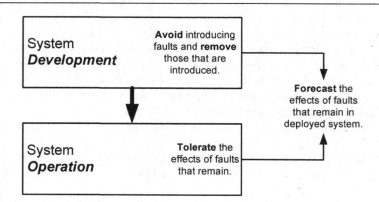

FIGURE 5.1 The four approaches to dealing with faults—avoidance, elimination, tolerance, and forecasting.

eral million hours. The probability of degradation faults occurring is so low that there is little value in trying to deal with them.

In practice, careful manufacturing and operational techniques permit many degradation faults to be ignored in computer systems. The rate of failure of modern microprocessors is so low that we rarely experience failures of the processors and memories in desktop machines. In part, this extraordinary reliability is the result of manufacturing techniques that avoid faults. Certainly we see failures of disks, power supplies, connectors, cooling fans, and circuit boards, and fault avoidance for these components has not progressed as far as fault avoidance in integrated circuits. These devices are dealt with using the other three approaches to dealing with faults.

5.2.2 Design Faults

For design faults, fault avoidance is entirely possible because of the basic notion of a design fault; something is wrong with the design. If we design a system with great care, we can, in fact, preclude the introduction of various classes of design faults. The way that this is done is by the use of systematic design techniques in which certain faults are precluded by the nature of the technique.

As far as software is concerned, faults can enter at any stage in the lifecycle. To avoid software faults, avoidance techniques have to be applied, therefore, at every stage. We will examine two important techniques for fault avoidance in Chapter 8 and Chapter 9. Here we look at a simple example to illustrate the idea.

A common example of software fault avoidance is to preclude certain constructs and to require others in high-level-language programs. These rules are often so simple that they can be checked by compilers or similar tools. Here are some simple cases:

Initialize all variables in a prescribed program location. If all variables are initialized to a known value, errors such as non-determinism and erroneous calculation associated with uninitialized-variable faults can be completely avoided. A typical location for such initialization is immediately after declaration.

Always include an `else` **clause in a** `case` **statement.** There is no possibility of software failing because of a missing case if this rule is followed. The semantics of `case` statements differ in different languages, and engineers can easily get confused.

Similar rules to these apply to hardware. Software rules are often developed in significant numbers in what are often called *style guides* to try to avoid faults of many types. An example is *Ada 95 Quality and Style: Guidelines for Professional Programmers* [34]. This is a comprehensive guide to developing software in Ada, and the text contains many hundreds of guidelines in all areas of the language. Such standards are discussed in Section 9.4.

5.3 Fault Elimination

Fault elimination is the active examination of a system to locate faults and to remove them. Fault elimination is conducted prior to the deployment of a system since the necessary examination cannot really be carried out with a system in operation.

5.3.1 Degradation Faults

Elimination of degradation faults seems like a strange idea. Since fault elimination takes place for the most part before a system is deployed, how can degradation faults have arisen before deployment? There are two aspects to this, each of which might arise inadvertently:

- Defective components might have been used in the construction of the system, and these components need to be found and replaced.

- Components might have been used that are subject to infant mortality, and a period of performance designed to cause such components to fail is needed.

Thus, elimination of degradation faults is an important part of system development. Designers must be sure that all of the system's components are functioning as expected prior to deployment, and they must be sure that the probabilities of degradation faults for the system's components have dropped below the infant mortality rate.

5.3.2 Design Faults

Design faults are the major target of fault elimination. Since design faults do not arise spontaneously, they are present and unchanging from the point in time when they are introduced until they are actively removed. To seek out and eliminate design faults from a system during development is an essential activity.

To eliminate a design fault, four critical steps are necessary:

- The presence of the fault has to be detected.

- The fault has to be identified.

- The fault has to be repaired.

- The resulting new design has to be verified so as to ensure that no new fault has been introduced as a result of the removal of the original fault.

The first three of these steps seem reasonably intuitive, but what about the fourth? Experience has shown that the repair of faults in software is often itself faulty. The changes made to software to correct a fault are actually incomplete or incorrect in some way, and often the effect is to create a false sense of security.

Design faults arise in all aspects of system design, and attempting to eliminate all of them is crucial. The most important class of design faults, however, is software faults, because they are the most common type of design fault and because they are so difficult to deal with. Much of the material in the latter parts of this book is concerned with the elimination of software faults.

5.4 Fault Tolerance

5.4.1 Familiarity with Fault Tolerance

Fault tolerance is a technique with which we are all familiar, because we come across examples regularly in our everyday lives. Examples include:

- Automobile spare tires allow us to deal with punctures, and dual braking systems provide some braking when the system loses brake fluid.

- Overdraft protection on bank accounts avoids checks being returned if the account balance drops below zero.

- Uninterruptable power supplies and power-fail interrupts for computer power sources allow action to be taken, such as safely saving files and logging off, when the primary source of power fails.

- Multiple engines on an aircraft allow safe flight to continue when an engine fails.

- Emergency lighting in buildings permits safe exit when the primary lighting systems fail.

- Backup copies of disk files provide protection against loss of data if the primary disk fails.

- Parity and Single-bit Error Correction Double-bit Error Detection (SECDED) in data storage and transmission allow some data errors to be detected (parity) or corrected (SECDED).

Although fairly simple, these examples illustrate the power that fault tolerance can have in helping to implement dependability.

5.4.2 Definitions

In order to enable a systematic and precise basis for the use of fault tolerance in computer systems, various authors have provided definitions of fault tolerance. Here are two definitions from the literature:

Sieworek and Swarz [131]:

"Fault-tolerant computing is the correct execution of a specified algorithm in the presence of defects"

This definition is a useful start, but there are two things to note. First, "correct execution" does not necessarily mean that the system will provide the same service when faults manifest themselves. Second, "the presence of defects" does not mean all defects. Defects might arise for which correct execution is not possible. Both of these points should be clear in a definition like this.

Anderson and Lee, paraphrased [10]:

> "*The fault-tolerant approach accepts that an implemented system will not be perfect, and that measures are therefore required to enable the operational system to cope with the faults that remain or develop.*"

This definition adds the explicit statement that a system will not be perfect, and this is a helpful reminder of what dependability is all about. Unfortunately, this definition also includes the phrase "*the* faults that remain or develop", and there is an implication that a system which utilizes fault tolerance can cope with all of the faults that remain or develop. This is not the case. There is a second implication in this definition that the "measures" will be successful when called upon to operate. They might not be. Again, such implications should not be present, and any definition of fault tolerance should not make them.

These observations lead to the following definition that is derived from the two definitions above:

Fault tolerance: A system that incorporates a fault-tolerance mechanism is one that is intended to continue to provide acceptable service in the presence of some faults.

Although well meaning, this definition is still not what we want. All three of these definitions actually refer to a mechanism, not the underlying concept. Here is the definition from the taxonomy:

Fault tolerance: Fault tolerance means to avoid service failures in the presence of faults.

This definition is the correct one. Avoiding service failures does not imply identical service. That some faults will not be tolerated by a particular mechanism does not mean that the definition of the concept is wrong.

Fault tolerance is an attempt to increase the dependability of the computing system to which it is applied. Elements are added to the computing system that, in the absence of faults, do not affect the normal operation of the system.

Fault tolerance is a complex topic. Essentially, what we are asking a system to do is:

- Deal with a situation that is to a large extent unpredictable.

- Ensure that the external behavior of the system that we observe is acceptable, either because the service provided is identical to the service we would receive had the fault not manifested itself or because the service provided is acceptable to us in a predefined way.

- Do all of this automatically.

Achieving this functionality is a tall order.

The unpredictability of the situation arises from many sources. For an anticipated degradation fault, the manifestation of the fault will occur at an unpredictable time. We cannot know when a component will fail. For degradation faults that we do not anticipate, the error, the failure semantics, and the time of manifestation will all be unknown.

For design faults, the situation is yet more complex. By their very nature, we cannot anticipate design faults very well. We know that software faults are likely to occur, but we have no idea about:

- What form a software fault will take.

- Where within the software a fault will be located.

- What the failure semantics of a software fault will be.

If we knew that a software fault lay within a certain small section of code, we would examine that section of code carefully and eliminate the fault. If we knew that a software fault would always have simple failure semantics, e.g., the software would stop and not damage any external state, we could plan for such an event. In practice, neither of these conditions occurs.

In practice, all we know is that design faults might occur, and that we will know little about their nature. Design faults are, therefore, difficult to tolerate, and efforts to do so are only of limited success. We will examine this topic in more depth in Chapter 11.

For Byzantine faults, the basis of such faults is some form of hardware degradation coupled with a transmission mechanism of the state. As a result, Byzantine faults are somewhat amenable to fault tolerance. An immense amount of work on the subject has been conducted and several efficient and effective mechanisms have been developed for Byzantine faults. We will examine this topic in more depth in Section 5.7.

With these various difficulties in mind, we now proceed to examine some of the important principles of fault tolerance.

5.4.3 Semantics of Fault Tolerance

If a mechanism acts to cope with the effects of a fault that is manifested, what do we require the semantics of the mechanism to be? This question is crucial. The semantics we need vary from system to system, and different semantics differ in the difficulty and cost of their implementation.

There are three major dimensions to the semantics of concern:

- **The externally observed service provided by the system during the period of time that the fault-tolerance mechanism acts.**
  In some cases, *any* deviation from the planned service is unacceptable, in which case the fault-tolerance mechanism has to *mask* the effects of the fault. In other cases, the planned service can be replaced with a different service for some period of time.

- **The externally observed service of the system after the fault-tolerance mechanism acts.**
  If long-term deviation from the planned service is unacceptable, the fault-tolerance mechanism has to ensure that the actions taken allow normal service to be continued. Otherwise, the planned service can be replaced with a different service. Maintaining the same service can be difficult primarily because of the resources that are needed.

- **The time during which the service provided by the system will be different from the planned service.**
  If this time has to be zero, then the effects of the fault have to be masked. If not, then there will be an upper bound that has to be met.

5.4.4 Phases of Fault Tolerance

In order for a fault to be tolerated, no matter what type of fault is involved and no matter what the required semantics are, four basic actions are necessary: (1) the error has to be detected; (2) the extent of the error has to be determined; (3) the error has to be repaired; and (4) functionality has to be resumed using the repaired state. These actions are referred to as the four phases of fault tolerance:

Error Detection.	Determination that the state is erroneous.
Damage Assessment.	Determination of that part of the state which is damaged.
State Restoration.	Removal of the erroneous part of the state and its replacement with a valid state.
Continued Service.	Provision of service using the valid state.

The second and third phases together are sometimes referred to by the comprehensive term **error recovery**.

The way in which these phases operate varies considerable. For some systems, no interruption in service is acceptable, in which case the effects of a fault have to be *masked*. The detailed semantics of these four phases are discussed in detail in Section 5.4.3.

All fault tolerance mechanisms employ these four phases. In some cases, a mechanism might appear to deviate from them, but a careful examination will reveal that they are, in fact, all there, although perhaps in a degenerate form. An example of such a mechanism is a system that intentionally shuts down whenever an internal component fails. Such systems are sometimes called *fail safe*, and there does not appear to be any continued service. In fact, the continued service is the provision of a benign interface. Although there is no functionality, there is a precise and well-defined interface upon which other systems can rely.

With the four phases of fault tolerance, we could, in principle, tolerate any fault. If we knew that a fault might manifest itself, then we could tolerate the fault by detecting the ensuing error, determining the damage to the state, repairing the state, and then taking steps to provide continued service.

This statement is correct, but does not say anything about how we can implement the four phases. And therein lies the problem. All four phases are difficult to achieve for virtually any fault, and so a great deal of care is needed if we are to develop a mechanism that can tolerate a fault properly.

Despite the difficulty that we face in implementing the four phases, they do provide us with two valuable benefits. Specifically, the four phases provide us with:

- A model that can be used to guide the development of mechanisms.

- A framework for evaluation of any particular fault-tolerance mechanism.

In the remainder of this book, we will frame our discussions of fault tolerance using these four phases.

5.4.5 An Example Fault-Tolerant System

To see how the four phases of fault tolerance operate, we look at an example. One of the most widely used fault-tolerant system structures is known as *triple modular redundancy* or TMR. An example of TMR is shown in Figure 5.2. In this example, three processors are operated in parallel with each receiving the same input. Each computes an output, and the outputs are supplied to a voter. By comparing the three values, the voter chooses a value and supplies that value as the TMR system's output. The TMR structure can be used for any type of component (processor, memory, disk, network link, etc.)

The faults that this TMR system can tolerate are degradation faults in the processors, including both permanent and transient faults (see Section 3.4). Transient faults can be caused by nuclear particles and cosmic rays impacting silicon devices.

Tolerating such transient faults is generally important but especially so for computers that have to operate in high-radiation environments.

Hardware degradation faults in processors are important, but there are many other classes of faults that will not be tolerated. Faults not tolerated include degradation faults in the input and output mechanisms, the voter and the power supplies, and all design faults.

Even within the class of processor degradation faults, TMR is limited. TMR can tolerate at most two permanent degradation faults that occur serially. In order to tolerate the second fault, the fault cannot arise until after the process of tolerating the first fault has been completed. This limitation is not especially severe. If degradation faults in the processors arise independently and with small probability p per unit time, then if tolerating a fault can be completed in one time unit, the probability that a second fault will occur so as to interfere with tolerating the first is of order p^2.

TMR can tolerate an arbitrary sequence of transient faults provided (a) the hardware is not damaged by the cause of the transient fault and (b) each transient fault does not overlap the previous transient fault.

The four phases of fault tolerance are implemented in TMR as follows:

Error detection. Errors are detected by differences in the outputs that the triplicated processors compute. These differences are present because of a fault, but the limitation of TMR only being able to tolerate a single fault arises, in part, because of

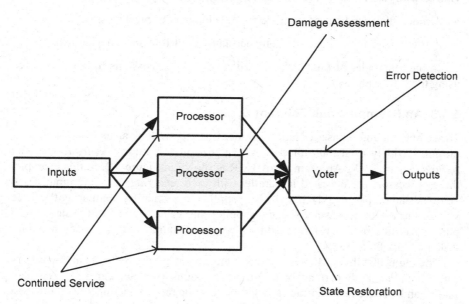

FIGURE 5.2 Triple Modular Redundancy and the phases of fault tolerance.

error detection. The occurrence of a single degradation fault means that only one processor will produce incorrect output values. Since the other two processors are fault free, the voter is able to detect the difference.

Damage assessment. The actual damage that occurs in processors when they fail is usually quite limited. In integrated circuits, for example, a single gate getting stuck at a fixed logic value is common. This can occur when one out of millions of transistors fails or when a single wire out of thousands in the circuit breaks. Outside of integrated circuits, a single wire in a single connector can fail. Despite these circumstances, TMR with triplicated processors does not have sufficient information to do other than assume that the entire processor has failed. So, in TMR, damage assessment is to diagnose the failure of an entire unit. Damage assessment is also, in part, the reason for TMR's ability to tolerate only a single degradation fault. With this restriction, the voter will see two identical sets of outputs and a single set of outputs that differs from the other two. If two degradation faults were possible, then two processors that were faulty could supply identical incorrect outputs to the voter, thereby defeating damage assessment.

State restoration. State restoration is achieved by removing the faulty processor. Removal is achieved by the voter merely ignoring subsequent outputs. Given the assumption of a single degradation fault only, this approach to state restoration provides a valid state from which to continue.

Continued service. Continued service is provided by the remaining two processors. Since they are assumed to be fault free, their outputs can continue to be used. With just two remaining processors, the ability of the system to tolerate faults has been reduced even if in this state the system can continue to provide service.

Once a TMR system has removed one of the processors from the set of three in order to tolerate a single degradation fault, the system is able to tolerate a second degradation fault but with very limited continued service. Since two processors remain functional, a second fault in either will be detected by the voter. In this case, however, there is no way to determine which processor experienced the fault. Thus damage assessment is limited to assuming the entire system is in error and continued service has to be limited to cessation of output.

Note carefully that the ability of a TMR system to tolerate faults has dropped as the two permanent degradation faults are tolerated. These issues are discussed in more detail in Section 6.3.3.

5.5 Fault Forecasting

For any fault that we cannot avoid, eliminate, or tolerate, we have to use fault forecasting. The idea is to predict the effects of the faults and to decide whether those effects are acceptable. If failures could be shown to occur at a rate below some pre-scribed value, the stakeholders of the system might be prepared to operate the system anyway.

The complexity of fault forecasting is increased by the need to be concerned with both degradation and design faults. Throughout this book we examine every-thing about dependability with the different characteristics of these two fault types in mind. When attempting to estimate probabilities of failure of components, both fault types need to be considered. Not surprisingly, the two fault types present differ-ent challenges in fault forecasting.

5.5.1 Fault Forecasting Process

Fault forecasting requires that a precise process be followed, because, by choosing to deal with faults by forecasting, the developer is admitting that anticipated faults *will* cause failures during operation. The process that has to be followed is:

- A high degree of assurance that the faults in question cannot be avoided, elimi-nated, or tolerated in a cost-effective way has to be established.

- The consequences of failure for each of the faults has to be quantified and assessed.

- An accurate statistical model of the rate of occurrence of failures from each of the faults has to be established.

- The ensuing system risk has to be computed (see Section 2.7.4).

- The acceptability of the risk to the system's stakeholders has to be determined.

Of the various elements in this process, by far the most difficult is the third step. Accurate statistical models of the type required are notoriously difficult to develop.

5.5.2 The Operating Environment

The issues in fault forecasting are not merely mathematical. The manifestation of faults is influenced considerably by the operating environment. The system under development will be used in an operational environment that must be modeled accu-rately if the rate of occurrence of failures is to be properly predicted.

In practice, the inputs that a system ends up facing are rarely exactly as expected. For degradation faults, the problem lies in the circumstances of the physi-cal environment. Temperature, humidity, vibration, and physical trauma all affect the types and frequency of degradation faults that will be manifested yet they are difficult to predict.

The operating environment is central to the modeling of design faults, as we see in Section 5.5.4.

5.5.3 Degradation Faults

As we noted in Section 3.5, degradation faults are fairly familiar. The notation that they are stochastic is familiar also. Incandescent light bulbs burn out with some probability per unit time, and the manufacturer can estimate the mean time to failure of the company's light bulbs by measuring a sample. A similar but enhanced approach to quantitative assessment can be applied to degradation faults in the physical components of a computer system. Those components are much more complex than a light bulb and cost a lot more, and so modeling enters the picture (see Section 12.2.3).

5.5.4 Design Faults

Unfortunately, quantitative modeling and therefore fault forecasting of design faults is much less familiar and much more difficult than fault forecasting of degradation faults. To see why, consider the following hypothetical program fragment:

```
while true loop
    read(sensor_value);
    calculate(actuator_setting, sensor_value);
    if actuator_setting = 0.46617815
        then fail;
    write(actuator_setting);
end while;
```

In this fragment, a sensor is being read and an actuator setting is being calculated and written. At the heart of the fragment is a software fault. For a particular value of the actuator setting, the software will always fail but only for that particular value.

The fault is, of course, a design fault. The software will always fail if the actuator setting is this special value. Unlike degradation faults, there is nothing stochastic about this behavior. If the specific input value for which the software fails arises, then the software will fail; otherwise it will not.

The fact that design faults are not stochastic in the same sense as degradation faults raises the question of whether metrics such as probability of failure per unit time are meaningful for artifacts like software. To the users of a software system, the software seems to fail in a stochastic manner. Poor software fails more often than good software, and this behavior seems to be stochastic. The reason for this apparent dilemma is that, for design faults, the randomness is in the *inputs* that are presented to the system. Input values are usually stochastic, and, if particular inputs arise by chance, then the associated design faults are triggered by chance.

This effect is illustrated in Figure 5.3. In the figure, software is shown as being part of a larger system, and that larger system is shown operating in an environment. The larger system might be something like an embedded computer network used in

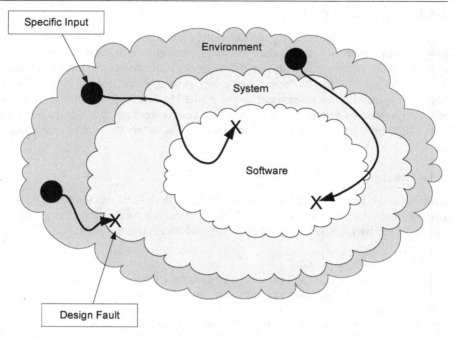

FIGURE 5.3 The basis for the stochastic analysis of design faults.

an automobile, in which case the environment will be the driver and all of the elements of the automobile.

In the figure, the system contains a design fault and the software two design faults, and input is shown originating in the environment. In the automobile example, the design fault in the system might be a wiring defect in the sensor or actuator network. Various inputs are supplied to the software by the system after they are presented to the system by the environment. Two specific inputs are shown that will trigger the design faults in the software, and one specific input is shown that will trigger the design fault in the system.

The stochastic nature of failures that derive from these design faults arises in both cases from the randomness of the inputs arising from the environment, not the faults themselves. Thus modeling of the stochastic nature of failures with design faults has to start with models of the environment.

5.6 Applying the Four Approaches to Fault Treatment

The four approaches to dealing with faults differ in their applicability, degree of success, and cost, and the differences are most significant when comparing degradation faults and design faults. Engineers must keep in mind that each approach has a role to play, and that the selection of approaches used will be system dependent.

Fault avoidance should always be our priority, but avoidance is much harder to practice with degradation faults. The success of fault avoidance depends upon the developers' ability to identify the faults to which the system is subject and to effect appropriate avoidance measures. The cost of fault avoidance is really the lowest since no resources are needed beyond identifying the fault classes of interest and seeking ways to avoid them.

Fault elimination is difficult with both design and degradation faults. Not only do the fault types have to be identified, but mechanisms are need to try to identify the faults that might need to be eliminated. And then the elimination process has to be conducted. The cost is higher than fault avoidance, because fault elimination is usually conducted in addition to fault avoidance.

Fault tolerance is much more difficult to apply to design faults than to degradation faults and tends to be less successful. The cost of fault tolerance is always high, because enabling a system to tolerate residual faults, no matter of what type, requires the addition of system components that are not otherwise required.

Finally, fault forecasting relies upon modeling of fault behavior and the associated failure semantics. This modeling is much more difficult for design faults than for degradation faults. Fault forecasting is the most expensive approach to dealing with faults, because the approach literally is to allow the system to fail at a rate deemed sufficiently small by the system's stakeholders. System failures can be costly, hence our interest in dependability.

5.7 Dealing with Byzantine Faults

The basic idea of Byzantine faults was introduced in Section 3.7. Byzantine faults are subtle, difficult to avoid or tolerate, and can have serious consequences. Recognizing their existence and serious nature has also allowed a serious problem in distributed systems to be uncovered and solved.

Byzantine faults can occur in essentially any real system, and engineers must either show by some means that such faults cannot arise in their specific system or show how the effects of such faults will be tolerated.

In dealing with Byzantine faults, engineers must understand how complex the problem is. Being lulled into a false sense of security is common as is thinking that a solution one has derived is correct. The solution might be correct, but experience has shown that the majority of people are convinced by informal arguments that are, in fact, wrong. In this area, analyzing algorithms mathematically is important. Even with mathematics, the analysis can be very subtle, and there have been cases in which people were convinced by *formal* arguments that were, in fact, wrong.

A complete and detailed treatment of the topic is beyond the scope of this book, and the interested reader is referred to the research literature on the subject. Many approaches to tolerating Byzantine faults have been developed along with some approaches to avoiding them. The necessary mathematics for all of this has been completed by the authors of the papers, and so using established results is likely to be much more successful than trying to develop solutions oneself.

From the perspective of the software engineer, understanding these issues so as to gain a healthy respect for the problem is the key requirement.

5.7.1 The Byzantine Generals

The concept of Byzantine faults was first introduced by Lamport, Shostak, and Pease in what they called the *Byzantine Generals Problem* [83]. The problem is a clever explanation of the underlying idea and is worth repeating.

As shown in Figure 5.4, several divisions of the Byzantine army are camped outside an enemy city, and the generals — the commanders of the divisions — have to decide whether they should attack the city or retreat. The generals need to agree on what the strategy is going to be, attack or retreat, because if some attack and some retreat they will obviously be in trouble.

The generals can only communicate by sending messages to each other. Under normal circumstances this restriction would be dealt with easily, but the army has been infiltrated by traitors. Some generals are traitors, and these traitors will attempt to disrupt the process of reaching agreement.

The army has two goals:

- All loyal generals must decide on the same strategy.
- A small number of traitors must not cause loyal generals to agree on a bad strategy.

These goals are stated informally, and in order to see how they apply and how they can be met, the goals are restated more formally.

Consider the role of just a *single* general. The general's goal is to get the message about the strategy that he has selected to all of the other generals whom we will refer to as lieutenants. The general and any number of the lieutenants might be traitors. The goal of this communication is for the commanding general to send an order to his $n-1$ lieutenants so as to ensure that:

IC1:   All loyal lieutenants obey the same order.

IC2:   If the commanding general is loyal, then all loyal lieutenants obey the order he sends.

Do we attack in
the morning?

Divisions of the
Byzantine Army

Messengers

FIGURE 5.4 The Byzantine army surrounding an enemy city.

IC1 and IC2 are called the *Interactive Consistency Conditions*, and these conditions provide us with a formal statement that can both be the basis of seeking a solution and the basis of understanding the Byzantine Generals Problem as the problem applies to computers.

5.7.2 The Byzantine Generals and Computers

When one is initially presented with the Byzantine Generals Problem and the Interactive Consistency Conditions, one is tempted to ask what on Earth either has to do with computers. In particular, how could something this esoteric have anything to do with the dependability of computers? To see this, we need to refine the problem statement a little.

The relevance to dependable computing comes from the need to transmit data from one computer to another. The "general" is the computer that originates the transmission and the "lieutenants" are the receiving computers. In terms of computers, the Interactive Consistency Conditions become:

IC1:   All non-faulty computers operate with the same data.

IC2:   If the originating computer is non-faulty, then all non-faulty receiving computers operate with the data sent by the originating computer.

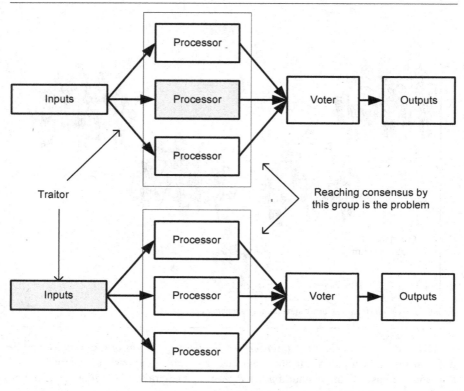

FIGURE 5.5 The Byzantine Generals Problem in a TMR system.

These conditions seems reasonable, perhaps even trivial in a sense. So, where are these conditions a problem and why should engineers care? The answers to these questions can be seen if we look at a simple triple-modular-redundant system, as shown in Figure 5.5. In a TMR system, the three different processors *must* operate with the same data if the system is to have the performance that is expected. If they operate with *different* data, then obviously the individual results of the different computers are likely to differ. In that case, the voter might conclude *incorrectly* that one or more processors has failed.

The problem seems to be limited to making sure that the input is distributed properly, and in a sense input distribution is the problem. Unfortunately, this distribution is far from simple. All the processors need to operate with the same input data, but they cannot be sure that the input distribution mechanism is not faulty. The obvious "solution" is to have the three processors exchange values, select a value to use if they are not identical, compare the values they received, and agree about which value they will use by some sort of selection process.

If the input source were the only problem, that would be fine. But the exchange of values by the processors is precisely the Byzantine Generals Problem. So we have to examine that carefully and make provision for the situation in which the processors themselves might be faulty.

The overall structure of the solution is to treat the input source as possibly faulty and accept that the three processors might have different data. The processors then need to reach a consensus about the value they will use in computation by undertaking some sort of algorithm that will allow the restated Interactive Consistency Conditions above to hold. Once this consensus is reached, the processors can continue with the application they are executing and know that the results presented to the voter by non-faulty processors will be the same.

There is just one problem with all this: there is no solution to the Byzantine Generals Problem if there are m traitors and no more than $3m$ generals. For the TMR case, what this means is that three processors cannot reach consensus as desired if one of them is faulty, i.e., the case $m = 1$.

This result is truly remarkable, because the result tells us that we have to be much more careful with redundant computer systems. Specifically:

- We must pay attention to Byzantine faults in such systems.

- We cannot distribute data as we need to in an N-modular redundant system (a generalization of triple-modular redundancy where $N > 3$) with m faulty computers unless N is greater than $3m$.

An important discussion of the practical elements of the Byzantine Generals Problem was presented by Driscol et al [38]. The paper presents a discussion of how Byzantine faults arise in the analog electrical circuits used to implement digital functionality. Of special note are examples that illustrate clearly how specific instances of Byzantine behavior can arise and how the effects are propagated throughout complex electronics.

5.7.3 The Impossibility Result

Surely, if we look carefully, we can find an algorithm that will allow the processors in a TMR system to reach consensus. This is a tempting thought, but do not bother looking. There is no such algorithm. To see why, we need to look carefully at the TMR case, although things are a bit easier to follow if we go back to using generals and messages as the context.

We begin with the commander and two lieutenants, as shown in Figure 5.6. The commander transmits a message to the two lieutenants, and they exchange values so as to try to determine a consensus. As shown in Figure 5.6(a), lieutenant 1 sees "attack" from the commander and "retreat" from the other lieutenant. In order to be sure that he obeys IC2, lieutenant 1 must decide to "attack" because that is what he got from the commander. To do otherwise, irrespective of what lieutenant 2 claims,

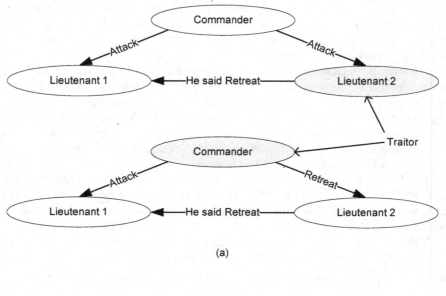

(a)

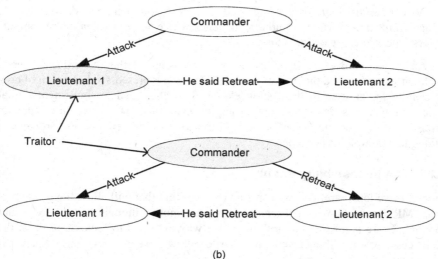

(b)

FIGURE 5.6 The inconsistency at the heart of the impossibility result.

would mean the possibility of violating IC2 because lieutenant 1 cannot tell which of the other two participants is a traitor.

Now consider how things look to lieutenant 2, as shown in Figure 5.6(b). In the case where he receives "retreat" from the commander, he too must obey this order or risk violating IC2. But by doing so, he violates IC1. In the case where the commander is a traitor, both lieutenants are required to do the same thing by IC1 and they do not. This surprising result can be generalized quite easily to the case of m traitors and $3m$ generals [83].

5.7.4 Solutions to the Byzantine Generals Problem

For $3m+1$ generals including m traitors, a solution to the problem exists that is based purely on voting. The solution requires multiple rounds of data exchange and a fairly complicated vote.

An intriguing solution exists if generals are required to sign their messages. The solution works for $3m$ generals in the presence of m traitors so the solution bypasses the impossibility result. The solution with signed messages is a great advantage in practice, because the solution offers an approach to fixing the situation with TMR.

In this solution, generals are required to sign their messages, and two assumptions are introduced about the new type of messages:

- A loyal general's signature cannot be forged, and any alteration of the contents of his signed message can be detected.

- Anyone can verify the authenticity of a general's signature.

At first glance, these assumptions seem quite unrealistic. Since we are dealing with traitors who are prepared to lie, does that not mean that they would happily forge a signature? At this point the analogy with generals does us a disservice, because we are not thinking about what the computers (the things we care about) are doing.

The notion of lying derives from a failed computer failing to transmit a message with integrity. Because the computer is faulty, we cannot be sure what effect the computer's fault might have on the content of a message. One thing we can assume is that the actions of a faulty computer are not malicious. So the idea of "lying" is not quite correct. The faulty computer is actually babbling in a way that we cannot predict.

What this means for signatures is that forging a signature will only occur with a very small probability. To forge a 32-bit signature, for example, would require a babbling computer to generate a valid signature by chance. If the computer were to generate a 32-bit string at random, the probability that the random string matched a signature would be 1 in 2^{32}, or about one in four billion.

The same argument applies to detection of a faulty computer's possible changes to the message. The use of parity and other checks to make sure that the contents have not been changed randomly is both simple and effective. Thus, in practice, the extra two assumptions are quite reasonable, and the solution using signed messages can be used quite effectively.

Since the introduction of the Byzantine Generals Problem, variations on the different circumstances and assumptions have been developed along with many refined and special-purpose solutions.

Key points in this chapter:

- The four approaches to dealing with faults are avoidance, elimination, tolerance, and forecasting.
- The four approaches should be applied in order.
- All four approaches can be applied to all three fault types: degradation, design, and Byzantine.
- All fault-tolerance mechanisms operate in four steps: error detection, damage assessment, state restoration, and continued service.
- Byzantine faults can arise in a wide variety of computer systems.
- Byzantine faults are difficult to detect and tolerate.
- The impossibility result for Byzantine faults shows that three computers cannot tolerate a Byzantine fault; four are required.

Exercises

1. Explain the preferred order of applying the four approaches to fault treatment and explain why that order is preferred.

2. The notion of failure probability cannot be applied to a software system in the same way that it can be applied to a system subject to degradation faults. Explain why.

3. Explain how the notion of failure probability is applied to a software system.

4. Give examples of three instances of fault tolerance that you have seen in everyday life that are different from the list in Section 5.4.1.

5. For the programming language with which you are most familiar, search for a set of rules about programming designed to promote fault avoidance as discussed in Section 5.2.2.

6. What type of approach to dealing with faults is software testing? Explain your answer.

7. For a software fault in a program that you have written, document the fault and discuss the failure semantics of the fault.

8. For the software fault that is the subject of Exercise 7, discuss what would be needed to tolerate the fault during execution.

9. In general, degradation faults are easier to tolerate than design faults. Explain why this is the case.

10. The primary lighting systems in buildings are often supplemented by emergency lighting systems that come on when the primary system fails. The system is using fault tolerance to try to avoid service failures. For such a lighting system:

    (a) Identify the four phases of fault tolerance in the lighting system.

    (b) Determine the required semantics of fault tolerance in this case (see Section 5.4.3).

11. Locate the original paper that introduced the Byzantine Generals Problem [83], and explain the problem to a colleague.

12. Implement the voting algorithm contained in the original paper that introduced the Byzantine Generals Problem.

13. A sophisticated automobile cruise-control system provides automatic acceleration and braking to maintain speed equal to the vehicle ahead (if there is one) and a speed set by the driver otherwise. The system provides accident prevention by braking the car automatically if the system detects an imminent collision. If the system detects skidding during emergency braking, then the separate ABS is turned on. A variety of sensors monitor vehicle conditions, and a small radar monitors the vehicle ahead and attempts to locate obstacles ahead. A computer system provides all the various services. The system performs numerous self

checks on the hardware whenever cruise control is not taking place. If a self-check fails, cruise control is disabled and a light is illuminated to inform the driver. The following figure illustrates the system design:

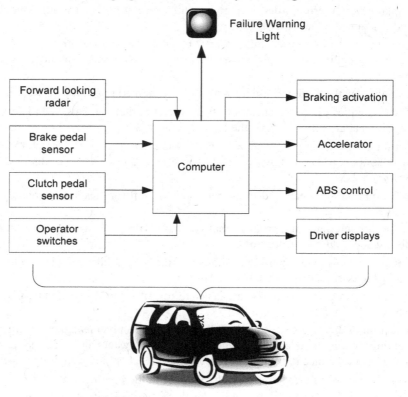

(a) Identify the hazards to which this system is subject.

(b) The failure semantics of the hardware sensors on the brake and clutch pedals are complex. When failed, they operate intermittently, and their behavior is inconsistent. These circumstances are common with degradation faults. What might the software monitoring these sensors do to try to detect the failures?

(c) What algorithms might the system employ in its self-checking process to detect faults in the brake activation and accelerator control mechanisms?

(d) Software failure of this system could be catastrophic, because the system has control of the accelerator and brakes. What checks might the software put into effect to detect its own failure in order to avoid excessive speed or braking? (Hint: whatever the software does, the commands to the accelerator and brakes should be "reasonable".)

CHAPTER 6   *Degradation Faults and Software*

Learning objectives of this chapter are to understand:

- The role of redundancy and replication in computer system architecture.
- The role of software in managing the redundancy in computer systems.
- The impact on software architecture of redundancy in computer systems.
- What software has to do to support redundant system architectures.
- The effects on software of operating on system architectures such as triple modular redundancy.

6.1 Impact on Software

Computer systems have to deal with degradation faults, and so the obvious thing to do is to use the four basic approaches, i.e., avoidance, elimination, tolerance, and forecasting, in a systematic way. In practice, that is what is done, but three of the four, avoidance, elimination, and forecasting of degradation faults, are quite specialized and beyond the scope of this book. Fault avoidance and elimination for computer hardware, for example, requires extensive, specialized knowledge of hardware technology, and fault forecasting requires detailed knowledge of the underlying probabilistic models and the associated methods of analysis.

In our discussion of degradation faults, therefore, we limit our attention to fault tolerance and, within that topic, to the aspects of the problem that are important to us as software engineers or computer engineers. Our goal is not to develop or analyze fault-tolerant structures that might be used for coping with degradation faults, although we will describe them. Our goal is to understand how such techniques impact software, both its development and its operation. This impact is quite extensive. The result of having to deal with degradation faults affects software in two ways:

Target Platform Architecture. The target platform upon which the software executes can be a lot more complicated than might be expected. Equipment is present that would not be needed if our goal was merely to execute the software. As a minimum, the software has to execute properly with this target.

Software Functionality. The software is usually called upon to help manage the target system. Tolerating degradation faults might require assistance from the software in all four phases. Software might be used (a) to detect errors by comparing data from different hardware elements, (b) to assess damage by examining data from the different components or running diagnostic tests designed to determine which components have failed, (c) to establish a consistent state by reconfiguring both the hardware components and the software itself, and (d) to provide continued service by stopping, starting, or reconfiguring either hardware or software components. Tolerating degradation faults might lead to different or reduced service, and that change might require extensive processing by the software.

As we proceed, we will assume that the degradation faults of interest are those which have been properly anticipated and whose existence has been analyzed using the techniques described in Chapter 5. We will also assume that the failure semantics associated with each degradation fault are properly defined and comprehensive.

6.2 Redundancy

6.2.1 Redundancy and Replication

Tolerating degradation faults relies upon *redundancy*. Redundancy does not mean simple replication, although replication is commonly used. Replication means having multiple instances of an entity that might fail available when fewer than that number are required to provide service. Having multiple instances of an entity leads to the obvious possibility that, when some of the entities fail, other replicates can continue to provide service. For example, if one entity is required but we have two, then service can be continued if one fails, at least in principle.

Clearly, replication is expensive. If we only need one of something to provide service, then having two will cost roughly twice as much. With this in mind, various less expensive techniques have been developed in which complete replication is not needed. Some additional, redundant equipment is required but less than would be needed with an exact copy.

Parity

A simple example of redundancy that is not replication is *memory parity*. Parity provides a form of degradation fault tolerance that is limited to error detection. A single parity bit is added to a set of data bits and is set to make the parity either even or odd. One parity bit might be used for many data bits, a byte, or a 32-bit word, for example. If a fault leads to one of the data bits or the parity bit being inverted, then the parity will be incorrect and specialized circuitry can detect the situation[1].

With parity, all that we have is error detection, because the location of the defective bit (or bits) is unknown. However, in many cases error detection is adequate. In terms of our notion of fault tolerance, error detection is achieved by observing the parity discrepancy, damage assessment is to assume that the entire set of data and parity bits is defective, and both state restoration and continued service are null. Thus, in terms of repairing the data bits, nothing useful can be done if parity checking is all that is available, and so continued service is limited to stopping.

Adding parity to a memory of any size is a useful capability. The system can detect an important class of errors, and measures outside of the basic memory mechanism can provide some form of alternate service at a higher level of abstraction. If these errors are not detected when they occur, the erroneous state could become much worse, as computing would continue with either incorrect data or incorrect instructions.

Note that parity deals with a particular type of fault, typically the loss of a single bit from a prescribed set. Thus, this has to be the anticipated fault for which parity is being added. Part of the process of anticipating the fault has to include the determination of the number of data bits for each parity bit and the failure semantics of individual data bits.

Error-Correcting Codes

Another example of a system that uses redundancy which is not replication is an *error-correcting code* for memory. In this case, the fault tolerance allows the effects of the fault to be masked. The data is not replicated, but additional information is stored along with the data. The additional information requires more bits than simple parity but fewer bits than the data.

If a bounded number of bits is lost either from the data or the additional information or both, then it can be recovered algorithmically. The most common instance of a code of this type is designed to deal with a loss of a single bit from a set of four. This requires three bits in addition to the four bits of data along with circuitry to make use of the additional bits. In this simple form, the additional bits are referred to as the syndrome. An error is signaled by the syndrome being non-zero. Damage assessment is to assume that only a single bit is erroneous, in which case, the non-zero syndrome is actually the location of the erroneous bit. State restoration is provided by inverting the erroneous bit, and continued service by resuming the operating software.

---

1. Actually, parity works if there is more than one changed bit as long as the number of changed bits is odd.

Mirrored Disks

An example of a system that uses redundancy which is replication to mask faults is a mirrored disk, as shown in Figure 6.1. In such a system, two disks are used in place of one, and each holds a complete copy of the data. If either disk fails as a result of an anticipated fault, the other disk can continue to support both read and write operations within the file system.

During the time that one of the disks is being repaired or replaced after a disk failure, the system is vulnerable to a second disk failure and so the probability of complete failure is non-zero. The system designers have to make sure that the probability of a second disk failure during that time is sufficiently small. Provided the failed disk can be replaced as a maintenance activity, the system can become fully replicated again as soon as all the data has been written to the replacement disk, a process called "resilvering".

RAID Systems

A generalization of the idea of mirrored disks is the set of architectures that is known as Redundant Array of Inexpensive Disk (RAID) systems [104]. There are several different disk architectures within the set, the simplest of which is exactly disk mirroring. Adding more complexity allows substantial benefits to be gained both in terms of performance and dependability. For example, the architecture known as RAID 2 uses an approach that is similar to error-correcting codes in memory. Instead of writing data sequentially on a single disk, a set of n bits is written across n disks, one bit per disk. The additional bits needed by the error-correcting

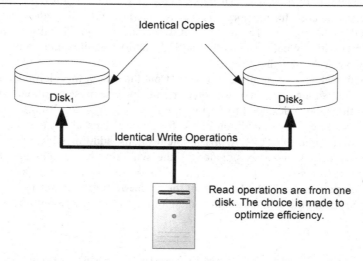

FIGURE 6.1 A mirrored disk system in which two identical copies of the data are maintained.

code are also written across a set of disks, one bit at a time. With this arrangement, a disk read failure can be masked, and a complete disk replaced if necessary without stopping the system.

6.2.2 Large vs. Small Component Redundancy

No matter what techniques are used to tolerate degradation faults, a decision has to be made about the size of the components to which fault tolerance will be applied. In the cases of parity and error correction discussed above, for example, deciding how many bits will be protected by a single parity bit or a single instance of error-correcting data is necessary. The reason for this choice is partly cost and partly the efficacy of damage assessment.

The issue of cost is fairly clear. Redundancy requires something additional in a system, even if that something is not complete replication, and so to keep costs down we would like to use as little redundancy as possible. In the case of parity, for example, the least additional memory requirement would occur if we used a single parity bit for an entire real memory (perhaps several gigabytes). The cost and organization of the parity generation and parity checking circuitry is another expense.

The problem of dealing with large components using minimal redundancy is that minimal redundancy limits the opportunity for damage assessment and therefore the continued service that can be provided. No matter what the size of a component is, the component to which redundancy is applied is the limit of damage assessment. During operation, complete failure of the component has to be assumed, even though this is rarely the case. Thus, of necessity, all of the working parts of a component are taken out of service along with those parts that have failed. If the designers' choice was to apply redundancy to large components, then large amounts of working hardware will be lost following any failure. If the choice had been to use redundancy on small components, reconfiguring what remains to assemble a working system is far more likely to be possible, albeit perhaps with reduced functionality.

The contrast is shown in Figure 6.2 In the upper diagram, a system consisting of an A component and a B component is replicated in its entirety. In the lower diagram, the individual components are replicated and connected in a flexible way. In the upper figure, a failure of component A makes the entire replicate unavailable, including a perfectly good B component. If the remaining B unit fails, the system will become non-operational.

In the lower figure, all that is lost if an A component fails is that A component. Subsequent failure of a B component (but not an A component) can be dealt with because the remaining A component can be connected to the remaining B component.

As an extreme example of the issues surrounding component size, consider the parity example again. If a single parity bit is used for an entire memory, then the entire memory is lost when a parity error is detected. However, if a single parity bit is used on each 32-bit word, then only one word is lost when a parity error is detected. Avoiding using part of memory is relatively easy for software if that part is known to be defective.

6.2.3 Static vs. Dynamic Redundancy

Although redundancy is needed for all aspects of fault tolerance, the same redundant elements are not necessarily used for all four phases. Certain elements might be used for error detection and entirely different elements used to provide continued service. The most important instance of this occurs with the notions of *static* and *dynamic* redundancy.

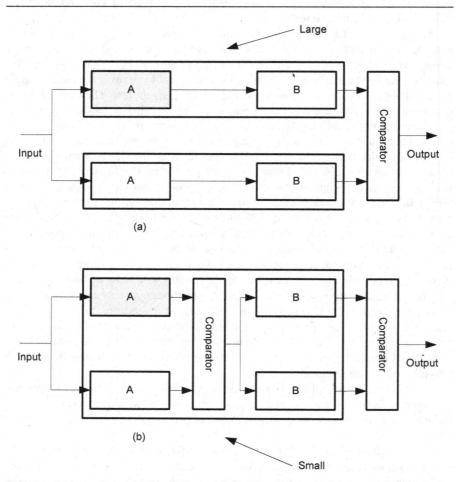

FIGURE 6.2 System in which redundancy is applied to (a) large components and (b) small components.

In practice, electronic components fail because of thermal stress, vibration, humidity, and physical damage. Thermal stress arises because of high absolute temperatures and temperatures that vary over time. Damage from thermal stress leads to an important idea, which is to extend the life of components intended to facilitate continued service by keeping them powered down. In other words, those components that are not needed for the provision of service are not operating. Keeping an electronic component powered down tends to increase the time to failure of the device.

Keeping a device powered down is not a panacea for longevity. The device is still subject to some temperature variation, vibration, and humidity, and possibly to physical damage. The most significant problem is the restoration of power when the device is needed. Failure rates at power on are relatively high. A second issue is that the power on operation is not transparent. Powering on a component frequently requires cessation of service while the new component is initialized, and other devices and the software are reconfigured.

Operating all of the devices in a system all the time is referred to as *static redundancy*. Keeping redundant devices powered down until needed is an approach called *dynamic redundancy*. In such a system, a set of j devices is needed to provide service and error detection, and these components are operated all the time. A set of k additional components is included in the system, and these devices are kept powered down until needed. The number of spares, k, can be set to provide an extended period of service if necessary. With the high reliability of modern devices, the value of k is sometimes just one or two.

The contrast between static and dynamic redundancy is illustrated in Figure 6.3. In Figure 6.3(a), static redundancy, the system begins with N operating units and the number of operating units decreases as units fail. In Figure 6.3(b), dynamic redundancy, the system begins with N−S operating units and S spares. The number of operating units remains the same at N−S as units fail, because spares are entered into the operating set.

6.3 Redundant Architectures

Many different redundant architectures have been developed, far too many to be discussed here. In practice, the design and development of the architecture for a specific system is a complex activity, and the purpose of discussing redundant architectures is twofold: (1) to review the basic architectural types and (2) to examine the implications on software of each architecture.

Employing redundancy in a system is an expensive and complicated undertaking. Any system that employs a redundant architecture incurs costs over and above those needed for the basic operation of the system. The additional costs incurred during development include:

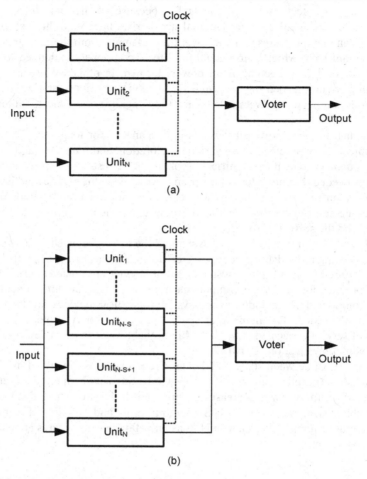

FIGURE 6.3 (a) Static redundancy versus (b) dynamic redundancy.

- Acquisition of hardware and software that constitute the redundant elements.

- Development of custom, system-specific hardware and software needed to effect the desired redundancy in the system.

- System verification and validation.

The additional costs incurred during operation include:

- Consumption of additional power.

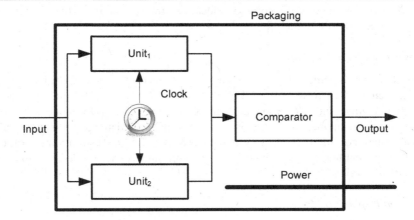

FIGURE 6.4 Dual-redundant architecture.

- Dissipation of additional heat.

- Supporting and perhaps moving additional weight.

- Provision of additional space.

Are these costs worthwhile? The value depends, of course, upon the probability of failure and the consequences of failure. Increased power demand might not be reasonable on a spacecraft if the spacecraft uses computer components that have demonstrated a small probability of failure. In an aircraft system, the weight of redundant components might be intolerable. On a submarine, power and weight are unlikely to be problematic, but the physical space required might not be available.

In this section, we review five basic redundant architectures. Each could be used as part of a strategy for tolerating degradation faults at the complete processor or memory level, at the functional unit or memory unit level, or at the component level. Significant enhancements would have to be made to the simple forms discussed here in order to deal with all of the anticipated faults at the processor or memory level. Those enhancements would be the subject of a great deal of analysis both to determine whether they should be used and what the effect would be.

In Section 6.4 we look briefly at the probabilities of failure of the various redundant architectures.

6.3.1 Dual Redundancy

A simple redundant architecture that is in common use is the *dual-redundant* architecture shown in Figure 6.4. In this architecture, two identical components are operated in parallel, and the results are compared. The operation of the components is synchronized by the use of a common clock, and the results of the two components are expected to be the same.

Phases of Fault Tolerance

Error detection is achieved by comparing the outputs of the two components. If they differ, then an error has occurred. Following error detection, determining what has failed — component 1, component 2, the comparator, the power source, or some other system component — is impossible. Thus, the only damage assessment that is possible is to consider the entire system to have failed. State restoration therefore is reduced to disabling the system entirely, and continued service is reduced to a total absence of service.

Effect on Dependability

The effect on dependability of a dual-redundant system is quite complex. Surprisingly, the MTTF is actually *reduced*. We examine this in section Section 6.4. So why would such an architecture even be considered? The reason is that a dual-redundant system provides *error detection*. Error detection is not possible with a single component unless the component is supplemented in some way, because there is nothing in the system to determine that the system's state is erroneous. The negative impact of an erroneous state arising and not being detected is obviously unbounded. This architecture is one of the simplest ways to create a supplement that can detect the effects of a substantial set of degradation faults. As expected, this architecture cannot detect design faults in the components.

Impact on Software

The impact on software of the dual-redundant architecture seems as if it would be minimal. The detection of errors is purely by hardware, and once an error is detected, the whole system is shut down. Thus, following error detection, the software has no opportunity to react. What might software have to do?

The impact on software is not as simple as it looks, because the software has to take precautions *before* a component fails. For both systems software and applications software, software developers have to be concerned about two things:

Deterministic environment. The software's operating environment must be deterministic. Although the two components are operating off a single clock, making the operating environment deterministic is still difficult. If the two software systems communicate separately with a peripheral device, they almost certainly would not see identical timing. The difference in timing could cause the two software systems to behave non-deterministically. Thus, provision has to be made for inputs to be distributed carefully from any source.

Even if the same scheduling algorithm is used, the processor timing will differ, thereby offering the possibility of divergence between threads if one gets ahead of another. This probably means no paging since that affects speed and requires a peripheral disk. Care has to be taken with cache management to be sure cache content is identical. Finally, various internal processor clocks could differ, so there is a need to synchronize the machines periodically.

Deterministic software. In a related issue, the software must not use any programming techniques that might lead to non-determinism. The most obvious example of such a technique is concurrency, the use of multiple threads or processes. Even if they are identical down to the bit level, making two concurrent software systems deterministic is essentially impossible.

One option, therefore, is to avoid concurrency completely. This option is not especially desirable, because many applications are built with concurrent algorithms. If threads are going to be used, then they must operate with a non-preemptive scheduler so that there is no dependence on a system clock for switching between threads. Non-preemptive scheduling means that threads stop executing when they block and not because some timer expires. Although the high-level architecture of such a system includes a "clock", that clock is not very well defined. Even if the clock meant the actual hardware oscillator, you could not count on precisely the same timing between the two units because of different individual delays.

Fortunately, there is a relatively simple way to deal with all the issues of determinacy identified above. The idea is to synchronize either (a) only when output is to be generated (as seen by the comparator) or (b) on some artificial fixed schedule. In most real-time systems, output is generated at the end of each real-time frame. If identical software is used in both processors, the effects discussed above can mostly be ignored, provided both systems operate with the same real-time clock and frame rate. For example, the Space Shuttle used four machines in the on-board Primary Flight Computer and they synchronized every 40 milliseconds.

Non-real-time systems can synchronize on a fixed time boundary, i.e., define a set of specific synchronization points in the code that requires the two units to synchronize.

Typical Application Domains

A dual-redundant architecture only provides error detection, and so the architecture cannot be used alone for systems that require high reliability or availability. Dual redundancy is a good approach to the design of monitoring systems, as discussed in Section 2.6.5 on page 40.

As we saw in Section 2.6.5, the utility of error detection followed by system shutdown should not be underestimated. Frequently, not knowing that something is wrong is far more important than something being wrong. In aircraft, for example, many systems are provided to help the pilot in various ways. In many cases, if these systems are unavailable, the situation is acceptable *provided that the pilot is aware of the lack of availability.* Thus, error detection coupled with a simple warning system is often sufficient.

Details of the Dual-Redundant Architecture

Before leaving the dual-redundant architecture, looking at the architecture in more detail is instructive. By applying fault tree analysis, we can quickly develop quite a long list of events that need to be addressed, but which are not addressed by the basic architecture since the concern is with the major, duplicated component. Specifically, we find the following events are not dealt with:

Comparator failure. If the comparator fails, there is no comprehensive error detection mechanism, and so the system might continue operating for an arbitrary time.

Clock failure. The clock is an important component, and clock failure might allow the duplicate units to diverge or cease operating completely.

Input distribution mechanism failure. If the input is not distributed correctly, the possibility exists for the duplicate units to generate different outputs even though they have not failed.

Distribution to comparator failure. The signals from the duplicate components might not be presented correctly to the comparator.

Output distribution failure. The output of the comparator, presumed correct, might not be supplied to the subsequent user of the output.

Power failure. Clearly, if all or part of the system loses power, the effect would be catastrophic.

These details and many more in a typical practical installation have to be addressed by system designers using a dual-redundant architecture.

6.3.2 Switched Dual Redundancy

The *switched, dual-redundant* architecture is shown in Figure 6.5. Despite the similarity, the switched dual-redundant architecture is quite different from the dual-redundant architecture. The philosophy is to supplement either one of the duplicate units or both with an error-detection mechanism, and to replace the comparator with a switch.

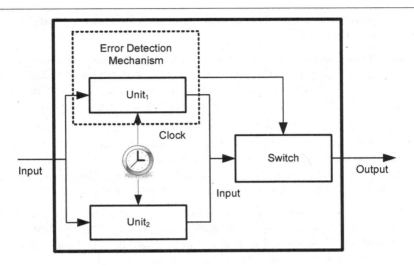

FIGURE 6.5 Switched dual-redundant architecture.

Error Detection Mechanisms

High-end computers frequently include extensive error detection as part of their basic design. An excellent example is the IBM Power6 [93]. There are many hardware techniques that can provide error detection without replication, including:

Parity. Parity can be applied to data buses in processors and to processor registers just as it can be applied to real memory. Hardware defects frequently manifest themselves as dropped bits that can be detected with parity.

Error Detection and Correction. Just as parity can be checked within non-memory components, more sophisticated error detection and error correction mechanisms can be used within non-memory components. Multiple-bit errors do occur and need to be detected, and additional value is gained by correcting single-bit errors.

Watchdog Timers. Timers that monitor temporal aspects of a system are often referred to as *watchdog timers*. They are set by either hardware or software to contain a value that is determined by the characteristics of the system. Separately, the watchdog timer is either reset if disabled by a subsequent event that is expected to happen. If the expected event does not happen, then the watchdog timer will expire and raise a signal of some sort. If a hardware failure within a processor causes the sequencing of events to be disrupted, then a watchdog timer can be used to detect the disruption. Clearly, watchdog timers are useful for software as well as hardware error detection. In particular, they can be used to detect and escape from infinite loops.

Memory Protection. Many hardware failures cause addresses to become damaged, and that damage could cause data to be read or written from a protected location. In that case, memory protection mechanisms can detect the event. In addition, marking the role of memory as read, write, or execute can prevent incorrect use of memory.

Integrity Checks. Various types of check can be performed on data to assess its integrity. Cyclic redundancy checks, for example, apply a function to blocks of data in series, and the result can be stored. If the computation is repeated, the result should be the same, and, if it is not, then an error has occurred.

Arithmetic Checks. Numerous properties of binary arithmetic have been studied that partition results into two equivalence classes, *feasible* answers and *infeasible* answers. Thus, many defects in computer arithmetic that result from defects in processing units can be detected without circuit duplication.

As well as error-detection mechanisms, many machines also include simple approaches to state restoration and continued service such as *instruction retry*. A processor that includes instruction retry makes provision for:

- Reversing the effects of a failed instruction in the local processor registers.

- Reissuing the instruction, perhaps multiple times.

Instruction retry works in circumstances where a transient degradation fault has occurred.

Even without techniques such as instruction retry, built-in error detection can be quite extensive. Thus, a switched dual-redundant system can be built quite effectively with off-the-shelf equipment, and the result is a system in which both units include extensive error detection. Provided the transition to an erroneous state is signalled suitably, the result is very effective.

Care has to be taken with the failure semantics of the processors. Although there are several techniques that can be used to detect errors in the primary component, modeling their coverage is difficult. This raises doubt about the quality of the error detection that can be achieved. Is it possible to actually miss an error? The answer is certainly "yes", and so error detection is stochastic. Even for well-defined but abstract failures, such as failure to compute an arithmetic result correctly, error detection is difficult unless full-scale duplication is used.

A second concern is that error detection might not occur until after the damage to the state has become serious. Thus, the software might have continued to operate *after* the state has become damaged but *before* the error is detected. Such an occurrence could be catastrophic.

Finally, if the processor fails and the failure is not detected, the possibility exists of unbounded damage. A solution to this is provided by *fail-stop machines*, which are discussed in Section 6.5.

Types of Spare

In a switched, dual-redundant system, one of the units, referred to as the *primary* unit, is used to provide service, and the other is referred to as the *backup* unit. Under normal operation, only the primary unit is used. The health of this unit is monitored by the error-detection mechanism, and the primary unit's outputs are made available by the switch. If the error-detection mechanism determines that the primary unit has failed, the backup unit becomes operational, and the switch supplies the output of the backup unit to the system. Since the service during normal operation is provided by the primary unit, the question arises of how the backup unit should be operated when it is not in use. There are three options:

Cold spare. The backup unit could be completely idle and not conduct any application-related computations at all. In fact, the backup unit could even remain powered off. In this case, the backup is referred to as a *cold spare*. In order to take over operation, the backup unit has to create all of the necessary state and then the switch has to start forwarding outputs from the backup to the rest of the system.

Warm spare. The backup unit could prepare to take over if needed but otherwise not conduct any of the operations that the primary unit does. Of particular importance for the backup unit is to maintain its disk status in a form that would allow it to take over service. In this case, the backup is referred to as a *warm spare*. In order to take over operation, the backup unit has to change its operation to compute everything that is required, enhance its state to match that of the primary unit just before it failed, and the switch has to start forwarding outputs from the backup to the rest of the system.

Since the backup has the capacity to provide the same service as the primary unit, the backup is largely idle when the primary unit is operating. The temptation to use the unit for some sort of additional service is rarely resisted, and running so-called non-critical functions on the backup unit when it is configured as a warm spare is common.

Hot spare. The backup unit could operate exactly as the primary unit does, including undertaking all computations but discarding them. In this case, the backup is referred to as a *hot spare*. In order to take over operation, all that is needed is for the switch to start forwarding outputs from the backup to the rest of the system.

Phases of Fault Tolerance

Since error detection does not involve the second of the duplicate units, damage assessment can be assumed to be restricted to the primary unit. State restoration is then relatively simple, because all that is needed is to start the backup unit operating and switch the source of outputs. Finally, continued service can be quite substantial since there is no net loss of operational equipment, although there is no longer a spare. Keep in mind that, following failure of the primary unit, there is no spare and that the system is vulnerable to complete failure. If the spare uses the same checking technology as the primary, then the error-detection mechanism will provide protection against continued operation with a failed unit.

Effect on Dependability

The effect on dependability of a switched, dual-redundant architecture is complex but quite substantial. An increase in the system's MTTF seems likely, because two separate units operate in series until failure of both occurs. This is only partially correct because of the action of the switch. By going to extraordinary lengths, the effects of the failure of the primary component can be masked, so that the system provides continuous service. Without these extraordinary lengths, the output is not continuous because of the need to initialize the backup unit and to make the switchover. Not masking the effect of the fault is the common case, because there are far more satisfactory ways of masking the effects of a fault.

Finally, note that all of the fault types not associated with the primary unit that were discussed in Section 6.3.1 have to be addressed with this architecture also.

Impact on Software

Software plays a major role in the switched, dual-redundant architecture. First, the backup unit has to have custom software if the unit is to be a warm spare. The state that the backup unit keeps is determined by the applications being supported and the mechanism to be used for switching units. For a backup that is operated as a cold spare, custom software is needed to initialize the spare when the spare has to take over. Finally, for a backup operated as a hot spare, custom software is needed just to support basic operation. The difficulty in this case is that the operation of a system is often intimately connected to the state of the operating environment.

Consider a web server, for example. The Hypertext Transfer Protocol (HTTP) employs the Transmission Control Protocol (TCP) and TCP requires various interactions between the client and the server. These interactions have to be "faked" for the hot spare because it actually has no interaction with the client. Faking will involve some synchronization between the primary unit and the backup unit so that the backup unit maintains exactly the same state as the primary unit.

Several system-level design issues are raised by this architecture that affect the software significantly, including:

- How the system's two halves are connected to the service network.
- Where the two halves are located.
- How the two halves communicate.
- Whether the various parts listed are handled as separate problems.
- The level of repeated activity that will be tolerated by the users.

As an example of the difficult issues that software has to deal with, consider the case of a cold spare. During normal operation, nothing need be done by the software because the spare machine, being cold, is doing other things. The problem is these "other things". If the primary fails, the secondary has to stop what it is doing. Thus, the secondary has to make sure that the shutdown times of the active applications that it is running are bounded. This is not necessarily trivial because every application has to be assessed for shutdown time.

Next, there has to be a complete system restart on the spare machine. Unless the operation of the primary was restricted to transactions (which is a common case), there is a good chance that the file system is in some sort of state of disarray. Thus, a check of the file system upon restart might be needed. In practice, many systems of this type are, in fact, designed for transaction processing, and so a great deal can be gained in terms of system recovery. In particular, if the system includes a database, then the database will be consistent and only contain completed and committed transactions.

In practice, for a system using a cold spare, complete replication is rarely used. Different components are treated differently. For example, application servers might be replicated, but the system might use a single, dependable database. If there is a single database, then the software only need be concerned about the servers. If there is, in fact, a replicated database, then the copy needs to be a true copy. Such a system could be built by just recording a log of database updates that is replayed when the backup system's private database has to go live.

Unless the system is restricted to transactions, there will have been incomplete operations underway, and that means various inconsistencies with application data structures. Software has to be available to make the data structures consistent. Finally, the applications designed to run on the primary have to be started on the secondary, and the secondary has to be linked into the system environment so as to be able to operate. This linking might mean redirection of communication links and switching of specialized peripherals such as special displays or printers.

Typical Application Domains

Given the limitations in error detection and the time required to switch between the primary and the backup unit with a switched, dual-redundant architecture, using the architecture to support a system that requires high reliability is unlikely. The architecture could be used for systems requiring high availability, although the difficulty of quantifying the performance of error detection makes quantifying the resulting availability difficult.

Faults cannot be masked effectively, so there will be a disturbance in service. The degree of disruption can range from an apparent lack of response as seen by a user to the user having to log on again, repeat certain activities, etc. What effect is seen will depend on various system characteristics, such as the start time for applications, whether the file system is damaged, the number of applications, the number of users, etc.

The switched dual-redundant architecture is most commonly used in systems where the expense of doing more is not considered cost effective or where the expense is prohibitive. Examples of the former are systems that provide business data processing. Such systems need to maintain levels of availability that are only moderate but which typically cannot be achieved without fault tolerance. Frequently, business data processing systems are complex because the associated business requires substantial amounts of data storage, transmission, and processing. The major service units, however, are often constructed as switched dual-redundant units.

An example of a system for which the cost of duplication is prohibitive but which still needs higher availability than would occur without fault tolerance is a wide-area network. Replicating the complete network is prohibitively expensive because the network includes compute and data-storage nodes, networking equipment, and so on. Consider, for example, the idea of building a complete duplicate of the Internet. This would, of course, be completely unrealistic. Instead, critical components such as servers are sometimes built as switched dual-redundant systems with the necessary repair times determining which type of backup — cold, warm, or hot — is used. In the case of a packet-switched, wide-area network there is no need to replicate the routing network explicitly because of the inherent redundancy in the packet network.

6.3.3 N-Modular Redundancy

The *N-modular redundant* architecture is shown in Figure 6.6. The concept is to operate a set of "N" identical units in parallel, and to vote on the collection of outputs. Since the units are identical, the expectation is that the outputs will be the same unless one or more of the parallel units is defective. An important special case is *triple modular redundancy* (TMR) in which N = 3.

N-modular redundancy is a generalization of dual redundancy (Section 6.3.1), i.e., dual redundancy is essentially N-modular redundancy with N = 2. With N greater than 2, a comparator is no longer sufficient because several output values have to be compared.

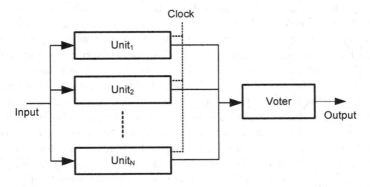

FIGURE 6.6 N-modular redundant architecture.

Phases of Fault Tolerance

Error detection in N-modular redundancy is based on the assumption that any difference in the values received by the voter indicate a failure of one or more of the N units. Provided there is a majority value, the units providing the majority value can be assumed not to have failed, and so damage assessment is to assume that units not in the majority have failed. State restoration is trivial because the states of the majority units can be assumed to be correct, and so all that is needed in state restoration is to arrange to ignore the units in the minority. Continued service is achieved by taking the outputs of the majority. Importantly, none of these steps needs to disrupt processing, and so the effects of a fault can be totally masked.

Effect on Dependability

The use of replication in the N-modular redundancy architecture provides a high level of assurance that errors resulting from degradation faults in the replicated units will be detected. This performance is in sharp contrast to the error detection that is possible with architectures such as switched dual redundancy. Since faults are masked with this architecture, the result is an increase in reliability, possibly a large increase. In fact, since N is not fixed, systems can be built in which reliability can be made quite close to one for protracted time periods.

As we have seen before, the complete analysis of this architecture as it might be instantiated in a real system is a complex and detailed process. Developing a high level of assurance that *all* single points of failure have been identified and properly dealt with requires comprehensive fault tree analysis, determination and assurance of the failure semantics of the components, and a comprehensive program of testing using fault injection to confirm that all anticipated faults will be treated properly.

The special case of the TMR architecture has an interesting extension that helps the overall dependability. This extension is called "TMR/Simplex" and it was originally proposed by Ball and Hardie [15]. The idea is that when a single processor fails in a TMR system, the remaining two processors constitute a self-checking pair. That is useful, but recall that the MTBF of a self-checking pair is less than that of a single processor. The TMR/Simplex idea is to avoid that reduction by using just one processor after the first failure. In other words, if one processor fails and two are left, turn off one of the remaining two good processors. The downside is that the system loses its error-detection capability. This is not an issue because a disagreement between processors in a self-checking pair leads to system shutdown and so a loss of service. If the system operates with just a single processor, the result is that there is a loss of service once the processor fails. But that would happen with the self-checking pair anyway and, on average, far earlier than with the single processor.

Impact on Software

The impact on software is essentially identical to the impact from the dual-redundant architecture discussed in Section 6.3.1. The key software issue is determinacy. The software running on the individual computer must operate so that the results supplied to the voter are identical or can be shown unambiguously to be equivalent.

Typical Application Domains

N-modular redundancy is the most expensive but also the most capable architecture that we have discussed. As such, NMR is used in application domains where reliability is the central attribute of dependability that is needed. Many aircraft systems that provide service that has to be continuous use some form of N-modular redundancy. Flight-control systems, for example, are the digital link between the pilot and the aircraft's control surfaces. As such, a flight-control system must be operating properly for the aircraft to be controllable. Clearly, some form of N-modular redundancy is the best choice for such applications.

6.3.4 Hybrid Redundancy

Hybrid redundancy is the architectural realization of dynamic redundancy. Essential hybrid redundancy is NMR with a set of spare units.

Basic Architecture

The basic architecture is shown in Figure 6.7. A total of N units are operated in parallel, and S of the units are not powered. Each of the S units is available to replace an operating unit that fails. If N–S is at least three, then failures of the operating units can be masked, provided a second failure does not occur during the repair. Repairs can continue until all S of the spare units has been brought into operation.

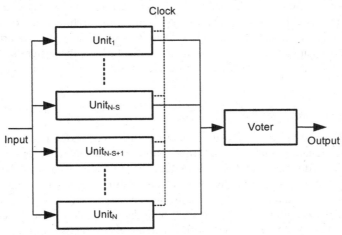

FIGURE 6.7 Hybrid redundancy with S spare units that are normally not powered.

Phases of Fault Tolerance

The phases of fault tolerance are similar to those in N-modular redundancy. The voter is responsible for detecting failure, and damage assessment assumes total failure of the replicated unit. State restoration and continued service are different because of the availability of a replacement unit. State restoration, therefore, consists of powering up one of the spare units and enabling its connections to the input and to the voter. Finally, continued service is identical to the service before failure, because the total number of units is unchanged.

Effect on Dependability

The effect on dependability of hybrid redundancy is the most substantial of all the architectures we have examined. Since degradation faults are masked, the architecture can be used for applications requiring reliability. The existence of multiple spare units that are expected to have long lifetimes means that the total service time can be very long.

Impact on Software

A lot of software is needed to enable the dependability potential of hybrid redundancy. The state of each spare has to be established when the spare is brought into operation. The issues are the same as those that arise in the switched dual-redundant architecture that operates with a cold spare (Section 6.3.2). In addition, the software running on the operating units has to be organized so that voting can operate correctly as with N-modular redundancy (Section 6.3.3). Finally, software is needed to monitor and model the complete architecture. Since the architecture provides long-term reliability, care has to be taken to maximize lifetime as the spares are used up. Rather than relying upon service remaining identical during the system's operational life, provision can be made to reduce service as the number of available spares declines.

Typical Application Domains

Hybrid redundancy is most often used in systems that require long periods of service without maintenance, such as spacecraft, remote monitoring systems, and systems located in hazardous environments. Care has to be taken to make sure that the non-transparency of the switchover that occurs when a unit is replaced is not a limitation. In spacecraft, for example, some systems, such as those that control engine burns, have to be reliable, although only for short periods of time. For these systems, either hybrid redundancy cannot be used or the switchover mechanism has to be disabled during certain operations. This restriction is not severe, however, because engine control is needed rarely and only for brief periods. By contrast, the command-uplink system has to be highly available and it has to operate for years at a time. Loss of the command-uplink system for brief periods when failed devices are being replaced is unlikely to be a problem.

6.4 Quantifying the Benefits of Redundancy

As we saw in Section 6.3, employing redundancy in a system is an expensive and complicated undertaking. Recall that the costs incurred during development include the additional hardware and software, the design effort, and additional effort in verification. The costs incurred during operation include additional space, power, and cooling. The benefits claimed are an improvement in dependability, but the improvement needs to be quantified if appropriate system trade-offs are to be made.

6.4.1 Statistical Independence

The benefit of hardware redundancy lies in the property that hardware components, when operating in a suitable environment, tend to exhibit failures that are *statistically independent*. The property of statistical independence is crucial, because this property allows a large improvement in system failure rate to be achieved by employing redundancy. Replication is the commonest form of redundancy, and we discuss a simple but illustrative probabilistic model of replication in this section.

The definition of statistical independence is that, if two events, A and B, have probabilities of occurrence p_A and p_B per unit time, then the probability that both events will occur in the same unit of time is $(p_A \times p_B)$. If these two probabilities are reasonably small, then their product is much smaller than either. The probabilities are also virtually constant through the useful lifetime of most devices, i.e., the period following infant mortality and prior to end of life on the bathtub curve (Section 3.5.1).

This remarkable outcome of statistical independence is the primary reason why we are able to build systems that can tolerate degradation faults and thereby to continue to provide service for protracted time periods. Statistical independence of failures is also the motivation behind the various architectures described in this chapter.

If two events are *not* statistically independent, the probability that both events will occur in the same time unit could be anything. If the two events are *disjoint*, i.e., they cannot occur together, then the probability that both events will occur in the same time unit is zero.

Statistical independence can be assumed for hardware degradation faults in different units under circumstances where there is no common cause of failure. Although this point seems obvious, its impact is considerable. In order to be confident that a probabilistic model based on statistical independence for a specific system can be trusted, the developers of the model have to be assured that there are no significant common causes of failure. For computers, the types of thing that can derail models include:

Common sources of power. If multiple devices are fed from the same power source, they will all fail at the same time if the power source fails.

Common sources of environmental degradation. Unexpected extreme temperatures, humidity levels, radiation levels, and vibration levels can lead to higher rates of failure in all the devices in the environment.

Common sources of physical trauma. If multiple devices are located close to each other and some sort of physical trauma occurs, then all of the devices will be affected.

Such common causes of failure apply to all of a computer system's components, not just the processing or storage elements. In particular, communications equipment that feeds data to replicated processors or storage units needs itself to be replicated. And for such communications equipment, geographic separation of the physical units (cables, modems, etc.) must be considered, especially cables. Cables are usually not in protected machine rooms, and frequently are miles in length.

6.4.2 Dual-Redundant Architecture

Recall from Section 6.3.1 that a dual-redundant architecture has no mechanism for damage assessment and so is forced to stop when one unit fails. This characteristic leads to an unusual and somewhat counter-intuitive result.

Suppose that the two units in a dual-redundant architecture have probability of failure per unit time p. For a single unit, the expected time to failure is $1/p$ time

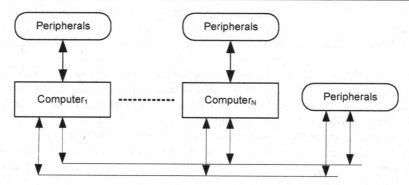

FIGURE 6.8 The basic architecture of a distributed system. Multiple computers communicate via one or more communications buses. The computers can be heterogeneous or homogeneous, and different computers within the system can have different peripherals attached. Peripherals for common use can be connected directly to the communications bus.

units. Ignoring the failure rate of the comparator, the probability of failure per unit time of the architecture, i.e., failure of either unit or both per unit time, is $2p - p^2$, and the expected time to failure is $1/(2p - p^2)$. This is about *half* the expected time to failure for a single unit.

Things seem to have gotten a lot worse, but that is not the case. The mean time to failure has been cut in half, but that is the price we pay for *error detection*. The great benefit of this architecture is that, for certain types of error, the architecture provides error detection. A single unit running in isolation cannot detect errors, and so operating just a single unit leaves us vulnerable to continuing operation with an undetected error.

6.5 Distributed Systems and Fail-Stop Computers

6.5.1 Distributed Systems

Distributed systems have become familiar because of their application in the networks that we use. A distributed system includes some number of computers that communicate via one or more communications mechanisms. Each computer could have peripherals connected, and other peripherals could be connected directly to the communications mechanisms. The basic architecture of a distributed system is shown in Figure 6.8.

The advent of distributed systems has brought many advantages, including:

Flexibility. Distributed systems provide flexibility by allowing differing numbers of computers to be used in different applications. Systems that require more computing resources can use more computers and vice versa.

Placement. Computers can be placed conveniently in the physical environment, thereby allowing more effective use of space.

Heterogeneity. Computers and peripherals can be heterogeneous, thereby allowing different types of computers to be used for different parts of the application.

Degraded Service. Computation remains feasible after some subset of the computers in the system has failed. Although some performance will have been lost, continuing to provide critical services can be considered.

Applications that require high dependability can benefit from all of these various advantages, but the last one — computation remains feasible after some subset of the computers in the system has failed — is clearly a major advantage. Obviously, the ability to provide service after a failure has to be designed into the system, especially the software, and this type of design is a challenging task. Nevertheless, from a dependability point of view, a distributed system offers a great deal of potential.

6.5.2 Failure Semantics of Computers

An important question that developers of distributed systems have to address is: "What happens to a computer when it fails?" This question is not obvious, and most system developers do not think of it. Answering this question is crucial, however, because a failed computer might do a lot of damage after it has stopped providing dependable service. For example, once failed, a computer might:

- Stop executing instructions and remain silent.

- Continue to fetch instructions but from the wrong address.

- Continue to execute instructions but compute incorrect values.

- Any combination of things like this in any order and with any duration.

Put more formally, the real question is: "What are the failure semantics of the computers in the system?" As we discussed in Section 3.8, the failure semantics of a component are the semantics presented at the component's interface when the component fails.

Anything other than immediately ceasing to execute instructions could cause harm to the state. Even if the computer ceased executing instructions, the way in which the computer ceased might mean that some data items were damaged or that correct data became inaccessible. Unless the failure semantics of failed computers in a distributed system are both well defined and assured, the benefits of having a distributed system are reduced significantly because the system's state post failure will be unknown. What is needed is the following:

- A precise definition of the failure semantics of a failed computer.

- A means of implementing those failure semantics.

The requisite definition and the associated implementation mechanism were developed in the theory of *fail-stop computers*. Although the technology of fail-stop computers was motivated by the needs of distributed systems, the technology obviously should be considered (and probably applied) to all the other architectures discussed in this chapter. Defining and assuring failure semantics are important.

6.5.3 Exploiting Distributed Systems

Before discussing fail-stop computers, we consider an intriguing idea for their application. The fact that losing some of the computers in a distributed system does not remove all computational capability suggests a technique based on the following four steps as a way to achieve dependability:

- Build computers so that they fail with precise failure semantics.

- Construct the system as a distributed system.

- Design the applications so that they can be reconfigured if necessary either to stop in a predictable way or be modified to reduce their computational demand in some way.

- Reconfigure the system to provide modified service after one or more computers fail.

These four steps are actually reasonably practical. The first step is provided by the theory of fail-stop computers, and the second is routine. The third and fourth steps require that we architect the system carefully.

This technique does not seem especially different or important until one realizes the following:

Building computers that are ultra reliable is difficult.

Building computers that fail with precise failure semantics is easier.

What these observations mean is that, if the goals of an application could be stated so as to make this technique applicable, we would have an easier task in developing the system. Another way to think of these observations is that focusing on perfection in dependable computing systems might not be the best approach. Instead, building computers that fail in a predictable way and combining such computers in a distributed system might be a better approach.

6.5.4 The Fail-Stop Concept

The concept of *fail-stop processors* was introduced by Schlichting and Schneider in 1983 [127]. Subsequently, Schneider presented an approach to their implementation [126]. The term that Schlichting and Schneider used was fail-stop processors, although their concept includes storage and so we use the term *fail-stop computers* here.

Informally, a fail-stop computer is a computer that becomes totally benign, i.e., does nothing, after the completion of the last instruction executed before the failure. Formally, Schlichting and Schneider defined a set of properties for fail-stop computers that are more than this simple notion of functional cessation. These properties make the fail-stop computer concept an ideal building block for constructing distributed systems.

From the perspective of the interface presented to the rest of the system, a fail-stop computer has three basic properties:

Halt-on-failure property. The halt-on-failure property means quite literally that the computer ceases all state changes after the last correct instruction was executed. Importantly, this property means that the computer does not "babble", i.e., constantly generate meaningless output values, nor does the computer generate erroneous but meaningful output values.

Failure-status property. The failure-status property means that other fail-stop computers in the system can tell that a failed machine has failed. Each machine being able to determine the status of the others is the key to recovery following failure of a machine.

Stable-storage property. A fail-stop computer has both volatile and stable storage. Stable storage is unaffected by failure and remains readable by all other processors in the system. Stable storage is used to hold application-related data that the system needs along with critical data such as the failure status of the associated computer. Volatile storage disappears on failure and is therefore not readable.

Off-the-shelf computers do *not* possess these properties with a high level of assurance. In particular, ordinary computers do not possess the halt-on-failure property. Without making provision for these properties in the design of a computer, the actions taken following failure could be arbitrary. Despite this limitation, the halt-on-failure property is often assumed. Any distributed system that is expected to continue processing after one or more nodes fail is relying upon the property, frequently without the system stakeholders realizing that they are making a critical assumption that might not hold.

Before discussing the implementation of fail-stop computers, we have to examine these three properties a little more carefully. Could they really be implemented as stated? The answer is "no" because the properties are stated as absolutes. No matter how carefully a computer was designed and built, if enough went wrong with the computer all at once, maintaining these properties might be impossible.

So, in practice, these properties have to be stated more carefully. We can guarantee these properties if the number of faults that are manifested with overlapping treatments is bounded. For example, if we could assume that no more than one fault would have to be dealt with at once, then we could design the computer to have these properties. If several faults were to manifest themselves, then the computer's behavior would be arbitrary.

The notion of a fail-stop computer, therefore, is one for which the three properties hold provided k or fewer faults are manifested with overlapping treatments, and such computers are known as k-fail-stop computers.

6.5.5 Implementing Fail-Stop Computers

Fail-stop computers using Schlichting and Schneider's design use a lot of hardware. A k-fail-stop computer uses $k+1$ computers to implement computation (the p computers) and $2k+1$ computers to implement stable storage (the s computers). This gives a total of $3k+2$ ordinary computers to implement a single k-fail-stop computer. These computers are connected together in various ways. For $k = 1$, we get a total of 5 computers, and the basic design of a 1-fail-stop computer is shown in Figure 6.9.

The p processors actually execute the software that runs on the fail-stop computer. Each p processor executes the same software. The output data of each p processor is sent to each of the s processors. The s processors provide the stable storage, and their memories are the implementation of stable storage. The s processors are connected to a communications mechanism by which they respond to reads of stable storage from other fail-stop computers in the system.

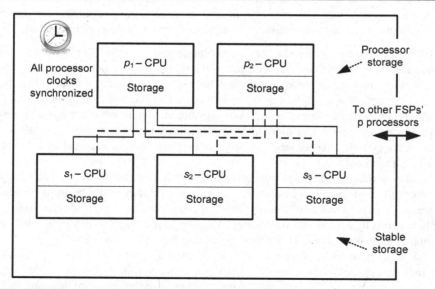

FIGURE 6.9 Basic architecture of a 1-fail-stop computer.

Each of the s processors performs a comparison to check that the $k+1$ outputs from the p processors are identical. If they are, then the data is part of the desired computation, and the s processors write the values into their own memory, thereby writing the data to stable storage.

If the $k+1$ outputs from the p processors are *not* identical, then some subset of the p processors has failed. In that case, the s processors do not write the data to their own memories, thereby excluding the corrupt data from stable storage. The s processors also set the status bit for their fail-stop computer to "failed" so that other computers can react as necessary. The structure used by the s processors is exactly an N-modular-redundant system as we discussed in Section 6.3.3 on page 164. The structure is used solely to detect faults in the p processors. There is no attempt to mask faults.

The computations by the s processors rely upon their having all received the same data from each of the p processors. Thus, the s processors must engage in a Byzantine agreement algorithm when they receive data from a p processor. If the values that any s processor obtains from the other $2k$ s processors are not identical to its own, then either one or more s processors have failed or the communication mechanism between the s processors has failed. In either event, the stable storage mechanism has failed, and the fail-stop computer has to stop. Stable storage is still operational, however, because sufficient of the s processors remain operational to maintain a majority.

6.5.6 Programming Fail-Stop Computers

The properties of fail-stop computers can now be exploited in distributed systems, because the failure semantics that we require are provided. With a little care, the programming task of fail-stop computers is fairly simple. Schlichting and Schneider defined a construct called a *fault-tolerant action* as the basic building block for writing applications [127].

Of course, a program executing on a fail-stop computer halts when a failure occurs. Execution can then be restarted on any remaining operational fail-stop computer that has sufficient resources. Keep in mind that the basic semantics of the fail-stop computer mean that the program will be in a well-defined and undamaged state. Although well-defined and undamaged, the state could be any state that could arise during execution.

When a program is restarted, the internal processor state and the contents of volatile storage are lost. Thus, some software is needed that can complete the state transformation that was in progress at the time of the failure and restore storage to a well-defined state. Such software is called a *recovery protocol*.

The syntactic structure that Schlichting and Schneider defined for the fault-tolerant action is:

```
FTA:action
    A
    recovery
    R
    end
```

where A is the basic action and R is the recovery protocol. So the meaning of this structure is:

```
execute A
if A completes
    then done
else
    execute R
```

Clearly, a recovery protocol must have the following three properties:

- The protocol can only use information that is in stable storage.
- The protocol must be kept in stable storage because the code for a recovery protocol must be available after a failure.
- The protocol must execute correctly when started in *any* intermediate state that could arise during execution.

Complying with the first two properties seems fairly simple. Stable storage is stable storage after all. But the third property seems quite tricky. What we have to do is to write a recovery protocol that could essentially finish whatever the main software, the action A, was doing when the failure occurred.

The key to programming the recovery action is stable storage. The action does not write everything to stable storage, only values that need external visibility. In practice, therefore, the programming of R can be facilitated by using stable storage carefully within A.

To see this, imagine an action that only writes once to stable storage, namely, at the end of its execution. In that case, R can be exactly the same as A, because, if R is invoked, it can start the computation over again. Schlichting and Schneider refer to such an action as a *restartable action.*

Schlichting and Schneider present an elegant proof structure for verifying properties of fault-tolerant actions in sequence and nested within one another, thereby providing the necessary logical framework for supporting the use of the concept in real programs. Fault-tolerant actions can be composed to allow the development of large programs, and they can be nested, thereby allowing the development of complicated programs.

To further illustrate the capabilities of fault-tolerant actions executing on fail-stop computers, Schlichting and Schneider present a realistic example of a process-control system in which they show both the overall approach to programming the system on a fail-stop computer and the proof of the essential fault-tolerant properties of the software.

Key points in this chapter:

- ◆ Software usually has to manage the effects of degradation faults.
- ◆ Hardware redundancy is used to deal with degradation faults.
- ◆ Replication is one form of redundancy.
- ◆ Several platform architectures have been developed that incorporate specific forms of redundancy.
- ◆ An important property that is present in many architectures is statistical independence of degradation faults between redundant entities.
- ◆ Fail-stop computers have ideal failure semantics. Whenever a failure occurs, the computer stops at the end of the last correctly executed instruction.

Exercises

1. Explain the difference between *redundancy* and simple *replication*.

2. If a memory system uses a single parity bit for each 32-bit word, what is the smallest amount of storage within which an error can be detected? What types of error could such a parity mechanism detect?

3. Are there errors in the memory described in Exercise 2 that parity could not detect? With parity operating on 32-bit words, is it possible for the memory system to repair errors?

4. Consider the *mirrored disk* structure. Writes go to two separate identical disks so that there are always two copies of the data. If one of the disks fails, that disk is replaced with a new unit. The new unit is then *resilvered*, i.e., made to contain the same data as the surviving original unit. Develop a resilvering algorithm that could be used by the recovery software.

5. Suppose a spacecraft computer system employs dynamic redundancy and begins with two computers of which one is powered and one is not. Both computers are self-checking. When operating, each computer has a probability of failure per hour of 10^{-6}. The probability of a processor failing immediately upon being powered up is 10^{-2}. Assuming that the spacecraft begins flight with one computer operating and one computer powered down, derive an expression for the probability that the spacecraft computer system will operate for at least one year.

6. Explain how the four phases of fault tolerance are achieved in the dual-redundant architecture.

7. Explain how the four phases of fault tolerance are achieved in the N-modular redundant architecture.

8. Consider the dual-redundant computer architecture:
   (a) What is the primary benefit that this architecture provides?
   (b) List the items whose failure will be detected by this architecture.
   (c) List the items whose failure will not be detected by this architecture.

9. Suppose a switched dual-redundant system is used for a business data-processing system that provides on-line sales from a Web-based catalog of products. Assuming a *cold* spare, summarize the *major* functions that the architectural support software has to perform (a) while the primary is running and (b) when the primary fails so as to get the backup functioning. Think carefully about how to handle the database, the active clients, the Web server, and whether faults are going to be masked.

10. Suppose a switched dual-redundant system is used for a business data-processing system that provides on-line sales from a Web-based catalog of products.

Assuming a *warm* spare, summarize the *major* functions that the architectural support software has to perform (a) while the primary is running and (b) when the primary fails so as to get the backup functioning. Think carefully about how to handle the database, the active clients, the Web server, and whether faults are going to be masked.

11. Suppose a switched dual-redundant system is used for a business data-processing system that provides on-line sales from a Web-based catalog of products. Assuming a *hot* spare, summarize the *major* functions that the architectural support software has to perform (a) while the primary is running and (b) when the primary fails so as to get the backup functioning. Think carefully about how to handle the database, the active clients, the Web server, and whether faults are going to be masked.

12. An important claim about the concept of a fail-stop computer is that such a computer is easier to build than a reliable computer. Explain why that is the case.

13. List the three major characteristics of a fail-stop computer. For each, explain what the characteristic means in terms of the computer's operation. For each explain how the characteristic is used in building a dependable computer system.

14. Consider the problem of developing a 2-fail-stop computer:

    (a) To what does the "2" refer in the phrase "2-fail-stop"?

    (b) How many p processors will be required?

    (c) How many s processors will be required?

CHAPTER 7   *Software Dependability*

Learning objectives of this chapter are to understand:

- The application of fault avoidance and fault elimination in the software lifecycle.
- The techniques available for avoiding faults in software.
- The techniques available for eliminating faults in software.
- Which phases of the software lifecycle tend to introduce the most faults.
- The best way to approach software dependability.
- Formal methods and why are they important.
- How an engineer can be reasonably confident that the various classes of faults that might occur in a system have been dealt with.

7.1 Faults and the Software Lifecycle

Software has been a causal factor in many failures of systems that required high levels of dependability. Knowing that, we must be aware of the potential that software has to affect dependability, and we must apply the right techniques when building software. The right techniques are not in one or even a small number of areas. All of the activities that we undertake when building software might be opportunities for defects to enter software and remain there.

There is no "perfect" way to develop dependable software that can be used on every project. Different projects have different goals and different stakeholders, and so the process used has to be tailored to the specific circumstances of a particular project. Many techniques can facilitate software dependability, however, and so it is important to be aware of them.

This book and therefore this chapter is not about software engineering in general, and so this chapter does not discuss complete and detailed software development processes and techniques. Rather, in this chapter Section 7.2, Section 7.3, and Section 7.6 summarize three important special software topics: (a) formal methods, (b) model checking, and (c) model-based development. Elements of these three top-

```
do {
    switch expression {
        ...
        case (value):
            if (logical expression) {
                sequence of statements
                break
            }
            else {
                another sequence of statements
            }
            statements after if...else statement
    }
    statements after switch statement
} while (expression)

statements after do...while statement
```

FIGURE 7.1 The general form of the code responsible for the failure of the AT&T long distance telephone system in January 1990.

ics are then part of general discussions of software fault avoidance in Section 7.8 and software fault elimination in Section 7.9. Managing software fault avoidance and fault elimination is discussed in Section 7.10, and common misconceptions about techniques for fault avoidance and elimination in software development are reviewed in Section 7.11. In the following three chapters, specific topics in fault avoidance and elimination are investigated in depth.

If achieving the necessary level of software assurance by fault avoidance and fault elimination is not possible, then our next goal is to tolerate faults. Software fault tolerance is covered in depth in Chapter 11.

Software fault forecasting is a specialized topic that involves the development and use of detailed probabilistic models of software dependability. This material is outside the scope of this book.

7.1.1 Software and Its Fragility

A Significant Failure

Software cannot be seen, felt, or touched, yet it is responsible for much of the functionality in critical systems and also for many failures. Sometimes, a single defective line of code in a software system is all that it takes to cause that system to fail. An example of this situation arose on January 15, 1990, when large sections of the AT&T long distance network failed.

The failure was determined later to have been caused by one line of a program written in C [102]. The general form of the code is shown in Figure 7.1. The fault in this code was the use of the `break` statement within the `if` statement. The semantics of a `break` statement are to terminate the enclosing switch or iteration statement. The programmer thought that the `break` statement was the equivalent of a branch out of the `if` statement, whereas, in fact, the enclosing `case` statement of the switch was terminated.

Generally, a single line of code is not expected to have such power, and that is why software failures are hard to predict and often hard to analyze. In a sense, the problem is akin to a large building collapsing when a single screw is removed from a door hinge on the fifth floor. Architects know that this will *not* happen to their buildings. Software engineers know that this *might* happen to their software.

Our concern with software, as with everything else, is to apply the fundamental principle of dependability, i.e., to capture the requirements correctly, to identify all of the faults to which the software is subject, and then to determine how to deal with all of those faults. Recall that software faults are always design faults, and so none of the specific techniques developed to deal with hardware degradation faults necessarily applies directly or with the same effect. Fortunately, however, the general concepts of fault avoidance, fault elimination, fault tolerance, and fault forecasting can be applied.

Logical Complexity

Although this book is about software, the difficulty we face is actually not software[1]. The real difficulty is logical complexity, and that complexity arises in both software *and* hardware. Logical complexity is sometimes expressed as bits in memory (software) and sometimes as patterns in silicon (hardware). The fragility of software arises from the associated complexity. But hardware is complex too, and hardware can be fragile in the same sense. Thus, the problems with design faults in software can and do arise in hardware.

The reason we use software is because we are trying to encode logical complexity, and software is a convenient means of doing so. The problem then is not that the entities with which we are concerned are software. Rather, the entities are complex, and we choose to implement them in software. In dealing with computer systems, keep in mind that both software and hardware are subject to design faults. The focus in this book is software, because software is often the choice we make to implement the complex entities that we need.

7.1.2 Dealing with Software Faults

In principle, systems can be built without design faults, and so, again in principle, we can build software without faults. To do so means relying upon fault avoidance

---

1. I am much indebted to Brian Randell for reminding me of the importance of the equivalence of software and the design of computer hardware.

and fault elimination, but in practice this is extremely difficult to do except in special cases. Establishing freedom from faults by analytic means is rarely possible, because much of software development remains informal and formal techniques cannot cope well with huge complexity.

Does this mean that we have to turn to fault tolerance and fault forecasting for design faults in general and software faults in particular? These two approaches play a major role in dealing with degradation faults in hardware. However, as we saw in Section 6.4, their application to hardware degradation faults relies in large measure on two powerful properties:

- For degradation faults, failures of independent hardware units tend to be statistically independent.

- For degradation faults, the probability of failure per unit time for hardware units is described quite accurately by the bathtub curve (see Section 3.5.1).

Unfortunately, software components do not display either of these characteristics, and the application of fault tolerance and fault forecasting to software is much more difficult as a result. Far more reliance, therefore, has to be placed on fault avoidance and fault elimination.

7.1.3 The Software Lifecycle

Faults can be introduced during virtually any stage of software development. Specifications can be wrong, designs can be wrong, and so on. To the extent possible, defects should be avoided at every stage and those introduced should be eliminated

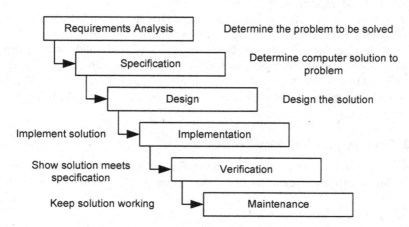

FIGURE 7.2 The classic software lifecycle and the introduction of faults.

at the stage in which they were introduced. Both fault avoidance and fault elimination techniques can and should be applied to all the artifacts as they are developed.

The classic software lifecycle is shown in Figure 7.2. This complete lifecycle provides a lot of insight into our task as software engineers when developing systems for which dependability is important. All the primary artifacts that we build are shown, and the lifecycle shows us, at a high level, where faults might be introduced and where we can try to deal with them.

7.1.4 Verification and Validation

Two terms that arise frequently in software dependability are *verification* and *validation*. For our purposes, we will use these definitions:

Validation. Developing the necessary assurance that the documented specification solves the problem stated in the abstract requirements (see Section 2.5), i.e., the system to be developed will solve the problem posed by the user.

Verification. Showing that one representation of software is a refinement of another, usually that the executable software is a correct implementation of the documented specification.

Informally, validation can be thought of as developers answering the question: "Did we build the *right thing*?". Verification is applied most commonly to show that an implementation implements a specification correctly, and so verification can be thought of as developers answering the question: "Did we build the *thing right*?". The basic relationships involved in validation and verification are illustrated in Figure 7.3.

Clearly the answer to either of these questions could be "no", in which case we would expect system failures in operation. The system might do one of two things:

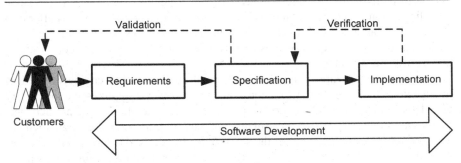

FIGURE 7.3 Validation and verification in software development.

- Something that the user did not want but do so correctly (erroneous specification, correct implementation).

- Something that the user wanted but do so incorrectly (correct specification, erroneous implementation).

The first statement of how software will solve the user's problem is the specification, and so validation is concerned with whether the stated specification provides the necessary functionality. Validation, therefore, is *precisely* what is needed to deal with the first issue raised by the Fundamental Principle of Dependability (Section 3.9) for software.

Verification is concerned with the various representations that are created during software development. Apart from the common use of verification in showing that a high-level-language implementation provides the functionality that is defined in a specification, other uses of verification include implementation to design and design to specification. Verification, therefore, is *precisely* what is needed to deal with the second issue raised by the Principle of Dependability for software.

Verification and validation are at the heart of the process of developing software for applications that require high dependability. All the other elements of the software lifecycle are concerned with fault avoidance or fault elimination. Verification and validation are concerned with showing that the Principle of Dependability has been satisfied.

7.2 Formal Techniques

7.2.1 Analysis in Software Engineering

One of the best hopes that we have for technological support in building dependable software is the use of *formal methods*. Formal methods employ mathematical rigor to help establish a variety of properties about software. The reason they are so powerful is that they can help us establish properties such as freedom from certain classes of faults. Thus, they are precisely what we need for software fault avoidance and elimination. Using formal methods is not a panacea, but their use does offer us a lot of value if applied carefully. Formal methods must always be supplemented with various informal techniques such as prototyping, inspection, proper documentation, and careful management.

Developing software is a major intellectual challenge, and engineers need as much help as they can get to tackle the challenge. In other disciplines, engineers rely to a large extent on mathematics to model systems and thereby to predict their dependability characteristics. In structural engineering, for example, finite-element analysis allows various aspects of the strength of structures to be predicted. The predictions are usually so accurate that structural failures resulting from design flaws (as opposed to things like faulty construction or poor maintenance) are rare. Similarly, aerodynamicists rely on the various forms of the Navier-Stokes equation to predict the flow of fluids (typically air) over surfaces. From the details of the flow, lift and drag can be predicted, from which many details of the flight characteristics of an airplane can be determined.

An important characteristic of the analysis undertaken in both structural analysis and fluid mechanics is continuity, i.e., these analyses rely upon continuous mathematics. This characteristic means that the analysis can call upon the entire body of classical mathematics, including the calculus. A second consequence of continuity is the ability to extrapolate to circumstances beyond experience by applying the available continuous functions. This second consequence enables prediction by analysis of the effects of, for example, structural changes. A structure can be made stronger by adding additional structural elements and analysis will predict the strength. Doubt in the adequacy of structural strength can thus be dealt with by making structures thicker or by duplicating them.

There are relatively few analysis techniques available in software engineering and even fewer that are routinely applied. In large measure, this lack is the result of software being discrete, i.e., not continuous. Software engineers rely upon natural language documentation and testing to a large extent in developing products. This approach produces products that work most of the time, but the type of prediction about performance that is common in other fields of engineering is not available. Software engineers are not able to predict that an aircraft's software-based autopilot will work as desired without testing it. By contrast, structural engineers can predict accurately that an aircraft's wings will not break off in flight and aerodynamicists can predict that the aircraft will fly, both without any testing. The contrast, illustrated in Figure 7.4, is between using testing to *establish* a conclusion (software engineering) and testing to *confirm* a conclusion (most other branches of engineering).

Aerospace Engineering	Software Engineering

Testing **Confirms** Analysis	Testing **Establishes** Conclusion

FIGURE 7.4 Analysis vs. testing in software and other branches of engineering.

A formal method is an application of mathematics, usually discrete mathematics, in software engineering. As such, a formal method provides the software engineer with a basis for analysis much like the capability that is common in other fields of engineering. The goals of formal methods are:

- To provide formal languages that replace much of the use of natural language in artifacts such as requirements, specifications, and designs.

- To allow properties of software to be determined without executing the software.

Rather than trying to establish those properties by executing large numbers of test cases, executing a relatively small number of test cases should work to confirm the results of analysis.

The uses of formal methods are summarized in Figure 7.5. The notations used are formal languages, and the artifacts produced are amenable to analysis because of the formal languages. Some analysis is limited to a single artifact, in which case the results of the analysis allow insights about that single artifact. Other analysis involves more than one artifact, in which case the analysis can be considerably more powerful. An example of the latter is the concept of *formal verification*. The implementation and specification are analyzed together and a proof established that the implementation is a refinement of the specification.

Some engineers have a negative impression of formal methods. In part, these impressions are based upon myths that have circulated, and two papers have been written to counter some of the common myths [54, 20]. The myths discussed and dispelled in these papers are:

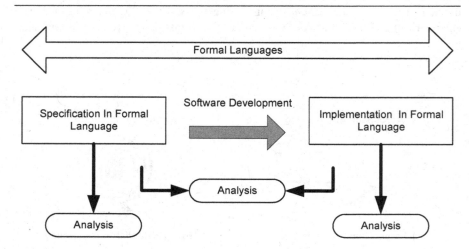

FIGURE 7.5 Formal languages and analysis in formal methods. Formal languages are used for both specification and implementation, and analysis can be performed on either or both.

1. "Formal methods can guarantee that software is perfect."
2. "Formal methods are all about program proving."
3. "Formal methods are only useful for safety-critical systems."
4. "Formal methods require highly trained mathematicians."
5. "Formal methods increase the cost of development."
6. "Formal methods are unacceptable to users."
7. "Formal methods are not used on real, large-scale software."
8. "Formal methods delay the development process."
9. "Formal methods lack tools."
10. "Formal methods replace traditional engineering design methods."
11. "Formal methods only apply to software."
12. "Formal methods are unnecessary."
13. "Formal methods are not supported."
14. "Formal-methods people always use formal methods."

None of these statements is true. Formal methods are neither a panacea that solves all problems nor a curiosity that provides no value. Formal methods are an important engineering technology.

7.2.2 Formal Specification

There are a variety of properties of specifications that are important: accuracy, completeness, consistency, freedom from ambiguity, and ease of change. Creating a specification that has these properties purely in natural language has proved to be difficult. Certainly, natural language has been used satisfactorily for specification, but the difficulties that arise typically have led researchers to seek better notations.

The result of the search has been the development of formal languages designed especially for software specification. All of the languages have mathematical semantics, i.e., the meaning of each of the various language elements is defined in terms of mathematics, and many (but not all) use a mathematical syntax. Some example formal languages are: Z [134], B [1], VDM [74], PVS [136], RSML [86], and Statecharts [57]. We examine Z in Chapter 7.

7.2.3 Formal Verification

Formal verification brings the rigor of formal methods to the challenge of verification. The primary application of formal verification is to establish that an implementation implies a specification. Such a proof is called a proof of *partial correctness*. If the program in question is expected to terminate, then a proof of termination can be added to the proof that the implementation implies the specification to produce a proof of *total correctness* (see Figure 7.6).

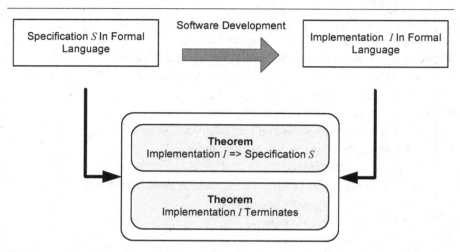

FIGURE 7.6 Proof of partial correctness and proof of termination provide proof of correctness.

7.2.4 The Terminology of Correctness

The use of the word "correctness" in formal verification is generally regarded as misleading. The problem is that people unfamiliar with the terminology will misinterpret the use of "correctness" in formal verification. Engineers in other fields, customers, regulators, or other stakeholders often assume that a program will do what they want if the program is "proven correct". This is not the case, because the requirements, the specification, or the proof could be wrong. In that case, the intuitive notion of correctness is deceptive. A better way to describe this notion of proof is as a *formal verification* proof.

7.3 Verification by Model Checking

7.3.1 The Role of Model Checking

Model checking is an important technique that is quite different from the other formal methods that we have been discussing. At the heart of model checking is the idea that analysis can be carried out on a *model* of an artifact rather than the artifact itself, hence the name.

This idea applies immediately to software and with great value. The most common application to software is in *concurrency*. The statements in a program that affect the program's concurrent behavior are largely independent of much of the rest of the program. For example, task creation and the synchronization of tasks do not

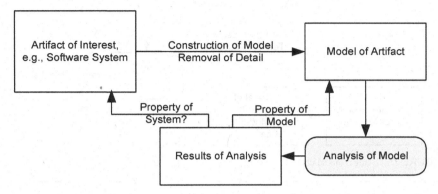

FIGURE 7.7 Analysis of a model and the relationship of the artifact to the model.

depend on arithmetic computations except to the extent that the latter affect normal control flow. A model of the concurrent aspects of a program can omit many of the details of computation.

Concurrent software is difficult for humans to reason about, to test, and to analyze using formal verification. A good example of the difficulties is deadlock. The concept of a deadlock and the conditions necessary for one to happen are relatively easy to state. But to show that a given set of concurrent processes will not deadlock under any execution circumstances can be difficult unless the set of processes is designed explicitly to avoid deadlock.

Difficulties such as showing freedom from deadlock arise because of the non-determinism that is inherent in concurrent programs. Each time a concurrent program executes, there can be large differences in the events that occur and in the sequence of these events. Reasoning about such circumstances is difficult because of the vast number of event sequences, and a successful test execution means that only one possible event sequence has been tested. Thus concurrency, one of the major challenges that arises in software verification, is well suited to analysis by model checking.

7.3.2 Analyzing Models

The idea of analyzing a model of an artifact rather than the artifact itself is familiar in engineering. Electrical engineers determine the characteristics of a circuit based on a mathematical model of that circuit. Similarly, structural engineers base their analysis on models of the structures that they build. In both cases, the details of the underlying systems are complex and do not contribute to the goals of the analysis. For example, an electrical circuit contains stray capacitance and inductance that do not contribute to the direct-current calculations of the circuit and so a model that ignores them is perfectly satisfactory.

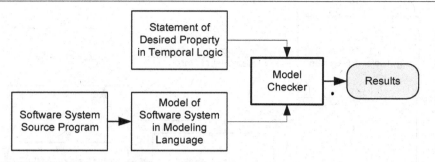

FIGURE 7.8 Using a model checker to analyze software.

Analyzing a model is illustrated in Figure 7.7 and means two things:

- The model is an abstraction of the artifact with much of the detail omitted. Only the aspects of the artifact that are relevant to the analysis are retained and so various forms of analysis become possible that would be impossible with the detail included.

- The analysis is carried out on a model, and the results of the analysis apply to the model. Provided the model is an accurate representation of the artifact, the results apply to the artifact. But the model must be accurate for the results to be useful.

An important example of the difficulty that can result from the use of models occurred in the field of civil engineering in the design of the suspended walkways in the Hyatt Regency hotel in Kansas City. Analysis of the forces on the walkway suspension system was *possible* because of the use of a model. The model was *an accurate representation of the design, but* the suspension system *as built* was different from the design and hence different from the model. The system as built was much weaker than the model predicted. The result was that the walkways collapsed on July 17, 1981, killing 114 people [105].

7.3.3 Using a Model Checker

The overall approach to using a model checker is shown in Figure 7.8. A model is prepared of the software system of interest in the modeling language that is supported by the model checker to be used. The model has to represent the necessary aspects of the program correctly and completely. Building models that have this property for large programs is difficult because of the amount of detail involved. As a result, various efforts have been undertaken to automate the model-building process by using tools that read the software and produce the model.

Next the properties that are desired of the software are formalized. This formalization is usually documented in a temporal logic known as *Linear Temporal Logic,* or LTL. LTL adds three new operators to predicate logic that allow the specification of the ordering of events. The three operators are:

- Eventually $\Diamond$
- Always $\Box$
- Until U

The operators from propositional and predicate logic are included in LTL, thereby allowing expressions such as the following examples to be written:

- $\Diamond p \vee \Diamond q$
  This expression reads "Eventually p or eventually q." In other words, no matter what state the computation is in, eventually either p or q will become true.

- $\Box(p \wedge q)$
  This expression reads "Always p and q." In other words, no matter what state the computation is in, p and q will always be true.

In these examples, p and q are machine states of interest. For example, in a safety-critical system, p and q might be safety properties such as logic combinations that prevent hazards. The second expression states that these properties will always hold no matter what the system does. If states exist in which this condition is not true, then a model checker will locate such states and, for each such state, provide a list of the events that could lead to the state, i.e., a counter example.

For more details of model checking in general and the Spin system [133] in particular, see the text by Holzmann [63].

7.4 Correctness by Construction

Humans are fallible. Relying on human intellect almost unaided to build large software systems is clearly not a good idea. There is plenty of evidence showing that relying on human intellect rarely works perfectly. The fragility of software and the difficulties that arise with software fault tolerance and software fault forecasting lead us to the conclusion that we should emphasize software fault avoidance and software fault elimination. By doing so, we will be aiming to produce software that is to a large extent free of faults as a result of the way the software was developed.

To meet operational goals, traditional software development relies to a significant extent on testing and repair. Ideally, when software is written, that software should be correct and known to be correct from the outset. Many other branches of engineering work this way, and the embodiment of the idea in software engineering is a technique called *correctness by construction* [8].

Correctness by construction is a comprehensive approach to software development that embodies the ideas of fault avoidance and fault elimination that are pervasive in this book. The goal of correctness by construction is to know that the implementation is correct as a result of the way that the implementation was built. This goal is challenging, but if the goal could be met, software engineering would be a much more effective discipline.

Correctness by construction does not rely on extensive testing, but that change in emphasis does not mean that the software is not tested. Correctness by construction means that elaborate test activities are not required to find the faults in the software. This situation is highly desirable for systems where dependability is the goal. Testing can then take its proper place as a different means of gaining confidence that the software contains relatively few faults. Correctness by construction has been pioneered by several authors, including Sutton and Carré [137], Hall and Chapman [55], and Amey [8].

The use of the word "correctness" in the phrase *proof of correctness* was discussed in Section 7.2.4, and now the word has arisen again. The idea of correctness by construction is to develop each of the necessary artifacts in a manner that ensures critical properties as a result of the development method. Proof might be used, but there is no mention of proof in the name and no implication that might mislead other engineers.

7.5 Approaches to Correctness by Construction

There are three different approaches to correctness by construction of an implementation, as shown in Figure 7.9. The three approaches are: *synthesis, refinement,* and *analysis*:

Synthesis. In construction of software using synthesis, the implementation in a high-level language is actually built automatically by an *application generator*. The application generator reads a formal specification and generates the application software automatically. In some application generators, the synthesis process is guided by humans, and in others synthesis is completely automatic.

Many application generators are available, including Mathworks Simulink, discussed in Section 7.6. When using Simulink, the input diagram is a formal specification and the code is generated mechanically.

Implementation correctness by construction is obtained using synthesis because the implementation (software) is written by a machine. Provided the synthesis mechanism is correct, we can be sure that the software implements the specification. The synthesis mechanism is a large program in its own right, and so assuming that synthesis does not introduce defects is a big assumption. The assumption is reasonable, however, because the synthesis mechanism will be used across many projects and by large numbers of engineers. Expending significant resources on this one artifact is likely to be worthwhile.

Refinement. In construction of software using refinement, software is built by developing a series of transformations from the high-level, abstract specification to a concrete implementation, usually in a high-level language. The key to fault avoidance is that transformations are selected and applied carefully, and proofs are constructed to show that, for each transformation that is applied, the properties of the input are maintained by the output. The transformations and proofs are usually developed by hand with extensive mechanical help. The transformations can be applied by sophisticated editors after being selected, and the proofs can either be generated mechanically or checked mechanically.

Refinement has been demonstrated with several formal-specification languages. The most extensive use of the approach has been with the B method. B includes a comprehensive treatment of refinement and is supported by a detailed textbook [1] and high quality tools [28]. The B method is discussed in Section 7.7.

Implementation correctness by construction is obtained using refinement because, when the implementation is complete, a proof exists from the software back to the specification. Provided the proof is correct, the verification argument is complete.

Analysis. In construction of software using analysis, the software is built by developing a series of program increments using a fairly conventional manual development approach. Design using procedural abstraction can be used to develop

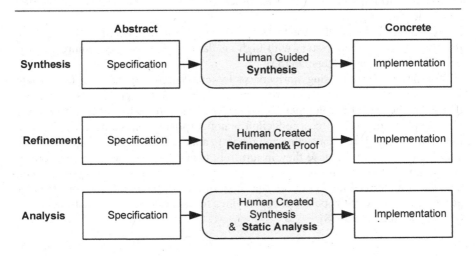

FIGURE 7.9 The three approaches to implementation correctness by construction.

the necessary procedures and functions, data structures can be designed in a manner that provides the semantics for the application, and so on.

The key to the use of analysis is the availability of a mechanism to verify each of the increments that is applied during development. In principle, any verification technique could be used, including testing, but in practice reliance is placed on static analysis. The important argument in analysis is to build a program in steps where the increment added at each step is followed by verification. Confidence begins with the first iteration in which a small program is verified. As increments are added to build a progressively more complete program, so the verification grows. Provided each step adds only a relatively small increment to the software, then verification after each increment is developed can rely upon the verification of the program in the previous step as a starting point. Also, since only a relatively small change will have been made to the software, the incremental verification challenge is reasonable. The SPARK approach to correctness by construction using analysis is discussed in Section 9.5.

To apply correctness by construction, the first step is to define the software development process to be used. Developers have to begin by seeking all of the places in which faults might arise during development. This information will allow the creation of a suitable development process for the system at hand. No single process is possible, because the circumstances of each system are different. A process for the development of custom software for an embedded system running on a high-performance modern microprocessor will be very different from the process used to develop an information system running on commodity hardware using commercial off-the-shelf (COTS) operating systems. A useful starting point for the development of a process to implement correctness by construction has been developed by Hall and Chapman [56].

A detailed example of correctness by construction in the development of a large distributed information system with high availability and security requirements is presented by Hall and Chapman [55].

Building software using correctness by construction seems as if it would increase development costs. Properly applied, it does not. In fact, there is strong evidence that the cost of development is reduced, often significantly, when compared to traditional methods. This cost reduction is not surprising when one considers that traditional methods rely on testing and repair to a large extent. Testing and repair are expensive activities, because they in turn rely heavily on expensive human effort. By eliminating much of this effort, correctness by construction can apply a small amount of additional human effort but do so differently and with greater effect. A particular example of the potential cost savings from correctness by construction has been reported by Amey [8].

7.6 Correctness by Construction — Synthesis

7.6.1 Generating Code from Formal Specifications

If the specification for a system is formal, then an implementation can, in principle, be created mechanically from that specification. In some cases, this idea is practical, and software can be created by machines rather than people. A general term that is sometimes used for this technique is *software synthesis*, and the tools used are sometimes referred to as *application generators*. One particular technique that has been developed is *model-based development*.

The concept is to develop a specification using a formal notation, and to have a tool translate that specification into an executable program, much as a compiler translates a high-level-language program into an executable program. This analogy points out the rather unfamiliar notion that what we call high-level-language programs are, in fact, specifications. A compiler writes the actual program, not the person who we usually call the programmer!

The specification languages used in model-based development are not those developed in the field of software engineering, such as Z and VDM. Rather, the languages are *domain specific*, i.e., each language is designed to be used by experts in a particular application domain rather than software engineers. Domain-specific languages are often graphical, and they permit domain experts to write formal software specifications in a notation with which they are familiar. The languages are essentially those developed within the application domain before computers came on the scene.

The term model-based development is most commonly associated with the field of control systems and related fields, such as signal and image processing. In model-based development of a control system, a controls engineer develops a specification of a control system using a standard graphic notation used by the controls discipline. This specification embodies the necessary control theory, but from the software perspective the specification is formal. This formal specification is translated into software in a high-level language using a synthesis tool.

Importantly, in this example of model-based development, the specification is developed by a controls engineer, not a software engineer. The notation used for the specification is a notation that comes from the field of control theory, not software engineering. And the actual software is synthesized by a powerful tool rather than being created by software engineers. Other than the development of the synthesis tools, software engineers do not play a central role in model-based development.

The way in which model-based development usually works is shown in Figure 7.10. Once an application expert has prepared a model of a system in a domain-specific language, the model can then be processed in two different ways —

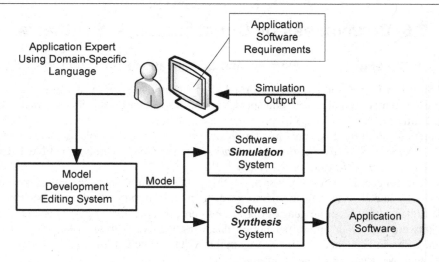

FIGURE 7.10 Application expert using domain-specific language to develop software.

simulation and *synthesis*. Many support tools for domain-specific languages provide a simulation capability that permits the expert to "execute" the model and observe its behavior. Extra facilities are available to play the role of input data sources and output data displays. With this capability, the expert can examine the dynamic behavior of the model and determine (at least in part) whether the model describes the desired solution. This activity is a major component of validation in model-based development.

Once the expert is satisfied with the model, synthesis is used to generate the implementation. The synthesis can often be tailored to specific targets and specific compiler options. Thus, the generated code can be created to meet the needs of complex target systems.

7.6.2 The Advantages of Model-Based Development

Many advantages are claimed for model-based development, including the following:

Less development effort. Much of the human effort that is needed in traditional software development is no longer needed. There is no software design or implementation, and verification is changed dramatically.

Closer to application, easier to validate. The specification is developed by an application expert in a notation with which he or she is familiar. Thus, validation is simpler and can be undertaken directly by the engineer who needs the system using a notation with which that engineer is familiar.

Independent of programming language. The source program created by the toolset is not determined by the skills and experience of programmers. Thus, any programming language could be used, and some synthesis systems actually support more than one. In fact, there is no technical need to generate source programs at all. A synthesis toolset could generate object programs directly. Most do not, however, because synthesis is used frequently in industries where software has to be approved by a certification agency. Most certification agencies undertake some of their responsibilities on software source programs.

No bugs from human development. In a sense, software synthesis is the best of all possible solutions to the problem of software dependability. Provided the tool that translates the specification to the executable program does so correctly, there is no possibility of faults being introduced in the translation. The requirement for accurate translation is not impossible to achieve. A translation tool would be widely used, and so exercising great care in the tool's construction would be worthwhile.

Successful software synthesis would provide accurate translation and require the use of formal specifications. Software synthesis thereby changes the field of software engineering considerably. Developers can turn their attention to dealing primarily with the requirements and the specification. The bulk of software development as currently practiced — design, implementation, testing, and documentation — is no longer needed.

7.6.3 Examples of Model-Based Development Systems

Examples of software synthesis tools are actually quite common. Here are some examples:

Parser generators. Parser generators such as YACC and GNU Bison are programs that read a context-free grammar and produce a parser for the language defined by the grammar. The parser produced is usually in a high-level language. The context-free grammar is the formal specification in this case.

Spreadsheet formulas. The formulas that define the computation for the cells in a spreadsheet are entered by the user in an algebraic form and evaluated by the spreadsheet program when the data in the associated cells changes. In most spreadsheets, the target of translation is not a high-level language. Most spreadsheets translate the algebraic representation of the desired computation into a synthetic internal form that is interpreted for evaluation of the expression. In no case does the developer of a spreadsheet have to write traditional programs.

Visual Basic. Visual Basic provides the user with a palette of typical GUI graphics and a blank window. The user selects graphics from the palette that he or she wants to use in a GUI for a piece of software and drags them onto the blank window. The graphics can be changed and repositioned as desired. The graphics palette and the mechanics of placing them to define a GUI constitute a formal specification of the GUI.

Functionality for the graphic elements is added in Visual Basic using a highly stylized program structure. To create the actual software, Visual Basic uses a variety of techniques, but the implementation of the graphics uses a library of program modules. The modules for the graphics that are actually in use are assembled automatically into a composite whole for execution. Thus, Visual Basic is partly a synthesis system and partly a specialized procedural programming system.

An important characteristic of software synthesis is that successful synthesis systems operate in narrow application domains. Each synthesis system is able to generate software for very specific types of software only. YACC, for example, generates high performance parsers, but YACC is of little use if software is needed for a device driver. Narrow domains of applicability do not seriously detract from the power of software synthesis. The availability of different synthesis tools broadens applicability, and several might be used for a given application.

7.6.4 Mathworks Simulink®

An example of a widely used, commercial tool that supports model-based development is *Mathworks Simulink* [95]. Simulink is designed primarily for use in the field of control systems, although many features have been added as the tool has evolved, and Simulink is widely applicable.

The specification language for Simulink is graphic and operates much like Visual Basic by providing the user with a palette of graphic icons representing various basic computation building blocks. Simulink provides building blocks for the supported application domains, including blocks for signal differentiation, signal integration, time delays, a wide variety of mathematical functions, input/output device interfacing, logic functions, and so on. Models are built by selecting icons representing functional blocks from the palette and dragging the icon to a window where the model is being built.

Simulink supports both model simulation and software synthesis. Building blocks are available for use with simulation that support a variety of input signal sources and display forms.

An example of a simple Simulink model is shown in Figure 7.11. Figure 7.11(a) is the complete model showing an input icon and an output icon marked "Scope1". The output icon is for display of the output of the model when it runs. Figure 7.11(b) is an expansion of the large central block (marked PID controller) in Figure 7.11(a). This shows Simulink's capability for abstracting sub-systems and allowing their separate development.

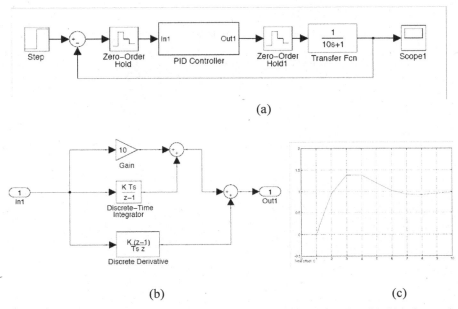

(a)

(b)   (c)

FIGURE 7.11 Simple PID controller represented in Simulink. (a) is the overall model; (b) is the actual controller, shown as a single block in (a); and (c) shows a sample of the output as displayed on the Scope component.

Figure 7.11(c) shows the output generated when this simple model was simulated. The output was directed to the building block labeled "Scope1" and, when the model was simulated, Simulink created a new window that displayed the output of the scope.

Figure 7.12 shows a small fragment of the C program that Simulink generated for the model in Figure 7.11. The source program is quite long, and the important thing to note about the part shown in Figure 7.12 is that, although the code was not written by humans, the code is readable (perhaps with difficulty) if necessary.

7.7 Correctness by Construction — Refinement

In the technique referred to as *development by refinement*, formal verification is woven throughout the development process. The basic idea is shown in Figure 7.13. Software is developed using a series of transformations or refinements, each of which makes the initial formal specification more concrete, and transformation is continued until an executable implementation has been produced.

```
/*
 * PID_Controlled_System.c
 *
 * Real-Time Workshop code generation for Simulink
 *          model "PID_Controlled_System.mdl".
 *
 * Model Version              : 1.9
 * Real-Time Workshop version : 7.0   (R2007b)  02-Aug-2007
 * C source code generated on : Tue Mar 24 10:41:24 2009
 */

#include "rt_logging_mmi.h"
#include "PID_Controlled_System_capi.h"
#include "PID_Controlled_System.h"
#include "PID_Controlled_System_private.h"

/* Block signals (auto storage) */
BlockIO_PID_Controlled_System PID_Controlled_System_B;

/* Continuous states */
ContinuousStates_PID_Controlled PID_Controlled_System_X;

/* Solver Matrices */

/* A and B matrices used by ODE3 fixed-step solver */
static const real_T rt_ODE3_A[3] = {
  1.0/2.0, 3.0/4.0, 1.0
};

static const real_T rt_ODE3_B[3][3] = {
  { 1.0/2.0, 0.0, 0.0 },

  { 0.0, 3.0/4.0, 0.0 },

  { 2.0/9.0, 1.0/3.0, 4.0/9.0 }
};

/* Block states (auto storage) */
D_Work_PID_Controlled_System PID_Controlled_System_DWork;
```

FIGURE 7.12 Sample of the code produced by Simulink for the model shown in Figure 7.11.

As each transformation is applied, a proof (actually a series of small proofs) that the transformation has produced a refinement that implies the original formal specification is developed. In this way, each refinement is verified formally as the refinement is applied. Taken together, the sequence of proofs produced for the sequence of refinements is then a verification proof that the implementation implies the original formal specification.

Development by refinement is a form of correctness by construction because the construction of the software is verified at each stage. Thus, no transformation is included in the sequence unless the necessary proof can be constructed. Finally, when the software is complete, so is the proof.

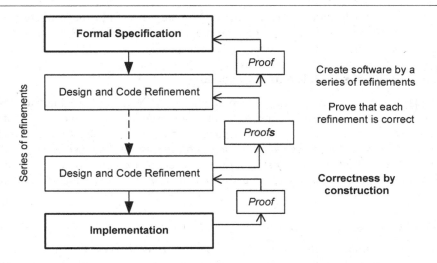

FIGURE 7.13 Software development by refinement in a form of correctness by construction.

The B Method is the most complete and most comprehensive instantiation of the refinement approach [1]. The method was developed by Jean-Raymond Abrial, who describes the method as follows:

"B is a method for specifying, designing and coding software systems."

The B Method includes various notations, but the starting point is the B specification language. The method of use and many aspects of the semantics are similar to Z, but the notation relies on an ASCII representation rather than the mathematical font symbols used in Z. As a result, the language looks somewhat more familiar to computer scientists and is easier to deal with using a conventional keyboard.

Several powerful tools have been developed to support the B Method, and the tools automate a lot of the process of applying refinement. See, for example, the Atelier B tools [28].

7.8 Software Fault Avoidance

Avoiding software faults should always be our goal. To avoid software faults, we need to have some idea of how they arise. For software developed using a typical process, the major source of defects is human error. The best way to avoid faults in such circumstances is to prevent engineers from undertaking practices that are known to be fault prone and to provide support for those engineers in avoiding software faults.

Some of the techniques that can be used for software fault avoidance are introduced in the remainder of this section to provide a summary of the available technology. Several are covered in depth in later chapters.

7.8.1 Rigorous Development Processes

The process is the focal point for much of what we do in software engineering. Processes do not have to be elaborate, restrictive, or prescriptive to be rigorous. What is required is a process that limits the opportunities for faults to be introduced to the extent possible. The processes used in any project must be designed to counter the introduction of faults at every stage of the lifecycle. A rigorous process, therefore, should include steps that address the *creation* and *assurance* of *all* the relevant artifacts.

Development Risk

The need to produce software that is adequately dependable is not the only thing that drives the overall form of a process. Development risk[2] is a major factor also. Development risk is the risk that the development process will fail in some way. Typical process failures include delivering software late, exceeding the budget for software development, delivering software that contains an unacceptable number of faults, and delivering software with reduced functionality. Process steps and decisions are more often than not undertaken as a result of perceived development risk. Thus attention to the determination of requirements in which prototypes are built and evaluated by customers is only peripherally related to dependability. We know that accurate requirements are essential for dependability, but the process activities undertaken to reduce the risk of requirements errors is only relevant to dependability in that it leads to the desired final result of accurate requirements.

Agile Development

Extreme Programming [17] and other agile methods have become popular in recent years, and that popularity raises the question: can agile methods be used in the development of software that has to meet high dependability requirements?

But this question is not the right question to ask. Agile methods target process efficiency. In essence, they are trying to make the best use of available resources by using them for process steps that are known to be efficient and effective. Agile methods can certainly be used for safety-critical systems. Such a process would not look like existing agile methods, but the underlying principles would be the same. For software dependability, the right question to ask of any process, not just agile

---

2. Note that this is not the same as operational risk that we discussed in Section 2.7.4.

methods, is whether the process has paid attention to all possible mechanisms for fault avoidance and fault elimination.

Cleanroom Software Engineering

Many process concepts and ideas have evolved in the search for ways of increasing software dependability. Cleanroom Software Engineering [112], for example, is an approach to rigorous software development that was developed by Harlan Mills and his colleagues at IBM.

Cleanroom addresses all phases of software development with the goal of excluding defects from the software development process. The name, Cleanroom, derives from the similarity that the developers sought with the use of cleanrooms in hardware engineering. A hardware cleanroom uses a variety of techniques to try to keep contaminants out of the hardware production process.

In the case of software, Cleanroom brings practical levels of formality to the challenge of software development by combining simple formal techniques with disciplined informal activities. Specification uses an approach called the Box Structure Method [96], and verification is accomplished by inspection so no formal proofs are involved. Testing is used to supplement inspection, but testing is performed using a statistical sampling approach. This approach to testing mimics the use of statistical quality control in industrial manufacturing. What this means is that testing is conducted typically by specialized test engineers, not the developers. In fact, since verification includes inspection, developers focus their attention upon informal reasoning about the software, not testing the software. Thus in the more common form of Cleanroom Software Engineering, software engineers do not execute the software they write at all.

Cleanroom has been used in industrial development and has been the subject of experimental assessment [130]. The experimental assessment yielded strong statistical evidence that applying Cleanroom has the potential to both increase the quality of software and reduce development costs. In the study, fifteen teams of three developed a small software system (several hundred lines) with ten teams using Cleanroom and five using a more traditional approach. One of the results of the study was:

The Cleanroom teams' products met the system requirements more completely and had a higher percentage of operationally generated test cases.

All ten Cleanroom teams made all of their scheduled intermediate product deliveries, while only two of the five non-Cleanroom teams did.

7.8.2 Appropriate Notations

We use a variety of notations to communicate among ourselves and with computers. We can and should use appropriate notations for all software artifacts. If we choose a notation that precludes certain fault types (as many as possible) in a certain artifact, then we have an excellent tool to facilitate fault avoidance.

As an example, consider programming languages. We know that programming languages cannot ensure good software, but they can certainly help its production. We get the most help from a language that:

- Supports modern software structures such as concurrency and data abstraction.

- Has a clear and unambiguous syntax.

- Implements strong typing.

The importance of these topics is easily seen from the much higher defect rates in software written in languages like C compared to software written in a language like Ada. C has a confusing syntax, does not support data abstraction explicitly, and has almost no type system. To use C in an application for which dependability is important is inappropriate unless there is a compelling practical reason for the choice, such as C being the only language available to a project for which a compiler is available. Ada was designed to support software dependability, and the language has many features designed to support software fault avoidance.

7.8.3 Comprehensive Standards for All Artifacts

Standards in software engineering provide a means of ensuring that things we want to happen actually do and that things we do not want to happen do not. Standards do this in situations where even the most well-meaning engineer might make a mistake, because he or she is unaware that certain things need to happen or need to be prevented. Standards in the field of software engineering have been developed for a wide variety of purposes by a wide variety of organizations, including the International Organization for Standardization [68], the Institute of Electrical and Electronic Engineers [64], the Department of Defense, and the RTCA [120].

As an example of the role of standards, consider their role in programming languages. There are many programming structures that are syntactically valid yet dangerous. The best-known example is the use of assignment in a conditional expression in C:

```
if (a=b) {...}
```

This statement is perfectly valid, but people new to C think that the "=" is a test of equality. In fact, the "=" is an assignment. Even engineers with a lot of experience can write a statement like this if they are not careful, and, although most modern compilers will issue a warning message, even experienced programmers sometimes ignore compiler warnings. Standards that prohibit such things and that are checked by tools go a long way to preventing common classes of faults.

In the same general area, some programming practices tend to be error prone because engineers find them hard to understand. Deeply nested conditional statements, for example, are error prone because engineers find reasoning about their logic to be difficult.

7.8.4 Support Tools

Tools, both simple and complex, help engineers. Tools, even simple ones, should be sought and used to the maximum extent possible. In everyday writing, most people appreciate spelling checkers even though the service they provide is quite simple and optional. In practice, spelling checkers ensure that sequences of letters which are not werds will always be detected. These sequences might not be detected if we relied on our own observation. Similarly, although they are not required, most software engineers appreciate sophisticated editors that highlight programming-language constructs and generally make software more easily understood. Such editors highlight things consistently and enhance the engineer's intellect. Some tools are so powerful and necessary that a software engineer would never dream of working without them, for example, a compiler when working in a high-level language. Surprisingly, there are a number of sophisticated tools that can establish important properties of software which are not commonly used, for example, static analyzers (see Section 7.9.1).

7.8.5 Properly Trained Personnel

At present, software engineering is largely a manual activity that depends heavily on the engineers involved being able to make accurate and appropriate technical decisions. Without the right training and experience, those decisions are frequently not the best. One of the most important and valuable assets that a software engineer can have is a clear picture of what he or she is *not* properly qualified to do. There is no reason to think that every software engineer knows all that is needed to tackle the engineering of every type of software.

7.8.6 Formal Techniques

As we saw in Section 7.2, formal techniques bring many benefits. The role of formal techniques in software fault avoidance is so important that we discuss that role at length in Chapter 8 and Chapter 9.

7.9 Software Fault Elimination

If we cannot avoid faults, then our next goal is to eliminate them. Many techniques have been developed to assist the engineer in eliminating software faults, and so choosing techniques is part of the problem. In thinking about software fault elimination, keep in mind that faults need to be eliminated from artifacts across the lifecycle, not just from source programs.

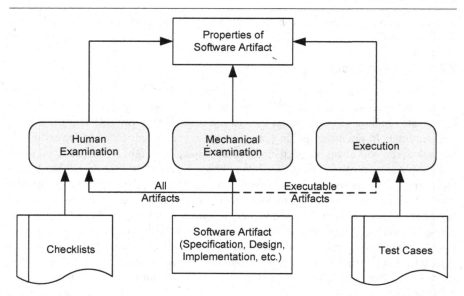

FIGURE 7.14 Static analysis can be either by human examination or mechanical examination. Dynamic analysis is only possible on executable artifacts.

Finding defects can be undertaken with two types of analysis: *static* analysis and *dynamic* analysis. These types of analysis are illustrated in Figure 7.14.

7.9.1 Static Analysis

Static analysis is the systematic examination of a software artifact either by a human or by a machine. Static analysis by humans is usually referred to as either a *review* or an *inspection*. The artifact is not executed during static analysis. Essentially, the software artifact is examined under a magnifying glass and defects are sought by various means. *All* software artifacts are candidates for static analysis, including those written in natural language.

Static analysis is associated most frequently with the execution of some form of analysis tool. For a list of static-analysis tools for various languages see the article in Wikipedia [151]. Different tools target different types of fault. Most target different types of software fault, but tools have also been developed to examine software systems and architectures to try to locate potential security vulnerabilities.

Many different human static-analysis (inspection) techniques have been developed and numerous experiments have been conducted to assess their effectiveness. In general, rigorous human inspections are very effective at locating faults.

Static analysis in essentially all forms is a cost-effective way to find faults. Comprehensive static-analysis methods in software development are not widely used, even in the development of systems that require high assurance, such as safety-critical and mission-critical systems. The cost of static methods is low compared to their benefits, and static methods can be cost-effective in virtually any software development.

Static analysis can and should be applied to any software development artifact. An engineer proofreading a document that he or she has written is a simple form of static analysis. Similarly, an engineer using a spelling checker on a natural-language document is a simple form of static analysis.

These examples illustrate two of the problems of static analysis: *false positives* and *false negatives* (see also Section 2.6.4).

False positive. A false positive is an indication that a problem exists when in fact there is no problem. False positives arise a lot with spelling checkers, because specialized words are often not in the underlying dictionary and so are flagged as mistakes. False positives arise with code-analysis tools also, although they tend to take the form of doubt: a variable *might* not be given a value in a particular block of code. For example:

```
if a > b then x := 1;
```

Typically, a static analyzer cannot determine the circumstances under which a will be greater than b and will issue a diagnostic that x might not have a value after the if statement. The programmer might have intended this, but the static analyzer cannot tell.

False negative. A false negative is a failure to indicate that a problem exists when in fact one does. This happens frequently with spelling checkers. Using the wrong word but spelling the word correctly is a common mistake, but the mistake will not be flagged. False negatives arise in code analysis tools where the tool cannot determine a condition with a high level of confidence such as might arise with a complicated sequence of function calls.

Almost all static analysis techniques can generate false positives and false negatives. These false results are more than a nuisance. There is a tendency for people to believe that, once a static-analysis tool reports no errors have been found, then there are no errors. Equally as bad is the natural tendency to ignore the results of static analysis if there are a lot of false positives. Engineers are not especially interested in having to take on the task of separating the false positives from the meaningful messages, and so they ignore all of them.

7.9.2 Dynamic Analysis

Dynamic analysis is the execution of a software artifact in a controlled environment with various properties of the artifact monitored in various ways. Execution could be using a real machine or a virtual machine. The execution of a software artifact in dynamic analysis has to take place in a controlled environment because:

- There must be a high level of assurance that the environment being used has properties that will actually be useful. The most common goal with the environment used in dynamic analysis is to make sure that the environment used is as close as possible to the expected actual operating environment. If it is, then the faults found will be especially important, because they were likely to have arisen in operation.

- There are plenty of circumstances in which an environment other than the expected operating environment needs to be used in dynamic analysis. The most common example is an environment that permits software to be analyzed in expected but unusual circumstances. A software system controlling a spacecraft, for example, would be designed to cope with a variety of failures of system components, and so analyzing the software in such a way that all anticipated component failures can be forced to occur (perhaps many times over) is a desirable additional operating environment.

- There must be mechanisms in place to record the data that results from the analysis. The reason for performing the analysis is to find faults, but faults can be subtle. We cannot detect faults directly by dynamic analysis. All we can do is to detect erroneous states. So the goal of the monitoring mechanism is to detect errors and provide enough information about the error that the associated fault can be located.

The fact that dynamic analysis requires execution suggests that the only target for dynamic analysis is an implementation, but this is not the case. An executable artifact could be source code, a model developed for a model checker, or a specification if the specification is written in an executable notation. In principle, any artifact written in a formal language could be executed provided certain restrictions are made. The restrictions that are needed are those that limit the defined computation to finite sets so that the computation can be stored in a computer. This general idea has led to the notion of *executable specifications*, i.e., specifications that define a computation in the usual way but which are executable. Although not common, some of the notations that support executable specifications are the model-based development systems Simulink [95] and the SCADE Suite [44], and the general specification languages Statecharts [57] and the Naval Research Laboratory's SCR notation [62].

7.9.3 Eliminating a Fault — Root-Cause Analysis

Fault elimination is a three-part activity: (1) locating the fault, (2) repairing the fault, and (3) determining how the fault got into the artifact in the first place. Surprisingly, repairing a fault in software is not without its problems. The probability that repairing a fault will introduce *another* fault is not zero. So fault repair has to be a rigorous process that is carefully checked.

A critical issue with design faults, including software faults, is *root-cause analysis*. This is the process of dealing with the question:

> *How did the fault get into the software in the first place, and*
> *how do we prevent whatever went wrong from happening again?*

If we are fortunate to find a fault using a fault-elimination technique, uncovering the mechanism whereby the fault got into the software is essential so that we can avoid similar faults in the future.

Root-cause analysis starts with a careful examination of the details of the fault itself, including determination of its severity and which stage of the development was likely to be the one in which the fault was introduced. The reason for this analysis is the need to address fault types rather than specific faults. Determining why a given fault arose is of only marginal value. Far more important is to determine details of the whole class of similar faults so as to try to prevent all of them in the future. If the details of the entire class can be determined, then fault avoidance or perhaps better or more powerful fault elimination techniques can be introduced into the development process.

Once details of the fault and its associated fault type have been determined, the changes in the process can be worked out. Some examples of fault types and ensuing process changes are:

Special processing case omitted. If fault elimination reveals an omitted special case, then the most likely process issue is either requirements elicitation or specification. Asking why the case was omitted usually reveals that "nobody thought of it". The solution is to review the validation procedures and make sure that proper requirements and specification models are being built, that the proper notations are being used, and that complete inspections are in effect for these artifacts.

Unexpected exception raised. An unexpected exception that is not handled properly is devastating in almost all cases. Exception semantics are complex in most programming languages and difficult for programmers to understand. Thus root-cause analysis must try to enhance the development process so as to provide assurance that unexpected exceptions will not arise *anywhere* in the software. To do so requires a determination of all types of exception to which a software system is vulnerable, location within the software of all the places where each type of exception could be raised, rigorous argument (or some other form of static analysis) that the exceptions could never arise, and changes to the development process to include these techniques in future developments.

Null pointer dereferenced. Dereferencing a null pointer is a common problem that is frequently devastating, because execution of the program is usually terminated. Again, the issue is not to determine why a specific pointer was null when the pointer was dereferenced. Rather, the issue is to determine how to be sure that no pointer anywhere in the program will be null when dereferenced. Getting this assurance requires that a rigorous argument be developed as to why pointer dereferencing is safe. Static software tools exist that can provide this type of assurance for many types of program, and the obvious process change is to introduce tool-based static analysis into the software development process.

7.10 Managing Software Fault Avoidance and Elimination

In considering how to proceed with fault avoidance and elimination, we have to establish a framework within which to work and within which we can understand the results of our activities. Viewing fault avoidance as finding a technique "to stop software developers from introducing faults" or fault elimination as finding a technique "to locate the software faults" is not sufficient because no single technique will do either.

Different techniques have different capabilities and different costs. Different techniques are applicable to different artifacts, and different techniques have different levels of effectiveness. In the end, what we have to do is to choose a set of techniques that will stop the introduction of or allow us to find as many defects as possible in the specific artifacts that we have, and do so within the budget and time constraints that we have to meet.

As they have been discussed so far, fault avoidance and fault elimination are both techniques that include a variety of techniques, but what does that tell us about the actual quality of the software that we are building? The answer lies in combining the two approaches and cataloging their results in a manner that allows us to draw useful conclusions about what we have and what remains to be done. We will refer to this approach as *fault freedom*, and the mechanism for achieving fault freedom is to characterize the results of fault avoidance and fault elimination as *properties*.

7.10.1 Fault Freedom as Properties

Properties of Artifacts

We begin by establishing a goal for fault avoidance and fault elimination that will help us to structure our thinking and assess our overall performance. A powerful way to do this is to establish useful properties of the artifact being examined. The properties might be freedom from certain classes of faults or possession of a characteristic that means certain faults can no longer be present. Whatever the property is, the intent is to establish the property either by blocking the faults associated with the property using fault avoidance or by suitable changes to the software using fault elimination. In the end, the property corresponds to a claim that a certain class of faults is not present.

Structuring software fault avoidance and fault elimination as establishing a set of properties allows progressively more comprehensive statements to be made about the target artifact. Once several properties have been established, the software artifact in fact has a "super" property that is the conjunction of those which have been shown.

Natural Language Properties

Because the final quality of a software system depends on all of the artifacts generated during the software lifecycle, we need to strive for fault freedom across the lifecycle. The properties that might be used for a specification written in natural language include simple but important ones such as:

- **Spelling errors removed from the document.**
  Without spelling errors, the document will be easier to read. This promotes fault elimination, because human reviewers are more likely to see technical flaws.

- **Document sections comply with organizational standards.**
  Ensuring that a document complies with organizational standards means that the document can become part of the organization's official collection, and the document will be more familiar to reviewers and again more readable.

- **Glossary of terms complete and all definitions checked by engineers in relevant domain.**
  A glossary of terms is an essential component of a specification, and the precision of the included definitions is key to reducing misunderstandings.

More complex properties of natural language specifications include the following:

- **Necessary functionality for all possible values of each input stream properly defined.**
  Systematic checking of the range of possible values of input and ensuring that the processing deals with each as needed is an important way of avoiding omission faults.

- **Necessary functionality for all possible device failures properly defined.**
  Similarly, systematic checking that the response has been defined to all anticipated device failures is also an important way of avoiding omission faults.

Properties such as these are often overlooked, because engineers tend to think about the functionality required of a system and not the actions that need to be taken when something is not part of the normal processing. Establishing that a common item which is easily overlooked has been checked is a simple but powerful property.

High-Level Language Properties

The properties that we might use for an implementation in a high-level language include:

- All identifiers in the source program are meaningful.

- All variables initialized at the point of declaration.

- Cases cover the selection type in case statements.

- Processing in place for all error conditions that might result from file operations.

- Handlers in place for all anticipated exceptions.

As with the properties of a natural-language specification, properties such as these seem simple, but they can be powerful. The notion of a meaningful identifier, for example, is that the identifier describes its use in a way that helps the reader. A variable called tmp is far less helpful to the reader than:

```
temperature_centigrade
```

Similarly, a function called cct is less useful than one called:

```
compute_centigrade_temperature.
```

Another useful property is the initialization of variables. A program will compile in most languages without variables being initialized, but the result is not likely to be the program that the engineer intended.

Collections of Properties

Although there is obviously a link, the properties discussed so far do not obviously relate to faults that lead to the wrong function being computed. Faults in the computation need to be eliminated, and the property-based approach can be applied to these faults also. For functionality, the requirements can be partitioned into individual elements in the same way as functionality is partitioned in functional testing.

For any given development, a list of properties needs to be developed to permit a comprehensive structured approach to fault avoidance and elimination. The list can be tailored to the type of artifact of interest, the technology used in that artifact, the resources available, the tools available, and the dependability requirements of the subject system. The relationship between the various parts is shown in Figure 7.15.

The process of analyzing the completeness of the properties is, of necessity, informal. The process needs to include a variety of checks ranging from the techniques used to elicit the requirements all the way to checks on the techniques used to handle configuration management. Documenting and reviewing these checks is best handled using a process of rigorous argument known as an *assurance argument*. We discuss assurance arguments in Chapter 12.

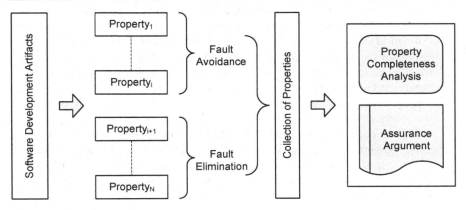

FIGURE 7.15 Establishing collections of properties about a set of software artifacts.

7.11 Misconceptions about Software Dependability

There are several widely held technical misconceptions about software dependability. In practice, these misconceptions tend to affect the choices of technology that engineers and managers make. The most commonly held misconceptions are:

Software defects are only introduced during implementation.

A common misconception is that software defects are only introduced during preparation of the source program and can only be found by testing. As should be evident from earlier parts of this book, this combination of ideas is a dangerous fallacy since both parts are wrong. Defects in the requirements, specification, and design of a software system are best dealt with in the requirements, specification, and design phases of development, not the subsequent implementation phase. For example, techniques for fault avoidance and fault elimination in specifications are far more effective than testing the subsequent implementation.

Experience has shown that, for many systems, the majority of software defects are actually introduced in the specifications but usually not found until testing. In some industries that develop systems with high dependability requirements, roughly two thirds of the defects that are detected either during testing or in the field were introduced in the specification. This statistic makes fault avoidance and elimination in specifications of crucial importance.

Small organizations cannot afford fault avoidance and elimination.

Another common misconception is that the cost of fault avoidance and fault elimination techniques early in the development process is not needed by and is beyond the means of a small organization. In view of the cost of failure for virtually all modern systems of any significant size and for all safety-critical systems, employing fault avoidance or fault elimination to the maximum extent possible is likely to be cost effective. The cost of a single failure can easily exceed the cost of any of the techniques discussed in this book. In addition, even if defects are located during development, the cost of removal usually exceeds the cost of applying rigorous development techniques. In dealing with software dependability, the cost of applying more sophisticated techniques can often be far less than the cost of *not* applying them. Defects that could have been avoided or eliminated during development might not get caught later.

Fault avoidance and fault elimination are impractical.

A third common misconception is that, in practice, when developing realistic software systems, employing ideas such as those discussed in this book is not possible. Various reasons are given to justify this claim. For example, some argue that proper specifications cannot be written, because the details of what the system is to do are not known when development begins. Such incompleteness is real and has to be addressed. But incomplete detail does not mean that specifications cannot be developed. Incompleteness means that specifications cannot be complete at the outset. Developing a partial specification and then determining the details of what is missing, perhaps by developing prototypes or holding detailed discussions with the customer, can be a perfectly rigorous process. Development risks such as incomplete specifications are part of the development process, but this does not mean that the process cannot be rigorous.

Project personnel cannot use the techniques.

A final common misconception is that software has to be written using tools and techniques with which the developers are familiar even if those tools and techniques are not entirely suitable for the subject software. C, for example (or one of its derivatives such as C++), is rarely suitable for use in developing safety-critical systems, yet C is often used and this use justified by claiming that C is familiar to developers. The benefits of other languages in terms of fault avoidance and fault elimination are lost as a result. In practice, learning an unfamiliar technology is rarely prohibitive, especially when major benefits ensue, and achieving dependability relies in many ways on employing the best technology available.

Key points in this chapter:

- Software can be very fragile. A large software system can fail because of a mistake in a single line of the source code.
- The software lifecycle helps identify both the points at which faults can arise and the points at which we might be able to deal with the faults.
- Validation can be thought of as answering the question: "Did we build the right thing?" and verification can be thought of as answering the question: "Did we build the thing right?".
- Correctness by construction is a concept in which developers attempt to create correct software by virtue of the technology used in construction.
- Formal methods provide a variety of analytic results about software artifacts.
- Model checking is an analysis technique for establishing properties of software by state space analysis.
- Model-based development is a technique for synthesized software from specifications written in application-specific languages.
- Various techniques can be utilized to effect software fault avoidance.
- Various techniques can be utilized to effect software fault elimination.
- A combination of techniques should be used to avoid and eliminate as many types of software fault as possible.

Exercises

1. Write a natural-language specification for a program that takes an integer in the range 0 to 10,000 and determines whether the year is a leap year.

2. Defects in software are a serious problem for safety-critical systems, but accidents occur as a result of defective *data* also. Things like defective navigation data, configuration data, and weight and fuel data have caused accidents even though the software was right. Discuss the application of fault avoidance to data.

3. Discuss the application of fault elimination to data.

4. Discuss the application of fault tolerance to data.

5. Explain the claim: Software engineering uses testing to establish a conclusion whereas other branches of engineering use testing to confirm a conclusion.

6. In Hall's paper, "Seven Myths of Formal Methods" [54], myth number 1 is "Formal Methods Can Guarantee That Software Is Perfect". In your own words, explain why this is a myth. Do not merely repeat the argument from the paper. Rather, show that you are aware of the argument details.

7. For myth 5 in Hall's article [54], discuss the overall economic effect of formal methods.

8. For myth 12 in Hinchey and Bowen's article [20], discuss the role of formal methods in software such as games, word processors, and operating systems.

9. Carefully explain the application of verification and validation to the requirements, specification, and implementation of a software system.

10. Explain why the use of formulas in spreadsheets is an example of model-based development.

11. Mathworks Simulink is a popular model-based development system. Itemize as a bulleted list the sources of software defects for a binary program created using Simulink and other associated utilities.

12. Consider the following program fragment:

```
for i in 1..5 loop
  for j in 1..3 loop
    if a > b then
      if c > d then
        compute_output(a, b, c, d);
      else
        compute_output(a, b, d, c);
    else
      if c > d then
        compute_output(b, a, c, d);
      else
        compute_output(b, a, d, c);
  end loop;
end loop;
```

Compute the total time needed to test the program if the test coverage required is to execute all paths of the program fragment and each execution requires one millisecond.

13. Several years ago, the Navy chose Microsoft Windows NT as the basis for many shipboard systems. The result was what is referred to as the USS Yorktown incident:

> http://en.wikipedia.org/wiki/USS_Yorktown_(CG-48)

The use of Commercial-Off-The-Shelf (COTS) computer components (both hardware and software) in safety-critical systems is viewed as highly desirable by developers and highly problematic by regulators. The advantage is the low cost. The disadvantages are many and obvious. Despite the problems, the use of COTS in systems requiring high dependability is continuing.

(a) Most COTS operating systems were designed for general-purpose use, not safety-critical use. Could a COTS operating system be modified and/or enhanced for use in a safety-critical application? If so, how? If not, why not?

(b) A COTS component that is often not recognized as such is a compiler. Compilers are essential for building safety-critical systems. Should COTS compilers be used for safety-critical systems? If so, why? If not, why not?

(c) Open-source software is viewed as a technology that might be exploited for safety-critical systems, because the source code of the software is open to public scrutiny. Does this fact make a difference to the suitability of the software for use in a safety-critical system? If so, why? If not, why not?

(d) COTS software is usually only available in binary form with no information about how the software was built. Such information is usually viewed as proprietary. This leaves open the question about what trust might be placed in the software as a result of knowing what the development process was. Discuss the possibility of an approach to trust in COTS software based upon a confidential assessment undertaken by a trusted third party.

CHAPTER 8

Software Fault Avoidance in Specification

Learning objectives of this chapter are to understand:

- The role and importance of software specification.
- The principles of formal specification in a declarative language.
- The mathematics of formal specification.
- How to read and understand formal specifications.
- How to write simple formal specifications.
- Why formal specifications are useful and when.
- How a formal specification is built.

8.1 The Role of Specification

The specification is the first statement of what a software system has to do. In essence, the specification is a statement about how the software will solve the problem posed by the requirements, and the specification is written in terms of the effect that the software has to have on its inputs and outputs.

The primary role of a software specification is to act as a reference for those who have to develop the associated software system, i.e., the role of a specification is *communication*. The specification is a repository for all the important information about what a software system is to do. As a repository, the goal is for the specification to convey to those who read it *all* the information they need. Those who write the specification possess information, and those who read the specification need that information. This communication must work correctly, and a lot of effort has been expended on specification technology precisely because of the importance of this communication.

Many different engineers use a software specification:

- Obviously, the engineers who actually implement the software will refer to it.

- The engineers who test the software will refer to the specification, because the specification tells them what the content of functional tests should be.

- Customers benefit from referring to the specification because the specification tells them what the system they are acquiring will do.

- For systems that are regulated, engineers working for agencies such as the U.S. Federal Aviation Administration (FAA), Food and Drug Administration (FDA), and Nuclear Regulatory Commission (NRC), and the U.K.'s Civil Aviation Authority (CAA) and Health and Safety Executive will require inspection of the software specification.

Having a specification from which to work is an important part of any software development process. Without an accurate specification, engineers have to proceed with at best an informal idea of what the software is to do. That informal idea is likely to be incomplete, inaccurate, and subject to change. We can achieve a great deal in the area of fault avoidance by paying careful attention to the specification of systems requiring high levels of dependability.

Defects in specification are the most expensive to repair. If a defect is present in the specification of a software system and that defect is not detected until after the system is built, the repair cost is as high as it can be, because all the software artifacts have to be changed. After the specification is corrected, the various designs have to be corrected and checked, the implementation has to be corrected, and the verification has to be repeated. There might also be various documents such as user manuals and maintenance manuals that have to be repaired.

Real specifications are large, complex, and difficult to write correctly and clearly. Developing complete and accurate specifications is a challenge in practice, but, as noted in Section 7.11, there are ways of dealing with the challenge. In this chapter we look at one of the most powerful ways to conquer the challenge, namely, *formal specification.*

In this chapter, we will look at formal specification with the goal of understanding how formal specifications are built. To do so, we will use one particular formal language, Z^1. Z is a powerful language, and there are several books on just that language [134, 108, 71, 154].

8.2 Difficulties with Natural Languages

Natural language is what we use every day when we communicate, but the use of natural language in software engineering is problematic for several reasons:

---

1. Details of Z are introduced in Section 8.6.

Ambiguity. Natural language is inherently ambiguous, because the meanings of words and phrases are determined by our experience. What is clear to the author of a statement might not be clear to the reader, and so the author and reader have different meanings, often without realizing that they have this difference.

Imprecision. Natural language is imprecise. In order for an author and a reader to communicate with a reasonable amount of text, many things that are expected to be common are assumed and omitted from the communication.

Informality. Natural language is not formally defined, and so there is no way to check the syntax or any other property mechanically in order to help locate deficiencies.

Dialects. There is no single definition of any natural language. English is not the same in any two countries and frequently is not the same in two regions of the same country.

Many attempts have been made to deal with these issues, including defining language subsets, developing natural-language analysis systems, developing glossaries of terms, relying on dictionaries, using special document formats, and training engineers.

None of these approaches nor any combination deals fully with the difficulties that arise with natural language. The only comprehensive solution is to turn to formal languages and formal specification. Yet practical circumstances often dictate the use of natural language in engineering. Thus, although efforts to deal with the various difficulties with natural language do not solve the problems, they can and should be used if one has to use natural language for specification, in order to comply with a standard, for example.

8.3 Specification Difficulties

8.3.1 Specification Defects

As we noted in Section 7.11, the majority of defects in a software system are introduced in the specification but usually not found until testing [108]. The situation is illustrated in Figure 8.1. What goes wrong in software specification? There are six major categories of defects that tend to arise:

Incorrect functionality. The stated functionality is not what the system is really supposed to do.

Missing functionality. The stated functionality omits something that the software is supposed to do.

Incompleteness. No functionality is stated for certain inputs or certain conditions that might occur.

Ambiguity. The stated functionality is open to more than one interpretation.

Inconsistency. Functionality is stated so that one part is inconsistent with another.

Naïveté. The specification documents a desired system that cannot be built because of technical limitations.

Dealing with these issues is obviously important. But, as long as we restrict our specification technology to natural language, we have no framework within which to attack the problems. Natural language has no precise syntax or semantics from which to derive helpful analysis.

8.3.2 Specification Evolution

Frequently, software engineers are told that no software specification is available, because the desired system is still being designed and so the associated software specification cannot be determined. Despite this, these engineers are asked to begin building the software for that part of the system that is specified even though the specification that is available is probably incomplete, poorly stated, and out of date.

Making things more difficult are the inevitable changes that occur as the desired system becomes more clearly defined. Early *system* design decisions change as more information becomes available, and this leads to changes in the specification of the *software*.

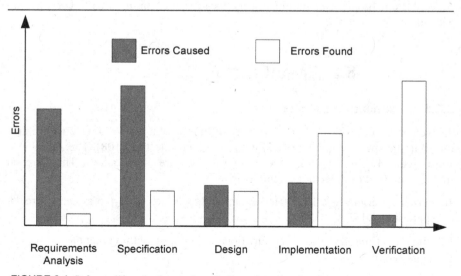

FIGURE 8.1 Software lifecycle phases where faults are introduced vs. located.

The ideal situation is to have a complete and accurate software specification before software design begins and for that specification to remain unchanged during development. In practice, this ideal is rarely, if ever, possible. Thus, specification techniques must take these realities into account and manage this development risk carefully.

Many techniques exist for dealing with the issue of incomplete specifications, including:

Throw-away prototypes. A *throw-away prototype*, as the name suggests, is a prototype that is thrown away after use [61]. The idea is to deal with a question of some sort by quickly building a prototype designed just to answer the question. Since the prototype will not be used as part of the system to be delivered, no attention need be paid to issues such as maintainability or documentation. Specification questions that might be answered using a throw-away prototype include user-interface features, performance measures, and detailed aspects of functionality. A partially complete but high-quality specification can define necessary throw-away prototypes based on incomplete specification details.

Evolutionary prototypes. An *evolutionary prototype*, again as the name suggests, is a prototype that evolves into part of the system under development. In effect, a system acts as its own prototype [61]. Provided care is exercised to ensure that prototypical elements do not remain incomplete or redundant in the delivered system, the resulting system is not affected negatively. That part of the system which is specified can be constructed carefully and used to help define the remainder of the system. This definition can take the form of a prototype implementation built using the completed system fragment to ascertain what the desired system functionality is. The benefit of having a partial but high-quality specification at this point is to permit the incremental development of the system to have a well-defined set of interfaces and functionality. Note that this process is designed to inform the specification, not replace the need for specification.

User interviews. Interviews with users and engineers in the application domain can be used to target questions about aspects of the specification that are uncertain.

System models. Development of system models such as data-flow models or models based on natural laws for physical systems can provide insight into how software systems need to operate.

Use cases. Use cases are a simple yet powerful way to investigate systematically the interaction between systems and their operating environment.

Specification reviews. Preliminary specifications can be reviewed with the final system's users to gather information even though the documented specification is known to be incomplete.

The use of formal specification is not precluded either by the problem of incomplete specifications or the use of these various mitigation techniques. No matter how little is established for a given specification and no matter how much of a specification is likely to change, the use of a formal language to document the specification is almost always beneficial. A formal specification facilitates the resolution of many of the issues with specification by providing a means of effective communication and a means of identifying specification weaknesses.

8.4 Formal Languages

8.4.1 Formal Syntax and Semantics

A formal language is any language that has a formal syntax and formal semantics. This idea is actually quite familiar to most people because *any programming language is a formal language.* In fact, almost all programming languages, and certainly languages like C++ and Java, are actually specification languages. Programmers think they are writing programs in Java, for example, but the compiler is really writing the program, i.e., the sequence of bits that executes on the computer.

Both syntax and semantics are important. A formal syntax means that there can be no doubt about what constitutes a statement in the language. If a language has a formal syntax, then text in the language can be processed mechanically to determine whether the text is a statement in the language. Again, this idea is familiar from the use of compilers that detect syntax errors in programs. With one common definition of what constitutes a statement in the language, there is no need for interpretation by the reader as occurs frequently in natural languages.

Formal semantics permit dependable communication between all parties who have to write or read statements in the language. Whereas natural language relies upon our experience to provide us with meaning, formal language semantics are defined in term of mathematics, and that provides completeness and freedom from ambiguity.

An important caveat has to be noted about formal semantics. The formal languages that we use typically in specification are not connected to any real-world concepts. Technically, formal languages are *uninterpreted*. Thus, using a term from the real world in a formal-language statement does not mean that the human concept is in any sense part of the semantics of the formal language. As far as the language is concerned, the term is just a symbol.

Formal semantics for a formal language define how the various constructs in the language manipulate the symbols being used. A simple example is the logical operator $\wedge$. Most people are familiar with the semantics of an expression such as $a \wedge b$. A more complex example is the semantics of an `if` statement in a high-level lan-

```
┌─── IntegerSort ────────────────────────────────────────────────
│  Input?     :    ℙ ℕ
│  Output!    :    seq ℕ
│
├──────────────────────
│  ( ( (#Input? < 100)                                        ∧       ⎫
│    (∀i       :    ℕ | i ∈ Input? • i < 1000)               ∧       ⎬ Pre-condition
│    (∀j       :    ℕ | j ∈ Input? • j ∈ Output!)            ∧       ⎫
│    (∀k       :    ℕ | k ∈ Output! • k ∈ Input?)            ∧       ⎬ Post-condition
│    (∀l       :    1..#Output!−1 • Ouput!(l) ≤                      ⎭
│  Output!(l+1) ) )
│
│                            ∨
│  (¬(#Input? < 100) ∨ (∃i : ℕ | i ∈ Input? • i > 1000) ∧
│
└────────────────────────────────────────────────────────────────
```

FIGURE 8.2 A simple formal specification of sorting written in Z.

guage program. Again, most people are familiar with the semantics of a statement such as:

```
if x > y then x := 1 else x := 2;
```

For both examples, however, note that the semantics refer just to how the formal language operates. Nothing is said about the real-world semantics in either example. What are a and b in the expression? What is x in the if statement? There is no real-world interpretation of any variable.

Formal language semantics do not include answers to questions such as these. The real-world semantics must be stated separately and have to be stated in natural language. This is why the notions of meaningful identifiers and comprehensive comments are stressed in efforts to make formal statements clear to their readers.

Except for programming languages, formal languages tend to be unfamiliar to software engineers. In fact, the languages are far easier to read and write than they appear. An example of a simple formal specification written in Z[2] is shown in Figure 8.2. Z is a convenient language to use, because much of the notation is identical to traditional discrete mathematics. So anybody who has studied things like sets and the predicate calculus in a course on discrete mathematics will find Z familiar and pretty much as easy to read as the original mathematical symbols.

Even without having studied Z, one can infer quite a lot about the meaning of this simple example. The name at the top seems likely to describe what the specification is about. Using that assumption, we can infer that this specification probably

---

2. Details of Z are introduced in Section 8.6.

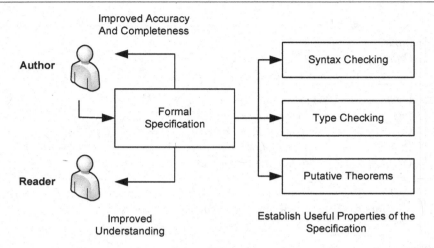

FIGURE 8.3 The benefits of formal specification include enabling improved accuracy and completeness by the author of the specification, improved understanding by readers of the specification, and the opportunity to analyze the specification by checking the syntax, type rules, and various properties.

describes integer sorting. The two labels, "pre-condition" and "post-condition", are not part of the specification. These labels identify (a) the condition that must hold before the specification can be applied, the *pre-condition*, and (b) the condition that must hold after the specification has be applied, the *post-condition*.

With these intuitive notions and a little background in discrete mathematics, the meaning of much of the specification is clear. For example, the first term:

$$\#Input? \quad < \quad 100$$

states that the cardinality (#) of the set *Input?* has to be less than 100. In other words, this specification is stating that the associated program need only deal with files containing less than 100 numbers to sort.

You can probably make good guesses about what most of the specification states. This insight is important, because understanding something like this example without much explanation illustrates the idea that using discrete mathematics in a formal specification is *not* especially difficult. At least, understanding something like this example is not very difficult. We will study this example in more depth in Section 8.7.

8.4.2 Benefits of Formal Languages

The formality of formal specification languages brings many advantages in the areas of understanding and analysis. These advantages, shown in Figure 8.3, are:

Improved understanding. Formal languages are much more precise than natural languages. A formal specification informs the reader much more effectively than a natural-language specification.

Improved accuracy and completeness. By writing specifications in a formal notation and using a rigorous structure, developers tend to create better artifacts. In part, this effect seems to be because of the relatively rigid structure of formal languages. Statements have to be made with a specific syntax, and the semantics available tend to constrain the way that statements can be made.

Syntax checking. The syntax of the language is completely formal, and that means that the syntax can be checked. Any deviation from the defined syntax of the language can be detected (by a program that is much like a compiler) and corrected by the author. Without syntax errors, a formal specification is much more likely to be correct.

Type checking. Just as strongly typed programming languages can help increase dependability so can strongly typed specification languages. Types are one of the basic building blocks of any formal language, and violations of the type rules in a specification are a strong indication of errors. The types can be checked to make sure that we have not violated the type rules, and some simple forms of completeness can be checked, case analysis, for example, to make sure that nothing has been left out.

The first two of these advantages accrue merely from the use of a formal specification language. No tools are needed and so they can be applied immediately. Importantly, these two advantages are also of great value. Understanding, accuracy, and completeness tend to be much higher with formal specification. The second two advantages require tools, but the ones needed are among the most commonly available.

A fifth advantage that arises with the use of formal specification languages is the possibility of analysis with *putative or speculative theorems*. With a specification written in a formal language, a determination can be made about whether the specification possesses certain expected properties. In general, a putative theorem is expected to be true, taking the specification as a set of axioms. For example, the engineer writing the specification might expect that (a) certain states can never be reached, (b) certain variables maintain a particular relationship, (c) certain events cannot occur, and so on. Such expectations can be stated as theorems, and, if the expectation follows from the specification, then the theorem can be proved from the specification. If the implementation implements the specification properly, then the implementation will have the same property.

The overall effect of using formal languages for specification is a significant reduction in specification defects. Some types of defect, such as those that come from the incorrect use of types, can be eliminated completely. Others, such as failing to state how certain input values are to be handled, can also be eliminated if the type of the input is properly stated. With the type properly defined, checking to see whether each element of the type has been included in the specification of input processing is possible. Finally, the clarity and structure of formal languages permit effective human review of specifications so that larger numbers of defects can be found by human inspections.

Many case studies on the use of formal specification languages have been conducted, and they have generally supported the notion that formal languages provide a variety of advantages. In particular, case studies have shown that formal languages tend to promote specifications of far higher quality than typically are produced when using natural language [27, 31, 39, 40, 72].

8.4.3 Presentation of Formal Languages

The benefit of using any formal language can be lost with sloppy presentation. This idea should be familiar from programming in high-level languages where engineers are admonished to indent carefully, to use meaningful identifiers, to leave white space between statements and subprograms to indicate structure, etc. Programs in high-level languages are often difficult to understand, and careful layout helps readers significantly.

The general rule to follow in specification is to do as much as possible to make the formal text as clear as possible. Simple rules to follow to promote clarity are:

- Use whatever structuring mechanisms are available in the language to structure the text. In Z, the primary structuring mechanism is the schema.

- Use vertical white space to delimit and emphasize major parts of the formal text. More space can be used before and after more significant parts.

- Use spacing within individual lines to separate operators and operands so as to delimit and emphasize the structure within the line.

- Use meaningful identifiers to help explain the formal statement to the reader. Long identifiers are not wrong and can add immense value. They take a little longer to type, but they can greatly reduce the time needed to read the formal statement.

- Where more than one adjacent line has the same overall layout, tab the contents so that the major constituent parts are in columns. Declarations, for example, often occur in groups with one per line, and declarations have a unique format in essentially all formal languages. The syntactic structure of a declaration is often something like this:

```
<variablenames>        :    <type>
```

By spacing within the lines to have the variable names begin in the same column, the colons to appear in the same column, and the type names begin in the same column, location of all the items is much easier for the reader. Here is an example in Z — understanding the syntax does not matter for the moment; appreciating the readability does:

Computers_on_line	:	$\mathbb{P}$ *Computers*
Number_of_servers	:	$\mathbb{N}_1$
Login_user_limit	:	$\mathbb{N}_1$
MAC_addresses	:	*Computer* $\leftrightarrow \mathbb{N}_1$

A good rule of thumb is that if the appearance of the text you are writing in a language like Z is not clear and attractive to you, then the text will probably quickly become impenetrable to others. In that case, rework the appearance. Some of the details of this topic are discussed in the example in Section 8.8.

8.4.4 Types of Formal Languages

High-level programming languages like Java are called *procedural languages*, because the program defines a procedure that the engineer wants the computer to follow. The program is essentially a sequence of statements saying to the computer:

> *"Do this,*
> *now do this,*
> *now do this,*
> *now do this,*
> *..."*

By stating the desired actions of the computer this way, the engineer is defining the algorithm and the data structures that are needed to achieve the desired computation. The actual desired computation is not stated explicitly, and determining what the desired computation is by looking at a procedural statement is usually quite difficult. Procedural languages say "how" something is to be done, not "what" is to be done.

Two different types of language are used for formal specification:

- **Declarative languages**. Declarative languages state the desired computation explicitly by defining the state in which the computer is required to be after the computation. Nothing is said about how the computation is to be achieved.

- **Functional languages**. Functional languages state the desired computation by defining a function that will achieve the computation. The computation is frequently stated in a declarative way, and so functional languages are in many ways special cases of declarative languages.

In practice, declarative languages are the most common and most important formal specification languages. Some example languages are Z, VDM, Larch, and RSML. PVS is an example of a functional specification language. In contrast to procedural languages, declarative languages say "what" is to be done, not "how" something is to be done.

8.4.5 Discrete Mathematics and Formal Specification

All general-purpose formal specification languages are based on discrete mathematics. In particular, the languages make heavy use of topics such as the propositional calculus, the predicate calculus including the quantifiers, set theory, relations, functions, and sequences.

An important difference between familiar procedural languages and declarative formal specification languages is the meaning of the equal sign, "=". In many programming languages, such as C, C++, and Java, the equal sign has been given the meaning of assignment. In C, for example, the statement:

```
c = a + b;
```

means fetch the values of a and b, add them together, and make the result the new value of c.

Assignment is not the meaning that the equal sign has in traditional mathematics, including discrete mathematics. In most cases, mathematics does not include the notion of assignment.

In formal specification, the meaning of the equal sign is *equality* in the sense of the predicate calculus. In a mathematical context, the statement above is a predicate that is true if c equal the sum of a and b, and the statement is false otherwise. Thinking of assignment rather than equality in specification (which is both tempting and easy to do) can be very misleading.

8.4.6 The Before and After State

In declarative languages, a mechanism is needed that permits reference to pieces of the state both before an operation has been applied and after the operation has been applied. For example, if an integer variable is part of the state and the integer's value is updated by an operation, reference to the variable both before the operation and afterwards is necessary in order to be able to describe the effect of the needed operation. If the variable is named i, then referring to i in two different ways is necessary, and so we need a notation that will identify the two circumstances.

In formal specification languages, a prime character is often used to indicate a reference to a variable, either before or after an operation. Which of the two uses the prime has depends on the particular language, although the use of the prime itself is almost universal.

As an example, suppose that an operation has to ensure that a variable named i in the system state has a value after the operation which is one more than its value before the operation. What that means is that the value of i in the state after the operation must be equal to the value of i in the before state plus one. Using the prime to designate the after state and the equal sign to mean equality, such a predicate might be expressed as:

$$i' = i + 1$$

Note carefully that this is a *predicate* and that the symbol "=" means *equality*.

8.4.7 A Simple Specification Example

An example that illustrates the contrast between procedural, declarative, and natural languages is the following simple specification of integer square root. For an integer square root of a positive integer input operand, the computation has to determine the greatest integer that, when squared, in less than or equal to the input operand. Admittedly, this is not a very useful computation.

The desired calculation in this example is the integer square root of a quantity x that is assumed to have a value by some means. The output is computed in the variable y:

- **Procedural specification:**

```
integer y;
read (x);

if x > 0 then
    y := x;
    while y**2 > x loop
        y := y - 1;
    end loop;
end if;

print (y);
```

This piece of program states how the computation should be carried out.

- **Declarative specification:**

$$(x > 0) \land (x \geq y'^2) \land (x < (y'+1)^2)$$

This logic statement states what properties the input parameter has to have in order for this operation to be applicable and what we want the final state of the computation to be. Note the use of the prime on y' to indicate the after state for the variable y.

- **Natural language specification:**

*The program **shall** read one positive input and write one output that is the integer square root of the input. The output squared **shall** be less than or equal to the input and the output+1 squared **shall** be greater than the input.*

The word "shall" is emphasized here because that has become common practice in the development of specifications in English. There is an informal and incomplete relationship between the use of "shall" and individual actions that the software has to perform. With the word "shall" emphasized, human review of specifications can be guided by the occurrence of the word.

8.5 Model-Based Specification

One of the problems with writing specifications in any notation is determining what the structure of the resulting specification should be. When writing a program in a high-level language, the language itself dictates what the overall form of a program has to be. Formal specification languages do the same thing for specifications.

In practice, the primary structure used with formal specification using declarative languages is *model-based specification*[3]. The name, model-based specification, derives from the fact that this structure is essentially a model of the desired system. This structure has two major parts:

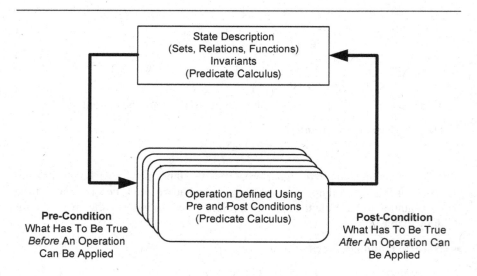

FIGURE 8.4 The basic structure of a model-based specification.

---

3. Model-based specification is not related to model-based development discussed in Chapter 7.

A definition of the state upon which the desired computation will operate.

This definition uses the various mathematical structures from discrete mathematics, such as sets, relations, and functions.

The state definition is itself in two parts: (a) the definitions of a set of variables and their associated types and (b) a set of invariants on the variables in the state. The invariants are predicates that must always be true for any implementation that meets the specification. A common use of invariants is to limit the range of values that a variable can take where the type of the variable does not permit the limitation.

Definitions of the operations in the desired computation.

The computations are expressed using *pre-* and *post-conditions* on the state. The pre-condition for an operation is a predicate that states what has to be true about the state before the operation can be applied, and the post-condition for an operation is a predicate that states what has to be true about the state after the operation is applied.

The structure of an operation is, therefore, quite simple. The structure will consist of the declaration of variables that the operation either reads or modifies together with a conjunction of the pre-condition and the post-condition. The pre-condition and the post-condition might consist of many terms and so could be quite long and complex.

The general form of a model-based specification is shown in Figure 8.4. There is a lot of similarity between this structure and programs written in high-level languages. A high-level language program declares a collection of variables that will be manipulated and subprograms or methods that will operate on those variables. For many people, developing specifications in formal languages turns out to be fun in the same sense as programming, despite the use of discrete mathematical structures!

The assumption with a model-based specification is that the various operations that have been defined could be applied to the state at any point. Control of operation sequences is specified using the various pre-conditions.

8.5.1 Using a Model-Based Specification

A model-based specification is fundamentally a collection of predicates, one for each invariant and one for each operation. This is quite different from what one might see in an ad hoc natural-language specification. A question that then arises is: "How is the specification used?" The answer is twofold:

- The specification defines for the developer precisely what the software has to do.

- The specification can be analyzed to provide all of the stakeholders with increased confidence in the specification.

The basic principle of model-based specification is that the specification is a statement of what the software has to make true during execution. There is an implied statement associated with the specification that says:

> *"Build an implementation that makes the*
> *logic statements in the specification true."*

Thus, the software developer's task is to write software to achieve this. In the case of the integer square root example (see Section 8.4.7), the output of a program could be anything, but, if the program is to implement the specification, then the output must make the predicate true. So if the input is 10, the output must be 3 because 3^2 is less than 10 and 4^2 is not. Similarly, the output could not be 2 because, although 2^2 is less than 10, 3^2 is also and the specification precludes that.

In developing a formal specification, we take advantage of the opportunity for analysis throughout the development. Thus, even when just a small part of the specification has been written, we can test what we have written to make sure that the embryonic specification obeys the language's syntax rules. We can do the same with the types. Developing the specification is best undertaken iteratively, so we can repeat these analyses periodically.

After syntax and type checking, the third form of analysis that we have available is to establish properties of the specification. There are many properties that can be established, but a simple example is to make sure that the invariants cannot be violated. Recall that an invariant is a predicate defined on the variables of the state that must not be violated by the various operations.

As an example, suppose that there is an integer, i, in the state, and that there is also an invariant which requires the value of i to always be less than 10. In other words, the specification states something like this (in no specific language):

```
i   :   integer
i   <   10
```

If there were an operation that contained the predicate:

```
i' =  i + 1
```

then an implementation of the operation should check that the invariant was maintained properly, but that check would require that the developer examine every operation and every invariant. If the implementation did not check, the invariant might be maintained during operation, or it might not. Maintenance of the invariant would depend on the actual sequence of operations that were executed.

The operation should have been specified to include either a pre-condition on the value of i or a check to make sure that the invariant would not be violated. A modification of the operation might then be:

```
(i < 9)    =>      (i' = i + 1)
```

In complex specification, making sure that such pre-conditions and checks are included in specifications cannot be completed properly and reliably by human inspection. The check can be completed mechanically, however. The approach is to state a theorem that the invariant will be maintained no matter what sequence of operations occurs, and then to try to prove that theorem using the statements in the specification as axioms. In the example above in its original form, attempts to prove such a theorem would fail.

8.6 The Declarative Language Z

Z (pronounced "zed") is a formal language that was originally proposed by Jean-Raymond Abrial in 1977. Z was developed subsequently at various locations but primarily the University of Oxford in the United Kingdom. Z has been used widely in industrial applications. There are several textbooks available for Z (for example [108, 71, 154, 134]), and a few tools that can check the syntax and types[4].

Z includes much of the discrete mathematics with which people are familiar, and the notation that Z uses is, for the most part, the same notation that is used in traditional discrete mathematics. Before discussing the use of Z, we review some of this mathematics using the Z syntax. This review is not a comprehensive introduction to the discrete mathematics of specification; the review is intended to be a refresher.

After the review of discrete mathematics, we look at the use of Z using two examples. This review of Z is also brief and covers only the major parts of the language. Z is a large language, and the details can be found in the texts mentioned above. The purpose of this survey is to look at specification in Z with sufficient depth that (a) you can see how a declarative language is used in specification, (b) become familiar enough with Z that you will be able to read and understand simple Z specifications, and (c) be ready to study Z further if necessary so as to be able to write Z specifications. With this background, you can easily acquire the details of the language using other sources.

8.6.1 Sets

A set is an unordered collection of items without replication. Sets can be defined either (a) by enumeration of all the elements as a list or (b) by comprehension in which a set is defined by selecting elements from an existing set. Here are some examples of each:

$$
\begin{aligned}
colors &= \{red, green, blue, orange, white\} \\
computers &= \{Lenovo, IBM, Dell, Gateway\} \\
squares &= \{i : \mathbb{N}_1 \mid i > 5 \wedge i < 10 \bullet i^2\} = \{36, 49, 64, 81\}
\end{aligned}
$$

---

4. A useful tool developed by Anthony Hall for working with Z using Word on Microsoft Windows can be downloaded from: `http://sourceforge.net/projects/zwordtools/`

The first and second examples are sets defined by enumeration. The third example is a set comprehension using the Z notation with the following parts:

$i : \mathbb{N}_1$ -   Declaration of the variable i to be a natural number.

$i > 5 \land i < 10$ -   Predicate restricting the values in the set to those for which the predicate is true.

i^2 -   Expression defining the values of the set elements from the values of the bound variable.

Z (like most similar languages) includes several predefined sets:

$\mathbb{N}$ –   *The set of natural numbers*:

   $\mathbb{N} = \{0, 1, 2, 3, 4, ... \}$

$\mathbb{N}_1$ –   *The set of positive natural numbers*:

   $\mathbb{N}_1 = \{1, 2, 3, 4, ... \}$

$\mathbb{Z}$ –   *The set of integers*

   $\mathbb{Z} = \{ ... -4, -3, -2, -1, 0, 1, 2, 3, 4, ... \}$

Sometimes we need to talk about a set for which we do not know the contents. In Z these are known as *given sets*, and their declaration just needs a name:

$$[files, \; users, \; cities]$$

In this example, three given sets are defined.

The basic set operators are shown in Table 8.1:

$\#A$	Cardinality	Number of elements in A
$a \in A$	Membership	a is an element of A
$A \cup B$	Union	Elements that are in A or B
$A \cap B$	Intersection	Elements that are in A and also in B
$A \subset B$	Proper subset	Elements of A are in B, but $\#A < \#B$
$A \subseteq B$	Subset	Elements of A are in B
$A \setminus B$	Difference	Elements in A but not in B
$\mathbb{P} \, A$	Powerset	Set of all subsets of A

TABLE 8.1. Basic set operators.

8.6.2 Propositions and Predicates

A *proposition* is a statement that is either true or false. Here are some examples in English:

   Valid user ID entered.

   Correct password entered.

   The file system is full.

The printer is out of paper.

The backup file system is not operational.

Propositional variables are associated with propositions to allow expressions to be defined conveniently. Natural language text is not part of Z. The first proposition above might be represented by the symbol "*ValidID*" and the second by the symbol "*CorrectPW*".

Separate propositions can be combined with the propositional operators:

$\vee$	*OR*
$\wedge$	*AND*
$\neg$	*NOT*
$\Rightarrow$	*IMPLICATION*
$\Leftrightarrow$	*EQUIVALENCE*

The meaning of each of the propositional operators is defined by the associated truth tables shown in Table 8.2:

A	B	$\neg A$	$A \vee B$	$A \wedge B$	$A \Rightarrow B$	$A \Leftrightarrow B$
F	F	T	F	F	T	T
F	T	T	T	F	T	F
T	F	F	T	F	F	F
T	T	F	T	T	T	T

TABLE 8.2. Truth tables for the propositional operators.

Here are some examples of useful propositional expressions whose meanings can be inferred immediately:

$$(ValidID \quad \wedge \quad CorrectPW) \vee (UserID = root) \Rightarrow Login$$

$$Filesystemfull \quad \Rightarrow \quad System\_Shutdown$$

A *predicate* is an expression that is either true or false when the variables in the expression are given values. Predicates are familiar from high-level-language programming, because predicates are used in Boolean expressions. Here are some examples:

$$CPUUtilization \quad > \quad 0.80$$

$$FileLength \quad < \quad 1000000000$$

Simple predicates like this can be combined with the propositional operators to form more complex and useful propositions such as this:

$$(CPUUtil > 0.80) \wedge (Filesyssize > 0.99) \Rightarrow SystemShutdown$$

Z includes "decoration" of variable names in the form of special characters appended to the name, to indicate something of their purpose. Of particular importance are the "?" that indicates an input variable, and "!" that indicates an output variable. Here are some examples:

$numberofnewrecords$?   : $\mathbb{N}_1$

$calculatedsizeoffile$!   : $\mathbb{N}_1$

8.6.3 Quantifiers

Propositions and predicates are useful tools, and they allow us to define conditions that are important in the specification of software. But propositions that need to be defined over sets of values can become too large to consider writing down. The quantifiers solve the problem.

There are two common quantifiers:

$\exists$ -   The existential quantifier meaning:
                             "there exists at least one".

$\forall$ -   The universal quantifier meaning:
                             "for all".

The quantifiers allow us to define predicates that cover a complete set without having to enumerate all the elements of the set. The syntax of the quantifiers is:

$\exists$ *declaration_of_bound_variables* | *predicate*1 • *predicate*2

$\forall$ *declaration_of_bound_variables* | *predicate*1 • *predicate*2

with the following meanings:

declaration_of_bound_variables :

   The declaration of variables whose scope is just the quantifier in which the declaration appears — the variables are "bound" to the quantifier.

*predicate*1 :

   This predicate restricts the values of the bound variables.

*predicate*2 :

   The predicate defines the truth value of the quantifier.

The symbols in the quantifiers can be read conveniently as English phrases:

$\exists$	there exists	|	such that	•	for which
$\forall$	for all	|	such that	•	it is the case that

Here is an example of an existential quantifier:

$\exists file : system \mid modified(file)$ • $size(file) > 1000$

In this example, a bound variable *file* of type *system* is declared. The quantifier reads:

"There exists a file of type system such that the file is modified
for which the size of the file is greater than 1,000 units."

Here is an example of a universal quantifier:

$$\forall file : system \mid modified(file) \bullet backup(file)$$

In this example, the quantifier reads:

"For all files of type system such that the file has been modified
it is the case that the file is backed up."

Once you gain confidence with the quantifiers and have some practice, you will be able to take these literal translations into English and rearrange the spoken or textual form to be less jaded. For example, you might read the first quantifier as:

"There is a modified system file that is bigger than 1,000 units."

Making this switch is fine as long as this informal version is not used in any engineering context other than you gaining insight into the formalism.

8.6.4 Cross Products

A cross product, denoted by the symbol ×, is a set of 2-tuples, i.e., a set of items that are ordered pairs. The two elements of each ordered pair come from sets. The elements of the product take on the value of every element in the associated source sets. Here is an example:

$$x \quad = \quad \{a, b, c\}$$
$$y \quad = \quad \{r, s\}$$
$$x \times y \quad = \quad \{(a, r), (a, s), (b, r), (b, s), (c, r), (c, s)\}$$

Interesting cross products can be defined even if the two sets are the same. Consider, for example:

$$\mathbb{N}_1 \times \mathbb{N}_1 \quad = \quad \{(1, 1), (1, 2) \dots (2, 1), (2, 2), \dots \}$$

This cross product defines all the points in the upper right quadrant of the plane that have integer coordinates.

8.6.5 Relations, Sequences, and Functions

A *relation* is a cross product (and therefore a set of 2-tuples) in which the 2-tuples are restricted to those that are defined by a binary relation. The binary relation can be anything useful to us in which we need to define ordered pairs.

The definition of the relation can be by enumeration or be algebraic. The set from which the first element of each 2-tuple of a relation is selected is the *source set*, and the subset of the source set that actually is used in the relation is the *domain* of the relation. The set from which the second element of each 2-tuple is selected is the *target set*, and the subset of the target set that actually is used is the *range* of the relation. Here is an example of a relation defined by enumeration along with its domain and range:

$$telephone\_numbers \quad = \quad \{john \mapsto 2673, jim \mapsto 2893, joe \mapsto 2806\}$$
$$dom\ telephone\_numbers \ = \quad \{john, jim, joe\}$$
$$rng\ telephone\_numbers \ = \quad \{2673, 2893, 2806\}$$

A *sequence* is a relation whose first element set is the integers in order beginning with one. Z has a special syntax to allow sequences to be defined conveniently. Here is an example of a sequence and what it means as a relation:

$$people\_in\_queue \qquad = \quad \langle john, joe, jim \rangle$$
$$\{1 \mapsto john, 2 \mapsto joe, 3 \mapsto jim\}$$

Sequences are a convenient structure for modeling information that we might implement with an array.

A *function* is a relation in which each element of the domain maps to at most one element of the range. The concept of a function leads to a set of special types of function shown in Table 8.3:

Function Type	Z Symbol	Meaning
Partial	$\nrightarrow$	The most general type of function. Some elements of the source set are not mapped.
Total	$\rightarrow$	All elements of the source set are mapped.
Injection	$\rightarrowtail$ $\rightarrowtail$	The inverse mapping is also a function. An injection can be partial or total.
Surjection	$\twoheadrightarrow$ $\twoheadrightarrow$	There is a mapping to every element of the range. A surjection can be partial or total.
Bijection	$\rightarrowtail\!\!\!\twoheadrightarrow$	The function is both an injection and a surjection.

TABLE 8.3. The various types of function and their representation symbol in Z.

8.6.6 Schemas

The basic structures of discrete mathematics provide much of the machinery needed for specification. What is needed next is a mechanism for organizing these structures into a form that can be used to describe large specifications. The mechanism used is Z is the *schema*.

A schema is a named graphic with two mathematical parts: the *signature* in which variables are declared and the *predicate* that is just a predicate on the variables. Both the signature and the predicate can refer to both before-state and after-state (primed) variables, thereby providing the facilities needed for model-based specification (see Section 8.5). An example of a simple schema is shown in Figure 8.5. The name of the schema is *Counter*. The schema declares a single variable called *CounterValue* that is an integer. From the type of *CounterValue*, $\mathbb{N}_1$, we know that the variable has to be positive. The predicate in the schema tells us that the value of the variable has to be less than or equal to 10.

Schemas whose predicates do not include after-state variables are used to define elements of the state in a model-based specification. Schemas whose predicates do include after-state variables are used to define operations. The predicate in a state schema defines an invariant on the state. Since the invariant might include several conjuncts, each involving a different variable, the predicate in a state schema is commonly thought of as a collection of invariants.

8.6.7 The Schema Calculus

Schemas have a precise syntax and semantics, and they can be manipulated as mathematical structures. The mechanism of this manipulation is the *schema calculus*. The schema calculus is a sophisticated and complex theory that we can only mention here. The schema calculus includes schema composition, schema expressions, and schema types. The calculus allows elaborate elements of specification to be defined simply and elegantly.

Decoration (such as the ? and ! decoration of variables described in Section 8.6.2) is also used for Z schemas in the form of prefix characters. The Delta symbol, Δ, when prepended to a state schema, defines a new schema consisting of the original together with the same text but with all variables primed. The invariant is included also with primed variables. This meaning is the result of using the Δ decoration, and the specifier can use the resulting schema freely without defining it. An example of the definition of the schema $\Delta Counter$ is shown in Figure 8.6. The Xi symbol, Ξ, when prepended to a schema name, creates a schema that consists of the Δ schema with an additional invariant that the state will not be changed. Including such decorated state schemas in operation schemas provides convenient access to the state and the invariant predicate.

```
┌─── Counter ──────────────────────────────────────
│   CounterValue        :    ℕ₁
├──────────────────────────────────────────────────
│   CounterValue        ≤    10
│
└──────────────────────────────────────────────────
```

FIGURE 8.5 A simple Z schema.

$$
\begin{array}{|l|}
\hline
\;\;\Delta Counter \rule{3cm}{0pt} \\
\;\;CounterValue,\ CounterValue' \qquad : \quad \mathbb{N}_1 \\
\hline
\;\;CounterValue \qquad \leq \quad 10 \\
\;\;CounterValue' \qquad \leq \ \ 10 \\
\hline
\end{array}
$$

FIGURE 8.6 The definition of a schema including the Δ decoration.

8.7 A Simple Example

Figure 8.7 is the same simple example that specifies integer sort which we saw in Figure 8.2 on page 227. The specification consists of a single schema. In the signature part, two variables are declared. The input variable, *Input?*, is a set of natural numbers. The output variable, *Output!*, is a sequence of natural numbers.

The predicate is a single expression that is eight lines long and is in two major parts. The first two and the seventh lines of the predicate are the pre-condition for the operation, and the third, fourth, fifth, and eighth lines are the post-condition. Line six is just an operator.

The meaning of these lines in the predicate is:

$$
\begin{array}{|l|}
\hline
\;\;\;\;\;IntegerSort \rule{3cm}{0pt} \\
\;\;Input? \qquad : \quad \mathbb{P}\,\mathbb{N} \\
\;\;Output! \qquad : \quad seq\,\mathbb{N} \\
\hline
\\
\;\;(((\#Input? < 100) \hfill \wedge \\
\;\;(\forall i \qquad : \quad \mathbb{N}\mid i \in Input? \bullet i < 1000) \hfill \wedge \\
\;\;(\forall j \qquad : \quad \mathbb{N}\mid j \in Input? \bullet j \in Output!) \hfill \wedge \\
\;\;(\forall k \qquad : \quad \mathbb{N}\mid k \in Output! \bullet k \in Input?) \hfill \wedge \\
\;\;(\forall l \qquad : \quad 1..\#Output!-1 \bullet Ouput!(l) \leq Output!(l+1))) \\
\qquad\qquad\qquad\qquad\qquad\qquad \vee \\
\;\;(\neg(\#Input? < 100) \vee (\exists i : \mathbb{N}\mid i \in Input? \bullet i > 1000) \wedge \\
\;\;(Msg! = ``Invalid\ input"))) \\
\hline
\end{array}
$$

FIGURE 8.7 Simple example of a declarative specification in Z.

- Line 1 states that the size of the input set must be less than 100.

- Line 2 states that the value of every element of the input set must be less than 1,000.
  These two lines ensure that the program which implements the specification will have to deal with less than 100 numbers, each of which must be less than 1,000. If either line 1 or line 2 were false, then this part of the pre-condition would be false.

- Line 3 states that every number that is in the input set must also be in the output sequence.

- Line 4 states that every number in the output sequence must appear in the input set.

- Line 5 states that all but the last number in the output sequence must be less than or equal to the next number in the sequence, i.e., the numbers in the sequence must be in sorted order.

- Line 7 is the opposite of lines 1 and 2, and so line 7 will be true if either of lines 1 and 2 were false. This expression ensures that the total pre-condition for the specification is *true*. In other words, the resulting program should be able to deal with any input. This does not mean that the program can sort any file. A pre-condition that is a tautology means that the program will never fail to do something that was specified, no matter what the input is.

- Line 8 states that a message is to be printed if the data is not suitable for sorting.

This example is reasonably complete, but makes a simplifying assumption that then makes the specification quite a bit simpler. The simplifying assumption is that there will be no repeated values in the input. This assumption is inherent in the fact that the input is stated to be a set. Uniqueness of the elements is a characteristic of sets.

The way that this simplifying assumption makes the specification simpler lies in the fact that the output of a sort has to be a permutation of the input. If there are no duplicate elements in the input, then the post-condition as stated in the example is sufficient. But if duplicate elements have to be included, the input structure can no longer be a set, and the post-condition stating that the output is a permutation of the input is correspondingly more difficult. Dealing with this is left as an exercise for the reader.

8.8 A Detailed Example

Suppose that a Z specification is required for a system to maintain a catalog of the books kept in a small library. To develop such a specification, just as with program-

[*ISBN*]

```
┌─── BookCatalog ──────────────────────────────────────────────
│  BooksInLibrary        :    ℙ ISBN
│ ─────────────────────────────────────────────────────────────
│  #BooksInLibrary       ≤    1000
└───────────────────────────────────────────────────────────────
```

```
┌─── AddBook ─────────────────────────────────────────────────
│  Δ BookCatalog
│  NewBook?              :    ISBN
│ ────────────────────────────────────────────────────────────
│  BooksInLibrary'       =    BooksInLibrary ∪ {NewBook?}
└──────────────────────────────────────────────────────────────
```

```
┌─── RemoveBook ──────────────────────────────────────────────
│  Δ BookCatalog
│  OldBook?              :    ISBN
│ ────────────────────────────────────────────────────────────
│  BooksInLibrary'       =    BooksInLibrary \ {OldBook?}
└──────────────────────────────────────────────────────────────
```

FIGURE 8.8 The first iteration of the specification for a simple library catalog system.

ming, things go much more smoothly if the specification is developed iteratively. Iterative development means developing a small part of the specification and checking it over carefully, and then repeating this process until the specification is complete. By proceeding iteratively, maintaining intellectual control of the specification is easier, and defects are much easier to locate.

Checking during each iteration includes visual inspection and analysis such as syntax and type checking. If the evolving specification passes visual inspection, syntax checking, and type checking, then many defects are likely to be absent, and the engineers building the specification will develop substantial confidence in the specification as they proceed.

To illustrate this iterative development approach, four versions of the library example are presented in the rest of this chapter. Each one either adds additional material to the specification or fixes a problem that comes up.

8.8.1 Version 1 of the Example

The first version of the specification is shown in Figure 8.8. At the top of the figure is a schema defining a given set, *ISBN*, that designates the complete set of unique numbers that are used to designate books, *International Standard Book Number*.

The second schema is the single state schema for the specification. In large specifications, the state might be defined by several schemas with various dependencies. In this first version of the example, a set of ISBNs will be used to model the catalog. The state schema includes a predicate which states that the cardinality of the set that models the catalog has to be less than or equal to 1,000. This invariant is to make sure that the catalog does not model more books than there is room for.

The third and fourth schemas are the two operation schemas. One describes how a book is added to the catalog; in the model, the book's ISBN is added to the set of ISBNs. The second operation schema describes how removing a book from the catalog is modeled; the book's ISBN is removed from the set of ISBNs. In both the third and fourth schemas, the post-condition of the operation is the complete predicate part of the schema.

Syntax and type checking of the specification reveal no errors. However, inspection of the operation schemas reveals three major functional mistakes:

- Modeling the addition and removal of books is basically satisfactory, but the addition schema does not necessarily maintain the invariant. The implementation could allow more than 1,000 books to be added.

- Adding a book to the library does not check to make sure that the book is not already in the library. Having multiple copies is something we might want to consider for an advanced version of the library software later, but in this specification, the library is modeled as a *set* of ISBNs, and so there are no duplicates.

- Removal of a book does not check to see that the book to be removed is actually in the library. If the book is not in the library, there is a chance that any implementation of this specification will not check and will try to remove the book from the catalog anyway. The result could easily be a damaged data structure.

These issues can be seen clearly in this preliminary version of the specification, and you might think that we have not achieved very much. But we have started down a path of precision and clarity in specification. The benefits of this path include our ability to see issues such as those we have just discussed. A little experience with the concepts of formal specification and a growing familiarity with notations like Z allow engineers to detect defects in specification with considerable speed and accuracy.

8.8.2 Version 2 of the Example

The second version of the specification is shown in Figure 8.9. All three of the problems noted with the first version have been corrected. In order to maintain the invariant correctly, the pre-condition for the add operation has been extended to include a clause which is false if the number of books in the catalog is not less than 1,000. A clause has been added to the pre-condition of the add operation to check to see whether the book is already in the library. In a similar way, the pre-condition for the remove operation has been extended to include a clause that will only be true if the book to be removed is actually in the library.

Unfortunately, visual inspection of this second version reveals that there is a subtle but important mistake. The mistake is in the post-condition for the operation schema *RemoveBook*. The mistake derives from the fact that the role of the specification is to say:

"Develop an implementation to make the specification logic true."

A careful examination of the post-condition for the *RemoveBook* schema reveals that the following implementation would satisfy the specification:

```
procedure removebook;
    print ("Book not in library.");
end removebook;
```

The reason that this implementation satisfies the specification is that this implementation makes the post-condition true even though this behavior is not what is desired. The post-condition is a disjunction, and the specification will be met by any implementation that makes *either* side of the disjunction true (remember, this is a logical "or"). By printing a message saying that the book is not in the library *even when the book actually is*, the program meets the specification by making line 5 of *RemoveBook* true. We need go no further with the implementation!

This might seem like a hypothetical case that would never arise in practice. Recognizing the mistake is easy with a specification of this size, but a mistake like this could be very difficult to find in a large specification. Thus, care with completeness of the pre- and post-conditions for operations is important.

8.8.3 Version 3 of the Example

The third version of the specification is shown in Figure 8.10. In this version, the error message about the remove operation failing will only be generated when indeed the book that is the subject of the removal is absent from the library.

Now that we have been through three iterations of the specification, we have a specification that passes visual inspection, and both syntax and type checking. The next thing to do is to add functionality to the specification so as to get closer to the final specification that we need.

[*ISBN*]

```
┌─⌐  BookCatalog ────────────────────────
│  BooksInLibrary      :    ℙ ISBN
├─────────────────────────────────────────
│  #BooksInLibrary     ≤    1000
│
└─────────────────────────────────────────
```

```
┌── AddBook ───────────────────────────────────────
│  Δ BookCatalog
│  NewBook?            :    ISBN
├──────────────────────────────────────────────────
│  ((#BooksInLibrary   <    1000                ∧
│  NewBook?            ∉    BooksIhave           ∧
│  BooksInLibrary'     =    BooksInLibrary ∪ {NewBook?})
│                      ∨
│  (#BooksInLibrary    =    1000                ∧
│  BooksInLibrary'     =    BooksInLibrary      ∧
│  Msg!                =    "Library Full.")
│                      ∨
│  (NewBook?           ∈    BooksInLibrary ∧
│  BooksInLibrary'     =    BooksInLibrary ∧
│  Msg!                =    "Book in already in library."))
└──────────────────────────────────────────────────
```

```
┌── RemoveBook ─────────────────────────────────────
│  Δ BookCatalog
│  OldBook?            :    ISBN
├──────────────────────────────────────────────────
│  ((OldBook?          ∈    BooksInLibrary ∧
│  BooksInLibrary'     =    BooksInLibrary \ {OldBook?})
│                      ∨
│  (BooksInLibrary'    =    BooksInLibrary ∧
│  Msg                 =    "Book not in library"))
└──────────────────────────────────────────────────
```

FIGURE 8.9 The second iteration of the specification for a simple library catalog system.

$[ISBN]$

BookCatalog

$BooksInLibrary$: $\mathbb{P}\ ISBN$

$\#BooksInLibrary$ $\leq$ 1000

AddBook

$\Delta\ BookCatalog$
$NewBook?$: $ISBN$

$((\#BooksInLibrary$ $<$ 1000 $\wedge$
$NewBook?$ $\notin$ $BooksIhave$ $\wedge$
$BooksInLibrary'$ $=$ $BooksInLibrary \cup \{NewBook?\})$
$\vee$
$(\#BooksInLibrary$ $=$ 1000 $\wedge$
$BooksInLibrary'$ $=$ $BooksInLibrary$ $\wedge$
$Msg!$ $=$ $"Library\ Full.")$
$\vee$
$(NewBook?$ $\in$ $BooksInLibrary$ $\wedge$
$BooksInLibrary'$ $=$ $BooksInLibrary$ $\wedge$
$Msg!$ $=$ $"Book\ in\ already\ in\ library."))$

RemoveBook

$\Delta\ BookCatalog$
$OldBook?$: $ISBN$

$((OldBook?$ $\in$ $BooksInLibrary$ $\wedge$
$BooksInLibrary'$ $=$ $BooksInLibrary \setminus \{OldBook?\})$
$\vee$
$(OldBook?$ $\notin$ $BooksInLibrary$ $\wedge$
$BooksInLibrary'$ $=$ $BooksInLibrary$ $\wedge$
Msg ' $=$ $"Book\ not\ in\ library"))$

FIGURE 8.10 The third iteration of the specification for a simple library catalog system.

$[ISBN, PeopleIKnow]$

```
┌─── BookCatalog ─────────────────────────────────────────────
│  BooksInLibrary     :   ℙ ISBN
│  BooksOnLoan        :   ℙ ISBN
│  Friends            :   ℙ PeopleIKnow
│  Loans              :   Friends ⤔ ℙ ISBN
│─────────────────────────────────────────────────────────────
│  #BooksInLibrary    ≤   1000
│  BooksOnLoan        ⊆   BooksInLibrary
│
└─────────────────────────────────────────────────────────────
```

```
┌─── BorrowBook ──────────────────────────────────────────────
│  Δ BookCatalog
│  RequestedBook?     :   ISBN
│  Borrower?          :   PeopleIKnow
│─────────────────────────────────────────────────────────────
│  ((Borrower?        ∈   Friends                        ∧
│  RequestedBook?     ∈   BooksInLibrary
│  BooksOnLoan'       =   BooksOnLoan ∪ {RequestedBook?}
│  Loans(Borrower?)'  =   Loans(Borrower?) ∪ {RequestedBook?})
│                         ∨
│  (Borrower?         ∉   Friends                        ∧
│  Msg'               =   "Books only loaned to friends.")
│                     ∨
│  (RequestedBook?    ∉   BooksInLibrary                 ∧
│  Msg'               =   "Book not in library"))
│
└─────────────────────────────────────────────────────────────
```

FIGURE 8.11 The fourth iteration of the specification for a simple library catalog system.

8.8.4 Version 4 of the Example

The functionality to be added is a mechanism to lend books from the catalog to friends. To do this, we do not need to modify the operation schemas for adding and removing books. We will need additional state information, because we will have to keep track of loans and the state schema will need to be extended. We also need to add operation schemas for lending and for returning a book.

The first question that needs to be addressed in this iteration is the approach we will use to modeling books on loan. We will only lend books to friends, but a friend could borrow several books. A suitable way to model this is to add a set of friends and a function that maps each friend to a set of books that the friend has borrowed. The function is partial because only friends who have actually borrowed books are included, and that is unlikely to be all of them.

Version 4 of the specification is much longer than version 3, so only part of the specification is shown in Figure 8.11. A new given set, *PeopleIKnow*, has been added, and a new set, *Friends*, has been added to the state to model the friends of the system user. Finally, a function, *Loans*, has been added to the state schema. *Loans* is a function whose domain is the set *Friends*, and whose range is a set of sets with one for each element of the domain. Thus, each friend who is in the domain of *Loans* maps to a set of books that the friend has borrowed.

The only operation schema shown is the *Borrow* operation. The pre-condition for this operation checks to see whether the request is from a friend and whether the requested book is in the catalog. If either condition is false, then the specification says to print an error message. If the pre-condition is true, then the book requested is added to the set of books in the possession of the person who requested it.

8.9 Overview of Formal Specification Development

Developing a formal specification is a significant challenge, but the challenge is manageable if we proceed carefully. And the benefits are considerable, so facing the challenge is worthwhile.

Using a declarative language that was designed for the task, such as Z, the specification is developed using the model-based specification structure. That structure consists of a set of declarations that define the state and a set of operations that define changes on the state.

The state and the operations are a model of the system being specified. Just like a model car looks like a car, so the model of the system being specified "looks" like the system being specified. Model cars are often used by automobile manufacturers to define what the real car should look like before the car is built. Similarly, architects often use models to describe what a planned building will look like. Sometimes models are graphical, but they still play the role of guiding the creative process and facilitating analysis.

In principle, a model car could guide the builders of the actual car. Always keep in mind that, just as a model car is usually not drivable and not intended to be, a specification is not executable and is not intended to be. There are exceptions to this general rule called *executable specifications*. Such specifications are executable so that the model can be tested in various ways.

The state in a model-based specification is a set of declarations, each of which is a mathematical structure. Some are simple scalar quantities such as integers, and others are more complex like sets and functions.

Operations in a model-based specification are defined by describing the state as it must be before the operation is applied, the pre-condition, and the state after the operation is applied, the post-condition. The pre-condition limits applicability of the operation, and the post-condition defines the desired state change.

The keys to the successful development of a formal specification are iteration and analysis. The specification should be built in a series of steps where a partial specification is constructed at each step. The first step will result in a simple specification in which only part of the state is defined, and in which only a small number of operations are defined. The operations might even be incomplete. At each step the evolving specification is subject to human inspection, and syntax and type checking.

Finally, we return to the topic of presentation introduced in Section 8.4.3. The use of techniques to make a specification more readable is illustrated in the example discussed in Section 8.8.1 to Section 8.8.4. The primary Boolean operators in each expression are carefully isolated so that they stand out. Boolean operators on adjacent lines with similar roles in the specification are placed in the same column. Finally, white space is used to structure and organize the mathematical expressions for ease of understanding.

Key points in this chapter:

- Specification is a critical aspect of software development.
- Natural language has been shown to be problematic as a notation for specification.
- Several formal languages have been developed to permit the development of formal specifications.
- Formal specification languages are typically based on discrete mathematics and are often declarative.
- Z is a specification language in fairly common use.
- Formal specifications enable clearer communication between engineers.
- Z specifications can be analyzed to show various properties.

Exercises

1. Write a *predicate* that is true for a year that is a leap year and false otherwise.

2. Define the *set* of leap years.

3. Write a *pre-condition* and a *post-condition* suitable for documenting a function that computes the maximum element of an array. Use any convenient array notation in the expressions.

4. Assuming the Z given set [Senators] is the set of all members of the U.S. Senate, defining any other items that you need, and using a mathematical notation:

   (a) Define the set consisting of all the Republican senators.

   (b) Define a predicate that is true if and only if there are 50 Democratic senators.

5. A computerized control system is used to control a building's hot water system. A hot-water tank has digital temperature sensors at the top and at the bottom and two heating elements, one at the top and one at the bottom. The control system has access to a simple clock that provides time of day as a count of the number of minutes since midnight. To ensure an adequate supply of hot water, the system uses the following algorithm (all temperatures are Fahrenheit):

   - From 6:00 a.m. to 9:00 a.m. if the temperature at the top of the tank is below 180, the upper heater is turned on and if the temperature at the bottom of the tank is below 120, the bottom heater is turned on.

   - From 1:00 a.m. to 6:00 a.m. if either temperature is below 160, the top heater is turned on.

   - At all other times, if any temperature is below 180, the top heater is turned on, but if the top temperature is below 140, both heaters are turned on.

   Write a formal specification for the water-tank control system in Z.

6. The specification for the water heater in Exercise 5 is quite simple but realistic. If you had this specification and an implementation in C, how would you go about testing the implementation? Pay attention to the real-time elements of the problem and the other basic testing issues that make testing difficult.

7. Define a suitable state and the pre- and post-conditions for each operation of a stack, i.e., develop a formal specification for a stack data structure.

8. Define a formal specification for a simple program that records the MAC addresses of the computers owned by an organization. Assume each computer only has one address, and identify the computers using a serial number assigned by the organization. Include operations to add and delete computers, and to change the MAC address of an existing computer.

9. Below is a possible Z state schema for the cruise-control application in Chapter 5, Exercise 13. The names of the variables indicate their purpose:

```
┌─── Braking_sensors_and_actuators ──────────────────────────
│
│   current_vehicle_speed        :    –31..255
│   speed_set_by_driver          :    32..255
│   current_radar_distance       :    0..4095
│   brake_pedal_pressure         :    0..255
│   acceleration                 :    -255..255
│
└────────────────────────────────────────────────────────────
```

Braking effect is linearly proportional to the brake pedal pressure, and brake pedal pressure is set as an integer in the range 0..255. If vehicle speed is above the set speed or the speed of the vehicle ahead, the brakes are to be applied with braking set to be proportional to the deviation from desired speed. If the radar detects an object at a distance less than 50% more than the vehicle's stopping distance, then the brakes are to be applied at the maximum level. The vehicle stopping distance in feet is (current speed in mph * 1.18).
Write a Z operation schema that specifies brake behavior.

10. After testing the cruise-control system, developers learned that maximum braking to avoid a collision might injure the vehicle's occupants. A linear accelerometer was added to the system, and the specification of emergency braking changed. The accelerometer returns an integer that is 100 times the acceleration in "g"s. Deceleration yields a negative integer from the accelerometer. If the absolute value of acceleration exceeds 1g, then emergency braking has to be reduced. The reduction has to be proportional to the measured deceleration so as to try to make deceleration –1g. Write a Z schema for emergency stopping.

11. The tracking system in the robotic surgery system described in Chapter 3, Exercise 9 monitors infra-red LEDs attached to the patient and the cutting equipment to determine their locations. Each has several LEDs attached. Sometimes the tracking system cannot "see" some of the LEDs because they are blocked by people or equipment. Accuracy requires the following: (a) no more than one LED is blocked on the patient and no more than one on the cutting head, *or* (b) no more than three LEDs are blocked on the patient and none on the cutting head, *or* (c) no more than two LEDs are blocked on the cutting head and none on the patient. Write a Z specification that will signal "off" to the drive motors if any of these conditions arises.

12. The software controlling the cutting mechanism in the robotic surgery system receives from the system's guidance software a three dimensional absolute coordinate to which the cutting head is to be moved from its current location. Each coordinate is a vector of three integers measuring millimeters within an estab-

lished frame of reference. Define suitable variables and write a pre-condition for the move operation which ensures that the requested move is (a) no further than *delta* millimeters from the current position, (b) no more than *gamma* millimeters travel distance in any dimension, and (c) that no coordinate value is greater than a maximum value of *omega* millimeters.

CHAPTER 9

Software Fault Avoidance in Implementation

Learning objectives of this chapter are to understand:

- How faults can be avoided in software implementation using correctness by construction.
- The role of programming languages in software implementation.
- The difficulties that arise with languages like C.
- The advantages of languages designed for dependability such as Ada.
- The role of programming standards.
- The SPARK approach to correctness by construction using low-level specification and mechanical verification.
- How formal verification can be applied easily by practicing engineers.

9.1 Implementing Software

Once we have a specification of what software is to do, we have to develop an implementation that can eventually be executed. Developing an implementation is usually undertaken in a relatively informal way by crafting each line of software by hand in a high-level language. The only exceptions are the application of model-based development and the use of reusable modules that come from libraries.

In this chapter, we resume discussion of the idea of correctness by construction that was introduced in Section 7.4. In particular, we look at the actual implementation of source code with an emphasis on one particular technique, the SPARK approach. We begin by looking at what goes wrong in implementing software so that we can see the scope of the problem and how correctness by construction can help.

9.1.1 Tool Support for Software Implementation

The quality of the finished product relies to a large extent on engineers not making mistakes while engaged for long periods of time in deeply intellectual activities. Fault avoidance is left to engineers' insight and chance, and a great deal of dependence is placed on fault elimination. Typically, engineers have to work without the support of tools that can help them to avoid mistakes. The tools that most software developers have available are:

Editors. Editors facilitate the development of designs in languages such as the various UML notations and source code. Many editors are tied to the syntax of the language that is being edited and provide features such as highlighting language structures. For artifacts that have to be developed in natural language, editors are far more limited.

Compilers. Compilers translate from source code to object code. Some compilers include checks on likely mistakes such as uninitialized variables.

Linkage editors. Linkage editors (or linkers) combine the outputs of multiple compilations together with libraries of standard subprograms.

File systems. File systems are usually just those provided by the underlying operating system.

Revision control systems. Revision control systems support the management of various versions of a software system so that new developments do not overwrite existing versions and that each instance of a system is created from the correct files.

Scripts. Scripts manage the translation process, allowing dependencies between files to be recorded and the necessity of recompilation to be determined.

Sometimes these tools are integrated into a single development environment such as Microsoft's Visual Studio or Eclipse. None of these tools, except compilers and sometimes editors, supports the intellectual activity of actually developing the source code itself.

9.1.2 Developing an Implementation

Software is a set of bits that is stored in the memory of a computer and interpreted by the processor(s). Programmers tend to refer to the source program as the software, but the source program is not the software. As shown in Figure 9.1, the *compiler* translates the source code to object files that are relocated to a standard address and contain symbolic references to other object files. Some of these other object files will have been created by separately compiling parts of a single application and others will have been created as reusable libraries. The *linkage editor* combines the different object files and resolves some of the symbolic references, those that are statically linked. Some links are resolved during execution using dynamic linking. Finally, the *loader* relocates the program to the desired operating address and places the memory image in memory.

Modern development environments effect translation quickly, but, in fact, the translation process is lengthy and complex. The relocated binary software that executes has been processed by three system utilities (although in practice they might be combined from the user's perspective), and these system utilities are themselves large programs. Thus, in thinking about dependability, we must keep in mind the possibility that the system utilities upon which we rely might themselves contain faults that affect software. Our focus in this chapter is on the source code for the software we build. The defects in the system utilities upon which we rely are few and far between, but such defects are not unknown.

9.1.3 What Goes Wrong with Software?

If we look carefully at the problems that arise in software implementation, we see a number of general areas of difficulty:

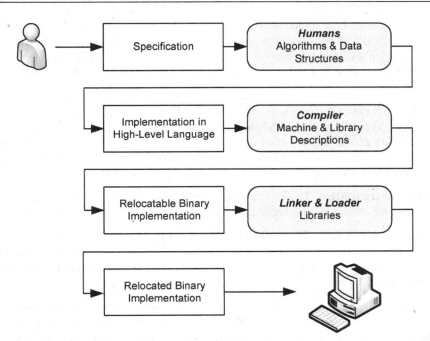

FIGURE 9.1 The creation of software actually requires a lot of processing after the source program has been created. That processing relies on several utilities, starting with the compiler, and any of those utilities might contain defects.

Incorrect functionality. The software implements the wrong functionality. Functionality might be incorrect if the specification was misunderstood, or if the engineer made a mistake in synthesizing the algorithms or data structures that were selected.

Missing functionality. The software omits some aspect of the desired functionality. Again, functionality might be missing if the specification was misunderstood, or if the engineer overlooked the stated specification of functionality.

Incorrect management of resources. The software functions correctly but exhausts available resources. Exhausting resources means running out of processor cycles and missing deadlines, running out of dynamically allocated storage and aborting, or running out of disk space and aborting.

Unanticipated exceptions. An exception is raised for which there is no handler. Exceptions are an unfortunate consequence of the design of many programming languages. Exceptions are raised when a program attempts to undertake some operation that cannot be completed, such as dividing by zero, generating a number that is too large or too small to be represented, or printing when there is no paper in the printer. If such exceptions are anticipated, then the software design will include handlers for the exceptions that will allow the software to continue in what must be assumed is the desired fashion (see also Section 11.6.4). Unfortunately, not all the exceptions that can arise are anticipated. If an unanticipated exception arises and no handler is present, then the software will be at the mercy of the exception semantics of the particular language in which the software was written.

Faults in libraries. Libraries upon which software depends sometimes contain faults. Typically, software depends upon both source and object libraries that are common across projects in an organization and which are, at best, only checked centrally. The libraries might contain faults unless they have been carefully engineered and maintained.

Defects in translation. These defects are those that might be introduced by the compiler, the linkage editor, and the loader.

Configuration defects. The software that executes is not the software that is desired. Configuration defects can occur if the software was linked from the wrong object files or libraries, or if the object files were created by compiling the wrong source files.

In this chapter, we concentrate on creating the source code in a high-level language. Issues such as whether a compiler translates the source code correctly are specialized, but they are also centralized in the sense that many engineers use the same compiler and so a single effort applied to a compiler will benefit many development activities. The source code for a given system is unique to that system, and so the engineers involved in implementation must have suitable techniques to allow the source code to be prepared properly.

9.2 Programming Languages

Programming languages are the primary tools used in implementation. As such, these tools should provide engineers with as much help as possible. That help comes in many forms, but from the perspective of dependability, the help that is needed is help with fault avoidance.

Programming languages cannot guarantee high-quality software. Merely using one language rather than another does not mean that all faults or even a significant fraction will be avoided. However, some language features offer the opportunity for excluding classes of faults from programs if the engineers using the language take advantage of the opportunity. Of course, languages that do not provide such an opportunity can be used to build high-quality software also, but the challenge is much greater because more reliance is being placed on human intellect.

Many features have been developed by programming language designers to facilitate the creation, understanding, and maintenance of software, and almost all of these features also facilitate fault avoidance. Some of the major areas of development in programming languages that support fault avoidance are:

Syntax. The importance of reading as well as writing software has led to substantial improvements in language syntax. Simple things like the alphabet used for symbols, the reserved words used to form language elements, elimination of special cases, and support for comments and "white space" facilitate readability greatly. More complex things like improved scope rules, procedure parameter semantics, and statement forms all tend to make programs clearer.

Basic structuring and abstraction mechanisms: Powerful structuring and abstraction mechanisms have been developed that facilitate both human understanding of software and software fault avoidance. One of the best examples is the notion of object-oriented programming. Objects provide a strong form of information hiding that compilers can check. Many inadvertent mistakes by programmers involve accessing or changing the wrong variable in a program. In an object-oriented language that is used correctly, a change to an instance variable requires the use of an access function. In fact, not only does the programmer not have direct access to instance variables and therefore most of the variables in the program, but he or she might not even know the names of those variables.

Strong typing. The type of a variable defines the set of values that the variable can take and the set of operations in which the variable can engage. An integer, for example, takes on values that are whole numbers which lie in a particular specified range. Integers can be used in arithmetic expressions, array indexing, and so on. Type checking is an analysis mechanism in which the types of variables are examined to make sure that the types of the variables being used match the associated operation. Compilers for languages that include strong type systems can check to make sure that the type rules are not violated, for example, attempting to add a string to a real.

Concurrency. Implementing concurrent activities is a common element of programming. Concurrency used to be restricted to the programming of operating systems, but many uses of concurrency arise in application software and software that covers both the application and systems areas, such as embedded software. Support for concurrency in a programming language allows engineers to state the necessary algorithms completely in one language and also to take advantage of the various creative features that language designers have developed.

Language definition. Increased attention has been paid to the definition of languages, because confusion and ambiguity in language definitions make the jobs of both the compiler writer and the programmer much more difficult. As languages have moved from being defined and maintained by organizations to become international standards, greater care has been exercised in the actual definitions of the languages themselves.

One of the reasons that is cited as a deterrent to the use of languages that support fault avoidance is that their syntax and type mechanisms are inconvenient to use because a lot of detail has to be specified. That detail is largely what helps to avoid faults, and so the detail has a specific purpose. But importantly, helping to avoid faults also helps to reduce the cost of testing and other forms of verification. Overall, therefore, software development costs can be and usually are lower when using these more sophisticated languages, sometimes substantially lower.

9.2.1 The C Programming Language

The impact that programming languages can have is amply demonstrated by C [69]. A brief examination reveals quickly that C provides little help with fault avoidance. The language has a confusing syntax and lacks a comprehensive type system. In addition, C has no language support for concurrency or real-time software, relying instead on the underlying operating system services. C also relies upon the operating-system-supplied linkage editor to support separate compilation, and so there is no type checking of parameters on calls across separately compiled entities. These issues remain for a lot of languages that are derived from C.

An Example of the Difficulties

An example of the difficulties that can arise in software implementation can be seen in a study of the software for the Lucent 5ESS telephone switch reported by

Yu [156]. Although undertaken several years ago, the results of the study are instructive and still relevant.

The 5ESS switch source code is several million lines long, and that software provides sophisticated telephone facilities. Most of the software is written in C. The types of defect reported in the study included:

- Use of uninitialized variables.
- Misuse of break and continue statements.
- Incorrect operator precedence.
- Incorrect loop boundaries.
- Indexing outside arrays.
- Truncation of values.
- Misuse of pointers.
- Incorrect AND and OR tests.
- Use of assignment when equality was intended.
- Bit fields not unsigned or enum.
- Incorrect logical AND and mask operators.
- Preprocessor conditional errors.
- Runaway comment delimiters.
- Unsigned variables and comparisons.
- Misuse of type casting.

All of the defects that were seen are common in programming, so the study was not merely looking at an unusual special case. At the beginning of the study, the subject software was afflicted with defects at a rate of roughly one every 200 non-comment and non-blank source lines. By careful introduction of root-cause analysis and systematic location and removal of the associated software faults, the study team was able to effect a large reduction in both fault density and system test time.

Static Analysis Support for C

Fortunately, separate static analysis systems have been developed for C, and so some of the difficulties can be mitigated in practice. The concept of such systems is to analyze a C program separately from a compiler and to look for violations of "common sense" rules rather than just the basic language rules. Thus, the diagnostics that are produced are not violations of the language definition. Note that the analysis here is *static*, meaning that the analysis is performed on the program without execution. Thus, any results are general and not tied to a specific test case.

Splint [135] is a sophisticated static analysis system for C. Checks on C that Splint makes include type checking across separate compilations, thereby ensuring that parameter type conflicts and differing numbers of actual and formal parameters will be brought to the programmer's attention.

Splint goes beyond common sense checks and provides a number of other powerful facilities. Programmers can annotate their code so as to inform Splint of their intent. The annotations are included as stylized comments so that compilers do not see them but Splint can. Splint reads the annotations and checks the program to the extent possible to make sure that the programmer's annotations hold.

An important property that Splint checks is the status of pointers. Dereferencing a null pointer is a fatal mistake in most programs, and yet a pointer being null on an obscure execution path is difficult to avoid. Splint checks for the possibility of a pointer being null at various points in a program's execution and warns the programmer about this possibility. Annotations can be used to adjust the default checks that Splint performs.

Management of dynamic storage is another major source of faults in software written in C. Not releasing storage that has been acquired from the heap is not initially fatal, but such a fault is, of course, a memory leak. A relatively small investment in annotations allows Splint to perform a fairly comprehensive static analysis of the use of dynamic storage in which many important classes of faults can be detected.

9.3 An Overview of Ada

Languages have been developed that provide substantial support for fault avoidance. One of the most notable is Ada. Engineers tend to be far less familiar with Ada than other languages, and so we present an overview of the major features of Ada in this section.

9.3.1 The Motivation for Ada

The development of Ada was sponsored originally by the U.S. Department of Defense with the specific aim of providing a single language that could be used for software development in many of the Department's complex systems. A project of the size of the development of Ada has many goals, but an important goal for Ada has always been to support the efficient development of correct software. This notion is best described by the following extract from the Ada 2005 Language Reference Manual [3]:

> *"The need for languages that promote reliability and simplify maintenance is well established. Hence emphasis was placed on program readability over ease of writing. For example, the rules of the language require that program variables be explicitly declared and that their type be specified. Since the type of a variable is invariant, compilers can ensure that operations on vari-*

ables are compatible with the properties intended for objects of the type. Furthermore, error-prone notations have been avoided, and the syntax of the language avoids the use of encoded forms in favor of more English-like constructs. Finally, the language offers support for separate compilation of program units in a way that facilitates program development and maintenance, and which provides the same degree of checking between units as within a unit."

Programmers misunderstanding language features is a major cause of faults in programs, and such misunderstandings arise when language designers provide ill-thought-out semantics and/or document language semantics inadequately. An overall feature of Ada that is of immense value in fault avoidance is the precision, care, and consistency of the semantics of language features and their documentation.

The first version of Ada was Ada '83, and there have been two major revisions since then, Ada '95 and Ada 2005. The language reference manual for the latest version of Ada, Ada 2005, documents the language and the standard libraries, and Ada is an international standard (ISO/IEC 8652:1995(E)) [4].

Ada is a large and powerful language with a multitude of features. From the outset, Ada has included support for all of the common programming features, but the language also includes support for concurrency, real-time processing, and operation on bare hardware, i.e., with no operating system. In part, these features are included in the language and defined carefully so as to ensure that Ada programs requiring a capability such as concurrency can be written fully within the language and therefore are able to take advantage of the precise semantics.

The language reference manual is divided into 13 sections that cover major language sections, together with 15 annexes that define additional information but no new language features. Annex A, for example, defines the predefined language environment, Annex B the interface to other languages including C and C++, and Annex C covers systems programming issues such as access to machine operations and interrupts.

9.3.2 Basic Features

Many of the basic features of the language are illustrated in Figure 9.2. This figure is a trivial program designed to show off several language features. As such, there is a lot missing that would be required if this program were to be used in practice, and there are several things in the program that are not needed but are included to make the example more comprehensive. Much of the syntax should be fairly obvious even if you have never seen Ada before, and a lot can be inferred by merely examining the program.

The first thing to note is that this example is a complete program that can be executed. The basic structure is a procedure that starts on line 4. The primary Ada encapsulation mechanism is the package, and lines 1 and 2 provide access to three

```
1      with Ada.Text_IO, Ada.Integer_Text_IO, Bank_Account;
2      use  Ada.Text_IO, Ada.Integer_Text_IO, Bank_Account;
3
4      procedure bank is
5         number_of_accounts    : constant Natural := 100;
6         type account_range       is range 1 .. number_of_accounts;
7         type transaction_type  is (deposit, withdrawal, balance, quit);
8         package Account_IO      is new Ada.Text_IO.Integer_IO (account_range);
9         package Transaction_IO is new Enumeration_IO (transaction_type);
10
11        transaction   : transaction_type;
12        amount         : access Natural;
13        accounts       : array (account_range) of account_type;
14        account_number : account_range;
15
16     begin
17
18        for i in account_range loop
19           create (accounts (i));
20        end loop;
21
22        amount := new Natural;
23
24        begin
25           Put ("Enter account number: ");
26           Account_IO.Get (account_number);
27
28           loop
29             Put ("Enter transaction type: ");
30             Transaction_IO.Get (transaction);
31             exit when transaction = quit;
32
33             case transaction is
34               when deposit =>
35                  Put ("Enter deposit amount: ");
36                  Get (amount.all);
37                  deposit (amount.all, accounts (account_number));
38               when withdrawal =>
39                  Put ("Enter withdrawal amount: ");
40                  Get (amount.all);
41                  withdrawal (amount.all, accounts (account_number));
42               when balance =>
43                  Put ("Balance is: ");
44                  Put (enquire (accounts (account_number)));
45                  New_Line;
46               when others =>
47                  Put ("Illegal action");
48             end case;
49
50           end loop;
51
52     exception
53        when Data_Error =>
54           Put ("Error in processing transaction.");
55        when Constraint_Error =>
56           Put ("Error in transaction amount.");
57     end;
58
59     end bank;
```

FIGURE 9.2 Simple Ada program that implements a trivial bank account system.

```
package Bank_Account is

     type account_type is private;

     procedure create (account : out account_type);

     procedure deposit (amount : in Integer; account : out account_type);

     procedure withdrawal (amount : in Integer; account : out account_type);

     function enquire (account : in account_type) return Integer;

limited private

     type account_type is record
        account_number   : Integer;
        balance          : Integer;
     end record;

end Bank_Account;

package body Bank_Account is

     procedure create (account : out account_type) is
     begin
        account.balance := 0;
     end create;

     procedure deposit (amount : in Integer; account : out account_type) is
     begin
        account.balance := account.balance + amount;
     end deposit;

     procedure withdrawal (amount : in Integer; account : out account_type) is
     begin
        account.balance := account.balance - amount;
     end withdrawal;

     function enquire (account : in account_type) return Integer is
     begin
        return account.balance;
     end enquire;

end Bank_Account;
```

FIGURE 9.3 Simple Ada package used by the program in Figure 9.2.

external packages. Two are part of the Ada system (packages Ada.Text_IO and Ada.Integer_Text_IO) and one is a custom package (Bank_Account) developed for this program. Package Bank_Account is illustrated in Figure 9.3.

On line 5 a constant integer is declared that is used in several declarations. Line 6 defines a new type that is a subrange of the integers. Line 7 defines an enumerated type. Lines 8 and 9 create new packages from library packages that provide extensive input and output facilities for variables of the types defined on lines 6 and 7.

Lines 11 to 14 are declarations of variables. Line 11 is a variable of the enumeration type defined on line 7. Line 12 declares a pointer to an object that will be of type Natural. Line 13 declares an array whose elements are of type account_type. This type is provided by the package Bank_Account. Line 14 declares a variable whose type is the subrange of the integers defined on line 6.

The body of the program starts on line 16. The program begins by initializing the array of accounts using the for statement on line 18. Space is allocated for an integer and the associated pointer stored on line 22. The heart of the computation is in the case statement starting on line 33. Users enter a transaction type that they want to carry out on an account (lines 26 and 30), and the case statement selects a code fragment suitable for the requested transaction. These code fragments accept details of a deposit or a withdrawal, or print the account balance.

Lines 52 to 57 are two exception handlers that will execute if either exception is raised. The two types of exception are associated with a particular condition that might arise in the program. The exception Data_Error is raised if the user enters an incorrect value for the enumeration type transaction_type. The exception Constraint_Error is raised if the user enters an account number outside the range of the associated type, account_range, because such a value would be outside the index range of the array of accounts.

9.3.3 Packages

The package Bank_Account is shown in Figure 9.3. The package is defined in two parts, the specification in the upper part of the figure and the body in the lower part. This structure facilitates the proper implementation of information hiding, a concept that is fairly common in modern programming languages.

The package specification defines a new type, account_type. The type is a record with two fields, and four operations are defined: create, deposit, withdrawal, and enquire. The implementation details are in the private part of the package and so they cannot be accessed directly. The keyword limited in the private part indicates that objects of this type cannot be assigned with the standard assignment operator, :=, and cannot be compared with the standard equality and inequality operators, = and /=. The package body defines the implementations of the four operations on type account_type, each of which is trivial.

9.3.4 Concurrent and Real-Time Programming

The task is the basic building block for describing concurrent computations. Ada provides extensive support for concurrent and real-time programming. Tasks are first class entities, and powerful and flexible tasking structures can be built quickly and easily within the language.

Ada's primary mechanism for communication between tasks is the *rendezvous*. A rendezvous is programmed with (a) an accept statement that defines an entry in one task and (b) any entry call in another. Each task executes independently until one reaches its accept statement or the other reaches its entry call, at which point the task stops and waits for the other task to reach its corresponding entity (either the `accept` statement or the entry call). When both tasks have arrived, the body of the `accept` statement is executed by one task while the other task waits. When the `accept` statement is complete, both tasks continue with their separate execution.

The accept statement is much like a procedure call, and parameters can be passed between the tasks when the rendezvous begins. Many other powerful features are provided to permit sophisticated multi-tasking programs to be written. Ada supports real-time processing in a comprehensive way with a variety of timing and control mechanisms.

9.3.5 Separate Compilation

Separate compilation is handled comprehensively in Ada. The language designers realized that separate compilation and the associated linking are crucial facilities and can be a major source of faults.

Software needs to be developed in pieces for several reasons:

- Compilation times of large programs can become excessive.

- Different parts of a program need to be developed by different engineers.

- Libraries of source code components often have to be available to permit convenient sharing.

- Isolating components into small parts with clean interfaces facilitates comprehension.

The approach to separate compilation in Ada has two major components:

- Separate compilation is equivalent to inclusion of source files. What this means is that separately compiling a set of parts is entirely equivalent to compiling the set of parts as one complete program. Thus, all checks that would be performed on a single program are completed in exactly the same way if the program were in several parts.

- Linking is included in the semantics of Ada in such a way that all dependencies between separately compiled parts are managed by the compiler. Thus, any change to one part that necessitates the recompilation of others is automatically taken care of by the compiler.

In thinking about the idea of separate compilation, note the fault avoidance capabilities that Ada provides. Faults cannot be introduced by engineers having to develop a program as a set of components. Whatever benefits that might accrue from building one large program are guaranteed to be in effect if the program is developed and built as a set of separate components.

9.3.6 Exceptions

Ada supports pre-defined and programmer-defined exceptions. Handlers are associated with program blocks that can be begin-end blocks, procedure or functions, or tasks.

When an exception is raised during execution, the Ada run-time system looks for a handler. If a handler is found in the block raising the exception, the handler is executed and the block is terminated. If no handler is found, the run-time system terminates the block in which the exception was raised, and attempts to re-raise the exception. For a begin-end block, the exception is reraised in the surrounding block. For a procedure or function, the exception is re-raised in the calling block at the point of the call and the procedure or function is terminated. Finally, if no handler for an exception is found in a task, the task is terminated and the exception is not re-raised.

These semantics can lead to difficulties if programmers are not careful with the placement of exception handlers. Re-raising an exception after a procedure with no suitable handler is terminated occurs at the point of the call. If the procedure containing the call has no suitable handler, that procedure is terminated also, and this propagation process continues until either a handler is found or the program is terminated. A sequence of program blocks was terminated because of an unhandled exception in Ariane V software written in Ada and the end result of those terminations was the Ariane V failure (see Section 1.4.1 on page 9) [89].

9.4 Programming Standards

9.4.1 Programming Standards and Programming Languages

Programming standards are sets of rules on the use of features in programming languages. Two examples are (a) the Motor Industry Software Reliability Association (MISRA) standard for C [97] and (b) Ada Quality & Style: Guidelines For Professional Programmers [34]. Several standards addressing a variety of language and related issues are available from the Free Software Foundation [50].

Rules in programming standards require one of the following for certain language features:

- They must be used.

- They must not be used.

- If they are used, they must be used in certain ways.

Many standards have been developed, and, in some cases, several different standards have been developed for the same programming language. In principle, programming standards can help by eliminating some practices that are known to be error prone. For example, a standard for C might require that Boolean expressions in conditional statements be free of assignment. In practice, this approach is only marginally effective for the following reasons:

- Standards can only draw attention to a small set of the mistakes that people make. The mistakes that can be controlled are those that either derive from improper use of a language feature or are easily defined by simple rules. Thus, standards are never and can never be complete.

- Although there are exceptions such as MISRA C (see below), standards are rarely enforced systematically by tools. Although a lot has been written about rules for the use of programming languages, few of the rules have been embodied in tools that can check for their violation.

- Fault avoidance is not the primary goal of most standards. Standards are designed to support a number of general quality goals for source programs, including readability, maintainability, performance, efficiency, and freedom from faults. Even though fault avoidance is recognized as important by those developing standards (although they might not use the term "fault avoidance"), fault avoidance is not covered comprehensively.

In looking at the defects reported in the Lucent 5ESS project mentioned in Section 9.1.3, one might ask whether the defects that were observed could have been avoided by using programming standards. One of the most prominent standards for C is that prepared by the Motor Industry Software Reliability Association (MISRA) [97]. Here are some examples of the rules in that standard:

MISRA-C Rule 47. "No dependence should be placed on C's operator precedence rules in expressions"

MISRA-C Rule 59. "The statements forming the body of an if, else if, else, while, do...while or for statement shall always be enclosed in braces"

MISRA-C Rule 66. "Only expressions concerned with loop control should appear within a for statement"

Systematic and complete enforcement of rules such as these would have been helpful in avoiding the faults seen by the authors of the Lucent study. Such enforcement could now be supported by comprehensive enforcement tools such as those from the Programming Research Group [109]. Manual enforcement would have been expensive to undertake.

Relying upon a set of rules to restrict the use of a programming language with a relatively ineffective design is not a good way to achieve the goal of fault avoidance in implementations. A far better approach is to rely upon a programming language that includes features designed specifically to avoid as many faults as possible.

9.4.2 Programming Standards and Fault Avoidance

That standards do not provide strong guarantees about freedom from faults does not mean that programming standards should not be used. In fact:

Programming standards should always be used.

Programming standards are sometimes the only realistic way to get valuable properties into software, and standards are always a useful supplement to the other techniques at our disposal. Properties that standards require can *assist* us in fault avoidance. The following are examples of guidelines for Ada [34]:

Readability. Readability refers literally to the ease with which a software developer can read and understand a source program. Often the reader is not the author. Readability can and should be promoted to facilitate fault elimination, especially through inspection. Various measures can be taken to increase the readability of source programs, including:

- Employ careful layout, spacing, and indentation of statements.
- Use meaningful identifiers.
- Avoid using magic numbers.
- Include clear and concise comments.
- Make proper use of types.

Concurrency. Concurrency is a magnet for faults. Concurrent software is difficult to write and to reason about. Concurrency can be made less complex and the resulting program made more amenable to analysis by the careful application of programming guidelines, such as:

- Ensure that exceptions can be handled properly during rendezvous.
- Do not share variables between tasks.
- Minimize the number of `accept` statements per task.
- Include an exception handler for `others` at the end of every task body.

Portability. Portability refers to the ability to move a program from one target platform to another. Porting a program to a new target can introduce faults that were not present on the original target. For example, numeric precision often changes, and the new target might not be able to support the numeric types used in the software.

Developers are presented with two challenges when porting software: (1) modifying the software so as to interface with the new target platform and (2) verifying that no new faults have been introduced.

Taking suitable precautions in the form of guidelines in a programming standard when preparing the original software can avoid subtle faults that arise on the new target. Some examples of such guidelines are:

- Encapsulate known dependencies on a specific platform into well-documented functions or classes.

- Avoid depending on compiler idiosyncracies such as the form or order of generated code.

- Do not depend on a platform-specific scheduling algorithm for concurrent tasks or threads.

Reusability. Software reuse is an established technique for improving the productivity of software engineers, but systematic reuse is also a valuable tool that helps with fault avoidance [79]. Software components in a reuse library, i.e., components designed properly for reuse, can be documented and verified carefully, so that their use brings not only their functionality but also their quality. Note that the same is not true of ad hoc reuse, i.e., components that just happen to be available. The difference is well illustrated by the Arianne V disaster (see Section 1.4.1.) in which one of the causal factors was the reuse of a component from the Arianne IV [89].

In general, reusing a software component is vastly cheaper than building an equivalent component. For systems requiring high dependability the cost imbalance can be high. The verification costs of an avionics software component that will be included in a product requiring FAA certification is inevitably substantial. Reuse does not avoid all of the cost, but significant savings are possible. Programming guidelines that promote reuse include:

- Use symbolic constants and symbolic expressions that compilers can evaluate to permit basic parameters (such as data structure sizes) of a reusable part to be tailored to the reuse target.

- Exploit the type system parameterization mechanism of the implementation language to allow types to be tailored to the reuse target.

- Provide iterators for data structures so that developers do not have to violate information hiding boundaries when working with data structures.

- Design reusable parts to use conditional compilation to delete implementation elements that are not needed for a particular reuse.

9.5 Correctness by Construction — SPARK

Analysis is the most general and most readily available of the three forms of correctness by construction. SPARK Ada is a programming language and system that has demonstrated this form of correctness by construction quite comprehensively.

SPARK is a practical, industrial-strength, and readily available example of implementation correctness by construction, and so engineers can use SPARK for development immediately. The approach requires that software be documented

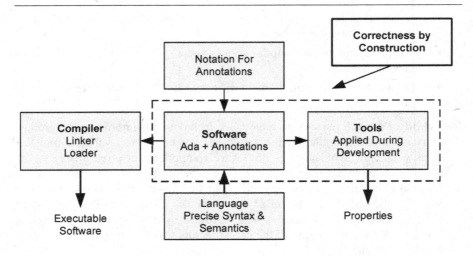

FIGURE 9.4 The SPARK concept of implementation correctness by construction.

using a low-level specification notation, and then a set of powerful tools is used to prove various properties of the software. The SPARK approach is described in detail by Barnes [16], and significant information about SPARK is available from the SPARK web site [110]. The SPARK Ada technology is commercially available and has a long record of accomplishment in the commercial, safety-critical software sector.

In SPARK, software is written in a carefully defined subset of Ada '95 [3][1], and the documentation is written in a special language that is structured as a set of *annotations*. The annotations are included in a program as comments so that they are unseen by compilers but are seen by the SPARK tools.

9.5.1 The SPARK Development Concept

The SPARK development concept is both elegant and simple. The end product of a software development activity using SPARK is a program in Ada together with a set of annotations that specify what the program does and a proof that the program implements the specification correctly. In order to be executed, the program has to be compiled, but any Ada compiler can be used. The development, analysis, and compilation concept is illustrated in Figure 9.4.

SPARK developers prepare the low-level specification for their software as they proceed with development. The general approach, shown in Figure 9.5, is much like

---

1. Ada '95 has been superceded by Ada 2005 [4].

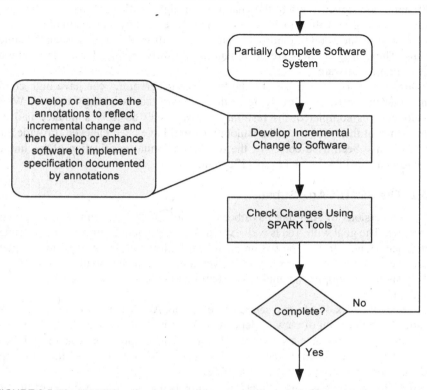

FIGURE 9.5 The SPARK iterative development approach to correctness by construction.

a typical "edit-compile" loop that many programmers use but with "analysis" replacing "compile", i.e., an "edit-analyze" loop. In a traditional development, the programmer edits the software to reach a short-term goal and then compiles the program to make sure that no new syntax errors have been introduced. The SPARK approach is similar, but the programmer uses the SPARK tools to analyze rather than compile the software.

Importantly, the "edit" phase of the development cycle starts with defining the annotations. Their role is to document the program, and the concept, therefore, is to develop the documentation first. Once the documentation is complete and checked, the implementation is developed to match the documentation. Finally, the combination of documentation and implementation is checked with the analysis tools.

Just as with compiling, if the results of an enhancement are checked only after extensive modifications and additions to the software, then there are likely to be many errors, including some that will require some of the modifications to be undone. The underlying principle in SPARK is for the programmer to reason carefully about a change, to effect the change with high confidence that the change is what is needed, and then to have the change checked by the available tools. A change will include both the introduction of new software and the associated annotations. Thus, programmers are documenting the software in a formal language as they build the software.

Once the change is checked by the tools, the programmer can have high confidence that the software is evolving to the software that is actually needed. When development is completed, the resulting software will be fully annotated and the compliance of the software to the annotations will have been checked. Provided all the tools have been used correctly, the result is a formal verification of the implementation against the low-level specification.

9.5.2 The SPARK Ada Subset

All three versions of Ada that have been produced ('83, '95, and 2005) are large languages. The goal with Ada is well explained by the quote from the Ada Language Reference Manual in Section 9.3 on page 264. Unfortunately, there is no complete formal semantic definition for any of the versions of Ada, and so none forms a suitable basis for developing an analysis system that could support correctness by construction.

Despite the lack of a formal semantic definition, Ada has many desirable characteristics from the point of view of dependability. With that in mind, the SPARK Ada developers chose to create a subset of Ada for which comprehensive analysis is possible. They selected from the complete language only those features for which the necessary proofs were known to be feasible.

SPARK Ada contains many language elements despite being a subset of the full language, and so a comprehensive definition has to be left to the SPARK literature [16, 111]. In summary, the SPARK subset of Ada includes the following:

- Scalar types — enumeration, character, Boolean, float, fixed.
- Fixed size array types and strings.
- Records.
- Full range of expressions.
- Statements including assignment, case, loop, if, exit, procedure call, entry call, return, and delay.
- Subprograms including both procedures and functions.
- Packages and therefore a complete separation of specification and implementation.
- Inheritance.
- Tasks including entries and entry calls.
- Separate compilation.

The SPARK subset of Ada omits the following from the full language:

Much of the tasking mechanism. What remains is referred to as the *Ravenscar* profile [23]. Many aspects of tasking inhibit proof.

Exceptions. The complex dynamic control flow associated with exception propagation and the dynamic location of handlers inhibit proof.

Generics. Generic definitions are convenient but really amount to an editing mechanism. Proof with generics essentially requires quantification over types.

Heap storage and associated access types (pointers). The difficulty with dynamic storage allocation really derives from the difficulty of proving that a program will not run out of space during execution. The notion of a pointer is also problematic, leading to issues such as dangling pointers.

Dynamically sized arrays. Dynamically sized arrays are arrays whose size is determined during execution based on the value of a variable. Their use precludes proof that storage limits will be met.

Implicit subtypes. An implicit subtype is a subtype that is included inline in the source text. The type definition is included where a type is needed; thus the type has no name. Implicit types make type checking difficult.

Goto statements. Goto statements permit arbitrary branches, and arbitrary branches lead to proof obligations that are often difficult and sometimes impossible to discharge. This omission will not even be noticed by most engineers since goto statements are rarely used.

One of the great benefits of these omissions is that programs written in the SPARK Ada subset do not require a lot of complex support during execution. The support necessary for tasking in full Ada, for example, is extensive but largely hidden from the programmer. A program in full Ada will be linked with the execution-time support mechanism that will come from a standard library. That mechanism is large and complex, always present, but not really visible in the source program at all.

In developing dependable systems, we have to include the execution-time support mechanism in our analysis, and we know that every effort has to be made in fault avoidance and elimination in that mechanism along with all the other software. By restricting the SPARK Ada subset in the way that they have, the designers have reduced the necessary execution-time support mechanism considerably, thereby making analysis of the mechanism much simpler.

9.5.3 The SPARK Annotations

The SPARK annotations are Ada comments with the text of the comment beginning with the "#" character. Following this character is a keyword that identifies the annotation and the keyword is followed by parameters.

The concept behind the annotations is to provide a means of specifying, in a declarative way, the functionality of the associated program text. The annotations are, therefore, similar in some ways to the declarative nature of Z (Section 8.6). The major difference between Z and the SPARK annotations is that Z is designed to document a program's specification at a high level, and the SPARK annotations are designed to document a program's specification at a low level.

The SPARK annotations play two different roles:

Defining a Program's Data Flow. These annotations define the dependencies between data items in the program. The SPARK documentation refers to these as the *core* annotations.

Defining a Program's Functionality. These annotations define the low-level specification of the program, and they are, for the most part, in the form of pre- and post-conditions for the various procedures and functions in the software. The SPARK documentation refers to these as the *proof* annotations.

The annotations are introduced in the next two sections, and the important topic of loop invariants is reviewed in Section 9.5.6. As an example, we will use a program for managing a simple bank account. For simplicity, this program is just part of the example shown in Figure 9.2 and Figure 9.3. Our simple Ada implementation of a program to calculate the balance in an account is shown in Figure 9.6.

Even if you are unfamiliar with Ada, this simple example should be fairly clear. Notice that the specification and implementation are completely separate. This separation is not necessary in a simple program like this, but it is important as we annotate the program.

As with any high-level language program, this is a purely procedural statement. The way engineers usually learn about a program that they did not write is to read the source text and mentally "execute" the program. We need more information both for human understanding and to support analysis, and crucial additional information is precisely what the SPARK Ada annotations provide.

9.5.4 Core Annotations

The locations of the declarations of variables and the Ada scope rules were designed to support information hiding. This separation is not quite what is needed for specification and verification so the necessary details are added by the core annotations:

```
--# global
```

Specification

```
package bank_account is
        procedure create;
        procedure deposit (amount : in Integer);
        procedure withdrawal (amount : in Integer);
        function enquire return Integer;
end bank_account;
```

Implementation

```
package body Bank_Account is
     balance      : Integer;

     procedure create is
     begin
        balance := 0;
     end create;

     procedure deposit (amount : in Integer) is
     begin
        balance := balance + amount;
     end deposit;

     procedure withdrawal (amount : in Integer) is
     begin
        balance := balance - amount;
     end withdrawal;

     function enquire return Integer is
     begin
        return balance;
     end enquire;

end Bank_Account;
```

FIGURE 9.6 Simple example Ada program.

```
--# derives

--# own
```

and we will look at each one separately.

```
--# global
```

The annotation --# global documents the fact that a variable referenced in a subprogram is a global variable. Much like a parameter, a global variable can be used as an input to a subprogram, an output from a subprogram, or both.

The --# global annotation uses the Ada reserved words in and out to indicate how the global variable will be used. In our example, the variable balance is global to the four subprograms (procedures and functions). In order to indicate our intent to the SPARK tools about this, we can use this annotation for each subprogram. The result is specification (a) in Figure 9.7.

```
(a)   package bank_account is
         procedure create;
         --# global out balance;
         procedure deposit (amount : in Integer);
         --# global in out balance;
         procedure withdrawal (amount : in Integer);
         --# global in out balance;
         function enquire return Integer;
         --# global in balance;
      end bank_account;


(b)   package bank_account is
         procedure create;
         --# global out balance;
         --# derives balance from ;
         procedure deposit (amount : in Integer);
         --# global in out balance;
         --# derives balance from balance, amount;
         procedure withdrawal (amount : in Integer);
         --# global in out balance;
         --# derives balance from balance, amount;
         function enquire return Integer;
         --# global in balance;
      end bank_account;


(c)   package bank_account is
         --# own balance;
         procedure create;
         --# global out balance;
         --# derives balance from ;
         procedure deposit (amount : in Integer);
         --# global in out balance;
         --# derives balance from balance, amount;
         procedure withdrawal (amount : in Integer);
         --# global in out balance;
         --# derives balance from balance, amount;
         function enquire return Integer;
         --# global in balance;
      end bank_account;
```

FIGURE 9.7   Partially annotated specification of the simple example Ada program.

```
--# derives
```

The annotation `--# derives` documents the dependencies of one variable on others, including global variables and parameters. In our example, the variable `balance` is set by the three procedures but not the function, so we need to indicate these dependencies. The result is specification (b) in Figure 9.7.

```
--# own
```

The annotation `--# own` documents variables that are defined by a package body. They are not visible in the package specification, but visibility is necessary so that other annotations can gain access to these variables. However, the visibility that is needed is purely for the annotations and hence the SPARK tools, and so opening up the visibility is done with this annotation. In our example, the variable `balance` is defined in the package body but needed by annotations in the specification and so needs to be made visible. The result is specification (c) in Figure 9.7.

The specification with which we started was 6 lines long and is now 14. This seems like a lot of work, but the important thing is that we have documented the program in an important way. A reasonable question that one might ask at this point is:

Why is all this annotation necessary?
Surely a tool could determine what the data dependencies are.

This is an understandable sentiment, but that sentiment is erroneous. The point of the annotations is to be able to state the data dependencies so that tools can *check* them. Thus, the idea is for the engineer to specify what the data flow is expected to be and then to have the tools check that the code (written by an engineer, perhaps the same one who wrote the annotations) actually does have that data flow. This enables the tools to check a wide variety of important properties of the code, including proper variable initialization, proper access to variables, etc.

9.5.5 Proof Annotations

The proof annotations define the functionality of the actual Ada source code. The basis of this specification is the use of pre- and post-conditions much as we saw in the use of Z for defining high-level specifications in Section 8.6. The big difference is the specification level. In the SPARK annotations, the goal is to define the functionality essentially one procedure or function at a time. The principles are the same, but the target is basic procedures and functions rather than high-level operations acting on a state. The proof annotations are:

```
--# pre
--# post
--# initializes
--# assert
```

and once again we will look at each one separately.

`--# pre`

The annotation `--# pre` documents the pre-condition that has to be true in order for the associated subprogram to be applied. Defining the pre-condition for a subprogram has to be done carefully, because a mistake could lead to a call that failed. The SPARK tools use pre-conditions as guarantees on the values of vari-

(a)
```
package bank_account is
    --# own balance;
    procedure create;
    --# global out balance;
    --# derives balance from ;
    procedure deposit (amount : in Integer);
    --# global in out balance;
    --# derives balance from balance, amount;
    --# pre amount < 100000;
    procedure withdrawal (amount : in Integer);
    --# global in out balance;
    --# derives balance from balance, amount;
    --# pre amount < 100000;
    function enquire return Integer;
    --# global in balance;
end bank_account;
```

(b)
```
package bank_account is
    --# own balance;
    procedure create;
    --# global out balance;
    --# derives balance from ;
    --# post balance = 0;
    procedure deposit (amount : in Integer);
    --# global in out balance;
    --# derives balance from balance, amount;
    --# pre amount < 100000;
    --# post balance = balance~ + amount;
    procedure withdrawal (amount : in Integer);
    --# global in out balance;
    --# derives balance from balance, amount;
    --# pre amount < 100000;
    --# post balance = balance~ - amount;
    function enquire return Integer;
    --# global in balance;
end bank_account;
```

FIGURE 9.8 Proof annotations for specification of the simple example Ada program.

ables, and they use these guarantees in their analysis both of the subprogram and of the code that calls the subprogram.

In our example, balance and enquire do not need pre-conditions, because they can always be called. The other two subprograms both need pre-conditions. For simplicity in this example, the pre-condition used is that the amount of money to be used in a transaction is less than $100,000. This is a reasonable approach, since we can assume an upper bound on bank account transactions that do not invoke special processing. The result is specification (a) in Figure 9.8.

--# post

The annotation --# post documents the post-condition that the subprogram will make true when the subprogram executes. Defining post-conditions for a subprogram has to be done carefully also, because the role of the post-condition is to define the computation. Fortunately, this definition is declarative, so, once again, we have a similarity with Z to provide some background.

In our example, all four subprograms need post-conditions. Fortunately, they are fairly simple and merely reflect the elementary arithmetic that is involved. Just as with Z, the notation needs to allow us to refer to a variable's value before the subprogram executes as well as after. Where Z uses a prime, " ' " to denote the before state, SPARK Ada's annotations use a tilde "~". After adding post-conditions for all of the subprograms, the result is specification (b) in Figure 9.8.

`--# initializes`

The annotation `--# initializes` documents variables that are initialized explicitly in a package body. This annotation goes with the `--# own` annotation. No such initialization occurs in our example, but we could modify the body to initialize the variable balance to zero when the package is elaborated. In that case, we would need to inform the SPARK tools using this annotation.

`--# assert`

The annotation `--# assert` documents a logical expression that is required to be true at the point where the annotation appears, i.e., an assertion. In the overall flow of a program, an assertion can be thought of as a combination of a post-condition for the code that preceded the assertion and a pre-condition for the code that follows the assertion. We have no use for assertions in our simple bank account example, but they play a big role in dealing with loops, as discussed in Section 9.5.6.

9.5.6 Loop Invariants

Loops present a difficult problem when dealing with verification. The problem derives from our efforts to answer the question:

How many times will the loop be executed?

We need to be able to write post-conditions for loops, but how can we do that if the loop might be executed zero, one, or many times?

The answer to the question lies in the notion of a *loop invariant*. Quite simply, a loop invariant is an algebraic predicate over program variables and any declared bound variables that is true both *before* and *after* the body of the loop. As a result, the loop invariant becomes the major part of the post-condition for the loop. If the loop is executed zero times, then the loop invariant is true after the loop, because it was true before the loop. If the loop is executed one or more times, then the loop invariant is true for any number of iterations because the invariant is true after the loop body is executed. The idea of a loop invariant and the points at which the invariant has to be true are shown in Figure 9.9.

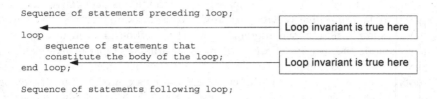

```
Sequence of statements preceding loop;

loop                                              Loop invariant is true here
        sequence of statements that
        constitute the body of the loop;         Loop invariant is true here
end loop;

Sequence of statements following loop;
```

FIGURE 9.9 A loop invariant is an *algebraic* relationship between the variables in a program. The invariant is true before the loop is executed and after the loop body is executed. The loop invariant is not necessarily true anywhere else.

The invariant is the major part of the loop post-condition, and the condition that terminates the loop is the other part. For example, a while statement terminates when the Boolean condition that controlled the loop becomes false. This condition will also be false if the loop is executed zero times. Thus, the negation of the while statement's Boolean condition is the second part of the loop post-condition.

A loop invariant is a predicate, and as such an invariant is an *algebraic* concept. Do not get confused into thinking that the condition depends on specific values of program variables. Not only is the invariant algebraic, but it is also *only* true at two points — before and after the loop body. Specifically, the loop invariant need not be true within the body of the loop.

An example of a loop and the associated invariant is shown in Figure 9.10 (a). The example is written in a simple hypothetical language and includes a program fragment that declares an array and two integer variables. The bulk of the program fragment is a loop that searches the array for the maximum value. The array is assumed to be initialized outside the fragment. The loop invariant indicates the state of the variable maximum. The first clause of the invariant says that maximum is greater than or equal to all the elements of the array in the range 1..counter (counter is the loop counter). The second clause of the invariant says that maximum is equal to at least one element of the array.

Figure 9.10 (b) shows the same example as in Figure 9.10 (a) but this time written in the syntax of Ada with the loop invariant stated as a SPARK annotation. The loop invariant does not include the second clause shown in Figure 9.10 (a), because that clause is trivially true. Only the essential declarations and loop are shown.

The first clause of the loop invariant in Figure 9.10 (b) says that the value of the variable maximum is greater than or equal to all of the elements of the array from location 1 up to location counter. This predicate is true before the loop is executed because in that case counter = 1 and maximum = data(i). The invariant is also true after the body of the loop is executed, but to establish that we would need to develop a proof. Notice in this example that the loop invariant is not true within the loop itself after the variable counter is incremented. But, provided the loop correctly implements the invariant, then the invariant will be true after the last statement in the body of the loop is executed.

A loop invariant always exists for any loop that an engineer writes. There is no difference between a loop for which we know the loop invariant and a loop for which we do not. The loop invariant actually documents the computation of the loop. We can write loops by defining the invariant and then writing the actual loop to make the invariant true where we need it to be true.

As an example of the use of loop invariants in verification with SPARK Ada, consider the example shown in Figure 9.11. This program performs integer addition by adding one in a loop to one operand a number of times equal to a second operand. This calculation is especially trivial but useful for illustration.

```
(a)    data       :    array[1..100] of integer;
       maximum    :    integer;
       counter    :    integer;

       counter    := 1;
       maximum    :=data[counter];
       repeat
          counter := counter + 1;
          if data[counter] > maximum then
             maximum := data[counter];
       until counter = 100;
```

```
       Loop invariant:
          (∀j : 1..100 | j ≤ counter • data[j] ≤ maximum
                              ∧
          (∃k : 1..100 | k ≤ counter • data[k] = maximum
```

```
(b)    type data_index_range is range 1..max_data_size;
       data           :    array(data_index_range) of Natural;
       maximum        :    Natural;
       counter        :    data_index_range := 1;
       ...
       maximum := data(counter);
       while counter < max_data_size
          --# assert for all i in 1..counter maximum >= data(i);
       loop
          counter := counter + 1;
          if maximum < data(counter) then
             maximum := data(counter);
       end loop;
```

FIGURE 9.10 (a) A simple program repeat loop that calculates the maximum element of an array and the associated loop invariant. (b) The same program written in Ada and using a `while` statement.

```
package simpleadd is
   procedure sum (X,Y : in Integer; Z : out Integer);
   --# derives Z from X, Y;
   --# pre (X>1) and (X<1000) and (Y>1) and (Y<1000);
   --# post Z=X+Y;
end simpleadd;

package body simpleadd is
   procedure sum (X,Y : in Integer; Z : out Integer) is
   begin
      if (X>1) and (X<1000) and (Y>1) and (Y<1000) then
         Z := X;
         for i in Integer range 1..Y loop
            Z := Z + 1;
            --# assert Z = X + i and Y = Y%;
         end loop;
      else
         Z := 0;
      end if;
   end sum;
end simpleadd;
```

FIGURE 9.11 Simple example of a loop invariant defined using a SPARK annotation.

The annotations in the specification should be familiar, but note the post-condition:

```
--# post Z=X+Y;
```

The loop invariant is in the body within the `for` statement. The invariant is expressed as an assertion. The first clause of the invariant says that the parameter Z is equal to the parameter X plus the loop counter i. The second clause says that the variable Y is unmodified by the loop. Even for this simple example, this loop invariant is useful. Can we be certain that this is the relationship or could we be off by one? Being off by one is a common problem in loops.

Recall from Figure 9.9 that the loop invariant has to be true *before* the loop is executed. In the example in Figure 9.11, the loop invariant is written in terms of the `for` statement counter i, but i is not given a value before the loop. So how can the loop invariant be true? This problem is a result of the semantics of the `for` statement in Ada. In Ada, the loop counter in a `for` statement is declared automatically at the start of the `for` statement, and the scope of the counter is just the `for` statement. Thus, the loop counter is not defined and has no meaning outside the loop. For purposes of analyzing loop invariants, the loop counter can be taken to be zero. With that assumption, the loop invariant in the example is true before the loop is executed. This problem does not arise in the other loop statements in Ada.

The use of a loop invariant is actually an application in programming of the mathematical proof technique of *induction*. Just as in a proof by induction in traditional mathematics, we have to establish the base step and the induction step. The base step is the proof that the loop invariant is true before the loop is executed. The

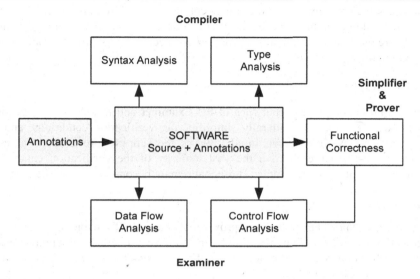

FIGURE 9.12 The SPARK Ada tools and their relationship to the various analyses.

induction step is the proof that the loop invariant is true after the body of the loop is executed provided the invariant was true before the body of the loop is executed.

The reason we have to discuss the concept of loop invariants is that they are used by the SPARK tools in establishing the proofs that a SPARK Ada program is a correct implementation of the specification documented by the annotations. Programmers are expected to know what the loops they write actually compute and therefore what the loop invariants are.

9.5.7 The SPARK Tools

Modern Ada compilers are powerful analysis tools, and so the starting point for analysis of a SPARK Ada program could be the compiler. But the SPARK tools will perform the analysis performed by compilers and more. There are three major tools, the Examiner, the Simplifier, and the Prover. The relationships between the compiler, the SPARK tools, and SPARK Ada software are shown in Figure 9.12. We can only discuss the tools here superficially. If you are interested in learning how to use them, see the textbook by Barnes [16]. The SPARK tools are freely available for non-commercial use.

The Examiner

The Examiner is the basic tool that is used to check that the subject software follows all of the SPARK Ada language rules. The Examiner also performs flow analysis so as to check the program against the core annotations. The third major function of the Examiner is to generate the necessary verification conditions. These are quite literally theorems about the logic of the program that need to be true for the code to correspond to the annotations.

The Simplifier

The Simplifier reads the output files of the Examiner and tackles the verification conditions. The Simplifier literally simplifies the verification conditions, and in many cases reduce them to true. In other words, the Simplifer proves them. In most cases, the Simplifier can prove the vast majority of the verification conditions because many of them are simple. Those that remain become the job of the Prover.

The Prover

The Prover is a mechanical theorem prover that is used to discharge, i.e., prove, the verification conditions left by the Simplifier. The Prover operates with human guidance, because the creation of proofs for verification conditions completely automatically is not always possible.

Key points in this chapter:

+ Programming languages can help avoid faults in software implementations.
+ Ada is an example of a programming language that includes features designed to help programmers avoid faults.
+ Programming standards provide sets of rules about the use of language features designed to help programmers avoid faults.
+ Correctness by construction can be implemented in three different ways: synthesis, refinement, and analysis.
+ SPARK is a programming technology based on Ada that provides a coupling between low-level formal specification and implementation together with tools that allow verification proofs of implementations.

Exercises

1. Read the paper entitled: "A Software Fault Prevention Approach in Coding and Root Cause Analysis" [156] and prepare a one page summary. Using your summary, explain the paper to a colleague.

2. Read the paper entitled: "Comparing Ada With C and C++" [128] and prepare a one page summary. Using your summary, explain the paper to a colleague.

3. Read the paper entitled: "Correctness By Construction: Better Can Also Be Cheaper" [8] and prepare a one page summary. Using your summary, explain the paper to a colleague.

4. For a programming language with which you are familiar, search on-line for programming standards that apply to that language. Determine the goals of the standards that you have located. Select a set of ten of the items in the standard and map each to a fault (or faults) that the item might help you avoid.

5. What are the two types of analysis that can be performed on properly annotated SPARK Ada programs?

6. The SPARK Ada annotation that documents data dependency (# derives) is supplying information much of which could be determined by a compiler. Why is this not left to a compiler (or similar tool)?

7. Consider the following piece of program:
```
i, n, factorial : integer;

i          := 1;
factorial  := 1;
read(n);

while i < n loop
   i := i + 1;
   factorial := factorial * i;
end loop
```
Determine the loop invariant.

8. Consider the following piece of program:
```
i, sum     : integer;
values     : array[1..100] of integer;

i    :=    2;
sum  :=    values[1];
while i <= 100 loop
   sum := sum + values[i];
   i := i + 1;
end loop
```
Determine the loop invariant.

9. Suppose the program fragment in the previous question were written as a procedure that takes an array as an input parameter and which computes an integer as

an output parameter. What SPARK annotations would you use to document the data dependencies that the procedure will have?

10. Suppose you have to develop a program in a high-level language to sort an array using Bubble sort. The array is to be sorted in place. To help you in the development of the program, you decide to document the main aspects of the program formally before you code anything. Assuming that all array elements are unique positive integers (i.e., no value is repeated) and each is representable on the target machine, what would you use for:

(a) The pre-condition

(b) The post-condition.

(c) The loop invariant.

Write each of these in a clear mathematical notation.

11. Consider the following fragment of SPARK Ada code:

```
procedure divide (in x, y: integer; out z: integer) is

begin
   z := 0;
   while x > y loop
      x := x - y;
      z := z + 1;
   end loop;
end divide;
```

(a) State the pre-condition as SPARK Ada annotation(s).

(b) State the post-condition as SPARK Ada annotation(s).

(c) State the loop invariant as SPARK Ada annotation(s).

12. How would you modify the postcondition from the previous question if the array could have duplicate entries?

13. Write the Bubble sort program as a procedure in a notation as close to SPARK Ada as you can manage. Include the SPARK annotations that you think should be used.

14. Consider the notion of exceptions in high-level language programs. Describe the major semantic models of exception propagation, location of exception handlers, and program processing after an exception.

CHAPTER 10

Software Fault Elimination

Learning objectives of this chapter are to understand:

- The role of inspection in software fault elimination.
- The various types of software inspection.
- The software artifacts to which inspection can be applied.
- The role of testing in software fault elimination.
- The issues in testing a software system for purposes of dependability.
- The role of test coverage metrics and which should be used.
- The difficulties that arise in testing real-time systems.

10.1 Why Fault Elimination?

Despite our best efforts to avoid faults, we have to assume that we have not been completely successful, and that faults remain in all the artifacts that are produced during software development. Finding faults in software artifacts is challenging because usually there are not a lot of faults, and they have an awful lot of places to hide.

One way to think about the problem, shown in Figure 10.1, is to imagine that we have a very large cake (software) that contains a few raisins (faults). The raisins were not in the recipe, but the raisins got into the cake because we were careless (or perhaps because we like raisins). The goal is to find the raisins. We do not know how many raisins there are, and the raisins can be anywhere in the cake. Several might be close together, even touching. There might be large regions of the cake with no raisins. If we examine the cake carefully, for example by cutting it into slices, some of the raisins might be revealed, but we will only see them where we slice the cake. Others might be lurking inside the slices, and cutting thinner slices does not ensure that we find all the raisins unless the slices are slimmer than a raisin. Remember, however, that the cake is *very* large.

When we proceed with development of a software product, we produce various artifacts, including (a) the requirements, (b) the specification, (c) the software architecture, (d) the high-level design, (e) the low-level design, (f) the implementation, (g) various test plans, (h) the maintenance guide, (i) the installation guide, and (j) the users' manual. Each of these might contain defects that could lead to a system failure during operation, and so we have to undertake fault elimination on all of them. Although most people concentrate on fault elimination in the software source program, viewing each artifact as a possible source of failure and taking appropriate measures with each one to eliminate faults that have crept in are both important.

A wide range of tools and techniques have been developed for fault elimination, and we cannot look at even a reasonable fraction of them. In this chapter we look at two important examples:

Inspection. Inspection is a *static* analysis technique in which human rather than machine examination is used. Many different inspection techniques have been developed. In general, inspection is a highly cost-effective technology.

Testing. Testing is a *dynamic* analysis technique. Everybody who has written any software has faced the challenge of testing. Literally thousands of papers and dozens of books have been written on the subject. Even within the field of testing, there is too much material to cover in any depth in this textbook. Rather, in this chapter we cover some of the basic principles of testing and one of the most important test coverage metrics, *Modified Condition Decision Coverage* (MCDC).

Returning briefly to the cake analogy, inspection would correspond to looking systematically for raisins by examining the material of the cake in various ways. We might miss raisins. Testing would correspond to eating samples of the cake. If we are to find the raisins by eating cake samples, we have to try to choose samples where raisins are hiding.

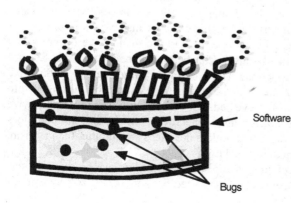

Software

Bugs

FIGURE 10.1 Finding faults in a large software system is much like finding a small number of raisins in a large cake. The raisins cannot be seen from the outside and might be hiding anywhere. There are nine in this cake.

10.2 Inspection

Any artifact created as part of software development can be inspected, and that general applicability is one of the great advantages of inspection. Engineers can even conduct rigorous inspections on natural-language documents. Although a machine cannot check very much in a natural-language document, engineers can inspect such a document and check for various properties of interest. The inspectors might be engineers who are familiar with the technology being used, domain experts who are familiar with the application domain, or other experts.

There is considerable experimental data showing that inspection is very effective [2, 82, 107]. There is also considerable experimental data showing that inspection is very *cost* effective. In other words, inspection works well and is not very expensive to perform. Inspections are a good idea for any software development, but for a system that requires a high level of dependability, a comprehensive program of inspections is essential. The rule, therefore, is:

Rigorous inspection should always be applied to all artifacts in software development.

Surprisingly, inspection is hard to do well in practice and the benefits are sometimes not as large as they could be, even though inspection is known to be effective in general. A variety of different inspection techniques have been developed in order to try to increase inspection performance and efficacy. In this section, we examine the technology of inspection, review several related but different approaches to inspection, and examine the reasons why specific inspection techniques are less effective than they might be.

10.2.1 Artifacts and Defects

Although our interest here is in fault elimination, the defects being sought by inspection can be anything of interest to the development organization, not just faults that affect functional correctness. A defect might be unrelated to functional correctness but might instead be failure to adhere to an important rule associated with quality. In practice, many other quality attributes of the different artifacts can be and should be checked. Inspections are used, for example, to detect aspects of software source code that will make the code difficult to maintain even though this is not directly related to fault elimination.

Table 10.1 illustrates the types of artifact to which inspection can be applied together with examples of the quality attributes that can be checked. The list in the table is merely a set of examples. In any specific development, the actual list of appropriate artifacts needs to be determined and the specific quality attributes for each artifact need to be listed.

ARTIFACT	QUALITY ATTRIBUTE
Development process	Comprehensive development steps and sequence, appropriate process documentation, properly defined milestones and schedule, suitable technologies selected for all process steps, overall use of configuration control tools and techniques.
Requirements	Completeness and accuracy, proper techniques selected, e.g., comprehensive use cases, suitable requirements documentation technology, validation approach properly defined and implemented.
Specification	Complete coverage of requirements, correct documentation style, structure, and layout, correct use of notations (formal language vs. natural language), verification technology appropriate.
Software architecture	Functional correctness and modifiability, resulting system performance, attention to reuse of existing templates, comprehensive treatment of exceptional conditions.
Low-level design	Functional correctness, proper use of object-oriented design if appropriate, required performance achievable, real-time deadlines achievable, memory management appropriate, maintainability, algorithmic efficiency.
Implementation	Programming standards defined and met, proper use of language features, file naming convention used correctly, system build scripts checked for content and sequence.
Documentation	Completeness, format, accessibility, grammar, overall presentation, notations to be used, schedule, author designations.

TABLE 10.1. Software artifacts and examples of the associated quality attributes that can be checked by inspection.

Note that this table includes the *development process*. A process might not appear to be an artifact in the same sense as the others shown. But the process is an artifact that should be documented, and the process should have quality attributes, although probably not a lot. Consideration of the development process often is viewed as an unimportant and unnecessary distraction. Yet the process is the "glue" that holds all of the other activities together. A missed development step or a step that is not completed carefully could have severe negative consequences for the final software product, including the product's dependability.

Essentially all inspections are conducted with a checklist of issues that have to be examined. These checklists correspond to elemental properties in which the development organization is interested. Brief samples from a typical checklist for a source code inspection for software written in C are shown in Figure 10.2. In a realistic development, checklists typically contain dozens of explicit checks.

Check list 1:	Introductory comments in source file follow the institutional structures that are required. Comments include copyright notice.
Check list 2:	Program does not use `goto` statements.
Check list 3:	Program does not use assignment in conditional expressions.
Check list 4:	Functional and variable names are meaningful.
Check list 5:	Program does not use problem functions such as strcpy().
Check list 6:	Program does not use "magic numbers", i.e., unusual constants that appear in the code itself but which should be defined as symbols in a prescribed section of the program.
Check list 7:	Functions always define their return type explicitly.
Check list 8:	Variables are given initialization values when declared.

FIGURE 10.2 Example items from a source code inspection checklist.

10.2.2 Fagan Inspections

The best known and most popular inspection technique was devised by Michael Fagan (hence the name) in the 1980s [45]. The technology has been through numerous revisions since its inception, but the basic principles are essentially unchanged.

Inspection Participants

In a Fagan inspection, the participants are:

- The **moderator** who manages the process.

- The **author** who developed the artifact to be inspected.

- The **reader** who provides the focus during the inspection meeting.

- **Inspectors** who are general participants.

- **Specialists** who provide expertise in particular technical areas.

Fagan Inspection Process

The steps in the Fagan inspection process are:

Planning. The planning phase is carried out by the *moderator* and involves deciding what will be inspected, selecting and getting the agreement of the various participants, developing a schedule, identifying appropriate meeting space, and distributing the various materials. Planning is a critical activity for two major reasons. First, the selection of the artifact to be inspected has to be done carefully. The artifact must be ready for inspection, and inspection must be an appropriate analysis technique at the point in time when it is being considered. If the artifact is large, as is likely to be the case with any realistic software artifact, then the artifact has to be inspected in parts, and the selection of the part for any given inspection has to be done carefully. The most critical criterion is artifact size. The chosen artifact must be long enough to be useful yet not so long as to require an inspection of unreasonable length. For source-code inspections, a typical inspection would target perhaps a few hundred lines.

The second reason that planning is critical activity in Fagan inspections is because appropriate participants have to be selected. The participants must have the necessary technical skills, but they must also be able to work in the setting of inspections in an effective way. Many engineers think (mistakenly) that inspections are not useful and resent participation. Needless to say, they do not make effective participants in inspections.

Overview. In the overview, the *author* of the artifact to be inspected presents general details of the artifact. For a source program, the overview might include an explanation of the functionality that the software provides, the major data structures and algorithms used, the history of the software's development, the status of the software, and a guide to the files in which the software is stored.

If the artifact is a specification written in natural language, the overview might include an explanation of the structure of the document, including how the specification is actually stated, the functionality that the system is expected to provide, the context in which the system is to operate, the implementation plan that is expected to be followed, and the customer's dependability requirements.

Preparation. Working alone, each *inspector* and *specialist* in a Fagan inspection is expected to prepare for the inspection by undertaking a review of the artifact. This activity might take several hours over several days. The goals of preparation are (a) to become familiar with the artifact and (b) to detect defects of interest in the artifact to the extent possible. There is no prescribed format for the preparation process. Preparation usually consists of the inspector reading the artifact.

Inspection. The inspection itself is a meeting attended by all the participants in which the artifact of interest is examined by the group. A single inspection meeting should not last more than two hours because groups find concentration and productive discussion difficult in longer meetings.

The mechanism of the inspection process is that the reader literally reads the artifact aloud as the other participants follow on their own copies of the artifact. The purposes of this approach are (a) to provide a focus for the deliberations and discussion and (b) to make sure that the entire artifact is actually examined. Of course, participants frequently stop the reading and discuss specific points in detail as the inspection proceeds.

An inspection is expected to reveal defects, and defects are recorded as they are identified, usually by the moderator.

Specialists are engineers with expert knowledge that is needed for or used by the artifact being inspected. Knowledge of concurrency or real-time processing, for example, is important in systems using those techniques, but expertise and experience in these areas is not common. Participation in the inspection by an engineer who has this expertise and experience would be important if the subject artifact used these techniques.

Rework. Rework is the activity undertaken by the authors of the artifact to repair whatever defects were found in the inspection. The time taken depends on what defects were identified during the inspection.

Follow-up. The final phase is the follow-up, in which the moderator checks to make sure that the defects identified have been properly repaired. Follow-up is not necessarily a straightforward activity. If a defect involved a lot of the artifact, then extensive changes might have been made. The inspection team needs to know that the repaired defect was not replaced with one or more new defects. To gain this assurance, reconvening the inspection team and reviewing the changes in an inspection setting is sometimes necessary.

Improving Fagan Inspections

Inspection is a powerful technology, and we rely on inspection quite extensively. Thus, considering ways in which the basic Fagan inspection process might be improved is important and has been the subject of extensive study. Some of the issues that have been raised with basic Fagan inspections are:

The overview should not be necessary. The overview is given by the author and is intended to assist the inspection team in understanding the artifact. However, the information supplied in the overview should be written down. Once written down, the information is still available if the author becomes unavailable and the inspection team can read and refer to the information throughout the process.

There is no enforced preparation. Inspectors are not required to proceed in any specific manner during preparation. The result is that in many cases they do either minimal or no preparation. This is a serious problem because the success of the process depends in part on thorough and comprehensive preparation.

Inspection is based on paper documents. Inspections tend to be dominated by paper documents. This eliminates most computer support and makes the whole process less reliable.

The inspection is not rigorous. When an inspection is completed, what new information is available to the development team? A number of defects will have been found and corrected in the subject artifact, but what new properties of the artifact does the development team have? There is no reason to believe that the artifact possesses specific properties of interest, such as freedom from a certain class of faults.

Inspections are impacted by social factors. Many aspects of the inspection process and in particular the actual inspection meeting tend to be affected by social concerns. These concerns then affect the results of the inspection. There is evidence, for example, that the rate of examination of the subject artifact can be driven by the clock, e.g., the rate of inspection tends to increase significantly toward the end of the inspection meeting.

A second example of this problem is that inspection meetings can be dominated by strong-willed individuals. Some people feel intimidated and refrain from adding their contributions to the discussion.

Inspector skill levels are not matched to activities. Many different properties, ranging from simple to complex, are checked in a typical inspection. Despite the range, all are reviewed and discussed by the entire inspection team. This mismatch means that the most senior engineers present are involved in checking even the simplest properties. More could be achieved and more efficiently if inspector skill levels were matched to the technical properties being checked.

10.2.3 Active Reviews

Parnas and Weiss developed an inspection technique called Active Reviews as part of the Naval Research Laboratory's Software Cost Reduction project [103]. Active Reviews are quite different from Fagan inspections and deal effectively with many of the issues listed above. The major differences are:

Inspectors work alone and only within their area of expertise. In an Active Review, the subject artifact is examined by each inspector working alone. There is no inspection meeting. The inspectors examine the artifact looking for properties in their own areas of expertise.

The author poses questions to the inspectors. The author poses technical questions about the subject artifact to the inspectors, who have to answer them after examining the artifact. The effect is to present the inspectors with a goal (answering the questions) for their inspection activities. Having to answer the questions ensures that the inspectors have studied the artifact to some degree, and, if the questions are chosen carefully, there is a high degree of coverage of the technical details of the artifact.

The questions posed to the inspectors by the author are designed to literally discover whether the inspectors have reviewed the artifact sufficiently carefully. To make this discovery, the questions need to challenge the inspectors' understanding and cover the whole artifact. Questions about source programs that might be used include:

- Under what circumstances would variable <x> take on a value in the range <a,b>?

- Under what circumstances would the return parameter <r> in method <m> be set to the value <c>?

- Why does the `if` statement at line <l> in method <n> not require an `else` clause?

- What is the role of parameter <q> in method <v> of function <w> and what values can it take?

Active Reviews are a considerable advance, and they offer the opportunity to deal effectively with several of the limitations of Fagan inspections. The remaining limitations are addressed by *Phased Inspections*.

10.2.4 Phased Inspections

Phased Inspections were introduced by Myers and Knight [98]. Phased Inspections provide a more rigorous inspection process than either Fagan inspections or Active Reviews. The general concept of a Phased Inspection is shown in Figure 10.3.

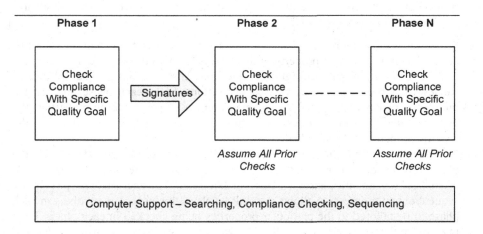

FIGURE 10.3 The Phased Inspection concept.

A Phased Inspection is composed of a series of mini inspections called *phases* that are carried out in sequence. Each phase is dedicated to examining the artifact to establish as comprehensively as possible that the artifact possesses one or a small number of properties. Phases are conducted in series, with each assuming all the properties established by earlier phases. Thus, initial phases are used to check elementary (but important) properties, and later phases focus on technically complex or advanced topics. Thus, inspectors involved in later phases can assume properties checked in earlier phases.

Phased Inspections are composed of two different types of phase — *single inspector* and *multi-inspector*. As the name suggests, a single-inspector phase involves just one inspector working alone. Also as the name suggests, a multi-inspector phase involves multiple inspectors and is organized into two parts. In the first part of a multi-inspector phase, the inspectors work alone and in parallel, each trying to establish the desired property. Once they have completed their inspection, they meet to *reconcile* their results. This second part of the phase is not an inspection. In principle, each inspector in a multi-inspector phase should come to the same conclusion. This is rarely the case in practice, and so the inspectors compare and merge their conclusions in the reconciliation.

For properties that can be checked and potentially established with certainty, a single-inspector phase is used. Examples of properties that would be checked by a single-inspector phase in a source-code inspection include:

- The correct use of required source-code layout and formatting rules.

- Complete and correct use of local programming practices such as always checking the status of a file after a read operation.

- Complete and correct use of all global programming practices such as always freeing storage explicitly after use.

Properties that cannot be established with certainty are checked in a multi-inspector phase. The most common property of this type is functional correctness.

The concept of author-originated questions that was introduced by Active Reviews has been adopted by Phased Inspections. Since each phase, including a multi-inspector phase, covers only a small number of very specific properties, the questions that the author prepares are different for each phase and tailored to the specific properties to be checked.

Each phase establishes a prescribed set of properties of the artifact. Because the phases are conducted in series, each phase can assume the properties that were established by all the phases carried out before it. The fact that the phases are sequential and progressive allows the skill levels of the inspectors involved in each phase to be tailored to the particular properties being checked in each phase. Each phase is dedicated to a narrow technical area, and so the inspectors who conduct the phase can be selected so as to maximize their suitability. Thus, junior engineers can conduct the earlier phases that check the elementary properties and senior engineers can check complex properties. In this way, specialists will not need to concern themselves with elementary properties. Taken together, the complete set of phases is able to establish the complete set of desired properties of the artifact.

To emphasize the importance of inspection, the inspector or inspectors conducting each phase sign a statement after the phase indicating their belief that the artifact has the properties which were the target of the phase. This type of responsibility coupled with the thorough nature of the phase structure helps to ensure that the artifact actually possesses the property that was the subject of the phase. The combined set of properties and the rigour with which they are established provides developers with a high degree of confidence that the various artifacts actually possess the properties checked by inspection.

The developers of Phased Inspections created a toolset to assist with the process [98]. The tool was used to present the artifact being inspected to the inspector, to display relevant checklists, to facilitate navigation throughout the artifact, and to check that the inspector at least displayed all of the artifact during inspection. For some properties, such as establishing the property that all loops in a source program had upper bounds on their numbers of iterations, the tool checked that all loops had been displayed by the inspector.

Phased Inspections have to be designed by developers for the artifact they are developing and for the properties they desire. Clearly, a Phased Inspection for a specification will differ considerable from a Phased Inspection for a source program. An example of a Phased Inspection that might be used for a source program in a high-level language is shown in Figure 10.4. In this example, there are five single-inspector phases and a single multi-inspector phase. In practice, each phase will be accompanied by a checklist that will define the specific characteristics that make up the property of interest. The phases focus on the following properties:

Internal documentation meets requirements. This single-inspector phase checks all of the source-code comments for accuracy, completeness, compliance with rules of the organization, layout, and placement.

Source code meets format requirements. This single-inspector phase checks the source code for statement layout, spacing, indentation, and use of meaningful identifiers.

Source code complies with local programming practices. This single-inspector phase checks the source code for properties such as initialization of variables, use of parentheses in expressions to force evaluation order, freedom from the use of magic numbers, use of constant expressions, proper type definitions, freedom from programming "tricks", completeness of methods in class definitions, completeness of coverage in case statements, and checks on failure modes from system operations such as opening files.

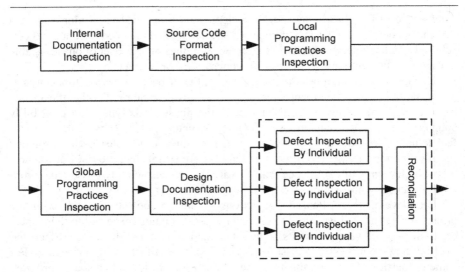

FIGURE 10.4 An example of a Phased Inspection.

Source code complies with global programming practices. This single-inspector phase checks the source code for properties such as proper and complete use of information-hiding interfaces, correct use of static versus dynamic memory, correct deletion (freeing) of dynamically allocated memory, correct locking and unlocking of shared resources, and correct use of concurrent-programming primitives.

Design documentation meets formal and coverage requirements. This single-inspector phase checks the documentation for the source program. This documentation might be merely the comments in the software or might include other, external documents. No matter what form, the documentation needs to be checked for accuracy, completeness, utility, and compliance with any requisite form that the organization dictates.

Source program is free of functional faults. This is the only multi-inspector phase that is included in this example, and the target of the phase is functional correctness. As such, the phase relies upon the individual inspectors both understanding and reasoning about the source program. To both facilitate and measure this, the phase makes use of author-supplied questions. These questions need to ensure that the inspectors have reviewed the source program sufficiently carefully. To do this, the questions need to force the inspectors to think about and reason about the whole program.

The phase structure of Phased Inspections is a considerable departure from previous methods. Clearly, conducting several phases will require a lot of effort by all involved, and the resources needed tend to be viewed as a disadvantage of the use of Phased Inspections. Importantly, however, Phased Inspections provide the known benefits of inspection along with three additional benefits:

Mapping of a complex activity to a rational process. There is too much to cover in a single inspection, and, if everything is forced into a single inspection, there are bound to be checks that are either omitted or not completed properly. This can easily occur with a Fagan inspection. A complete Phased Inspection will include several phases, and so an individual phase can be limited to one or a small number of properties.

Appropriate use of staff. The inspection staff can be tailored to the properties being checked. Each phase can employ a different staff, and so staff capabilities can be matched to the properties of interest in the phase.

High level of assurance that the artifact has needed properties. There is a high probability that the artifact possesses whatever properties of interest were the motivation for the various phases. The design of the phase mechanism is intended to promote that.

10.3 Testing

Testing is important in the development of software that has to achieve high levels of dependability. All high-dependability software systems have to be tested no matter what technology was used in the software's development. Testing complements whatever those methods were, and so testing *always* has a role to play:

> *Systems requiring high dependability must be tested thoroughly and comprehensively even if all other techniques for dealing with faults have been applied.*

Despite the importance of testing, we cannot cover the topic thoroughly in this textbook. Almost all of the general material on testing applies to high-dependability software and should be studied. In this section, we consider a few special topics that tend not to be discussed in more general textbooks.

10.3.1 Exhaustive Testing

Testing is the most common technique used in practice for fault elimination. When considering testing, especially in the context of systems that require high dependability, the following quote from Dijkstra must be kept in mind [32]:

> *"Testing can show the presence of bugs but never their absence."*

In other words, we might be able to detect defects in software by testing, but we cannot tell whether we have found them all.

Although true for most software systems, this observation by Dijkstra is not always true. For software that has a relatively small number of inputs, testing the software with all possible inputs is possible in a process called *exhaustive testing*. The only limitation is resources. If we could run tests that covered all possible inputs, we would know that the software would never see an input during operation that was not seen and checked during testing. Done carefully, this would mean that we had removed all the faults.

As an example, consider the following. If a piece of software has a single input that can take on a total of 10^{12} values and we can execute 10^6 tests per second, then all possible inputs could be tested in about ten days. Provided we had a high level of confidence that fault avoidance and fault elimination had been successful prior to starting exhaustive testing, a ten day test period that yielded extreme confidence in the software would be a worthwhile investment.

The definition of "relatively small number of inputs" has changed over time as computers have gotten faster and cheaper. We can now consider exhaustive testing for software for which such testing would have been infeasible a few years ago. Faster computers mean more tests per second, and cheaper computers mean that we can operate more computers in parallel to reduce the total elapsed time. The value of testing all possible inputs is great, and so we should try to test exhaustively if at all possible.

In some cases, exhaustive testing is possible even though the time required appears to be unreasonable. The way in which exhaustive testing is made possible is to artificially restrict the number of inputs that the software will see. The approach to making the restriction is based on the observation that many inputs have more precision than is really needed. Most physical values such as speed and direction that are read from sensors are represented as either 32-bit fixed or 32-bit floating point numbers, because this precision is convenient. The input in such cases appears to have a large number of values. Nothing is lost, however, if several of the low-order bits are ignored. In the case of speed and direction, ignoring perhaps half of 32 bits would be unlikely to affect the system's actions. By doing so, the number of inputs that the software will see is cut down very significantly. This idea of intentionally limiting the precision of input data so as to facilitate exhaustive testing was first suggested by Knight et al. [78].

10.3.2 The Role of Testing

Software is designed to perform some function, and so the engineers who built the software will want to see what their creation can do. The customer who is expecting to use the software will want to see the software execute before putting it into production use, because actually seeing the software instills confidence in the software. However, in practice, testing serves three different roles:

Verification. By executing the software, it is possible to determine whether the software provides the expected output. In other words, developers can determine whether the implementation complies with the specification. This form of verification is quite limited, because all that is known after testing is that the software executed correctly for the test cases. What the software will do on other inputs is unknown, but the assumption is always made that the software will execute correctly, at least "most" of the time.

Debugging. If the output of the software when tested is not what was expected, then testing has shown the presence of a defect. The developers can use the details of the failing test and the details of the software itself to determine what the fault is. Although this is useful, the fact of the matter is that fault avoidance failed if a program fails during testing. This situation should lead to a determination of why fault avoidance failed and process changes to eliminate the process problem for future developments.

Validation. The customer can see what the software does for each test case and can determine whether that is what is needed. This role of testing allows all the stakeholders in the system to determine whether the software provides the desired service, i.e., validation.

Surprisingly, some people think that testing software is a waste of time and money if the testing process does not reveal defects. Nothing could be further from the truth. Although testing is not ideal as a verification technique, testing *is* a verification technique. As such, testing that does not reveal any defects has performed two valuable tasks:

- A limited form of verification that the software implements the specification.

- Confirmation that the measures undertaken to avoid faults have performed as desired.

The three roles for testing — verification, debugging, and validation — are all useful, but testing should not be relied upon for all three. There are better ways to do debugging, for example. More importantly, validation is an activity that should take place during requirements acquisition and specification development.

10.3.3 The Testing Process

The general test process is shown in Figure 10.5. The *software under test* is instrumented to collect *test metric data* using a *test metric tool*. The software is then placed into a *test execution harness* that controls the execution of the software as it is tested. The various *test case inputs* that are needed come from a file and the *test case outputs* that the software generates are stored in a second file. The test case outputs are checked to see whether they are correct by comparing them with the *expected outputs*, and the *test metric data* is collected. The test metric data is used to determine whether testing can be considered adequate.

In practice, this general testing process is complex and difficult to conduct for any system, but testing is especially difficult for any system requiring high levels of dependability. The major issues that arise are:

- The form of the software that is tested.
- Determining the correctness of the output when a test case is run.
- Deciding how many test cases to run.
- Automation of the test process.

In this section, we deal with each of these issues.

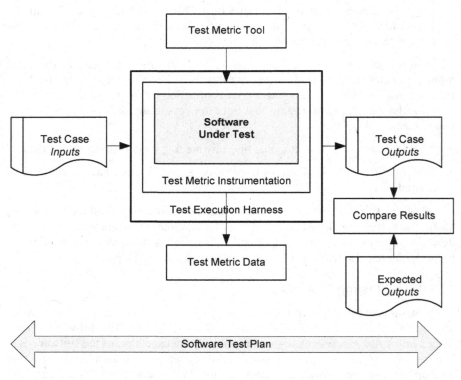

FIGURE 10.5 The general testing process includes creation of test inputs, executing the software, observing the software during testing, determining whether the software executed the tests correctly, and computing test metrics of interest.

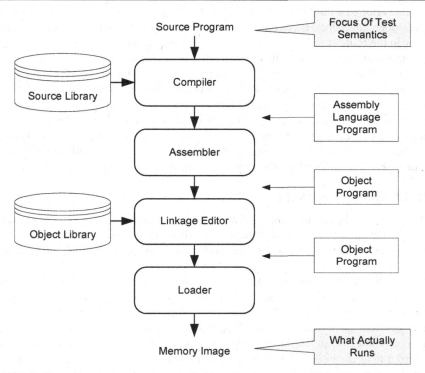

FIGURE 10.6 Translation of a source program to binary involves system utilities including a compiler, a linkage editor, a loader, and often an assembler.

10.3.4 Software Form

Much of the literature and theory of software testing is framed in terms related to the software *source* code. White-box test coverage metrics, for example, are defined in terms of source-code statements. Unfortunately, analysis at the source-code level does not account for the fact that the source code is not what executes.

The software that executes has been created from the source program by at least three system utilities: (a) a compiler, (b) a linkage editor, and (c) a loader, all three of which have to work correctly if the test results obtained from the source code of the program are to hold. In some cases a fourth utility is involved, an assembler. The use of an assembler is required when the output of a compiler is assembly language as is often the case. The role of the various utilities is shown in Figure 10.6.

When dealing with a system requiring high levels of dependability, the role of these system utilities must be kept in mind. We might know a great deal about the source program as a result of analysis of the source program. For example, if we have developed a model and used model checking to confirm that a concurrent program does not enter undesired states, the binary program might fail because of an error in the translation process. Compilers, linkage editors, and loaders are complex programs, and reports of faults in these utilities are not unusual.

The fact that the source program is not the program that runs has led many who develop software for systems with high dependability requirements to prefer testing to analysis. This situation is quite a dilemma, however. As we discuss in Chapter 12, testing cannot provide adequate assurance that a system has a high level of dependability. Yet other analysis techniques, including coverage metrics, operate typically on the source program. In practice, the best option is to use both analysis of the source program and testing of the binary program.

10.3.5 Output Checking

Determining whether the output of a program is correct requires either (a) that we know what the correct output should be so that we can compare the actual output with what we expect or (b) that we have some way of distinguishing the correct value by some other means.

In order to know what the correct output should be, we have to have a method of computing the output separately from the program. In general, having such a method is unlikely. Presumably, we wrote the program so as to compute something that we needed and did not already have a means of computing. In some cases, engineers attempt to compute the expected output of a program by hand in an approach referred to as *desk checking* There is an implication that humans will repeat the calculation at their desks. For most realistic programs, such repetition is completely unrealistic.

To see how difficult output checking is, consider checking the output of a program that computes the average of 100,000 numbers. Except for special cases where the numbers have some simple pattern, checking the average requires repeating the entire calculation.

If you are not convinced about the difficulty of output checking, consider checking the output of a program that inverts $1,000 \times 1,000$ matrices or a program that solves the travelling-salesman's problem for 100 cities. Neither is feasible by hand.

Given this difficulty, how can testing software ever be useful? Is output checking always bordering on the impossible? There are several indications that provide *partial* information that the output of a program is correct:

- The program does not crash when executing tests.
- The program does not raise any unexpected exceptions.
- The program does not enter an infinite loop and execution time is not excessive.
- The interactive response rate is uniform and reasonable.
- The output values are within the set of values of the associated type.

- The output values are "reasonable" for the associated type.
- Graphic output looks "reasonable" to the eye.

All of these indications are helpful in that if they were not true we could be sure there was something wrong. But the fact that a program does not crash or raise unexpected exceptions and so on does not mean that the program is fault free.

In some cases (but relatively few), there are simple techniques that allow us to determine whether a test case has been executed successfully:

- A program for which correct output has a property that is simple to check, e.g., a sort program where the output is sorted. Note, however, that sorted order is not the only property that the output of a sort has to have. A second is that the output has to be a permutation of the input. This property is difficult to check.

- A program for which the correct output has a simple relationship to the input, e.g., a program to compute the inverse of a matrix in which the output multiplied by the input should yield the identity matrix.

- Special input cases that generate output which is easy to check, e.g., a set of identical numbers that are input to a program that computes the average should yield the obvious output.

No satisfactory general solution to the problem of output checking exists. In practice, most testing relies upon the list of items of partial information above together with human assessment of functionality.

10.3.6 Test Adequacy

Everybody who has ever tested a program has faced the dilemma of how many tests to conduct. If we could run as many tests as we wish, how many would be sufficient?

Although we should not rely on testing alone for assurance, successful execution of a suite of test cases does provide some confidence in the dependability of a system. Thus, software engineers developing systems for safety-critical, security-critical, or mission-critical applications must decide on the number and form of the test cases that they run.

Test adequacy is usually determined by measurement of a *test-coverage metric*. A test-coverage metric is a measure captured during testing that is related in some way to the goal of comprehensive testing. As shown in Figure 10.5 on page 306, measuring a test metric requires:

- A tool that instruments the software so as to capture and record the necessary data.
- Execution of the software under test and capture of the coverage-metric data during execution.

- Computation of the value of the metric once testing is complete.

Notice that this process raises several issues for software developers. The instrumentation used to capture coverage-metric data will affect a program's real-time performance, and so testing while capturing coverage-metric data might be impossible for software with hard, real-time requirements. Also, the introduction of probes to capture coverage-metric data will change the software no matter what the software's requirements are. Thus, the software for which metric data is captured will not be exactly the same as the software that is used in the associated application.

The following are the most common test metrics:

Functional coverage. Functional coverage is a measure of how many of the basic functions that the software has to provide have been executed during testing. A calculator program, for example, might offer functionality that includes the four basic arithmetic operators, and functional coverage would measure how many of the four were actually tested.

Statement coverage. Statement coverage is a measure of how many of the high-level language statements in the software have been executed during testing. Statement coverage might seem simple because engineers often assume that executing a program means executing all of a program. In practice, most runs of a given program actually execute only a small fraction of the statements. The combined statement coverage results of many tests frequently do not cover all of the statements in a program.

Branch coverage. Branch coverage is a measure of how many of the branches in the software have been executed for each of the two possibilities at each branch (branch taken and branch not taken). For branches that are part of the implementation of a loop control statement, the definition is often extended to include zero, one, and more than one executions of the loop.

Branch coverage might seem to be the same as statement coverage. If all the statements in a program have been executed, haven't all the branches been executed? The answer is "yes" but not for both branch decisions, and that difference is important. Consider the following example:

```
if a > b then a := a + 1; endif;
```

There are two statements in the example, and they would both be executed by a test for which a > b. But that test would only execute the if statement with the associated branch not taken.

Modified condition/decision coverage (MCDC). MCDC is a sophisticated test-coverage metric that was developed primarily for use in the commercial aviation industry [26, 58]. This metric is required by the FAA for some computer applications in commercial aircraft such as fly-by-wire control systems and autopilots. MCDC is sufficiently important that we deal with it more fully in the next section.

Note that a test coverage metric is not a test method; a test coverage metric is just a number. Thus, speaking of "branch testing", for example, is meaningless. The metric itself says nothing about how test cases will be selected, their output checked, how the testing process will be managed, and so on. The only meaningful statement in a testing situation is the value of the test-coverage metric that has been achieved.

Since each of the four metrics listed above relates to some aspect of a program, the value of a test metric is usually expressed as a percentage. For example, if a test process measures statement coverage, then the total number of statements executed in the test process divided by the number of statements in the program expressed as a percentage is the value of the coverage metric.

An assumption that is made about test metrics is that higher percentages are better. This assumption is perfectly reasonable, but leaves us with the problem that we do not have any link between specific values of test-coverage metrics and dependability metrics of interest.

Clearly, there are a few simple relationships upon which we can rely. If statement coverage is less than 100%, we know that some parts of the software have never even been executed, and program statements that have never been executed have certainly not been tested. The same is true with branch coverage. If there is a branch for which only one side has been executed, then we certainly have not tested to see what happens if the other side is executed.

Unfortunately, that is about all we have. There is really no stronger link between test-coverage metric values and aspects of dependability. Despite that, reaching 100% statement or branch coverage is clearly a good idea and a goal that developers should strive to meet. In practice, getting high levels of coverage is very difficult, and a great deal of effort is usually required to generate a set of tests that will lead to coverage metrics with values much above about 70%. The reason for this difficulty lies in the role of the code that is not executed. That code is usually associated with obscure circumstances such as failure conditions and handling interrupts. To execute this code means that the obscure circumstances have to be generated, and tests that force these conditions are often tedious to develop.

10.3.7 Modified Condition Decision Coverage

Modified Condition Decision Coverage is an elaborate special case of branch coverage [26, 58]. The reason that MCDC was invented was to deal with some of the limitations of branch coverage.

To see the problem, consider the following simple statement:

```
if A or B then ... else ... endif;
```

Branch coverage would be complete once we had tested the associated program and both the then clause and the else clauses had been executed. We could achieve that by having a test case in which A and B were both true and a second in which they were both false. We designate these values of A and B as TT and FF.

Why is this insufficient? Merely having A and B take on the values TT and FF leaves doubt about the other combinations of values of A and B. Would the software operate correctly with A and B taking on other values? There is no indication and no requirement to check if we limit coverage to branch coverage.

Concerns such as these led to the introduction of a new term, **decision coverage**, which is equivalent to branch coverage, and two new coverage metrics:

Condition coverage: A condition is any Boolean variable or predicate in the expression controlling a branch. In condition coverage, all possible values of all conditions in a branch expression are taken during testing.

Condition/decision coverage: In condition/decision coverage, all conditions and all decisions must evaluate to both T and F during testing.

All this seems elaborate and somewhat confusing. An obvious question that comes to mind is: "Doesn't condition coverage include decision coverage?" If all of the Boolean variables and predicates in a branch expression have taken on the values T and F, then surely both sides of the branch must have been executed.

The answer, surprisingly, is "no". To see this, consider tests of a program that included the simple if statement above. If the values used for A and B in two tests were TF and FT, then both variables have taken on both truth values, but only the then clause of the statement will have been executed.

Condition/decision coverage seems to solve the problem. Since decision coverage is not implied by condition coverage, we will insist on decision coverage separately. This change is helpful and brings a lot of benefits, but there remains a

A	B	A or B
F	F	F
F	T	T
T	F	T
T	T	T

FIGURE 10.7 Logical values of conditions in a simple if statement and the resulting value of the decision. From this truth table, values that have to be generated during testing to achieve MCDC can be determined.

problem with the form of logical expressions. Condition/decision coverage fails to reveal logical expressions that might be erroneous. To see this, consider again the simple if statement above, and assume that tests were conducted so that A and B took on the values TT and FF. Both condition and decision coverage requirements would be met, but the testing would not distinguish the expression A or B from the expression A and B.

This limitation led Chelinski and Miller to introduce yet another coverage metric, Modified Condition Decision or MCDC [26, 58]:

Modified Condition Decision Coverage: In Modified Condition Decision Coverage, testing must show that every condition in the branch expression affects the outcome of the decision *independently*.

In essence, what this amounts to is showing that the decision is affected by having each condition take on the values T and F while all the other conditions remain fixed. For the simple if statement example, in order to achieve MCDC, the values of A and B would have to take on the values TF, FT, and FF. This is illustrated in Figure 10.7. The solid lines bounding the T and F values of A show that the value of the expression is determined by A with the value of B fixed at F. Similarly, the dashed box shows that the value of the expression is determined by B with the value of A fixed at F. The union of the two sets of values shows the values that A and B have to take in order to obtain MCDC.

So far, we have discussed branch expressions assuming complete evaluation. Some languages, C++ and Java, for example, always implement short-circuit evaluation in which evaluation of a Boolean expression ceases once the value of the expression is determined. In our simple if statement example, the evaluation of the expression A or B would cease without evaluating B if A were T. For such languages, MCDC is equivalent to condition/decision coverage.

10.3.8 Test Automation

Having an engineer just sit in front of a workstation and arrange for each test to be run is an appealing idea. In practice, however, the number of tests that are typically needed makes this impractical. A second concern is the almost certain need to rerun the same tests many times. Running a set of tests more than once will be necessary for many different reasons. Automation is essential in such circumstances.

The basic structure of the setup we need for test automation is shown in Figure 10.5 on page 306. This picture is fairly simple, but a little investigation reveals that the task of test automation needs more care for other than fairly simple systems. The main issues are:

Graphic user interfaces. Most user interfaces are graphic, and so to test a program we need to effect mouse movements, text input, menu item selections, and interaction with dialog boxes. This is easy for a human user, but if we are going to test a program with a graphical user interface we need to automate the interaction.

Many systems have been developed, including some which attempt to record user actions for later automatic playback. This approach is not really adequate because the automatic generation of test cases is precluded.

Embedded systems. Many systems requiring high levels of dependability are embedded and are responsible for controlling some sort of physical device. Many times the thing that is controlled is subject to change according to the laws of physics. To test such a system, the embedded execution environment needs to be enhanced to allow test-case input to be supplied, output values to be captured, and coverage metric data to be collected. For an embedded system, these types of enhancement impact the operating environment in such a way that the system as tested is not the system as deployed.

10.3.9 Real-Time Systems

Real-time systems are especially difficult to test. The difficulty of automating testing noted above with embedded systems becomes more significant for real-time systems. The establishment of a suitable test environment can affect the real-time behavior of the system to a point where testing the real-time performance is meaningless.

Real-time systems are much more difficult to test than non-real-time for three reasons:

Nondeterminism. Real-time systems are typically concurrent and so the test engineer has to deal with the potential for nondeterminism.

Instrumentation. Any attempt to introduce test instrumentation into a real-time system will inevitably disturb the timing of the system.

Inconsistency. Hardware timing is inconsistent. Modern hardware is so complex that timing varies from execution to execution for the same instruction sequence.

The first two items are closely coupled since any effort to make a system deterministic is going to affect timing. The biggest problem is the difficulty of capturing the data needed to compute coverage metrics. Real-time systems can be run with no instrumentation, but that severely limits the value of testing and precludes any easy way of determining that the system has missed a timing requirement.

There is no good solution to this problem. Hardware can be used to create probes that do not affect software timing, but this solution is difficult and expensive. One common approach for simple systems is to use a *hardware emulator*. The CPU is replaced by a larger, faster CPU that emulates the original but has cycles left over for collecting data.

The approach that is often used for unit and subsystem testing is to separate real-time testing from functional testing. The software is instrumented and operated with simulated peripheral devices, and tests are run just to check correct functionality. This can be done with full test-coverage instrumentation. Separately, the software is tested with no internal instrumentation but with simulated peripherals that are instrumented. These peripherals can check the values that are being used and the timing of output presentation.

An approach that is used in some system developments is to try to model the timing of software and predict whether the software will meet its deadlines. For simple, sequential software, this amounts to looking at the machine instructions and estimating their timing. The timing of basic blocks is estimated and then the timing of complete subsystems is estimated using the control-flow graph and estimates of branch frequencies. The most important metric is *worst-case execution time* (WCET). If the worst case could be estimated and shown to be less than the deadline, then the deadline would always be met.

The use of WCET has been made much more difficult by the third problem, hardware timing inconsistency. This problem is the result of modern processor designs. These designs are so complex that the timing of any given instruction sequence is hard to determine. The worst case is easy; just assume no overlap in the pipeline, no out-of-order issue, incorrect branch prediction, conflicts on every memory access, and no cache hits. This provides such a poor estimate that the result is useless unless the designer wants to have the processor idle most of the time when the system runs.

The idea of measuring processor timing, though seemingly attractive, is actually very difficult. If the designer develops careful probes and measures the actual timing of an instruction sequence, he or she will not know how close this value is to the actual WCET that will be seen during operation. Even if many measurements are averaged, the result might not be close to the WCET that the system will experience. The benefit of this approach is that if sufficient data is obtained, then the developer can build a statistical argument about the value of the WCET.

In practice, designers have to address this issue, but there are no really good solutions. The best approach is to begin by disabling some of the hardware that causes timing variation if possible. Some systems, for example, disable caching. The next step is to test the software in its operational environment and measure the actual timing that is seen over as wide a range of inputs and environmental conditions as possible. This data can then be used to obtain the best statistical estimate possible of the likely WCET.

Key points in this chapter:

- Inspection is a powerful technique for finding faults in all artifacts.
- A variety of inspection techniques has been developed.
- Verification by testing only applies to executable artifacts.
- The most difficult aspect of testing is determining output correctness.
- A variety of test metrics have been developed to provide engineers with a means of assessing the test process.
- Modified Condition Decision Coverage (MCDC) is a sophisticated test-coverage metric used primarily by the FAA for critical aircraft systems.
- Testing complex modern systems that include graphic user interfaces or that are embedded is challenging because of the difficulty of controlling the test environment.

Exercises

1. Consider the role of inspection in the development of a safety-critical computer system. To what artifacts should inspection be applied? What conclusions can be drawn about a safety-critical system as a result of the inspection that has been applied? What classes of fault could be the target of inspection for the various artifacts inspected?

2. For a program that you have written, develop a set of questions about the program that could be posed to inspectors in Active Reviews or Phased Inspections. Make sure that the questions are precisely stated and that each one will force the inspector to understand as much of the program as possible.

3. Specialists are important contributors to a Fagan inspection. Develop a checklist that might be used by a specialist in real-time system design when inspecting a program that has to operate in hard real time.

4. For a programming language with which you are familiar, search on-line for a tool that will enable you to determine branch coverage of a program. Assess the tool by applying it to specimen programs that you have written.

5. Achieving high levels of statement and branch coverage for any realistic program is difficult, because test cases have to be contrived to force the software to execute special cases and error processing code. Of particular concern are exception handlers. Exceptions have to be raised at a point in the software where the handler of interest is the one called. For a program that you have written, develop test cases to exercise as much of the exception handling code as possible. Determine the fraction of the exception handling code that you were successful in executing.

6. Following on from the previous question, suppose that you attempted to "test" the exception handling elements of the software by inserting additional software into code blocks that allowed you to trigger the exception handlers. Would that be adequate to allow you to draw conclusions about the software?

7. Consider a software system that was written from a formal specification in Z. Discuss the concept of generating test cases from the specification. How would such an approach work? How useful would the test cases be?

8. Consider the following fragment of Ada source code:

```
PressureAlarm := (Pressure < PLimit);
if (Temp > TLimit) and PressureAlarm then
    if CoolingPumpState= On then
        EmergencyIndicator:= On;
    else
        ReactantPump := On;
    endif;
endif;
```

    (a) What are the *decisions* in this code in the sense of MC DC test coverage?

    (b) What are the *conditions* in this code in the sense of MC DC test coverage?

9. Java uses a garbage collection approach to reclaiming dynamic storage. Is it possible for a Java program to "leak" memory? If so, why? If not, why not?

10. Dynamic memory management is problematic for safety-critical systems. What are the issues that make dynamic memory management problematic?

11. In full Ada, exceptions are propagated up the dynamic call chain until a handler is found. SPARK Ada specifically disallows all exceptions because they are not easy to analyze. Would the inclusion of exception handlers in every function and procedure along with a *static* check of the handlers being there be a way to allow Ada exceptions in SPARK Ada? If so, why? If not, why not?

12. The C programming language is difficult to analyze by tools attempting to measure MC DC coverage, because C has no Boolean type. Although decision points in source code can be found, the conditions upon which they depend are difficult to determine automatically. Why is this the case?

13. The test coverage metrics that are commonly measured are based upon the source form of the software, but the binary form is what executes. How might you verify that the binary form of the software properly implements the source program?

CHAPTER 11

Software Fault Tolerance

Learning objectives of this chapter are to understand:

- The difficulty of tolerating design faults.
- The role of fault tolerance in software dependability.
- The limitations of fault tolerance in achieving software dependability.
- The various techniques available for providing fault tolerance in software.
- The effectiveness of the mechanisms for tolerating software faults.
- The cost of software fault tolerance during development and operation.

11.1 Components Subject to Design Faults

In the past four chapters, we have focused on software fault avoidance and software fault elimination. Now we move on to look at software fault tolerance, and we will be looking at a completely different form of fault tolerance from that which we examined in Chapter 6.

Although our primary interest lies in software dependability, in considering the development of a dependable computing system, identifying all of the system components that might be subject to design faults is important. The real issue is to tolerate design faults, and the techniques developed for software fault tolerance apply to design fault tolerance in other complex logical structures such as processors.

We have mentioned several system components subject to design faults already, but here is the complete list:

System software. All forms of system software upon which we rely are subject to design faults. This includes operating system kernels, file systems, network protocol stacks, compilers, debugging systems, configuration management systems, device drivers, linkers, and loaders.

Application software. Most people think of the software that they write as being the only application software with which they have to be concerned. In doing so, they are forgetting the plethora of libraries that are part of the implementation of high-level languages, the run-time support that the language requires, and the software that is written by others with which their code interacts.

Embedded firmware. Many safety-critical systems use *application-specific integrated circuits* (ASICs) and *field-programmable gate arrays* (FPGAs) as part of their implementation. The logic they contain is often referred to as *firmware*, and such devices are often thought of as "hardware" and thus somehow different. But, in fact, they are just another manifestation of the complex logic that we find in software and so, from the perspective of faults to which they might be subject, they are just as subject to design faults as software. Importantly, they are also subject to degradation faults and so designers have to deal with both. From the perspective of the software engineer, ASICs and FPGAs are best thought of as software.

Processors. In the early days of computing, processor faults were mostly degradation faults. The processors were much less complex than those of today and so were somewhat easier to design. Also, manufacturing techniques were not as good, and so the probability of failure was higher. This situation has reversed in recent years. Processors are much more complex and manufacturing techniques are vastly better. The result is that design defects in processors now tend to dominate. You can probably see this yourself if you ask yourself whether one of the computers you use has ever failed because of processor degradation. Certainly many people have experienced disk and power supply failures, but most people have never experienced a processor degradation fault because such faults are so rare.

Design faults in processors are a different story, and they are now a major area of concern. The most famous design defect (but far from the most serious) is the Intel Pentium FDIV bug in which the original Pentium processor did not compute floating-point division correctly in some obscure cases [152]. In order to seek some protection from processor design faults in the Boeing 777 flight control system, Boeing used three different processors operating in parallel in each channel of the system [155].

Power supplies and wiring. Experience shows that power supplies and power sources tend to suffer from degradation faults at a fairly high rate, but design faults in power supplies are not uncommon. Similarly, design faults in wiring do occur, although the relative simplicity of wiring tends to keep the occurrence of wiring design defects quite low. Obviously, degradation faults in wiring are common and have to be dealt with carefully. Chafing of wiring tends to occur unless routing is done carefully and wiring is restrained from movement. Also, the insulation in wiring tends to degrade over time and so is subject to cracking.

11.2 Issues with Design Fault Tolerance

11.2.1 The Difficulty of Tolerating Design Faults

In general, design faults are much more difficult to tolerate than degradation faults. The reasons for this difficulty are:

Design faults are more difficult to anticipate than degradation faults. We know that things break, i.e., degradation faults will occur, and, in general, we know how they break. Anticipation of the failure of a disk, for example, is fairly easy. All disks will fail eventually. But anticipating the way that things will be *designed* incorrectly, or, in the case of software, how the software will be written incorrectly, is difficult. From experience, we probably suspect that any piece of software of any significant size will have defects, but we cannot easily anticipate what the faults will be. Fortunately, we can mitigate this problem somewhat by using software techniques that allow us to predict that certain types of fault are absent (see Chapter 8, Chapter 9, and Chapter 10).

The effects of design faults are hard to predict. Since design faults are hard to anticipate, it follows that we cannot predict their effects. A software defect in one program could send corrupt data to multiple other programs. Any of the programs could send corrupt data to peripherals and over network links. How bad the damage is depends upon how quickly the erroneous state can be detected and measures taken to stop the spread of the error. An error that was not detected could continue to spread for an arbitrary time. In some cases, errors have spread to file backups, because they have persisted for protracted periods.

We discussed the complexity of erroneous states in Section 3.2. Figure 11.1 is the same as Figure 3.2, and shows a system consisting of several interconnected computers, one of which has an attached disk and printer. The damage to the state from a single fault in Program$_1$ on Computer A ends up affecting the state of three programs on Computer A, one program each on Computers B and C, a disk, and the output from a printer.

A practical example that demonstrates both the difficulty of anticipating design faults and the difficulty of predicting their effects occurred in February 2007. Many of the avionics systems on six Lockheed F22 Raptor fighter aircraft failed as the aircraft crossed the International Date Line [33]. The aircraft were flying from Hawaii to Okinawa, Japan. The aircraft were able to return safely to Hawaii with the assistance of tanker aircraft that had been accompanying them.

The failure semantics that components exhibit are difficult to define. A consequence of the previous point, that the effects of design faults are hard to predict, is the fact that failure semantics for design faults are hard to define. Having well-

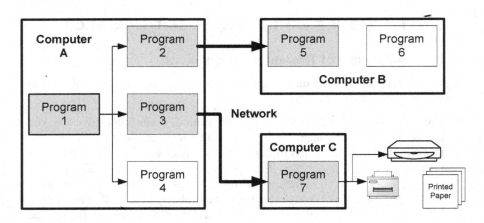

FIGURE 11.1 Possible effect of a single bug on the state of a computer system.

defined failure semantics is essential if we are to tolerate faults. But how will anything that is subject to design faults appear after a design fault has manifested itself? In particular, how will a piece of software appear after a software fault has caused an error? Software might terminate, but, if it does so, there is no guarantee that the state that is left will be predictable in any way. Also, as we noted in the previous point, making things worse (if that is possible) is that software might continue to execute and keep generating more and more defective state. The creation of defective state could continue for an arbitrary period of time, because there is no guarantee that the offending software will terminate.

Having well-defined failure semantics is so important that, even for degradation faults, provision is sometimes made to force the state following a failure to be predictable. Power supplies, for example, employ over-current and over-voltage mechanisms so that the semantics of failure of the power supply or the associated wiring will be that power is withdrawn. Given the difficulty we face with failure semantics for design faults, we have to consider explicit measures to provide predictable failure semantics.

To get a sense of the problem of building fault-tolerant software, think about a piece of software that you have written. Did you know whether the software contained bugs or not? Did you know what the effect of the bugs that at least you suspected would be? Did you know how your software would fail when a bug manifested itself? In particular, did you know whether the software would terminate or keep executing?

Continuing with this challenge, consider the following four questions:

1. Could you modify your software so that it could detect that it was in an erroneous state?

2. Could you modify your software so that it could clean up the operating state and make the state one from which execution could proceed correctly?

3. Could you modify your software so that it could continue execution from the corrected state either with the original functionality or with modified functionality?

4. Could you build the entire software system so that these three activities could be completed automatically?

The point of these four questions is to ask you whether you could make your own software *fault tolerant*, since these questions are a restatement of the four phases of fault tolerance: error detection, damage assessment, state restoration, and continued service.

11.2.2 Self-Healing Systems

A further question to contemplate is whether you could modify your own software to go beyond fault tolerance into fault repair. Tolerating a fault is difficult and not always successful. A much better situation would be one in which software was written so that when a fault manifested itself, the fault was located and *corrected* automatically. This is the essence of research on self-healing software systems.

Although self-healing software is a nice idea, building software that can repair faults automatically is probably a long way off. One example of a promising approach is the use of genetic algorithms. In this approach, when an error is detected, the path taken through the software is identified and compared with the paths taken when the software executed test cases for which the software was known to work. Using the collection of paths, the likely location of the fault within the software is identified, and then a series of source-code transformations (mutations in the genetic sense) are applied. Each transformation produces a slightly different program and each of these is executed with both the known good test cases and the failing case. If one of the transformed programs executes all test cases correctly, then there is a chance that the fault has been corrected. For more details on this approach see the work of Weimer et al. [147].

There are examples of systems that can "heal" hardware degradation faults although, inevitably, self-healing in that case consumes components as failed components are replaced by operating spares. The simplest example of this approach is in hybrid redundancy, in which failed components are detected by a voter and replaced with spares that typically are unpowered so as to maximize their "shelf" life (see Section 6.3.4, page 166).

11.2.3 Error Detection

Error detection in fault tolerance for software is essentially the same problem as occurs with testing. How can we tell, reliably, whether or not the software has computed the correct output? When software fails, the symptoms are often complex and include outputs that are "close" to those expected. Software failures can even look like hardware failures. Finally, software failures are often intermittent, i.e., they are due to Heisenbugs (see Section 3.4), and so, even if software fails in a detectable way, the software might well work as desired if we try to re-execute the software as part of an effort to locate the fault.

Software error detection becomes a lot more practical if we merely look for certain types of failure. For example, for software that is operating in real time, failure includes failure to deliver the requisite results by a deadline. Monitoring the software's output provides an easy way to detect failure to provide output on time. Similarly, some issues with concurrent software can be detected quite easily. A deadlocked system, for example, can be detected by observation of process progress. The fact that error detection is more practical for certain types of failure has led to powerful results in the field of dependability that we look at in Section 11.6.

11.2.4 Forward and Backward Error Recovery

Error recovery is the combination of state restoration and continued service. The basic idea with state restoration is to create a state from which continued service can resume satisfactorily. The way that this is done for degradation faults is to remove the failed component (and frequently much more) from the system in service. If spares are available, they are introduced into the system in service. If no spares are available, the system has to operate without the removed component. This type of state restoration is referred to as *forward error recovery*, because the state that is produced during state restoration is a new state, not one that existed in the system's past.

In systems where no spares are available, the system has lost resources with forward error recovery. Since the loss might be substantial (e.g., a complete processor, memory unit, disk system, etc.), the opportunities for continued service are restricted. Continued service almost certainly cannot be the same as the original service, because the overall loss of resources can be considerable.

Error recovery is more flexible and therefore more complex when tolerating software faults than when tolerating degradation faults. The reason for the difference is that, with errors arising from software faults, the possibility exists of returning the system to a state that existed in the past in order to achieve state restoration and provide sophisticated continued service as a result. This technique is called *backward error recovery*.

When dealing with software, backward error recovery can be very useful. Since we can recreate a state that existed before a fault manifested itself and damaged the

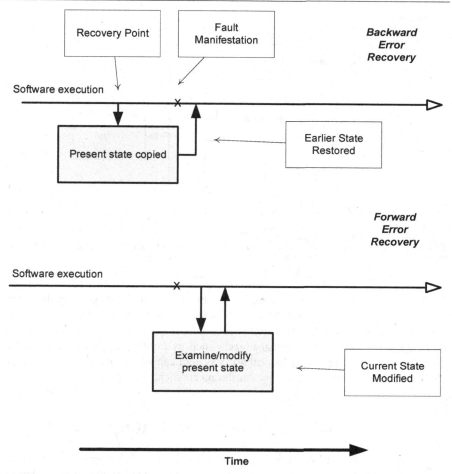

FIGURE 11.2 Backward and forward error recovery. Time is shown from left to right. In the case of backward error recovery, the state of the system is restored to a previous state. In forward error recovery, the new state is created by modifying the erroneous state to produce a possible, consistent future state.

state, continued service can be based on a complete and consistent state, and full service could be provided, at least in principle. The notions of forward and backward error are illustrated in Figure 11.2.

If the provision of continued service is able to avoid the fault that damaged the state, then the effect is to reverse time so as to make the system state revert to what it was in the past (hence the name *backward* error recovery) and "rewrite" history. Provided this is acceptable to the application, then the approach is quite powerful.

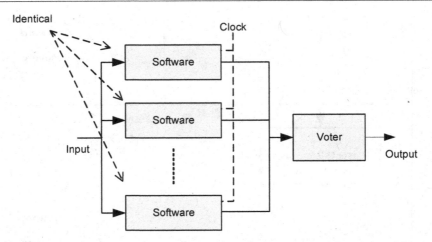

FIGURE 11.3 N-modular system for software in which software is merely replicated. Except for non-determinacy, all copies generate the same output and there is no benefit from the replication.

Backward error recovery is a desirable approach, but it has to be applied carefully. Reversing time means that the entire system state has to be taken back in time, and there has to be certainty that such reversal is complete. Part of a system's state is its peripherals, including physical objects such as printed paper. Paper cannot be "unprinted", and so restoring the state of a system cannot include restoring paper to its unprinted condition or any other similar mechanical change.

11.3 Software Replication

Replication worked for degradation faults, so it is tempting to turn to replication again for design faults. A software version of N-modular redundancy for software in which the software is replicated (as we did for hardware when dealing with degradation faults) is shown in Figure 11.3.

This approach seems unlikely to provide any benefit. If the software components are just copies, then surely if one fails, they will all fail. This observation is correct provided two conditions hold:

Each copy receives the same data. Clearly if the copies receive different data, they are likely to act differently. Since we are dealing with copies, supplying them with the same data seems both obvious and essential.

The software is deterministic. If the software is not deterministic, then the different copies might do different things, although the different behaviors are not necessarily useful.

Thus, if these two conditions hold, there is no gain from executing copies of the software in terms of tolerating design faults in the software.

These two conditions are, in fact, rather important, because they need not hold. If they do not hold, then the copies might behave differently, and that might be an advantage to us. Surprisingly, in practice, software designers can force these conditions to be violated quite easily, and violating the conditions can have considerable benefit. The major benefits that ensure occur in dealing with *Heisenbugs*, which we discuss in Section 11.5.2, and with a general approach to software fault tolerance that is called *data diversity*, which we discuss in Section 11.5.

11.4 Design Diversity

By definition, design faults are characteristics of design. This observation suggests that, if two or more software systems are built to provide the same functionality but with different designs, they might not all fail on the same input. Exploiting this possibility has led to a technique that is referred to as *design diversity*.

How might different software systems be built with different designs? The basic idea is to focus on independent development by teams that do not communicate with each other. This isolated development is illustrated in Figure 11.4. Several specific techniques have been proposed:

Different development teams. The idea with different development teams is to have groups of engineers working independently develop two or more versions

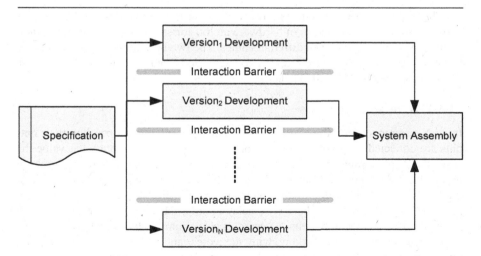

FIGURE 11.4 N-modular system in which different teams develop different versions of the software in isolation.

of a software system. Once the versions are complete, the system is assembled. The different teams must not communicate, because, if they did, they might be influenced in some way to make the same mistakes. Thus, there has to be a way to ensure that the different teams do not discuss their implementations. If a single organization is responsible for more than one implementation, then that organization has to partition its staff, house them in separate sets of offices, ensure that they have no need to communicate for other professional reasons, and provide them with different computers, printers, etc.

Different software development tools. The use of different development tools is typically used in addition to the use of different development teams. Different tools begins with things like different programming languages (and therefore compilers), and extends to different linkers and loaders, different software development environments, and so on.

Different software design techniques. A special case of using different software development tools is the explicit use of different software design techniques. Comparison of software systems built using functional decomposition with those using object-oriented design reveals apparently considerable differences. Each design technique brings its own software-engineering advantages, and so the choice of technique is usually made using criteria other than dependability.

Different versions over time. Software systems are updated, extended, and enhanced quite often. One way to obtain multiple versions is to use up-to-date and older versions. Provided they supply the same functionality, there is a chance that the defects they contain will be different.

The multiple software systems built with any of these methods could be configured in various ways, much as in hardware architectures. Different software system architectures have been given different names. The two best known architectures are (1) the *N-version System* introduced by Avizienis and Chen [25] and (2) the *recovery block* introduced by Randell [114].

11.4.1 N-Version Systems

In an N-version system, the N different versions are executed in parallel, their outputs are collected by a voter, and the voter makes a decision about what value the system's output should be. The organization of an N-version system is shown in Figure 11.5. An important advantage of an N-version system with $N \geq 3$ is that faults are masked. Provided that the voter is able to select the correct output from the set of available outputs, there is no delay or other interruption of service.

A disadvantage of an N-version system is clear from the figure. All of the N versions have to be executed along with the voter, and so considerable hardware resources are needed over and above that needed for a single version.

A clock is needed in an N-version system to synchronize the execution of the different versions and the voter. The versions cannot operate in lockstep, because their execution times will differ. The voter has to be protected against the different execution times of the various versions and against the possibility that versions might fail. If the voter were merely to await the arrival from all the versions and one of them had failed, the voter might wait forever.

Output selection by the voter can use one of several different techniques that have been developed:

- The simplest technique is to choose the value supplied by the majority, if there is a majority.

- Sometimes groups of versions produce the same output, but there is more than one group. In that case, the value returned by the largest group can be used.

- The median value can be used.

- The middle value of the set ordered according to some function can be used.

- The average of all the values can be used.

Designing a voter for a specific system is quite complicated, because outputs can differ in ways that prohibit simple approaches to voting, specifically, numeric differences and algorithmic differences:

Numeric difference. The values supplied by different versions can be correct but differ because of rounding errors or similar numeric issues. Floating-point output values, for example, will not be bit-for-bit the same. The degree of difference

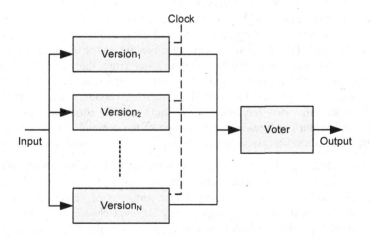

FIGURE 11.5 Operational organization of an N-version system.

that can be expected is system specific and so has to be analyzed for each individual system.

The fact that there can be a difference raises a new and important concern. The differences between values returned by different versions must be readily distinguished from erroneous values. Different values that appeared to differ because of rounding error, for example, might actually be different because of a fault. The designer has to answer the question "At what point is the difference in values to be deemed the result of a fault so that erroneous values can be ignored?"

This might seem like a problem that is solved easily by setting a limit, but the problem is much more subtle than it appears. Prior to the time at which the value received is deemed to indicate failure, the system will have been operating with the assumption that the value was trustworthy. If the voter used was based on averaging, mid-value selection, or median selection, then the output value could change suddenly as the voter decides that a version has failed and that the version's output could no longer be trusted.

As an example, consider the hypothetical data in Table 11.1. The data in the table

Time Frame	1	2	3	4	5	6	7
Version 1	180.0	181.0	179.0	180.0	180.0	179.0	180.0
Version 2	179.9	180.9	179.0	179.9	179.9	179.0	179.9
Version 3	180.1	183.1	186.1	189.1	192.1	195.1	198.1
Output	180.0	181.6	181.4	183.0	184.1	185.4	179.5

TABLE 11.1. Three-channel system with a failed version (number 3) that drifts.

is assumed to come from a three-version system (i.e., $N = 3$) that operates in real time and produces headings (in degrees) for an aircraft. The first row of the table indicates the timeframe for the hypothetical data, and rows two, three, and four are the outputs of the three versions for each frame. In the example, the third version is defective and is drifting slowly away from the correct value that is needed. The voting algorithm being used is the average of the three values, but at timeframe 7, the voter decides that the value from version 3 is sufficiently different from the other two versions that version 3 must be considered failed. At that point, the output becomes just the average of the remaining two versions. As a result, there is a relatively large (six degrees), sudden change in the output value.

Algorithmic differences. Another problem with voting is the possibility of two correct outputs being substantially different. Two software versions calculating the roots of a polynomial should compute the same set of values. But if only one value is needed, the versions might select different choices to return. Consider, for example, the computation of a square root. An application might under specify square root, expecting that the positive value would be assumed. If a version returns the negative square root, this value might not be expected, and a simple voter might infer that the associated version had failed.

A more elaborate example of the problem of multiple different correct solutions occurs in navigation systems. If two versions compute routes independently, the routes are likely to differ since they will be based on different heuristics. The only way to avoid this is to vote on small increments in the route (perhaps single direction decisions). This approach requires that the versions engage in a vote frequently during the computation using a technique called "cross-check points". A major disadvantage of introducing cross-check points is that they severely limit the design choices that can be used in the versions. The designs must be able to create the detailed data used in the cross-check points. This limitation is precisely the opposite of what is desired with design diversity, because it limits design choices.

Just as with N-modular redundancy in degradation fault tolerance, a decision about damage assessment has to be made if any of the versions fails to deliver an acceptable value to the voter. Again by analogy with degradation fault tolerance, the usual choice is to assume that the entire version is defective and to omit any values that the version produces in subsequent votes. By doing so, N-version systems are implementing forward error recovery.

Some techniques have been developed to restart failed software versions. The simplest technique is to reset the version and allow it to resume membership in the active set of versions. Resetting a version is problematic if the version maintains state, because the state has to be re-established. The state might have been created over a long period of execution, and this means that special and probably extensive actions need to be taken to re-initialize a failed version.

11.4.2 Recovery Blocks

In a recovery block, the versions, referred to as *alternates*, are executed in series until one of them, usually the first one, referred to as the *primary*, is determined to have completed the needed computation successfully. Assessment of the computation of an alternate is by error-detection mechanisms built into the alternate and by a final, external error-detection mechanism called an *acceptance test* [114]. To the extent possible, the acceptance test is designed to determine whether the output meets the system's specification. The organization of a recovery block system is shown in Figure 11.6.

The recovery block operates by storing the system's state, executing one alternate (the primary), and subjecting the primary's computations to the built-in error-detection mechanisms and the output to the acceptance test. If the built-in mechanisms do not detect an error and the output passes the acceptance test, i.e., meets the specification as defined by the acceptance test, then the output is supplied to the system and the recovery block terminates. If the primary fails, the recovery block restores the system's state and executes the next alternate. This process continues until the output is determined to be acceptable by the acceptance test or the recovery block runs out of alternates and fails.

The recovery block architecture implements backward error recovery, because the previously stored state is restored whenever an alternate fails. Thus, following state restoration, alternates can assume the complete state, so the alternate can undertake any processing that is deemed appropriate. Specifically, alternates do not have to meet identical specifications provided the acceptance test is properly defined.

Unlike an N-version system, a Recover Block system is not able to mask faults because any faulty alternate is guaranteed to cause a delay as the state is restored and other alternates are executed. Also, since an arbitrary number of alternates might be executed, up to and including the maximum number available, the execution time of a recovery block is unpredictable.

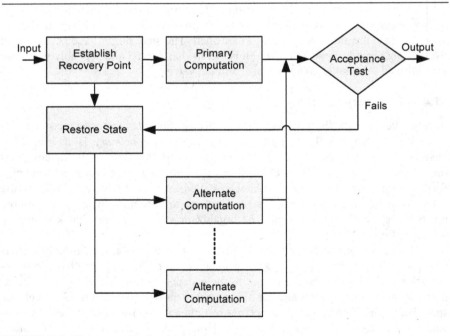

FIGURE 11.6 The recovery block software system architecture.

11.4.3 Conversations and Dialogs

Concurrent Systems

The recovery block framework was designed for sequential programs and has to be enhanced for concurrent programs. In a concurrent program, multiple processes or threads will be operating concurrently and asynchronously. Thus, to provide backward error recovery using recovery blocks, each of the concurrent entities will have to be structured as a recovery block. The issue that arises is the possibility of interacting states because of communication. Parallel processes, for example, are usually written to communicate with each other because the processes are merely building blocks for a larger entity.

The Domino Effect

When processes communicate, the data that passes from one to the other becomes part of the state of the recipient. Thus, in order to effect backward error recovery of the recipient, the sender has to be backed up to a point before the communication took place. To do so requires that the sender actually be backed up to a recovery point that the process established. This recovery point might be well before the point at which the problematic communication took place. The problem gets worse, however, when we realize that between establishing the recovery point and communication with the receiving process, the sending process might have been a recipient itself. Thus, the sender in that communication has to be backed up, and so on and so on. In the end, any number of processes might have to be backed up an arbitrary amount of time to reach a point that is truly a valid earlier state for all of the processes involved. This unconstrained rollback is called the *domino effect*.

Conversations

To avoid the domino effect, an enhancement to the recovery block structure was devised called a Conversation [114]. A Conversation is a structure covering a group of processes that want to communicate. As each process enters the Conversation, the process establishes a recover point as if the process were entering a recovery block. The most important aspect of a Conversation is that all of the processes that enter must synchronize the evaluations of their acceptance tests. If all acceptance tests pass, then the Conversation is complete and the processes proceed to their subsequent actions. If a process fails its acceptance test, then *all* of the processes must effect local backward error recovery and reestablish their stored states. Then each process executes an alternate and attempts to reach a point where the process can pass its acceptance test. Recovery and execution of alternates continues until all the processes pass their individual acceptance tests or no more alternates remain.

Dialogs

In related work, Knight and Gregory pointed out that the basic idea of a Conversation is potentially too rigid for many practical situations [53]. All of the processes in a Conversation are expected to eventually pass their individual acceptance tests and this might be impractical. A more effective approach in practice might be to dissolve the Conversation when the processes have to recover and allow the process to undertake an entirely different form of processing. Some processes might need to abandon their interaction with the group and effect some entirely different control path. Others might want to effect some different or reduced form of processing with the group that required an entirely different form of processing, including none. The structure that Knight and Gregory introduced for this flexible form of backward error recovery for communicating sequential processes is called a *Dialog* [53].

11.4.4 Measuring Design Diversity

Diversity Metrics

No matter what software system architecture is being used, successful fault tolerance using design diversity relies upon the different versions having different designs. How might the difference between designs be measured, or, more formally, how might design diversity be measured? Dealing with this question is a difficult challenge for many reasons. The first problem is to answer the question: "What does it mean for two software systems to have different designs?" In practice, there are no metrics that can measure design diversity in a meaningful way.

Statistical Independence

Even if there were metrics for design diversity and we could be confident that two designs were "different" according to the metric, this would not necessarily mean that the different designs had different faults. If they are to be effective, all of the various design-diverse software architectures rely upon the assumption that versions developed independently will have small probabilities of failing on the same input. Clearly, if versions developed independently fail frequently on the same inputs, then the improvement in dependability that can be expected from the multiple versions is small. As we saw in Section 6.4, large improvements in hardware dependability can be achieved where failures of different components are statistically independent. Unfortunately, statistical independence of faults is known not to be the case for software [80] and probably does not hold for any type of design fault.

   If versions that are developed independently do not necessarily fail in a statistically independent way, then how are their failures related and what effect does this have on system dependability? For any given system, there is no known way of predicting the failure rate of the system. Failures for a given system might be statistically independent, might be totally correlated, or anything in between. This range of possibilities means that no specific improvement in dependability can be expected from a design-diverse system, although improvements have been reported in various experiments (e.g., [80]).

For safety-critical systems, the systems most likely to be seeking dependability, the assumption has to be that no improvement in dependability will result from design diversity, because safety-critical systems need high levels of assurance. Indeed, since a design-diverse system is more complex than a single system, a failure rate greater than a single, carefully engineered system is entirely possible.

Modeling Design Diversity

A theoretical model of the failure rate of design-diverse systems was developed by Eckhardt and Lee [41]. This model predicts the failure rate extremely well but can only be used for theoretical studies. The model relies upon the distribution of the probability of failure of a set of versions for each vector of values in the input space. This distribution exists for any given system but cannot be known. If the distribution were known, the points in the input space where coincident failures occur would be known, and so the versions could be repaired.

The Eckhardt and Lee model does enable important "what if" questions to be answered about the effect of different distributions. If specific distributions are assumed, the model predicts the failure rate of the resulting design-diverse system. This work has enabled answers to be obtained to questions such as the optimal number of versions. The model shows, for example, that with reasonable assumptions about the correlation distribution, the benefit of an N-version system increases with N up to a specific value and actually decreases thereafter.

11.4.5 Comparison Checking

The availability of several versions when developing a design-diverse system has led many developers to use the N-version structure during system testing. Since the basic structure is intended to provide error detection during execution, obviously the same approach could be used for error detection during testing. Test inputs can be created by any suitable means, the versions executed, and then the outputs compared. The basic structure is shown in Figure 11.7.

The idea of using the N-version structure during testing has been referred to as *back-to-back testing*, although this term is misleading [145]. The structure does not provide all the elements of testing, just error detection. A more accurate term is *comparison checking*, and so that is the term used here.

Comparison checking seems like a good idea for two reasons:

- The technique does not require a lot of additional resources because the primary constituents of a comparison-checking system are the software versions that have to be developed anyway.

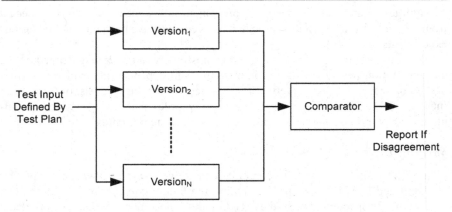

FIGURE 11.7 System structure for testing using comparison checking.

- The major problem in software testing, i.e., determining whether the output of the software is correct, appears to be solved.

In practice, comparison checking has a subtle problem that makes it far less attractive than it appears. When executing a test case using comparison checking, there are four possible outcomes:

All versions produce correct outputs. The comparator would indicate that the test was successful, and the test process would continue with the next test case.

Some versions produce correct outputs. The comparator would indicate that the test case was unsuccessful and identify the differences between the versions. The developers could then make the necessary corrections to the versions that failed.

All versions produce incorrect but different outputs. The comparator would indicate that the test case was unsuccessful and identify the differences between the versions. Again, the developers could then make the necessary corrections.

All versions produce incorrect but identical outputs. The comparator would indicate that the test was successful, and the test process would continue with the next test case.

The first three outcomes are productive and help developers to improve the software. There will be an unknown but potentially large number of false alarms because of the same set of issues raised with voting in N-version systems. Whether the false alarms become an impediment to development will depend on the rate that they arise for a specific system.

The real issue with comparison checking is the fourth outcome. A set of versions producing identical but incorrect outputs will not signal failure during testing. The defects that are the greatest concern for an operational N-version system or a recovery block, identical failures in all versions, will not be detected during testing. As testing proceeds, the faults that can be detected, i.e., those which cause the versions to have different outputs, will be detected and removed. In the limit, if a set of versions is tested with comparison checking, the versions will converge to compute the same function, including the same *erroneous* outputs for some inputs. An N-version system constructed from such a set of versions will be no more useful during operation than any of the individual versions.

11.4.6 The Consistent Comparison Problem

The Consistent Comparison Problem (CCP) is a problem that applies only to N-version systems [81]. The problem arises whenever comparisons (if statements, etc.) are used in the logic flow of the software. The problem is:

Without communication, two or more versions in an N-version system cannot ensure that, for any given comparison, the result of the comparison obtained by all the versions will be the same.

Thus, where the versions are making a comparison that relates directly to the application, such as comparing a computed flying altitude in an autopilot against a threshold, the versions might conclude differently about whether the altitude is above or below the threshold.

Unfortunately, there is no algorithmic solution to the problem [81]. In other words, there is no change to the software that can be made which will avoid the problem. Making things worse is that the problem will *always* occur, even with versions that are individually considered perfect. The rate at which the problem manifests itself is application dependent, and so modeling the effects of the Consistent Comparison Problem in general is problematic.

An example of the problem based on a simple thermostat is illustrated in Figure 11.8. Suppose that a 2-version system is developed to implement a thermostat for a heating furnace. The simple algorithm that is used by the software is to read a temperature sensor periodically to see what the current air temperature is, and then to compare the value read with a set point, the desired temperature. If the air temperature read from the sensor is below the set point, then the software commands the furnace to turn on. The furnace is turned off if the observed temperature is above the set point. This computation is repeated every few seconds.

A complication is that the software is required to implement hysteresis to prevent the furnace from cycling on and off too frequently. The requirements for the system's hysteresis are to change the furnace state (on to off or vice versa) only if:

- The thermostat has indicated the need for a fixed number of cycles. The number of cycles might be quite high to prevent the effects of transient temperature changes from affecting the furnace state.

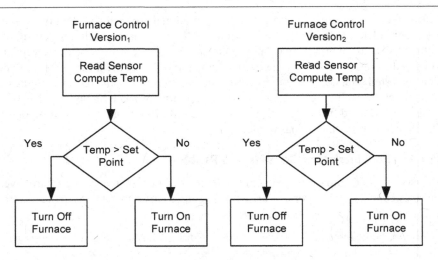

FIGURE 11.8 An example of the Consistent Comparison Problem.

- A specified period of time has passed since the last state change. The specified time period might be several minutes.

The two software versions are intentionally different because the designers are trying to achieve design diversity. Thus, (1) the internal representations of temperature used by the two versions might be different (one might use fixed point and the other floating point, for example); and (2) the algorithm used to transform the sensor reading (which is just bits from an analog-to-digital converter) into engineering units (degrees on an appropriate temperature scale) might be different. The hysteresis algorithms might be different, although this is unlikely because the requirements are quite specific.

Now consider the comparison used to determine whether the furnace should be turned on or off. If the value read from the sensor were close to the set point, the two different versions might well make different decisions, one concluding that the sensor value was below the set point and the other concluding that the sensor value was above the set point. In such a case, the two versions would supply different decisions to their individual implementations of the hysteresis algorithms. In the end, the two versions might supply *completely different* outputs to the comparator, and the comparator would be forced to conclude that the system had failed.

The idea that springs to mind when faced with this challenge is to suggest that there should be an interval around the set point within which care should be taken. But an interval does not help, because the Consistent Comparison Problem reappears when one asks whether the values to be compared lie within the interval.

Since there is no algorithmic solution to the Consistent Comparison Problem, the only thing to do is for the various versions to communicate. The versions exchange their computed values and compute a consensus value. All of the versions will use this consensus for comparison at any point where comparisons have to be made that derive from the requirements.

Such points of communication are just the cross-check points we saw in Section 11.4.1. This approach is a poor solution to the Consistent Comparison Problem, however, because the result is to restrict the designs of the versions in serious ways. For example, the designs of the versions have to be restricted to ensure that the cross-check points are present and have the proper form. Where several comparisons have to be made in sequence, the comparisons have to be made in the same order in all versions, and, if the exchange that is made at the cross-check points is of data values used in the comparison, then those data values either have to be of the same type or have to be of types for which type switching will not interfere with the comparisons.

The Consistent Comparison Problem occurs in practice, but the frequency with which the problem occurs depends upon the software system designs in the various versions and upon the frequency with which the application supplies values that could make the comparisons inconsistent. For any given system, predicting this frequency of occurrence is problematic.

11.5 Data Diversity

11.5.1 Faults and Data

Design diversity attempts to deal with design faults by having more than one implementation, each with its own design. Each of the *different* implementations is executed with the *same* data. What would happen if we executed instances of the *same* implementation with *different* data? Recall from Section 11.3 that one of the reasons for avoiding pure software replication was that the replicates would be subject to exactly the same faults if they used exactly the same data and were deterministic.

There is good evidence that software faults are, in many cases, data sensitive [9]. In other words, faults manifest themselves with certain data values yet do not do so with data that is very similar. How this might happen is easy to see when one thinks of the situations in which software fails for special cases. Avoiding the exact data values associated with the special case usually means that the software works.

As an example, consider the tangent of 90°. This particular tangent is undefined, and so if computation of the tangent is included in a program, the programmer must be careful to avoid calling the tangent function with this special value. Failing to check and calling the function will almost certainly lead to failure. Yet a value that is very close will work correctly. The calculator in Microsoft Windows XP indicates (correctly) that 90° is an invalid value, but the calculator is quite happy to calculate the tangent of 89.9999999999° (that is, 89 followed by ten nines). That any application would care if this value were used instead of 90° seems unlikely.

This extreme sensitivity of many software faults to particular data values suggests an approach to dealing with faults that is, in some sense, the opposite of design diversity. The approach is to use multiple instances of a single design but to execute each with different data. Rather obviously, the technique is called *data diversity* [9].

If data is to be varied in a data-diverse system, where does the variation come from? Implementing data diversity in general seems impossible, because the data is not under the control of the software developer. But in practice, getting different data is not hard.

11.5.2 A Special Case of Data Diversity

Several special cases of the data diversity have been reported, although they were not referred to as data diversity. The best known and most significant of the special cases was developed at Tandem Computers by Jim Gray [51]. The Tandem computer system was developed to provide a platform for applications requiring high availability. Various special facilities were included in the hardware design, the operating system, and in the support offered to application software so as to enable high availability for database applications.

In 1985, Gray was examining failures of Tandem systems reported from the field, and he noticed that some faults in the Tandem system software did not always manifest themselves when the software was executed. In other words, sometimes the software would fail and sometimes not, and this phenomenon occurred even on the same data. Gray coined the phrase *Heisenbug* to describe this behavior (see Section 3.4).

The observation about Heisenbugs led to the introduction of a form of data diversity in the Tandem system. Since the primary use of the system was database applications, in many circumstances software could be re-executed without harm fairly easily. If software failed while processing a transaction and before the transaction was committed, the transaction could be applied again without harm. When this was done, the processing of the transaction succeeded quite frequently.

Since the transaction that was attempted a second time was the same as the transaction that led to the software failure, why did the software not fail during the second execution? The reason is the inherent non-determinacy in transaction processing that derives from concurrency. Transaction processing involves many steps, some combination of which is executed concurrently. Although the transaction data was the same, the actual sequence of events undertaken by the software was different. By chance, sometimes the fault that led to the failure did not manifest itself during the second execution.

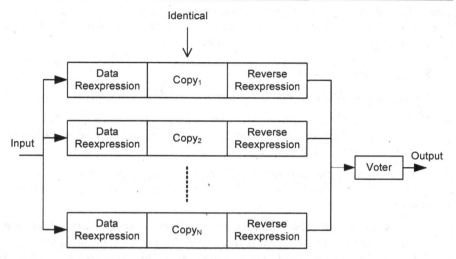

FIGURE 11.9 The N-copy data-diversity software system architecture.

11.5.3 Generalized Data Diversity

The most general form of a data-diverse system was introduced by Ammann and Knight [9]. General data diversity operates by executing *identical copies* of the software with *different data* being supplied to each copy. As with design diversity, different system architectures have been developed to implement data diversity. The most important is the N-copy architecture shown in Figure 11.9.

The N-copy system architecture is the data-diverse version of the N-version system architecture from design diversity. An N-copy system operates by having N identical copies of the software executing concurrently. The input data is transformed differently for each of the copies using a technique called *data reexpression*. The outputs of the copies are transformed so as to recover the expected outputs from the program had it been operating on the original input. The algorithmic means by which the output to be used is obtained from the output that the software produced with reexpressed input is *reverse reexpression*.

The outputs from the N copies are supplied to a voter. Except for the effects of non-determinacy against which measures have to be taken, copies that executed correctly will have the same outputs. Thus, provided a majority of the copies execute correctly, the voter can select the system output using a simple majority vote.

As an example of data diversity, consider a program designed to sort a file of integers. An N-copy structure can be constructed by operating N copies of the sort program in parallel. A suitable data reexpression algorithm would be to form a permutation of the input values. Each copy of the software is given a different permutation and so operates with different data. However, the copies should all produce the same result, a sorted file, and, in this case, reversing the reexpression is unnecessary. Voting can proceed directly on the output of the copies.

11.5.4 Data Reexpression

Data reexpression is the algorithmic manipulation of data such that:

- The reexpressed data is different from the original data in some way. The difference could be different values, different order of values, different encodings of engineering values, different precision, and so on.

- The software will execute with the different values. The reexpressed data must still be within the expected set of valid inputs for which the software was designed.

- The expected output values can be recovered from the actual outputs generated by the software. Since the data was changed by reexpression, the output might be different from that produced by the original data. This difference will not be a problem as long as there is an algorithmic way to recover the expected outputs.

Data reexpression can be achieved in two different ways: *exact* reexpression and *inexact* reexpression. These two terms are defined as follows:

Exact reexpression: An exact reexpression algorithm changes the input data for a program in such a way that the exact output which would have been obtained from the original data can be obtained from the output of the reexpressed data by an algorithmic means.

Inexact reexpression: An inexact reexpression algorithm changes the input data for a program in such a way that the output obtained from the reexpressed data remains acceptable to the application.

Some examples of exact reexpression are:

- Permuting the input data to a sort program. There is no need to reverse the reexpression.

- Adding a constant value to data that comes from a linear scale such as coordinates in a two- or three-dimensional coordinate system. For computations that do not depend on absolute location, the actual coordinates can be translated or rotated. The reverse reexpression that is needed will depend on what the calculation is.

- Reordering the records in a file. Many computations that process large data volumes from files are independent of the order of the records. There is no need to reverse the reexpression.

- Changing the order of the transactions in a transaction-processing system. Large on-line service systems such as reservation systems, many financial systems, and e-commerce web sites complete transactions for a variety of clients, and the order of processing can be varied with no ill effects and with no need for reexpression.

Some examples of inexact reexpression are:

- The time at which sensors are read can be varied between the channels in a real-time system that uses redundant channels. Since the datum read by a sensor is a sample of a real-world physical value that changes over time, sensor readings taken at different times are likely to be slightly different. There is no need to reverse the reexpression.

- Non-integer numeric data values can be changed by small amounts. As with the previous example, a sensor datum is usually represented in digital form with a precision far greater than that which is warranted by the sensor's accuracy. Thus, small changes to the value are likely to be acceptable to the application. Again, there is no need to reverse the reexpression.

11.5.5 N-Copy Execution and Voting

The execution of the copies in an N-copy system is much simpler than the execution of the versions in an N-version system. The copies are all the same software, and so their execution times are likely to be almost identical, even operating with reexpressed data. An overall synchronization mechanism is still required to make sure that voting takes place only after all the copies have produced a result. Failure of copies is possible, and so the execution system needs to be prepared to manage failed copies by eliminating them from the operating set.

Voting in an N-copy system is also much simpler than with an N-version system. There is no chance of multiple solutions being produced that are correct but different. The data values used in voting will not necessarily be identical, but the values will be very close for most N-copy systems. The range of values that can be produced and for which the voter needs to take account is much simpler to derive because the copies are all the same software.

An important question that developers ask is "How many copies should be used?" Fortunately, there is no major development cost incurred by using more copies rather than less. The copies are exactly that, copies, and so any number can be used. The cost of development of an N-copy system is low, because the only items needed over and above the application itself are:

- The execution framework, including the copy-synchronization facility and the voter.
- The reexpression algorithm.
- The reverse reexpression algorithm.

Usually, these costs are small compared to the development cost of the application itself.

Naturally, there is an operational cost, because the copies all have to be executed. This cost will limit the number of copies, although the advent of multicore processors promises to reduce the impact of this cost. Only a single instance of the software needs to be kept in memory because all of the copies will use the same instructions. Similarly, only one instance of the reexpression and reverse reexpression software need to be available. The system in operation will actually use one process for each actual copy, and the memory needed to add a copy therefore is just the memory needed to support a process.

11.6 Targeted Fault Tolerance

The goal with both design and data diversity is to provide a general approach to fault tolerance that provides protection against a wide variety of software faults. Since neither can do so with a level of assurance that is quantifiable, the value of each for any given system is unknown. For safety-critical applications, this means that choosing to use a general diversity technique is a difficult decision. There might be an improvement in dependability, but for a specific system this cannot be modeled. There is certainly a cost, and that suggests that a better approach might be to use the resources for fault avoidance and fault elimination instead.

An alternative approach is a middle ground in which the application of fault tolerance in software is targeted to specific fault classes. In some systems, certain fault classes lead to errors that are especially serious, and so looking carefully at those fault classes is constructive.

With targeted fault tolerance, the fault classes of interest are identified, and then all the phases of fault tolerance are tailored to those fault classes. The errors associated with the fault classes of interest can usually be determined, and so error detection is much easier. Similarly, once error detection is accomplished, damage assessment, state restoration, and continued service can usually be tailored to the system and the fault classes of interest.

In this section, we examine four different targeted fault tolerance mechanisms. Each of these four techniques is in common use. Keep in mind that each of the techniques is targeting *specific* fault classes, and so faults outside those targeted classes might manifest themselves during operation with effects that could be serious. If a class of faults that could lead to hazards is missed, then serious failures are possible.

As we have noted elsewhere, fault tolerance, including targeted software fault tolerance, should be considered only after fault avoidance and fault elimination have been applied comprehensively.

11.6.1 Safety Kernels

In safety-critical systems, there is a set of hazards that must be avoided. These hazards are usually relatively few in number and relatively easy to define. Statements that define transitions to hazardous states are referred to as *safety policies*. In discussing the notion of a hazard in Section 3.11 on page 94, we used the following as an example of a hazard:

> *An elevator shaft with a door open but with no elevator car present.*

Avoiding opening a door to the elevator shaft when no car is present is clearly something that we want, and this is an example of a safety policy that needs to be enforced.

An important technology that is most commonly known as a *safety kernel* is to architect the system so as to check explicitly for system transitions that lead to hazards and stop them. The safety kernel concept as discussed here was proposed originally by Rushby [122], although many other authors have discussed the topic [22, 148, 149].

As an example, consider a controller for a simple microwave oven. The most serious hazard would be to have the microwave generator on when the door was open. The result would be to expose people nearby to high levels of microwave energy. The software in a controller such as this is not especially complicated, but the hazard is very dangerous and so designers want a high level of assurance that the hazard is unlikely to arise. Other software faults might cause problems, such as the timer functioning incorrectly, the display malfunctioning, and so on, but none of these is serious. Dealing with the serious hazard is a candidate for targeted fault tolerance using a safety kernel.

A simple safety-kernel structure in software for this microwave oven controller would consist of:

- A well-protected software component placed between the generator activation logic and the output port that connects to the generator. The role of this software component would be to allow the generator to be turned on only if the door were closed.

- A supplement to the processor's interrupt handler. The purpose of the supplement would be to intercept the interrupt from the door-opening hardware and turn off the microwave generator if it were on.

The software component needs to have a form like this:

```
procedure turn_on_generator (in door_status : door_state) is
    if door_status = closed then
        generator_output_port := on;
end turn_on_generator;
```

This software would avoid the hazard if there were an attempt to turn on the microwave generator when the door was open for *any* reason, including faults in the remainder of the software.

This type of protection would not deal with the case where the door was opened while cooking was in progress. Turning off the microwave generator if the door were opened has to be triggered by an interrupt, with the interrupt handler's first action being to turn off the generator. The code for the interrupt handler might look like this:

```
On door_open_interrupt begin
    generator_output_port := off;
end;
```

There are several important things to note about this example:

- When operating with a structure like this, the software that contained the generator-activation logic could contain any number of faults, but the hazard could not arise provided the simple check was executed (i.e., not circumvented in some way) and this checking software was not damaged by faults elsewhere in the software. With a small software component of this form, we do not need to have high levels of assurance of the remainder of the (possibly complex) software.

- If this simple safety-kernel structure is to provide a high degree of protection, the kernel has to operate as designed no matter what goes wrong with the application software. In other words, there must be no way for the application software to interfere with the safety-kernel software. A simple example of interference would be if the application software went into an infinite loop so that the safety kernel could not execute.

  Making sure that there is no interference is complicated in its own way because of the high level of assurance that is required. What is needed is to construct a fault tree for the hazard:

  Safety kernel does not prevent system from entering a hazardous state.

  The events in the fault tree will include:
  - Application software enters infinite loop.
  - Safety-kernel software damaged by other software.
  - Microwave generator power switched on from another location.

  As with any hazard, preparation of the fault tree has to be careful, thorough, and systematic (see Section 4.3). Such fault trees are relatively easy to build; see, for example, the work of Wika [148]. A fault tree for a safety kernel is likely to reveal that modifications such as the addition of an external hardware watchdog timer are needed because that is the only way to be sure that an infinite loop in the software will be stopped.

- A software safety kernel for an application like a microwave oven will have a simple structure much like the example, and so verifying the software fragment is far easier than verifying the software that contained the generator-activation logic. From a practical perspective, this property is useful, because assurance efforts can be focused on the simple structure.

- What happens if this simple safety kernel has to act is not defined. A "fail" indicator could be illuminated for the user, or some other action taken.

In practice, most safety-critical systems are much more complicated than this simple example, and the associated safety kernels are correspondingly more complex. The benefits remain, however. A safety kernel is present to stop the system from transitioning to a hazardous state, and those states are identified during hazard analysis. With a properly designed safety kernel in place, failures of the bulk of the software in the safety-critical system can be tolerated. Finally, the relative simplicity of the safety kernel makes verification a more manageable task.

11.6.2 Application Isolation

Consider the problem of separating different applications in a safety-critical computing system so that they do not interfere with each other. Multiple safety-critical applications often have to be run on a *single* computer. Being sure that the failure of one does not affect others is important. This topic is an issue in fault tolerance because, in effect, faults in one application are being tolerated so that they do not interfere with other applications.

The requirement here is to guarantee separation of applications or achieve separation with a high degree of assurance. This requirement is brought about by the fact that different applications might fail, but, if they do, they should not affect others. If a failing application causes one or more other applications to fail, then the dependability assessment of those applications will, in all likelihood, not be valid. That makes the system both less dependable and less predictable.

In some systems, this separation is achieved by using one computer for each application. In some sense this is the ideal. Provided the communication system between computers has certain properties, then the separation that is required is present.

If more than one application operates on the same machine, then the ideal of separate computers needs to be effected on the single machine. How could one do this? The approach to follow is to view a separation failure as a *hazard* and to apply fault-tree analysis. Once a draft fault tree is in place, one can use the fault tree to develop techniques that will reduce the probability of the hazard to a suitably low level.

From the fault tree, for example, one can see the effects of an architectural feature such as memory protection and the effects of changing or improving that feature.

Viewing this informally, the types of questions that come up as concerns in separation are:

Architecture: How are processes separated in memory? Could one process read/write the memory of another? How is processor dispatching done? Could one process entering an infinite loop inhibit another process?

Operating System: How does the operating system provide inter-process communication? How does the operating system provide process separation?

Application Development: How are the operating system services provided to applications and can applications abuse the operating system's interface either accidentally or maliciously? How does an application determine that it is in trouble with excess resource allocation? Could an application deadlock? Does that matter? What could be done to ensure that the application has certain desirable, non-interference properties? Could it be shown that an application could never enter an infinite loop?

Programming Languages: What facilities does the language provide to effect control of memory protection mechanisms, if any? How is concurrency provided? Could a process change its priority and thereby affect another process or application? What can be done in the programming language to support analysis so that we might be sure that there is no interference provided we trust the compiler?

Interference can either be through the processor, memory, or the peripheral devices. Interference through the processor would occur if one application were able to gain control of the processor and fail to relinquish it. Interference through memory would occur is one application were able to write into the memory allocated to another. Finally, interference through a peripheral device would occur if one application could access a peripheral being used by another.

Achieving proper separation without hardware support is impossible. Necessary hardware support includes facilities for timer interrupts and memory protection. Trustworthiness of the operating system is essential also since the operating system is relied upon to provide basic separation services.

To deal with the processor, the existence of a timer interrupt that returns control to the operating system and that cannot be masked by any application no matter what the application does has to be shown. To deal with memory, the hardware protection mechanism has to be shown to stop erroneous writes no matter what an application does. In practice, this can usually be shown quite elegantly using a typical virtual memory mechanism.

Finally, to deal with peripherals, many techniques are possible. Coupling direct memory access with virtual memory provides a fairly simple approach.

The modern implementations of machine virtualization are beginning to have an impact in this area. With systems like VMWare, supporting one virtual machine for each application is possible. The issue of separation then reduces to showing that the virtual machine mechanism works correctly.

11.6.3 Watchdog Timers

In real-time systems, states that systems enter if real-time deadlines are missed tend to be hazards. The system's designers based their design on a real-time deadline, and so failing to meet that deadline is potentially serious. As an example, consider a simple heart pacemaker that provides pacing stimuli to a patient after calculating whether a stimulus is needed for the current heartbeat. If the software that determines whether a stimulus is needed takes too long to execute, that software will miss its real-time deadline and fail to generate a stimulus if one is needed.

Meeting deadlines in a real-time system is an example of a safety policy. Failing to do so is likely to be hazardous, and the policy needs to be maintained all the time. This policy could be included in a set that was implemented by a safety kernel, but systems frequently deal with the safety policy of meeting deadlines as a special case. The technique used is to implement a *watchdog timer*.

A watchdog timer is a countdown timer that is set by an application and which raises an interrupt when it expires. The value used to set the timer is beyond the time that the application expects to take to conduct some predefined unit of processing. Normally, when that unit of processing is complete, the timer is reset by the application with a new value. If the application fails to complete the unit of processing before the timer expires, the timer interrupt occurs, allowing some action to be taken to correct what is an unexpected situation.

A typical use of a watchdog timer is to gain control if a real-time deadline is about to be missed. An application is expected to manage time with sufficient care that real-time deadlines are met. By setting a watchdog timer, control can be given to a different piece of software that can take corrective action.

11.6.4 Exceptions

Exceptions are often associated with software fault tolerance, but they are really not intended for that purpose. Some exceptions are raised to indicate an expected and perfectly normal event, such as a printer running out of paper. In such cases, exceptions are being used as asynchronous signals. In other cases, interrupts are defined for custom use in specific programs. Ada, for example, allows programmer defined exceptions and provides a `raise` statement so that exceptions can be raised explicitly. Using this mechanism, programmers can define their own asynchronous signals. Finally, exceptions are raised because of what most engineers consider to be faults, division by zero and floating point overflow, for example.

The concept of an exception seems as if it ought to be applicable to software fault tolerance. For things like division by zero, the error is detected automatically, and a branch is executed to software that could perform the other three phases of fault tolerance.

Exceptions are not designed as a comprehensive approach to software fault tolerance, and their utility as a fault-tolerance mechanism is limited. The problems with exceptions as a mechanism for software fault tolerance are as follows:

Error detection is incomplete. Detection of things like division by zero and floating-point overflow is all very well, but such events do not cover the space of errors that might arise. In fact, they cover an insignificant fraction of the errors that might arise in a typical large program even if the basic interrupt mechanism is complemented with programmer-defined exceptions.

Damage assessment is difficult. If an exception is raised, all that is known about the system is that the local state associated with the exception is erroneous, e.g., a divisor is zero and should not be. Nothing else is known about the state, and so the software that is executed in the exception handler has to be smart enough to determine what parts of the state are erroneous.

State restoration is difficult. Even if damage assessment were completed satisfactorily, restoring the state is difficult with the semantics of almost all programming languages. The difficulty arises because of the context within which the interrupt handler has to execute. The variables that are in scope are defined by the particular language, and these variables are not the entire set in the program. In languages like Ada, for example, exception handlers are associated with the block in which the exception was raised. Variables not accessible to the block are not accessible to the exception handler. For concurrent programs, the problem is even worse because exception handlers do not necessarily have any access to the concurrent objects.

Continued service is difficult. The semantics of languages dictate what the flow of control has to be when an exception handler completes. The two most common semantics are *termination* and *resumption*. In termination semantics, the exception handler and some parts of the associated program are terminated. The parts of a program that are terminated depend on the details of the programming language and the circumstances during execution. In Ada, for example, the block raising the exception is terminated along with the exception handler if there was one. If no handler was provided, the exception is re-raised in the calling program unit, and that unit is terminated if no handler is provided. This process continues until a handler is found or the complete program is terminated. An example of the seriousness of these semantics is evident in the Ariane 5 disaster that was attributed to an unhandled exception [89].

In resumption semantics, the code following the point where the exception was raised is resumed. Doing so assumes that the exception handler was able to deal with whatever caused the exception to be raised in the first place. Gaining a high level of assurance that this is the case is unlikely at best.

11.6.5 Execution Time Checking

An error-detection mechanism can be woven through any piece of software, and the error-detection mechanism can be associated with mechanisms to provide the other phases of fault tolerance. Sophisticated mechanisms have been developed to facilitate the description of erroneous states starting with the simple notion of an assertion and extending through design by contract to comprehensive program specification mechanisms.

An assertion is a predicate (a Boolean expression) that should evaluate to true when the program executes. The expression documents an invariant about the program's state that follows from the basic design set up by the developers. If the assertion evaluates to false, then some aspect of the state violates the invariant that the developers expected to be true, i.e., an error has been detected.

Some languages, including C, C++, Java, and Eiffel, provide assertion statements as part of their basic syntax. The semantics of the assertion failing vary with the language, but the most common action is to raise an exception.

In a more extensive form, assertion systems allow the documentation of much of the software's specification within the source code. Eiffel is a good example of this type of language, where the concept is known as *design by contract*[1] [42]. In design by contract, assertions in the form of pre- and post-conditions document the interfaces that software components either assume or provide. These assertions are compiled into the program and evaluated during execution.

A comprehensive system for documenting the specification of a program within the source code is the Anna language defined for Ada '83 [91]. Anna text is included in the program as comments and is processed by a precompiler into corresponding Ada statements. When compiled, the result includes execution-time checks of the specification description included in the Anna text.

Anna is much more than an assertion mechanism. The notation includes annotations for all of the Ada '83 language elements, allowing, for example, much of the detail of types, variables, expressions, statements, subprograms, and packages to be defined.

Note carefully the difference between the way in which pre- and post-conditions are used in the concepts described here and the way they are used in SPARK Ada. For assertions and all of the concepts associated with them, the determination of compliance with the conditions is checked during execution, and the checks apply to

---

1. Design by contract is a trademark of Interactive Software Engineering, Inc., Goleta, CA.

that specific execution only. In SPARK Ada, the conditions are established by static analysis, and so they are shown to hold *before* execution and for all possible executions.

Execution-time checking is a starting point for a mechanism to provide software fault tolerance. However, as with the other mechanisms in this section, the use of execution-time checking does not provide a comprehensive approach to software fault tolerance upon which we can rely in our efforts to achieve dependability. The problems with execution-time checking are:

Error detection is incomplete. Although valuable, execution-time checking does not provide a comprehensive approach to error detection. Simple assertions, for example, are introduced by programmers in an ad hoc manner for which there is no way to determine coverage. The assertions might catch the error resulting from a fault and they might not. The facilities provided by Eiffel and Anna are far more satisfactory and are potentially comprehensive. Even with these mechanisms, there is no explicit mechanism to check whether the stated pre- and post-conditions are, in fact, the complete conditions upon which a program component relies.

Other phases of fault tolerance are not supported. Execution-time checking is supported in the more advanced cases by language elements, but the semantics of those language elements end typically with either an interrupt being raised or the program terminated. No provision is made for proper damage assessment, state restoration, or continued service.

Key points in this chapter:

- Tolerating design faults is more difficult than tolerating degradation faults.
- Replication of software provides no protection against software faults.
- Design diversity is a general technique for software fault tolerance.
- Design diversity has a number of difficulties that limit its applicability and performance.
- Data diversity is a general technique for fault tolerance based on the notion of a "Heisenbug" introduced by Jim Gray.
- Specialized fault tolerance techniques have been developed that target specific types of design faults.

Exercises

1. Configuration management systems are examples of system software that can be subject to design faults. A configuration management system is not directly involved in the correct creation of a software system as a compiler would be nor in the correct operation of a software system as an operating system would be. Explain how a design defect in a configuration management system could impact the correct operation of a critical computer system.

2. Navigation software is notorious for failing, especially on special cases such as the Equator, the Greenwich meridian, and the International Date Line. A particular ship's navigation system is based on high-precision latitude and longitude data obtained from GPS. To reach its destination, the ship's navigation system plots a course along the Earth's surface from its current location to its destination. Design reexpression and reverse reexpression algorithms that could be used to permit data diversity to be applied to the computations that use the latitude and longitude data.

3. Explain how data diversity might be employed in the navigation software discussed in the previous question.

4. For software faults associated with the troublesome special cases in the navigation software, estimate the reduction in failure rate that is likely to be produced by using data diversity. State carefully any assumptions that you have to make.

5. Suppose you decide to try data diversity on the software used to position the ship's rudder because you are worried about its dependability. That software takes a specific angle to which the final rudder should be set (a parameter between +60 degrees and −60 degrees) and calculates all the necessary rudder servo settings and actions. Could data diversity be used with this software? If so, how? If not, why not?

6. The failure of the computer system for the hot water tank in Chapter 8, Exercise 5, could be very serious. If the software turns on either heater and leaves the heater on for an extended time, the tank could explode. You decide to modify the software to include a safety kernel to make sure this does not happen. What safety policy would you enforce?

7. For the safety policy that you defined in the previous question, determine what events could allow the hazard "water tank overheats" to arise by building a fault tree for the hazard and assuming that the safety kernel is implemented correctly.

8. Suppose a 3-version programming system is built to compute the dosage in the radiation therapy machine described in Chapter 1, Exercise 13. The computed dose is returned as two floating-point numbers representing required duration and required beam intensity. The system's voter cannot base its decision on equality of results, because they might not be equal. How could the voter deter-

mine the output to be used in a way that preserved the fault-tolerance facilities of the system?

9. Develop a rigorous argument that the use of comparison checking in testing reduces any possible benefit of N-version programming (i.e., reduces the absolute decrease in the probability of failure that N-version programming might provide) with every test in which a difference between the versions arises. Show that in the limit any benefit from N-version programming vanishes.

10. Suppose a 2-version system includes a comparison that is subject to the consistent comparison problem. If the data with which the system effects comparison is randomly distributed between 0 and 1, and if the system computes a new output every millisecond, compute the rate at which the system will fail as a result of inconsistent comparisons if the maximum rounding error to which each version is subject is 0.000001.

11. Is fault tolerance a mechanism that can be used to help implement safety? If so how, and if not, why not?

12. Consider the problem of exploiting Gray's idea of *Heisenbugs* in a concurrent system that deadlocks. What would have to be included in the design of such a system to exploit the idea in order to recover from deadlocks?

13. *Software rejuvenation* [132] is a technique in which software is periodically restarted, e.g., an operating system is rebooted. Empirical evidence indicates that this idea is helpful in preventing failures.

    (a) Why does this technique make a difference?

    (b) Which attributes of dependability can be affected by this technique and how?

    (c) If you were to implement software rejuvenation, how would you determine the times when the restarts should be undertaken?

    (d) What are the impacts of this technique on normal operation?

    (e) What types of computer system would be most likely to benefit from this technique?

CHAPTER 12

Dependability Assessment

Learning objectives of this chapter are to understand:

- The concepts and limitations of quantitative assessment.
- The role and limitations of prescriptive standards.
- The use of rigorous arguments in dependability assessment.
- How the dependability of a system can be determined.
- Effective ways to approach the problem of dependability assurance.

12.1 Approaches to Assessment

Throughout this book, we have been concerned with creating dependable computer systems. In Chapter 2, we discussed the need for defining dependability requirements, and in subsequent chapters, we examined various ways in which we might meet the defined requirements for software while remaining aware of what is happening on the hardware side.

Our final task is to determine whether we have met the dependability requirements for a specific software system. Examining this issue is important, because otherwise we might end up with one of two unacceptable circumstances:

- The system that we have built has *lower* dependability than is required, and so the system might fail more frequently than is considered acceptable.

- The system that we have built has *higher* dependability than is required. Higher dependability might not seem like a problem, but we are likely to have expended more resources than needed to produce the system and perhaps lost a competitive edge as a result.

Dependability assessment of computer systems has been a subject of study for as long as there have been computers. A great deal of research has been conducted on probabilistic assessment, and the technology that has evolved is both elaborate and sophisticated. The greatest successes have been in assessing the effects of degrada-

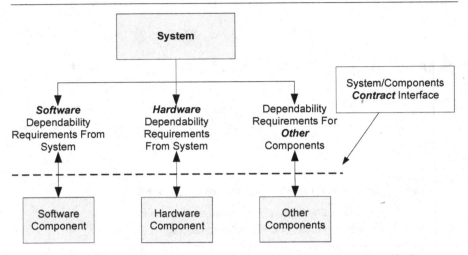

FIGURE 12.1 The contract model between the overall system and the components used in the system.

tion faults. Probabilistic assessment of the effects of design faults, especially software faults, has been far less successful.

Covering dependability assessment, particularly probabilistic assessment, in depth is beyond the scope of this book. Our emphasis will remain on dependability of the software system. Software engineers need to understand how overall system assessment is done, at least in part, because many of the techniques used in dependability assessment at the overall system level can be applied at the software system level. In this chapter we will discuss three different approaches to dependability assessment that are in more or less common use:

Quantitative Assessment. Quantitative assessment is the estimation of a probability associated with an entity either by direct measurement or by modeling.

Prescriptive Standards. Prescriptive standards base dependability assessment of an entity on the process by which the entity was built.

Rigorous Argument. Rigorous argument is a non-quantified approach to assessment in which an argument is created that the entity is suitable for its intended use.

Throughout this chapter, keep in mind the *dependability contract* concept that was introduced in Section 2.8.3. The general concept is repeated in Figure 12.1. The dependability requirements for a computer system derive from the design of the system of which the computer system is a component, and meeting those dependability requirements can be thought of as a contract between the systems engineers and the computer and software engineers.

12.2 Quantitative Assessment

Several attributes of dependability are probabilistic, and this suggests that we could use some form of measurement to see whether the requirement has been met. Reliability and availability, for example, are probabilities that we could assess perhaps by measurement. Similarly, performance metrics such as Mean Time Between Failures (MTBF) and Mean Time To Failure (MTTF) are expected values of distributions and so estimating these quantities by sampling should be possible. Such estimates can be obtained by operating the system of interest and noting when failures occur. Routine statistical procedures can be applied to estimate both the expected value of interest and the variance.

As we shall see in Section 12.2.4, quantitative assessment of dependability attributes faces several challenges that limit its applicability. Some attributes are not quantifiable, for some systems there are no reliable models to use, and some desired levels of dependability cannot be estimated in reasonable amounts of time.

12.2.1 The Basic Approach

Estimating probabilities in complex systems is achieved using a variety of sophisticated analysis techniques, including statistical sampling, Markov modeling, approximations, and so on. Fundamentally, however, quantitative estimates of system properties are derived by applying the following two-step process:

(1) **Estimate parameters of constituent part by life testing.** The quantitative properties of system constituent parts are estimated by observing a sample set of identical parts in operation and measuring their rate of failure.

(2) **Estimate system parameters by modeling.** Models that predict system parameters based on the parameters of constituent parts are developed. These models are then used with the data obtained in part parameter estimates to estimate the system parameters of interest.

As an example of quantitative assessment, consider the simple computer system shown in Figure 12.2. The computer is composed of six constituent parts: (1) a processor, (2) a memory, (3) a power supply, (4) a parallel data bus linking the processor and memory, (5) a collection of peripherals, and (6) a printed circuit board, often called the mother board, upon which the processor, memory, and ancillary electronics are mounted. Using life testing, the manufacturers of the components have determined that the probabilities of failure per hour for the constituent parts have mean values of 10^{-6} for the processor, 10^{-6} for memory, 10^{-5} for the power supply, 10^{-8} for the data bus, 10^{-3} for the peripheral system (meaning loss of at least one from per-

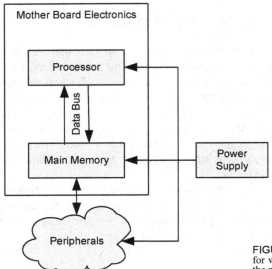

FIGURE 12.2 A simple computer system for which we need a quantitative measure of the probability of failure.

haps several), and10^{-4} for the mother board. We model the probability of failure of the system using the following assumptions:

- The six constituent parts fail with statistical independence (see Section 6.4.1).
- When a constituent part fails, the failure is fail stop (see Section 6.5.4).
- Failure of any of the six constituent parts causes the entire computer to fail.

Since we know the probabilities of failure of the individual constituent parts and we are assuming that part failures are independent, the probability of failure of the computer per hour is just the sum of the probabilities of failure of the six parts, i.e., 0.00111201. Clearly, this value is dominated by the probability of failure of the peripheral system.

As a second example of quantitative assessment, consider the dual-redundant architecture discussed in Section 6.3.1 on page 155. Suppose that the rate of failure per unit time of each processor has been determined by life testing to be 10^{-6}. In this case, both processors have to be operational or the comparator will be forced to shut the system down. Assuming that processor failures are independent, the failure rate of the system derived from processor failure is the sum of the two processor failure rates, $10^{-6} + 10^{-6}$. Thus the failure rate is much higher than that of a single processor and the MTTF has been cut by a half. Although that is the cost, recall from Section 6.3.1 that the important benefit gained is error detection.

12.2.2 Life Testing

Life testing is a process in which a set of identical parts is placed into an operational environment, and the performance of the members of the set is monitored. Life testing of personal computers is illustrated in Figure 12.3. The test environment includes a variety of environmental effects. Various part parameters can be estimated by observing the behavior of the parts being tested. In particular, failures can be observed. In Figure 12.3, one of the computers has failed.

The operational environment could be an artificial one in a laboratory or the actual environment in which the parts operate. In the laboratory approach, the operating circumstances can be both controlled and varied. For example, in the case of integrated circuits, the change in MTTF with case temperature, humidity, and vibration can be measured by conducting life testing with the environmental parameters set appropriately. Such measurement also allows assessment of the rate of infant

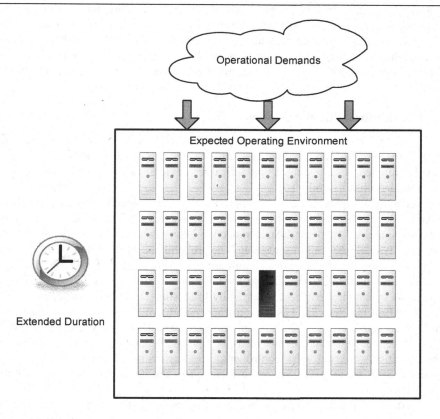

FIGURE 12.3 Long duration life testing of components using replication. In this case one computer has failed.

mortality so that volume development and delivery can take account of infant mortality properly.

Two difficulties that arise with life testing in a laboratory are:

- The cost of the laboratory itself.

- The difficulty in both determining and creating the correct operational environment.

Though often large, the cost issue is predictable and the cost/benefit analysis can be performed reasonably easily. Dealing with the operational environment is more difficult. If the environment used in testing is not that which the parts will experience in operation, the various estimates that are obtained by life testing might be inaccurate.

The problem of determining and creating the correct operational environment is a major difficulty. To see this, consider the problem of conducting life testing on DRAM integrated circuits. As noted above, the effect on the rate of failure of the case temperature, the humidity, and vibration can be measured in or predicted for the anticipated operating environment quite well. However, the rate of failure is also affected by data-access patterns, by physical shock, and by the thermal shock associated with powering the device on and off. These latter three factors are difficult to predict for consumer devices since operating patterns vary so widely.

12.2.3 Compositional Modeling

Life testing is practical for constituent parts that are less expensive and that can be both operated and monitored successfully without a lot of expensive and complicated equipment. Life testing is impractical for devices such as complete computers or even large disk assemblies.

For more complex devices, the approach that is followed is based on compositional models. The probabilistic parameter of interest for the device is estimated using a model of the device. Such models predict what will happen to the device when individual parts fail in some way. The probabilistic performance of the constituent parts from which the device is built are estimated using life testing.

In a large disk drive, for example, the failure distributions of individual electrical and some mechanical parts are assessed by life testing, and then parameters such as the MTTF of the device are estimated from a model of the device. In the case of a disk drive, some types of fault are intermittent because of the way in which disk drives operate. Many times, disk reads and writes succeed after an initial failure if the operation is retried. Disk controllers know that and exploit the effect to avoid failures. Such techniques have to be included in the dependability model for the device.

Models are difficult to build and in many cases are based upon sophisticated mathematics. In some cases, assumptions have to be made that are not completely realistic in order to make the mathematics tractable. To deal with the possibility of inaccuracies in models, system developers frequently observe the population of systems that have been deployed and check that failures are occurring at a rate no worse than the rate predicted by the model.

12.2.4 Difficulties with Quantitative Assessment

Despite the cost and difficulty of determining the operational environment, life testing and modeling work well in many circumstances, and so thinking that they could be applied universally is tempting. There are three issues that arise which preclude their use in a number of circumstances where we need dependability assessment:

Non-Quantifiable Attributes. Obviously, some attributes of dependability cannot be quantified. There is no useful metric for confidentiality, for example. For systems where confidentiality is important, some other mechanism of assessment is needed.

Unavailability of Models. Although the use of models in dependability assessment has proven useful, there are many circumstances in which models are either insufficiently accurate or just not available at all. The most important area in which models do not exist is in dealing with design faults. Compositional models for systems subject to design faults cannot be created by somehow measuring the rate of failure of the constituent parts and then trying to infer failure rates for the system.

This problem is especially serious for software, because the problem means that we cannot estimate dependability attributes of a million line software system from the measured attributes of ten thousand procedures, each one hundred lines long, or any other combination.

Without compositional models for design faults, the only alternatives are:

-   To develop quantitative estimates of dependability parameters using life testing alone, i.e., to subject the entire system to testing in the operational environment. For software, this means that complete instances of the software system of interest have to be operated and observed. The size and complexity of modern software systems usually preclude such an approach.

-   To develop system-level models of dependability parameters based upon system-level characteristics and sometimes performance observations. Examples for software dependability are *reliability-growth* models such as the Littlewood-Verrall model [90]. In a reliability-growth model, the reliability of the software is estimated by modeling the faults in the software and the repair process. The software is operated and repaired as failures occur, and the circumstances of the operation and the failure are used to calibrate the model. Once the model parameters are set, an estimate of the reliability of the software can be obtained.

Ultra-High Levels of Dependability. Life testing depends upon observing failures of a population under test in order to be able to estimate population statistics. Observing no failures allows a lower bound to be estimated but that bound could be far from the actual value.

If ultra-high levels of dependability are needed, levels such as 10^{-9} failures per hour, as is typical of critical elements of avionics systems, then the population will experience failures extremely rarely. Producing estimates in cases such as this has been shown to be essentially infeasible because of the time needed to obtain the necessary data [24]. In the case of a system required to demonstrate a failure rate of 10^{-9} per hour or less, for example, the total test time necessary is hundreds of thousands of years. Even with large numbers of replicates (if that were possible), the total time will still be a large number of years. Testing times of this duration are completely infeasible.

For more modest goals, such as systems that have to demonstrate a failure rate of less than 10^{-4} failures per demand, as might be the case for a protection system, the test time is still a factor that has to be considered carefully in determining how to assess a dependability metric.

In summary, dependability requirements are often defined in quantitative terms, and that means we have to show that the system, as built, will meet those requirements. For degradation faults, using life testing of constituent parts and modeling of systems, estimation of the required probabilities is feasible and successful in practice. For design faults, including software faults of course, quantitative assessment is problematic. Estimates can be obtained for systems with relatively low dependability requirements, but estimation becomes infeasible at higher levels. Finally, there is always a concern that data about rates of failure obtained by measurement of constituent parts might not reflect that which will be seen in practice, because the operational environment used for data collection might not be the same as the environment that is seen once the system is deployed.

12.3 Prescriptive Standards

Dealing with the challenges posed by quantitative modeling is sufficiently difficult that the preferred approach to building systems frequently has to be pushed to the side. Instead, *prescriptive* development standards are used. Requiring prescriptive standards is the approach chosen by many government agencies that regulate the use of computing systems.

A prescriptive standard is any standard that dictates development practice in some way. Typically, in order to comply with the standard, a prescriptive standard specifies that during development either:

(a) Certain work products must be produced.

(b) Certain specific development actions must be undertaken.

(c) Certain goals must be met.

(d) A combination of (a), (b), and (c) is required.

Earlier standards tended to focus on prescribed work products or development actions, i.e., (a) and (b) above. In some cases, prescriptive standards document what amounts to standardized development processes that are required for the construction of certain systems or system components. Implied in this approach is that such prescriptive standards essentially define dependability requirements for the systems being regulated.

Prescriptive standards often require the use of engineering techniques that are generally accepted to be useful in terms of achieving dependability. For example, a prescriptive standard for software might require that certain test techniques be used during software development. The use of a specific technique is usually justified, because, when used properly, the technique is known to have a particular benefit in terms of dealing with faults.

Typically, prescriptive standards address major aspects of dependability, and standards are, as a result, frequently lengthy and detailed. Despite their length, in many cases, standards are accompanied by even longer documents that explain how the standard should be interpreted and what is required for compliance.

The use of goal-based standards, i.e., (c) above, is emerging as a more flexible approach. The concept is merely to define the required outcome and to leave the approach to meeting these outcomes to the system developers.

Prescriptive standards have been developed for use at the levels of both the application system and the computer system. Some examples of prescriptive standards are:

Overall system level:

DoD Mil Std 882B	System Safety Program Requirements.
IEEE 1228	Standard for Software Safety Plans.
IEC 61508	Functional safety of electrical/electronic/ programmable electronic safety-related systems.
ISO/IEC 15026:1998	Information technology — System and software integrity levels.

Computer system level:

RTCA DO-178B	Software Considerations in Airborne Systems and Equipment Certification.
NASA-STD-8739.8	Software Assurance Standard.
UL 1998	Standard for Software in Programmable Components.
SAE ARP 4754	Certification Considerations for Highly-Integrated or Complex Aircraft Systems.

12.3.1 The Goal of Prescriptive Standards

The overall goal of prescriptive standards is to define and require development activities or artifacts that will effect fault avoidance and fault elimination such that the implied dependability requirements will be met. Engineers are then required to follow a development process that complies with the standard. Without such a requirement, regulators would have a difficult job determining whether a system submitted for certification has the necessary dependability properties. Regulators cannot rely exclusively upon quantitative assessment, as we discussed in the previous section. Thus, regulators can only proceed in one of two ways:

- Conduct some form of lengthy and expensive examination of the computer system in question in order to establish to their satisfaction that the necessary dependability requirements will be met. If no rules apply to the development process, then regulators are faced with a starting point for their examination of a system that would be completely arbitrary. This approach is hardly practical.

- Require a prescribed set of development artifacts or practices that, taken together, provide a high degree of assurance that fault avoidance, fault elimination, and fault tolerance have been applied properly and comprehensively. The role of the regulator is then to check that the prescribed development practices have been applied as desired. This approach is entirely practical.

Prescriptive standards come in a variety of forms and from a variety of sources. Government agencies that regulate software for use in situations where the public interest has to be protected usually require that software to be submitted for approval be produced using a prescribed standard. Other prescriptive standards have been developed by the International Organization for Standardization (ISO) and the Institute of Electrical and Electronic Engineers (IEEE). Such standards can be followed voluntarily.

12.3.2 Example Prescriptive Standard — RTCA/DO-178B

The Federal Aviation Administration regards compliance with a standard known as RTCA/DO-178B[1] [120] as an acceptable means of receiving regulatory approval for software to be used on commercial air transports. The title of the standard is "Software Considerations In Airborne Systems And Equipment Certification." EUROCAE is the European Organization for Civil Aviation Equipment, and EUROCAE ED12B is an identical standard to RTCA/DO-178B. DO-178B is not the only method of obtaining regulatory approval, but not following the standard requires showing that the development procedures followed are equivalent to DO-178B. In

---

1. DO-178B is copyright by RTCA, Inc. Excerpts are used with permission. Complete copies of DO-178B and other RTCA documents can be purchased from RTCA Inc., 1150 18th Street NW, Suite 910, Washington, DC 20036. (202) 833-9339.

practice, essentially all avionics software is developed in compliance with DO-178B. DO-178B does not apply to ground software such as that used in air-traffic-control systems.

Note that DO-178B is a software dependability standard, *not* a safety standard. This distinction is important, because safety has to be addressed separately. DO-178B was published in 1992, and various documents have been released by the FAA since the standard was published either to provide an interpretation of the standard or to offer guidance on compliance. Of special importance in terms of interpretation of DO-178B is RTCA/DO-248 [121].

Software can be found on board commercial air transports in autopilots, flight management systems, flight control systems, navigation systems, communications systems, engines controls, fuel management systems, brakes, and many other systems. For an overview of avionics functionality and development methods, see *The Glass Cockpit* [77].

The DO-178B standard plays an important role by providing the framework within which all of these computer systems are developed. Comprehensive compliance leads to regulatory approval. Thus such compliance implies for legal purposes that the necessary dependability requirements have been met.

Dependability Requirements

DO-178B defines five software levels for avionics systems designated A through E, with A as the most critical. The five levels and their definitions are shown in Table 12.1.

Level	Definition
A	Software whose anomalous behavior, as shown by the system safety assessment process, would cause or contribute to a failure of system function resulting in a catastrophic failure condition for the aircraft.
B	Software whose anomalous behavior, as shown by the system safety assessment process, would cause or contribute to a failure of system function resulting in a hazardous/severe-major failure condition for the aircraft.
C	Software whose anomalous behavior, as shown by the system safety assessment process, would cause or contribute to a failure of system function resulting in a major failure condition for the aircraft.
D	Software whose anomalous behavior, as shown by the system safety assessment process, would cause or contribute to a failure of system function resulting in a minor failure condition for the aircraft.
E	Software whose anomalous behavior, as shown by the system safety assessment process, would cause or contribute to a failure of system function with no effect on aircraft operational capability or pilot workload. Once software has been confirmed as level E by the certification authority, no further guidelines of this document apply.

TABLE 12.1. RTCA DO-178B criticality levels.

Although not labeled as such, the entries in this table are software dependability requirements. Devices such as flight-control systems and autopilots that have full control of an airplane are criticality level A since their failure could cause an accident. The other levels are progressively less critical. The actual software dependability requirements are implied rather than stated explicitly. At level A, for example, software failure could cause catastrophic consequences if failure of the software led to a failure of a critical aircraft subsystem such as the flight-control system.

Deriving a specific dependability requirement for software from these criticality levels is difficult, because the concern is with the associated system, not the software. The notion, therefore, is to begin at the critical-system level. Informally, the FAA requirement at level A is that system failure should be *extremely improbable*, and the FAA defines this term to be a probability of 10^{-9} per hour, i.e., the probability of correct operation for one hour is required to be $1 - 10^{-9}$ or greater [46].

The first step in applying DO-178B is to determine which criticality level has to be used for the critical system in question. The level is determined by the system safety assessment process based on the effect that failure of the system of which the software is a part would have on the aircraft. Establishing the criticality level of the system allows the software's dependability requirements to be defined and the dependability contract between the system and the software established.

Examining a couple of examples is helpful to see the difficulty here. A flight-control system is a computer that links the pilot's primary controls, the yoke and rudder pedals, to the control surfaces of the aircraft (flaps, rudder, etc.). Total loss of the system would almost certainly lead to an accident. Thus, the probability of failure of the flight-control system per hour has to be less than 10^{-9}. But this is for the entire flight-control system, not just the software. Even with great care, the probability of failure of the computer hardware might well be of this order. So the reliability requirement on the software would have to be even more extreme. The practical manifestation of this requirement is to designate the software level A.

Now consider a critical system whose failure would not necessarily endanger the aircraft immediately, e.g., an autopilot. An autopilot can fly the aircraft automatically under many flight scenarios and is usually determined to be level A. This requirement applies to an autopilot in a somewhat different way from the way the requirement applies to a flight-control system. The difference arises because catastrophic consequences can only occur if (a) the autopilot fails, (b) the failed autopilot flies the aircraft in a dangerous way during certain phases of flight, and (c) the human pilot is unaware of the failure. Again, much of the probability of failure that can be permitted will be taken up by the hardware. In dealing with the software, the dependability requirement that is paramount is error detection and fail-stop failure semantics.

Dependability requirements expressed as levels, such as those shown in Table 12.1, are used in many other standards and are often referred to as *software integrity levels.* For example, the ISO/IEC 15026 standard is entitled "Information technology — System and software integrity levels" and establishes a framework for the meaning and definition of software integrity levels [70]. Since software is tied to system dependability with the contract structure discussed in Section 2.8.3, software integrity levels are often included in system safety standards. The contract then defaults to the software meeting the required integrity level.

Process Activities

DO-178B consists of 12 sections, an annex, and three appendices. The major sections are:

- Section 2   -   System Aspects Relating To Software Development
- Section 3   -   Software Life Cycle
- Section 4   -   Software Planning Process
- Section 5   -   Software Development Processes
- Section 6   -   Software Verification Process
- Section 7   -   Software Configuration Management Process
- Section 8   -   Software Quality Assurance Process
- Section 9   -   Certification Liaison Process
- Section 10   -   Overview of Aircraft and Engine Certification
- Section 11   -   Software Life Cycle Data
- Section 12   -   Additional Considerations
- Annex A   -   Process Objectives and Outputs by Software Level

The majority of the DO-178B standard is a detailed explanation of the expected software development process together with extensive definitions of terms. As an example of the details of the standard, Section 4, "Software Planning Process", consists of the following six subsections:

- 4.1   Software Planning Process Objectives
- 4.2   Software Planning Process Activities
- 4.3   Software Plans
- 4.4   Software Life Cycle Environment Planning
-        4.4.1   Software Development Environment
-        4.4.2   Language and Compiler Considerations
-        4.4.3   Software Test Environment
- 4.5   Software Development Standards
- 4.6   Review and Assurance of the Software Planning Process

Section 4 does not prescribe a specific approach to process planning that has to be followed. Rather, the section defines detailed, low-level objectives. The introductory paragraph of section 4 states:

"This section discusses the objectives and activities of the software planning process. This process produces the software plans and standards that direct the software development processes and the integral processes. Table A 1 of Annex A is a summary of the objectives and outputs of the software planning process by software level."

Each subsection of section 4 is a detailed set of definitions and objectives. Subsection 4.1 of section 4, for example, is shown in Figure 12.4. Although stated as objectives, the details are so precise that they define many of the activities that must be present in the process.

The heart of the compliance mechanism for the standard is meeting all of objectives. As an aid, ten tables are listed in Annex A. The tables are essentially summaries of the objectives for various process requirements showing to which criticality level the objective applies, whether compliance has to be established independently,

---

The purpose of the software planning process is to define the means of producing software which will satisfy the system requirements and provide the level of confidence which is consistent with airworthiness requirements. The objectives of the software planning process are:

a.   The activities of the software development processes and integral processes of the software life cycle that will address the system requirements and software level(s) are defined (subsection 4.2).

b.   The software life cycle(s), including the inter relationships between the processes, their sequencing, feedback mechanisms, and transition criteria are determined (section 3).

c.   The software life cycle environment, including the methods and tools to be used for the activities of each software life cycle process have been selected (subsection 4.4).

d.   Additional considerations, such as those discussed in section 12, have been addressed, if necessary.

e.   Software development standards consistent with the system safety objectives for the software to be produced are defined (subsection 4.5).

f.   Software plans that comply with subsection 4.3 and section 11 have been produced.

g.   Development and revision of the software plans are coordinated (subsection 4.3).

FIGURE 12.4 Subsection 4.1 of DO-178B.

	Objective		Applicability by SW Level				Output
	Description	**Ref.**	**A**	**B**	**C**	**D**	**Description**
1	Software development and integral processes activities are defined.	4.1a 4.3	O	O	O	O	Plan for Software Aspects of Certification. Software Development Plan. Software Verification Plan. SCM Plan. SQA Plan
2	Transition criteria, inter-relationships and sequencing among processes are defined.	4.1b 4.3	O	O	O		
3	Software lifecycle environment is defined.	4.1c	O	O	O		
4	Additional considerations are addressed.	4.1d	O	O	O	O	
5	Software development standards are defined.	4.1e	O	O	O		SW Requirements Standards. SW Design Standards. SW Code Standards.
6	Software plans comply with this document.	4.1f 4.6	O	O	O		SQA Records. Software Verification Results
7	Software plans are coordinated.	4.1g 4.6	O	O	O		SQA Records Software Verification Results

FIGURE 12.5 Part of Table A-1 from Annex A of DO-178B.

and so on. Each table targets a major process area. Table A-1 entitled "Software Planning Process", is shown in Figure 12.5. This table is the summary for some parts of section 4.

As can be seen in Figure 12.5, the objectives stated in the left column of the table are all in the form of "yes/no" questions. Mere existence of an artifact is not sufficient. The artifact must meet the intent of the standard as interpreted by the inspector checking compliance.

12.3.3 The Advantages of Prescriptive Standards

Prescriptive standards have three significant advantages:

Targeted fault avoidance and fault elimination. Techniques can be included in the standard that are designed to avoid or eliminate certain classes of faults in a very specific way. For example, certain programming languages or test techniques might be required. The use of targeted techniques in standards is a special case of the concepts on managing software fault avoidance and elimination discussed in Section 7.10 on page 212.

Process guidance and coverage. Process structures can be included in the standard that are designed to ensure that crucial process steps are carried out in the right order and with the correct form. For example, rigorous and documented configuration management might be required so as to ensure that software versions are properly managed.

Enhanced engineering communication. The fact that engineers are following a prescriptive standard means that they have a comprehensive basis for communication. All the engineers involved in development know what has to be done, and what has to be done is largely defined in a small set of documents. The artifacts to be produced for submission to the regulating agency are well defined, and so the targets of engineering activities are fairly clear.

12.3.4 The Disadvantages of Prescriptive Standards

Despite their advantages, prescriptive standards suffer from two significant disadvantages:

Prescriptive standards are inflexible. By their very nature, prescriptive standards dictate details of the development process. Some standards dictate less detail than others and focus more on specific development objectives. Some standards also permit deviation from the prescribed approach provided the deviation is carefully documented and fully justified.

The challenge, however, lies in the spectrum of systems that are covered by a single standard. RTCA DO-178B/EUROCAE ED12B, discussed in Section 12.3.2, for example, has to cover *all* digital systems that fall within the definitions of level A through level D. A specific system might benefit from a different development technology, but such deviations are difficult to effect in practice. Despite efforts to make standards less constraining, the effect of a standard in the certification process makes engineers reluctant to deviate from the prescribed standard at all. To do so risks certification failure for the system they are developing.

Prescriptive standards rely upon an unjustified assumption. The use of a prescriptive standard includes the assumption that by following the complete standard, an *overall* dependability requirement for the developed system will be met.

That requirement might be quantitative, but by following the standard, there is no obligation to measure or model probabilities.

More specifically, in the context of dependability, prescribed processes rely upon the following assumption:

If a specific prescriptive standard is followed to develop a particular artifact, then that artifact will possess a certain dependability property as a result of having been developed according to the standard.

Unfortunately, there is no basis for the assumption that significant dependability properties will be met by following a documented set of development procedures. Even if somehow this were possible, there would be no guarantee that the developers followed the standard precisely as intended. Thus, relying on a prescribed standard is far from an assured way of meeting dependability goals about any system. In particular, there is no basis for assuming that *quantitative* dependability goals will be met by following a prescribed development standard.

Despite this disadvantage, the use of standards in a number of industries has proven quite successful. Although there is no basis for the fundamental assumption, experience has shown that large numbers of systems have provided service over a substantial period of time with an acceptably low failure rate. Thus, in a sense, the basis for the assumption has become the record of use.

Except for some situations in Europe, virtually all systems that have to achieve high levels of dependability and which are the subject of regulation rely upon prescriptive standards. In the United States, for example, the Federal Aviation Administration, the Food and Drug Administration, and many parts of the Department of Defense use prescriptive standards.

12.4 Rigorous Arguments

In order to deal with the difficulties of quantitative assessment and prescriptive standards, a new approach to dependability assessment has been developed that is based upon the use of *rigorous argument*. The concept is (a) to develop a system, and (b) to develop an argument to justify a claim about the system. Specifically, developers:

- Construct the system using a process and technology that they choose. Techniques can be chosen based upon the needs of the system being built, including elements of existing prescriptive standards if desired.

- Construct an argument that documents their rationale for believing that the system has certain important properties, usually those associated with dependability.

The argument makes the developers' rationale *explicit*, and this notion is what makes this technique unique. Developers of systems that have high dependability requirements always have a rationale for their choices of technology. Similarly, there is a rationale for the detailed content of any prescriptive standard, but the rationale is never written down in a systematic and comprehensive way.

12.4.1 The Concept of Argument

Much of the work on the use of rigorous argument in dependability is based on the work of Toulmin [139]. The idea of an argument is both familiar and unfamiliar to computer and software engineers. Everybody knows (or thinks they know) what an argument is. But few people are familiar with the idea of documenting an argument and even less familiar with the idea of a rigorous argument.

In essence, the argument contains the developers' thinking behind their choices of development processes, tools, and techniques. The argument says:

> *We, the developers, believe that the system we have built*
> *meets the dependability requirements because...*

The argument has to be a good one, because the argument is the primary means by which a decision is made about whether a system should be used. This decision about system use should not be based on anything but a strong argument combined with the associated evidence.

Informally, a rigorous argument about the dependability of a system is part of an overall dependability case that consists of the following five main parts:

- An overall, high-level dependability claim (the top-level goal) that has been established for the system.

- A definition of the context within which the top-level goal is expected to hold. Context includes everything that might be needed to constrain the applicability of the dependability argument to a given set of circumstances.

- An explicit argument that shows how the overall dependability claim can be reasonably inferred from the underlying evidence. In practice, multiple different argument strategies are sometimes used in conjunction to argue dependability in a given case.

- A collection of supporting evidence in the form of assessments of either system properties or properties about how the system was developed. These assessments come from techniques such as measurements, analyses, testing, modeling, and simulation.

- A list of the assumptions that have been made in the argument. Some aspects of the development and assessment process have to rely on assumptions that cannot easily be justified by available forms of evidence.

The fact that the argument is explicit, i.e., actually documented, brings several immediate advantages:

Argument review by developers. The developers of the target system have to construct the argument, and, in doing so, they have to think about the argument's contents. Thus, the argument is reviewed as it is built, and the argument can affect technology choices made by developers.

Argument review by other engineers. Engineers not involved in development of the system or the argument can examine the argument and determine whether they think the argument is convincing. This examination is a form of inspection and is an effective way of assessing arguments.

Argument review by regulators. Explicit arguments provide regulators with precisely the view that they need when they are trying to assess whether the dependability goals of a system have been met with sufficient fidelity to protect the public interest.

Argument permanence. The argument is always available, because it is written down. Thus, the rationale is never lost as it would be if the rationale were only discussed verbally.

Argument quality. The fact that the argument is rigorous means that the argument is more likely to be convincing, and, in some sense, "correct".

As with other topics in this book, we cannot cover rigorous arguments in depth. Our discussion begins in the next section with a review of the present major use of rigorous arguments, *safety cases*. In Section 12.4.3, we present some of the basic aspects of safety case and argument structure. The remaining sections present (a) an example of a safety argument and how the argument might be developed, (b) a popular notation, the Goal Structuring Notation, that has been developed for documenting arguments, and (c) the concept of using patterns in argumentation.

12.4.2 Safety Cases

The use of rigorous argument was pioneered in the field of system safety primarily in the United Kingdom (U.K.). Over a period of several decades, various significant accidents occurred in the U.K., including a fire at the Windscale nuclear reactor in 1957, an explosion at the Flixborough chemical plant in 1974, an explosion on the Piper Alpha oil platform in 1988, and a collision of passenger trains at Clapham in 1988. These accidents and other accidents and incidents over the past 50 years led to the development of a detailed safety culture that includes safety cases.

The concise definition of a safety case is:

"A safety case should communicate a clear, comprehensive and defensible argument that a system is acceptably safe to operate in a particular context." [75]

There are three important phrases to note about this definition:

"clear, comprehensive and defensible". The argument has to be *clear* so as to be accessible. The argument has to be *comprehensive*, because all aspects of safety have to be addressed. And the argument has to be *defensible*, because the argument must be convincing to all the stakeholders and not subject to a successful rebuttal.

"acceptably safe". Since systems cannot be shown to be completely safe, the argument has to show what is practical. Thus the level of risk that the stakeholders of the system will tolerate must be part of the goal that the argument addresses.

"particular context". A system is designed to operate in a specific context, and, if the system is operated in a different context, then the system could be unsafe. Thus, the operating context must be stated and considered in the use and evaluation of the argument.

Creating a safety case that meets the definition is an elaborate process. There are four major tasks that have to be undertaken:

Determine what level of safety will be acceptable. This determination is a process of negotiation driven primarily by those charged with protecting the public interest. For a medical device, for example, the prospect of patient injury is obviously the focus, but different patient injuries have different implications.

Determine what the operating context will be. The operating context involves a wide range of factors, each of which might have many attributes. For a medical device, for example, determining the operating context requires that those developing the context ascertain everything about where, when, by whom, for what purpose, and how the device will be used.

Determine all the relevant system details. Many different engineering disciplines are involved in the development of any modern engineered system. Medical devices, for example, are motivated by medical professionals, but the creation of the device is likely to involve mechanical engineers, materials scientists, electrical engineers, computer engineers, software engineers, and probably others.

Create an argument that is clear, comprehensive and defensible. In practice, documented arguments tend to be large. They depend on many other documents that provide the context, the evidence, and so on. The totality of the materials that constitute the safety case will often be hundreds of pages. An argument can seem reasonable to one engineer but not to another. An argument can be malformed in subtle ways that are hard to see but which make the argument insufficient.

12.4.3 Regulation Based on Safety Cases

Safety cases are used extensively in the United Kingdom (U.K.) as the primary means of documenting safety and demonstrating compliance with associated regulation. The following U.K. agencies require safety cases in some areas of their jurisdiction:

- The Health and Safety Executive for various elements of the nuclear industry and for offshore installations such as oil platforms.

- The Office of Rail Regulation for rail signaling and management.

- The Ministry of Defence for all safety-critical defense systems.

- The Civil Aviation Authority for air-traffic services safety requirements.

An important example of regulation based on safety cases is U.K. Ministry of Defence, Defence Standard 00-56 [140]. This standard is *goal-based* and different from the standards mentioned earlier in this chapter. The standard is only 18 pages long yet it covers a wide range of systems. The standard states:

The purpose of this Standard is to set requirements that enable the acquisition of systems that are compliant with both safety legislation and MOD safety policy.

In other words, the standard is considered all that is needed to protect the interests of the various stakeholders for U.K. defence systems. The heart of the standard is the requirement that a safety case be supplied for any compliant system. The standard states:

The Contractor shall produce a Safety Case for the system on behalf of the Duty Holder. The Safety Case shall consist of a structured argument, supported by a body of evidence, that provides a compelling, comprehensible and valid case that a system is safe for a given application in a given environment.

A second important example of regulation based on safety cases is the U.K. Civil Aviation Authority's CAP 670 Air Traffic Services Safety Requirements [141]. This is also a goal-based standard. The standard states:

Whilst the contents of the document may be of interest to other parties, this document is addressed to ATS providers who are expected to demonstrate compliance with applicable requirements either directly or through the provision of safety assurance documentation which may be in the form known as a safety case.

At the time of writing, no regulating agency in the United States requires the use of safety cases as discussed here. The Food and Drug Administration (FDA) does not currently require them but has issued guidance for particular devices that permits their use [48].

12.4.4 Building a Safety Case

The Structure of a Safety Case

A complete safety case is the composition of the safety argument, all the information used by the argument such as the evidence and the context definitions, and any ancillary materials such as informal descriptions that might be considered useful. The argument provides the reader with the rationale, and the other materials provide the details to which the argument refers.

The high-level structure of a safety case is illustrated in Fig. 12.6. At the top right is the safety claim (a requirement that has to be met) that is expressed as a goal. At the bottom right is the body of supporting evidence that will be used as the basis of the safety argument. Linking the supporting evidence to the top-level goal is the safety argument. This argument should show how the top-level goal follows from the supporting evidence.

To the left in the figure are the details of the operating context, a set of explicit assumptions that are being made and which will be used as part of the basis for the argument, and a set of justifications that explain why certain strategies were used in the argument and why they should be accepted.

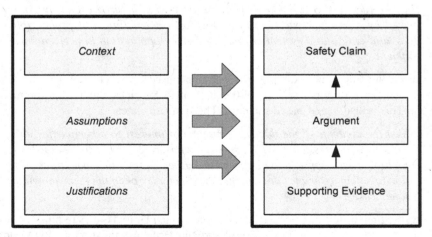

FIGURE 12.6 The overall content and basic structure of a safety case.

The Structure of a Safety Argument

The structure of a safety argument is a hierarchy of goals. A higher-level goal is decomposed into a set of lower-level goals that, if satisfied, can be combined according to a strategy to argue that the higher-level goal is satisfied. Decomposition is applied to all goals until low-level goals can be reasonably inferred from available evidence.

The process of building a safety argument begins with defining the top-level goal of the argument. This goal is the fundamental claim that is being made about the system. Essentially, the form of the goal is a statement of the safety requirement for the system. This goal is decomposed into lower-level goals, and this process continues until the entire hierarchy is complete.

The basic building blocks of a safety argument are:

Goals. A set of goals in which a top-level goal documents the safety claim and other subgoals help to structure and elaborate the argument. Goal statements have the form of a proposition in order that they may be evaluated as true or false.

Contexts. Context is needed to establish the expected operating environment for the system itself and also for the environments in which some of the evidence was obtained.

Strategies. A strategy shows how a higher-level goal will be inferred from lower-level goals.

Solutions. Solutions are the composition of all forms of evidence. Solutions might include data from tests, details of a process step, and so on.

Assumptions. As the name implies, assumptions document the assumptions being made in the argument.

Justifications. Justifications basically provide the reasoning behind the use of a particular strategy.

12.4.5 A Simple Example

To illustrate the basic elements of a safety argument, consider the simple problem of arguing that using a match in an office to light a candle is safe. The top-level safety goal used might be:

> **Goal**: *Lighting a candle using a match in my office is adequately safe.*

In order to make this goal meaningful, we need to state the context and the meaning that we want for "adequately safe". This could be done in the following way:

> **Operating Context**: *The lighting of the candle will take place in an office that is identified by building number and office number. The details of the*

office location, dimensions, content, accessibility, and construction materials are provided in certified documents at a specified location.

Adequately safe: *Adequately safe means that burning or setting fire unintentionally to anything other than the subject candle is* **reduced As Low As is Reasonably Practicable (ALARP)**.

The definition of adequately safe uses the ALARP principle, because that principle provides the form of the claim that is most useful. ALARP in this case means:

- There is no known means of burning or setting fire to an object in the room other than the subject candle that has not been properly identified and made inoperative. Thus, fire can only result from an ignition process that has not been identified, and the expense of seeking other highly unlikely (hopefully non-existent) ignition processes is grossly disproportionate to the expected reduction in risk.

- The cost of installing additional risk-reduction technologies such as a building sprinkler system is grossly disproportionate to the expected reduction in risk.

The only significant hazard that we need to address is a state in which something other than the candle could be set on fire or burned. So the definition of adequately safe is basically that this hazard is as unlikely to occur as we can reasonably make it.

Notice the amount of detail that this goal and the context statement contain, and how the planned notion of "safe" is defined. Also note that this is just the top-level goal statement, not the whole safety argument.

In order to complete the safety argument for this example, the remainder of the argument needs to be developed and the associated evidence generated. The strategy that we will use is to argue that the top-level safety goal follows if the following subgoals holds:

- No children are present in the room when the candle is ignited.
- The room cannot be accessed in an unplanned manner by children.
- There are no combustible materials within a three-meter radius of the location at which matches will be used.
- There is a non-combustible mat below the candle and the space in which the lighted match will be present.
- The contact information for the fire department is accurate and prominently visible.
- The fire department is available at all times that a candle might be ignited.
- The office communications equipment provides highly reliable facilities to contact the fire department.
- There are no combustible gases present.
- The match does not explode or burn out of control.

- No burning matches are present once the candle is alight.
- The candle does not explode or burn out of control.
- The operator is competent to use a match in the required manner.
- The candle cannot be moved out of the office once ignited.

The development process that has to be followed for refinement of any goal is to determine the argument strategy to be used, define the set of subgoals, and review this elaboration of the top-level goal so as to remain convinced that this refinement is valid. Where assumptions have to be made or where additional context has to be added, these need to be documented as part of the refinement also.

The evidence that will be used in this argument includes (but is not limited to):

- All personnel in the room have been checked and found to be adults.
- Materials in the office within three meters of the location at which matches will be used have been shown to be non-combustible by an independent laboratory.
- The office has been checked for explosive gases by an independent laboratory within a short period of time so that explosive gases could not have built up since the test was conducted.
- The candle brand has been tested for burn characteristics by an independent laboratory and found to be adequate.
- The match brand has been checked for burn characteristics by an independent laboratory and found to be adequate.
- The equipment available to extinguish a burning match and to dispose of a hot match has been thoroughly tested by expert fire-prevention engineers.
- The operator has been given training in (a) lighting a candle with a match and (b) determining where within the office space the use of a match would be at least three meters from combustible materials.

Even though this example is simple and is incomplete, note the length of the argument so far, the amount of evidence needed, and the rigor yet relative informality of the approach.

Completing this example, a simple one, requires that we expand all of the subgoals. One might conclude from the evidence listed above that the subgoals are all valid. But there is at least one flaw in that argument. The flaw is the assumption that if all personnel in the room are adults, then there are no children present. Since people come and go all the time, we need at least two lower-level goals to be able to justify the claim that no children are present. To argue that the operating context is limited to adults, there needs to be a strong argument that children cannot reach the environment. Thus, we need two subgoals:

- All personnel in the room are adults.
- Children cannot gain access to the room.

This second subgoal seems simple since the area in question is an office, and apparently a secretary guards the office in question. In practice, the simplicity of this example is deceptive, and that deception is precisely where the need for a comprehensive argument is greatest. If an error is made so that a child can obtain access to matches, the consequences could be serious. Consider that the argument so far says nothing about what happens if the secretary is not at her desk, whether the office is locked during non-business hours, whether the secretary was trained not to admit children, and so on.

We can (and, of course, should) modify the system and the argument to take care of these omissions. That is simple to do once we have the initial form of the argument. The argument that we obtain will be fairly comprehensive, because we will deal with locking the office, secretary training, and so on. That evidence now includes (hypothetical) documents about company procedures that define secretary training and scheduling.

But the power of rigorous argument is well illustrated at this point, because, when we review the argument, we detect several weaknesses:

- Demanding that the secretary be trained to deny children access to the office does not mean that the secretary either fully understood the training or that he or she would properly enforce the rule of denying children access.

- Requiring that the secretary lock the door whenever he or she is absent does not mean that the secretary will always remember to lock the door.

- There is no indication that the secretary would prohibit the introduction of explosive gases or combustible materials into the office. Even though our top-level goal is argued, in part, by the checks on explosive gases and combustible materials, there is no provision in the system as described to maintain that state.

The fact that the safety of the system depends on significant but subtle details is not necessarily revealed by a rigorous safety argument, but the chances are high that the argument will reveal subtle errors if we build the argument carefully and inspect the argument systematically.

12.4.6 The Goal Structuring Notation

In practice, arguments are large, complex artifacts that have to be read and understood by a variety of people. If they were documented in an ad hoc manner, the chances are high that the reader of an argument would be unfamiliar with whatever notation was used. Having a single, well-designed notation for documenting arguments is important.

The example of lighting a candle given in the previous section demonstrates why rigor and precise notations are needed. The example is for illustration of basic ideas only, and documenting the complete safety case is not necessary. Were the complete safety case needed, informal and unstructured English text would not be satisfac-

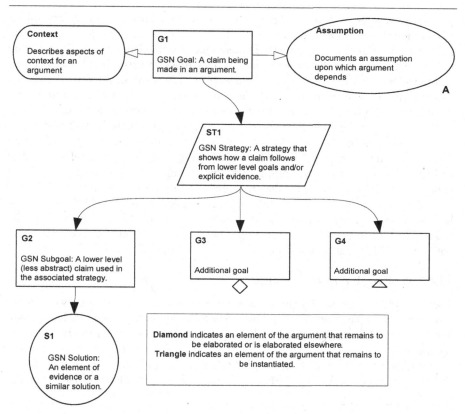

FIGURE 12.7 The graphic elements of the Goal Structuring Notation (GSN).

tory. Various notations have been developed for documenting arguments, but we will concentrate on just one, the *Goal Structuring Notation* (GSN).

The Goal Structuring Notation is a graphic notation that has been developed to provide a complete and unified approach to documenting safety arguments [75]. Tools have been developed to facilitate the editing and analysis of safety cases documented in GSN including ASCE [5], ISCaDE [119], and the University of York add-on for Microsoft Visio [142].

The graphic elements that are used in the representation of an argument in GSN are shown in Figure 12.7 and are just the argument building blocks. Each element has an identifying symbol in the top left of the element. The character used indicates the type of element, e.g., "G" for goal, and the integer identifies the specific element. The primary purpose of the identifying symbol is to allow reference to the element in all the associated documentation.

An example of a simple top-level goal and the associated context description for a hypothetical unmanned aircraft system (UAS) is shown in Fig. 12.8. The arrow from the goal element to the context element indicates the dependence of the goal on the context. Note that the contexts in the GSN diagram refer to associated documents, the Safety Manual and the Concept of Operations for the aircraft. These documents will be included in the complete safety case. Note also that the context will include the definition of exactly what the word "safe" is to mean in this case.

With a top-level goal of the form shown in Fig. 12.8 properly stated and the context fully documented, the next step in the development of a safety argument would be to determine the strategy that will be used to argue that the top-level goal is met and the subgoals that will be employed in that strategy. This process of refinement continues until the leaf nodes in the argument are solutions or assumptions.

An example of part of a hypothetical argument documented in GSN for the top-level goal and contexts in Figure 12.8 is shown in Figure 12.9. In this example, the top-level goal is argued using a strategy based on the idea that the risks associated with all credible hazards should be reduced to an acceptable level.

12.4.7 Software and Arguments

The example in Figure 12.9 does not mention software. This is not an omission. Software is not mentioned, because the safety argument is for an application system. The argument decomposition shown has not reached the level where software enters the picture.

Refinement of the argument for goal G8 is shown in Figure 12.10. In this subargument, the focus is on a hypothetical ground-based surveillance radar. The radar

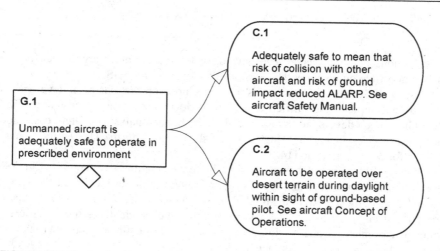

FIGURE 12.8 Top-level goal and context example.

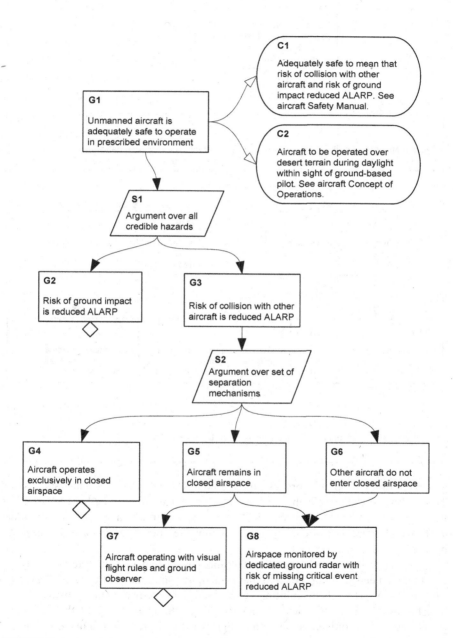

FIGURE 12.9 · A small fragment of a safety argument documented in GSN.

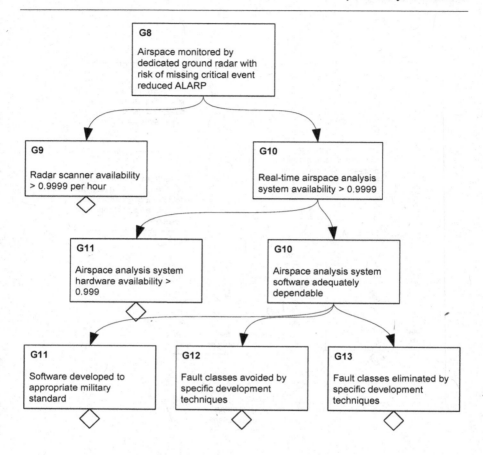

FIGURE 12.10 Refinement of UAS argument down to software level.

generates raw data that is processed by a complex computerized analysis system. The analysis system tracks the subject aircraft and determines whether the aircraft is in danger of exiting the airspace within which it is authorized to operate. The radar also looks for intruder aircraft that might enter the operating airspace for the UAS by mistake.

In order to have confidence that the analysis system will operate correctly, an argument is needed about the computer system that implements the analysis system. The argument proceeds by splitting the problem into hardware and software claims. The hardware claim includes a statement about the availability of the hardware. Assuming that the only concern with the hardware is degradation faults, this claim is quite reasonable.

Unfortunately, a similar claim cannot be made in this case for the software. The use of fault avoidance and fault elimination techniques can provide assurance that whole classes of faults are missing, but for the remainder of the software faults the argument has to appeal to the process by which the software was constructed. Thus, the argument in the end will rest, in part, upon the assumption that the software has the necessary dependability properties as a result of the development process used. This situation is common and leads us to a discussion about the different types of evidence that can arise.

12.4.8 Types of Evidence

The evidence used in safety arguments can take various forms, and the different forms provide different levels of support for the claims to which they contribute. The fundamental difference is between *direct* and *indirect* evidence:

Direct evidence: Direct evidence is evidence about the product itself.

Indirect evidence: Indirect evidence is evidence about how the product was produced.

Direct evidence is preferred, because such evidence derives from and is evidence about the product itself. Indirect evidence has the disadvantage of requiring the basic assumption that a product property can be inferred from the indirect evidence. This problem is the same as the problem we noted with the use of prescribed standards (see Section 12.3.4).

Evidence can be broken down into subtypes that characterize the evidence further. The breakdowns differ between different sources, and so here we will use the characterizations from the U.K. Ministry of Defence in Defence Standard 00-56 [140].

Defence Standard 00-56 distinguishes five types of evidence:

Direct evidence from analysis. During development, various types of analysis are performed on systems and system components, including software. The result of an analysis is typically the establishment of a property of the artifact. Static analysis of software, for example, can establish that certain faults are absent from the software (see Section 7.9.1, page 208). Analytic evidence provides strong support for any claim, although a convincing argument about a general software claim will require a lot of evidence.

Direct evidence from demonstration. Demonstration evidence includes the results of testing, simulation, modeling, and possibly operational use. Testing is, of course, common for many different components of a system, especially software. Simulation and modeling are special mechanisms that correspond roughly to the idea of "testing" algorithms.

Clearly, evidence from operational use is not an option except under special circumstances. Any operational use that is to be included as evidence must have come from some version of the system that is different from the system that is the subject of the safety case. If that were not the situation, the system would have been operating without the planned safety case and presumably with some form of restricted or preliminary authority to operate.

Situations in which operational evidence arises and can be used include operation in an environment different from that for which the safety case is being developed. For example, an unmanned aircraft might be operated for substantial periods of time over an uninhabited desert area and substantial operational experience gained without harm. That evidence about the aircraft system in general and the avionics, navigation, engine-control, and communications software in particular might be used in a safety case for the operation of the aircraft over a populated area.

Direct evidence from the review process. Review evidence is the evidence obtained from rigorous inspection. As discussed in Chapter 10, inspections are highly effective and can be applied to virtually any artifact.

Indirect evidence from a process. As we discussed in Section 12.3.3, there are advantages to the use of prescriptive standards, and citing the use of such standards is of value despite the fact that the evidence is indirect. Care must be taken, however, with any prescriptive standard to seek ways in which the standard might be missing something. Typically, software standards require some form of testing and rely upon that testing for verification. Such testing does not necessarily test the subject artifact in such a way as to reveal application-specific faults. Software testing that relies on branch coverage, for example, will not necessarily reveal faults that cause real-time deadlines to be missed.

Indirect qualitative evidence. Qualitative evidence includes assessment that an artifact has certain properties that are not related quantitatively to the artifact but tend to correlate with a "better" artifact. For software, there are many useful metrics about software design that tend to correlate well with software that is more dependable. Also for software, expert judgment is a valuable form of evidence. Experts with substantial experience can judge various attributes of a software system, including items such as likely completeness of documentation, appropriate types of data structures, appropriate coding techniques, and so on. Such judgment is useful evidence.

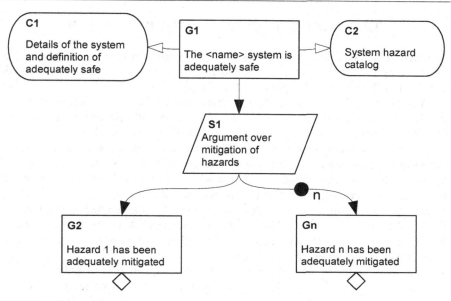

FIGURE 12.11 A commonly occurring high-level safety argument.

12.4.9 Safety Case Patterns

Arguments relate evidence to claims and are rarely unique. In fact, commonly used arguments exist, including high-level argument fragments that are distinct from evidence and special arguments that are specific to particular domains. Arguments can be reused by starting with what is usually called a template. Safety case templates are called *patterns*.

Patterns capture successful argument approaches so that they may easily be reused. They document "best practice" arguments, such as specialized domain expertise, successful certification approaches, and "tools of the trade".

Various safety case pattern catalogs are available (for example in [76] and [146]), and they should be consulted any time that a safety case is being built. If a suitable pattern is found, that pattern can be instantiated for a specific use, although instantiation must be done carefully to ensure that the argument limitations or restrictions that apply have been properly respected. GSN includes symbols for pattern support.

A commonly occurring high-level safety argument is shown in Figure 12.11. This pattern was the basis of the example in Figure 12.9. The strategies in this pattern can be elaborated with the help of other patterns that address the strategies specifically.

12.5 Applicability of Argumentation

As noted in Section 2.8.1, there is no such thing as safe software or secure software. Software by itself cannot do any harm to people, equipment, the environment, or information. These notions apply to application systems.

Arguments have been applied to all of the dependability attributes that are meaningful at the application system level. When speaking of a dependability attribute other than safety, the term that is sometimes used is an *assurance* case.

The notion of safety arguments is well established. In practice, outside of equipment safety, assurance cases are being applied primarily in the fields of security and location safety. Security arguments have been the subject of preliminary research and evaluation. An argument that a system is secure in some sense is a valuable complement to the qualitative assessment that has been attempted in the security field in the form of security audits. In the field of location safety, assurance cases have been applied to the assurance of various properties of nuclear fuel handling and to the Yucca mountain nuclear waste repository.

Also as we noted in Section 2.8.3, computer systems in general and software in particular have dependability requirements that are derived from the needs of the overall system within which the computer system will operate. These derived dependability requirements constitute a contract between the computer system and the overall system within which the computer system will operate.

The use of arguments for software is restricted to the meaningful dependability properties of software. Rather than develop separate technologies for arguments about software reliability, software availability, and so on, the more common practice is to create an assurance argument. Such an argument is used to provide assurance that the software meets the dependability requirements derived from the application system.

Why Rigorous Arguments Rather Than Quantitative Assessment?

How does the use of argument mitigate the difficulties with quantitative assessment? As we saw in Section 12.2.4, the three areas of difficulty with quantitative assessment are (1) non-quantifiable attributes, (2) unavailability of models, and (3) ultra-high levels of dependability. Rigorous arguments provide an approach to dealing with all three areas of difficulty:

Non-quantifiable attributes. Non-quantifiable attributes are usually dealt with by either fault avoidance or fault elimination. Provided the techniques used are comprehensive, the required attribute is present *in theory*. The major problem that arises is a lack of assurance that the various techniques have been applied properly. By using a rigorous argument, (a) the details of the techniques and their application can be documented and (b) the rationale for believing that the techniques provide the necessary attribute and that the techniques have been applied properly can be properly stated and examined.

Unavailability of models. Without models, the applicability of quantitative assessment is severely restricted. By using a rigorous argument, developers can show that all possible or at least all reasonable measures have been taken in the development of the subject software. This approach does not provide a quantitative assessment, but the approach does provide a strong basis for believing that the ALARP principle has been applied systematically and thoroughly.

Ultra-high levels of dependability. Ultra-high levels of dependability cannot be determined by quantitative means, as we noted in Section 12.2.4. Again, by using a rigorous argument, developers can show that all possible or at least all reasonable measures have been taken in the development of the subject software.

Why Rigorous Arguments Rather Than Prescriptive Standards?

How does the use of argument mitigate the difficulties with prescriptive standards? As we saw in Section 12.3.4, the disadvantages of prescriptive standards are their inflexibility and their dependence on an unjustified assumption. As noted in Section 12.4, there is always an *implicit* argument associated with any prescriptive standard. This idea is easy to see if one asks the following question for any prescriptive standard:

Why does the standard require what it does?

For each entity that a prescriptive standard requires, there must have been a rationale, and that rationale must have been in the mind of the developers of the standard when the standard was written. Properly composed, structured, and documented, the rationales for the entities could constitute a complete and comprehensive overall argument addressing a suitable top-level claim. Unfortunately for existing standards, this preparation has not been done.

Turning this situation around, we can document our rationale for some aspect of a system's or software's dependability attribute and associate that rationale with the process steps that we take to achieve it. Thus, the inflexibility of prescriptive standards is eliminated, because we can tailor the standard to a specific process and justify our process steps with the dependability argument.

Key points in this chapter:

- There are three general approaches to dependability assessment: quantitative assessment, prescriptive standards, and rigorous argument.
- In most cases, quantitative assessment cannot be applied effectively to software dependability assessment.
- Prescriptive standards are applied regularly to software development.
- Prescriptive standards are generally of only limited flexibility and so cannot accommodate well the idiosyncracies of systems.
- There is no generally applicable relationship between the details of a prescriptive standard and the ensuing dependability of software built using the standard.
- Rigorous argument is used to document the rationale that developers have for believing in the dependability attributes of a target artifact.
- A rigorous argument is embedded within a comprehensive safety case to provide documentation of the rationale for believing a system is safe.
- Safety cases can be scrutinized by independent entities such as certification agencies to allow assessment of the safety of a given system.

Exercises

1. DoD Mil Std 882D is a standard that is available for download [35]. Examine the standard and identify several prescriptive processes and several prescriptive artifact elements that the standard requires.

2. Review Mil Std 882D and determine how the standard requires that hazard identification be conducted.

3. Download a copy of MoD Defence Standard 00-56 [140]. The standard requires that a system developer deliver a safety case to the regulators and that the safety case be "compelling". The standard does not define compelling for an argument. Develop an argument of your own for the term "compelling".

4. Sketch out an argument in GSN for the candle example discussed in Section 12.4.5.

5. Software is neither safe nor unsafe (see Section 2.8.1), but rigorous argument can be applied successfully to software. In that case, the argument is referred to as a software assurance argument. Top-level claims in such arguments are the dependability requirements for the software. Develop a GSN pattern that might be used as a starting point in developing an assurance argument for software.

6. In a software assurance argument, determine whether each of the following items of evidence is direct or indirect: (a) report of the inspection of the specification, (b) results of the static analysis of the source program, (c) report of the successful completion of the exit criteria for software testing, and (d) report of test coverage analysis.

7. Concisely explain what is meant by a *safety case* for a safety-critical system.

8. How is *safety* defined for a safety case?

9. Critics have claimed that fault trees and safety arguments in the GSN are basically the same thing. If this is the case, explain why. If not, explain why not.

10. Consider an expression in a piece of software that contains 24 inputs (variables or functions that are either true or false). How much time would it take to execute all of the tests required for multiple condition coverage (exhaustive testing) if you could run 200 tests per second?

11. Briefly explain the meaning and significance of the Butler and Finelli result [24].

12. A safety case documented in GSN is a directed, acyclic graph (DAG).

   (a) What would be found at the root of the DAG and what would it say?

   (b) What major types of nodes are typically found within the DAG?

   (c) Would details of a system's fault tree analysis be included in a typical safety case? If so, how and, if not, why not?

Bibliography

[1]   Abrial, Jean-Raymond, *The B Book: Assigning Programs To Meanings*, Cambridge University Press (2005)

[2]   Ackerman, A., L. Buchwald, and F. Lewski, Software Inspections: An Effective Verification Process, *IEEE Software*, Vol. 6, No. 3 (May 1989)

[3]   Ada Information Clearinghouse, *Ada Reference Manual*, ISO/IEC 8652:1995(E) with Technical Corrigendum 1 and Amendment 1
        http://www.adaic.com/standards/05rm/RM-Final.pdf

[4]   Ada Information Clearinghouse, *Ada Reference Manual*, ISO/IEC 8652:1995(E) with Technical Corrigendum 1
        http://www.adaic.com/standards/95lrm/html/RM-TTL.html

[5]   Adelard LLP, Adelard Safety Case Editor
        http://www.adelard.com

[6]   Akera, A., The Circulation of Knowledge and the Origins of the ENIAC: (Or, What Was and Was Not Innovative About the American Wartime Project)
        http://ghn.ieee.org/wiki/images/b/be/Akera.pdf

[7]   American Nuclear Society, ANSI/ANS-2.29-2008: *Probabilistic Seismic Hazard Analysis* (2008)

[8]   Amey, P., Correctness by Construction: Better Can Also Be Cheaper, *Crosstalk: The Journal of Defense Software Engineering* (March 2002)

[9]   Ammann, P. and J. Knight, Data Diversity: An Approach To Software Fault Tolerance, *IEEE Transactions on Computers*, Vol. 37, No. 4 (April 1988)

[10]   Anderson, T. amd P. Lee, *Fault Tolerance: Principles and Practice*, Prentice Hall International (1983)

[11]   Australian Transport Safety Bureau, *In-flight upset event 240 km north-west of Perth, WA, Boeing Company 777-200, 9M-MRG*
        http://www.atsb.gov.au/publications/investigation_reports/2005/AAIR/pdf/aair200503722_001.pdf

[12]   Automotive Industry Action Group (AIAG), *FMEA-3: Potential Failure Effects Analysis*
        https://www.aiag.org

[13] Avizienis, A., J.-C. Laprie, B. Randell, and C. Landwehr, Basic Concepts and Taxonomy of Dependable and Secure Computing, *IEEE Transactions on Secure and Dependable Computing*, Vol.1, No.1 (January-March 2004)

[14] Bahr, N., *System Safety Engineering And Risk Assessment: A Practical Approach (Chemical Engineering)*, Taylor and Francis (1997)

[15] Ball, M. and F.H. Hardie, *Architecture for an Extended Mission Aerospace Computer*, IBM No. 66-825-1753, Owego, New York (May 1969)

[16] Barnes, J., *High Integrity Software: The SPARK Approach to Safety and Security*, Addison Wesley (2003)

[17] Beck, K. and C. Andres, *Extreme Programming Explained: Embrace Change*, Pearson (2004)

[18] Borkar, S., Designing reliable systems from unreliable components: the challenges of transistor variability and degradation, *IEEE Micro*, Vol. 25, No. 6 (November/December 2005)

[19] Bose, P., Designing reliable systems with unreliable components, *IEEE Micro*, Vol. 26, No. 5, (June 2006)

[20] Bowen, J.P. and M.G. Hinchey, Seven More Myths of Formal Methods, *IEEE Software* (July 1995)

[21] British Standards Institution BS 5760-5, *Reliability of systems, equipment and components. Guide to failure modes, effects and criticality analysis (FMEA and FMECA)* (1991)

[22] Burns, A. and A. Wellings, Safety Kernels: Specification and Implementation, *High Integrity Systems*, Vol 1, No 3 (1995)

[23] Burns, A., B. Dobbing, and T. Vardanega, Guide for the Use of the Ada Ravenscar Profile in High Integrity Systems, University of York Technical Report YCS-2003-348 (2003)

[24] Butler, R. and G. Finelli, The Infeasibility of Quantifying the Reliability of Life-Critical Real-Time Software, *IEEE Transactions on Software Engineering*, Vol. 19 , No. 1, pp. 3-12 (January 1993)

[25] Chen, L. and A. Avizienis, *N-version Programming: A Fault-tolerance Approach to Reliability of Software Operation*, Eighth International Symposium on Fault Tolerant Computing, Toulouse, France (1978)

[26] Chilenski, J. and S. Miller, Applicability of Modified Condition/Decision Coverage to Software Testing, *Software Engineering Journal*, Vol. 9, No. 5, pp.193-200 (September 1994)

[27] Clarke, E. and J. Wing, Formal Methods: State of the Art and Future Directions, *ACM Computing Surveys*, Vol. 28, No. 4 (December 1996)

[28] ClearSy System Engineering, Atelier B toolset
http://www.atelierb.eu/index-en.php

[29] Cole, G., *Estimating Drive Reliability in Desktop Computers and Consumer Electronics Systems*, Seagate Technology Paper TP-338.1 (November 2000)

[30] Computerworld, March 29, 2007
http://www.computerworld.com/action/article.do?command=viewArticleBasic&articleId=9014782

[31] Craigen, D., S. Gerhart, and T. Ralston, An International Survey of Industrial Applications of Formal Methods, National Institute of Standards and Technology, GCR 626 (1993)

[32] Dahl, O., E. W. Dijkstra, and C. A. Hoare, *Structured Programming*, Academic Press, New York (1972)

[33] Defense Industry Daily, F-22 Squadron Shot Down by the International Date Line
http://www.defenseindustrydaily.com/f22-squadron-shot-down-by-the-international-date-line-03087/

[34] Department of Defense, Ada Joint Program Office, *Ada 95 Quality and Style: Guidelines for Professional Programmers*
http://www.adaic.org/docs/95style/95style.pdf

[35] Department of Defense, *Mil-Std-882D, Standard Practice for System Safety*
http://www.denix.osd.mil/shf/upload/MIL-STD-882D.pdf

[36] Department of Defense, *MIL-STD-1629A: Procedures for Performing a Failure Mode, Effects and Criticality Analysis.*

[37] Dobson, J. and B. Randell, *Building Reliable Secure Computing Systems Out Of Unreliable Insecure Components*, Proceedings of the IEEE Symposium on Security and Privacy, Oakland, CA (1986)

[38] Driscoll, K., B. Hall, M. Paulitsch, P. Zumsteg, and H. Sivencrona, *The Real Byzantine Generals,* 23rd Digital Avionics Systems Conference, Salt Lake City (October 2004)

[39] Droschl, G., W. Kuhn, G. Sonneck, and M. Thuswald, *A Formal Methods Case Study: Using Light-Weight VDM for the Development of a Security System Module*, Lecture Notes in Computer Science, Vol. 1943, Springer Verlag (2000)

[40] Easterbrook, S. and J. Callahan, *Formal Methods for Verification and Validation of Partial Specifications: A Case Study*, NASA Independent Verification and Validation Facility, Morgantown, WV (1997)

[41] Eckhardt, D. and L. Lee, A Theoretical Basis for the Analysis of Multiversion Software Subject to Coincident Errors, *IEEE Transactions on Software Engineering*, Vol. SE-11, No. 12 (December 1985)

[42] Eiffel Software
http://www.eiffel.com/

[43] Ericson, C., *Fault Tree Analysis—A History*, Proceedings 17th International System Safety Conference, International System Safety Society, Orlando FL (1999)

[44] Esterel Technologies, SCADE Suite
http://www.esterel-technologies.com/products/scade-suite/

[45] Fagan, M.E., Design and code inspections to reduce errors in program development, *IBM Journal of Research and Development*, Vol. 15, No. 3 (1976)

[46] Federal Aviation Administration, System Safety Handbook
http://www.faa.gov/library/manuals/aviation/risk_management/
ss_handbook/

[47] Finkelstein, A. and J. Dowell, *A Comedy of Errors: The London Ambulance Service Case Study*
http://www.cs.ucl.ac.uk/staff/a.finkelstein/papers/lascase.pdf

[48] Food and Drug Administration, Guidance for Industry and FDA Staff, Total Product Life Cycle: Infusion Pump — Premarket Notification [510(k)] Submissions, DRAFT GUIDANCE (April 2010)

[49] Garman, J., The "Bug" Heard 'Round the World, *ACM Sigsoft Software Engineering notes*, Vol. 6, No. 5 (October 1981)

[50] GNU Coding Standards
http://www.gnu.org/prep/standards/

[51] Gray, J., *Why Do Computers Stop and What Can Be Done About It?*, Tandem Computers Technical Report TR 85.7 (June 1985)
http://www.hpl.hp.com/techreports/tandem/TR-85.7.pdf

[52] Gray, J. and C. van Ingen, *Empirical Measurements of Disk Failure Rates and Error Rates*, Microsoft Research Technical Report MSR-TR-2005-166 (December 2005)

[53] Gregory, S. and J.C. Knight, *On the Provision of Backward Error Recovery in Production Programming Languages*, Nineteenth Annual Symposium on Fault-Tolerant Computing, Chicago, IL (June 1989)

[54] Hall, A., Seven Myths of Formal Methods, *IEEE Software* (September 1990)

[55] Hall, A. and R. Chapman, Correctness by Construction: Developing a Commercial Secure System, *IEEE Software*, Vol.19, No. 1, pp. 18-25 (Jan/Feb 2002)

[56] Hall, A. and R. Chapman, Correctness by Construction
http://www.anthonyhall.org/Correctness_by_Construction.pdf

[57] Harel, D., Statecharts: A Visual Formalism for Complex Systems, *Science of Computer Programming*, Vol. 8, pp. 231-274 (1987)

[58] Hayhurst, K., D. Veerhusen, J. Chilenski, L. Rierson, *A Practical Tutorial on Modified Condition/Decision Coverage*, NASA Langley Technical Report TM-2001-21087 (May 2001)

[59] Health and Safety at Work etc. Act 1974
http://www.healthandsafety.co.uk/haswa.htm

[60] Health and Safety Executive, *ALARP Suite of Guidance*
http://www.hse.gov.uk/risk/theory/alarp.htm

[61] Hekmatpor, S. and D. Ince, *Software Prototyping, Formal Methods and VDM*, Addison-Wesley (1988)

[62] Heitmeyer, C., M. Archer, R. Bharadwaj and R. Jeffords, Tools for constructing requirements specifications: The SCR toolset at the age of ten, *International Journal of Computer Systems Science & Engineering*, Vol. 20, No. 1 (2005)

[63] Holzmann, G., *The Spin Model Checker: Primer and Reference Manual*, Addison Wesley, Boston (2004)

[64] Institute of Electrical and Electronic Engineers
http://www.ieee.org/portal/innovate/products/standard/
ieee_choice.html

[65] International Electrotechnical Commission IEC 61025, Fault tree analysis (FTA) (2006)

[66] International Electrotechnical Commission IEC 60812:2006(E), Analysis techniques for system reliability – Procedure for failure mode and effects analysis (FMEA) (2006)

[67] International Electrotechnical, Commission IEC 61882. Hazard and operability studies (HAZOP studies) – Application guide (2001)

[68] International Standards Organization
http://www.iso.org/iso/home.htm

398

[69]   International Standards Organization/International Electrotechnical Commission 9899 - Programming languages - C (2005)
         http://www.open-std.org/jtc1/sc22/wg14/www/docs/n1124.pdf

[70]   International Standards Organization/International Electrotechnical Commission 15026:1998 -- Information technology -- System and software integrity levels (1998)

[71]   Jacky, J, *The Way of Z: Practical Programming with Formal Methods*, Cambridge University Press (1996)

[72]   Jetley, R., C. Carlos, and S. Iyer, A case study on applying formal methods to medical devices: computer-aided resuscitation algorithm, *International Journal on Software Tools for Technology Transfer*, Vol. 5 No. 4 (May 2004)

[73]   Johnson, C.W., *A Handbook of Incident and Accident Reporting*, University of Glasgow Press, Glasgow, Scotland (October 2003)
         http://www.dcs.gla.ac.uk/~johnson/book/

[74]   Jones, C., *Systematic Software Development Using VDM*, Prentice Hall (1986)

[75]   Kelly, T.P., *A Systematic Approach to Safety Case Management*, Proceedings SAE 2004 World Congress, Detroit, MI (2004)

[76]   Kelly, T.P., Arguing Safety — A Systematic Approach to Managing Safety Cases, D. Phil Thesis, University of York, U.K. (September 1998)

[77]   Knight, J., The Glass Cockpit, *IEEE Computer*, Vol. 40, No. 9 (September 2007)

[78]   Knight J.C., A.G. Cass, A.M. Fernandez, and K.G. Wika, *Testing a Safety-Critical Application*, ISSTA `94, International Symposium on Software Testing and Analysis (workshop section), Seattle, WA (August 1994)

[79]   Knight, J. and M. Dunn, Software quality through domain-driven certification, *Annals of Software Engineering*, Vol. 5 (1998)

[80]   Knight, J. and N. Leveson, An Experimental Evaluation of the Assumption of Independence in Multiversion Programming, *IEEE Transactions on Software Engineering*, Vol. 12, No. 1 (January 1986)

[81]   Knight, J. and N. Leveson, The Consistent Comparison Problem in N-Version Software, *IEEE Transactions on Software Engineering*, Vol. 15, No. 11, (November 1989)

[82]   Laitenberger, O., Cost-effective Detection of Software Defects through Perspective-based Inspections, *Journal of Empirical Software Engineering*, Vol. 6 (2001)

[83] Lamport, L., R. Shostak, and M. Pease, The Byzantine Generals Problem, *ACM Transactions on Programming Languages and Systems*, Vol. 4, No. 3 (July 1982)

[84] Leveson, N., *Safeware: System Safety and Computers*, Addision Wesley, (1995)

[85] Leveson, N. and P. Harvey, Software fault tree analysis, *Journal of Systems and Software*, Vol. 3, No. 2 (1983)

[86] Leveson, N., M. Heimdahl, H. Hildreth, and J. Reese, Requirements Specification for Process-Control Systems, *IEEE Transactions on Software Engineering*, Vol. 20, No. 9 (1994)

[87] Leveson, N. and J. Stolzy, Safety Analysis Using Petri Nets, *IEEE Transactions on Software Engineering*, Vol. 13, No. 3 (1987)

[88] Leveson, N.G. and C.S. Turner, An Investigation of the Therac-25 Accidents, *IEEE Computer*, Vol. 26, No. 7 (July 1993)

[89] Lions, J.L., *Ariane 5 Flight 501 Failure, Report by the Inquiry Board* http://esamultimedia.esa.int/docs/esa-x-1819eng.pdf

[90] Littlewood, B., The Littlewood-Verrall model for software reliability compared with some rivals, *Journal of Systems and Software*, Vol. 1, pp. 251-258 (1979-1980)

[91] Luckham, D., F.W. von Henke, B. Krieg-Brueckner, O. Owe, *ANNA: A Language for Annotating Ada Programs*, Springer-Verlag Lecture Notes in Computer Science 260 (1987)

[92] Mackall, D., *Development and Flight Test Experiences With a Flight-Crucial Digital Control System*, Technical Report NASA TP-2857, Research Engineering, NASA Dryden Flight Research Center (1988)

[93] Mack, M.J., W. M. Sauer, S. B. Swaney, and B. G. Mealey, IBM POWER6 Reliability, *IBM Journal of Research and Development*, Vol. 51, No. 6 (2007) http://www.research.ibm.com/journal/rd/516/mack.html

[94] *Mars Climate Orbiter, Mishap Investigation Board Phase I Report* ftp://ftp.hq.nasa.gov/pub/pao/reports/1999/MCO_report.pdf

[95] Mathworks Simulink http://www.mathworks.com/products/simulink/

[96] Mills, H., R. Linger, and A. Hevner, *Principles of Information System Analysis and Design*, Academic Press, Inc. (1986)

[97] Motor Industry Software Reliability Association, *MISRA-C:2004 Guidelines for the Use of the C Language in Critical Systems*
http://www.misra-c2.org/

[98] Myers, E. and J. Knight, An Improved Software Inspection Technique and an Empirical Evaluation of Its Effectiveness, *Communications of the ACM*, Vol. 36, No. 11, pp. 50-61 (November, 1993)

[99] National Highway Transportation Administration, *Fatality Analysis Reporting System Encyclopedia*
http://www-fars.nhtsa.dot.gov/Main/index.aspx

[100] National Transportation Board, *Aviation Accident Statistics*
http://www.ntsb.gov/aviation/stats.htm

[101] National Transportation Safety Board, *Aircraft Accident Report: Controlled Flight into Terrain Korean Air Flight 801, Boeing 747-300, HL7468, Nimitz Hill, Guam, August 6, 1997*, NTSB No. AAR-00/01
http://www.ntsb.gov/publictn/2000/AAR0001.htm

[102] Neumann, P., Risks to the Public, *ACM SIGSOFT, Software Engineering Notes*, Vol. 15, No. 2, page 11ff (April 1990)

[103] Parnas, D. and D. Weiss, *Active Design Reviews: Principles and Practices*, International Conference on Software Engineering, London, U.K. (1985)

[104] Patterson, D., G. Gibson, and R. Katz, *A Case for Redundant Arrays of Inexpensive Disks (RAID)*, Proceedings of the ACM International Conference on Management of Data (SIGMOD), Chicago, IL (1988)

[105] Petroski, H., *To Engineer Is Human: The Role of Failure in Successful Design*, St. Martin's Press (1985)

[106] Pinheiro, E., W. Weber, and L. Barroso, *Failure Trends in a Large Disk Drive Population*, FAST '07: 5th USENIX Conference on File and USENIX Association Storage Technologies (2007)

[107] Porter, A., et al., An Experiment to Assess the Cost-Benefits of Code Inspections in Large Scale Software Development, *IEEE Transactions on Software Engineering*, Vol. 23, No. 6 (June 1997)

[108] Potter, B., J. Sinclair, and D. Till, *An Introduction to Formal Specification and Z — Second Edition*, Prentice Hall (1996)

[109] PQRA, http://www.programmingresearch.com

[110] Praxis High Integrity Systems
http://www.spark.com

[111] Praxis High Integrity Systems, *SPARK Ada Reference Manual*
http://www.sparkada.com/downloads/SPARK95.pdf

[112] Prowell, S., C. Trammell, R. Linger, and J. Poore, *Cleanroom Software Engineering: Technology and Process*, SEI Series in Software Engineering (1995)

[113] Randell, B., The Colossus, in *A History of Computing in the Twentieth Century* (N. Metropolis, J. Howlett and G. C. Rota, Eds.), pp. 47-92, Academic Press, New York (1980)

[114] Randell, B., System Structure for Software Fault Tolerance, *IEEE Transactions on Software Engineering*, Vol. SE-1, No. 2, pp. 220-232 (1975)

[115] Random House, *Dictionary of the English Language*, Second Edition, unabridged (1987)

[116] Redmill, F., M. Chudleigh, and J. Catmur, *System Safety: HAZOP and Software HAZOP*, John Wiley (1999)

[117] Redmill, F., *ALARP Explored*, Technical Report CS-TR-1197, Department of Computing Science, University of Newcastle upon Tyne (March 2010)

[118] Report of the Loss of the Mars Polar Lander and Deep Space 2 Missions
ftp://ftp.hq.nasa.gov/pub/pao/reports/2000/2000_mpl_report_1.pdf
ftp://ftp.hq.nasa.gov/pub/pao/reports/2000/2000_mpl_report_2.pdf
ftp://ftp.hq.nasa.gov/pub/pao/reports/2000/2000_mpl_report_3.pdf
ftp://ftp.hq.nasa.gov/pub/pao/reports/2000/2000_mpl_report_4.pdf
ftp://ftp.hq.nasa.gov/pub/pao/reports/2000/2000_mpl_report_5.pdf

[119] RCM, Integrated Safety Case Development Environment, ISCaDE
http://www.iscade.co.uk

[120] RTCA/DO-178B/ED-12B, *Software Considerations in Airborne Systems and Equipment,* Federal Aviation Administration software standard, RTCA Inc. (December 1992)

[121] RTCA/DO-248, *Final Report for Clarification of DO-178B, "Software Considerations in Airborne Systems and Equipment,"* Prepared by SC-190, (October 12, 2001)

[122] Rushby, J., Kernels for Safety?, in *Safe and Secure Computing Systems*, T. Anderson, Ed., Blackwell Scientific Publications (1989)

[123] SAE International, *ARP 5580, Recommended Failure Modes and Effects Analysis (FMEA) Practices for Non-Automobile Applications*
http://www.sae.org/technical/standards/ARP5580

[124] SAE International, J1739: Potential Failure Mode and Effects Analysis in Design (Design FMEA), Potential Failure Mode and Effects Analysis in

Manufacturing and Assembly Processes (Process FMEA)
http://www.sae.org/technical/standards/J1739_200901

[125] Schneier, B., Attack Trees, *Dr. Dobbs Journal* (December 1999)
http://www.schneier.com/paper-attacktrees-ddj-ft.html

[126] Schneider, F., Byzantine Generals in Action: Implementing Fail-Stop Processors, *ACM Transactions on Computer Systems*, Vol. 2, No. 2, pp. 45-154 (May 1984)

[127] Schneider, F. and R. Schlichting, Fail-Stop Processors: An Approach to Designing Fault Tolerant Computing Systems, *ACM Transactions on Computing Systems*, Vol. 1, No. 3, pp. 222-238 (August 1983)

[128] Schonberg, E., *Comparing Ada With C and C++*,
http://www.adaic.org/whyada/ada-vs-c/ada-vs-c.html

[129] Schroeder, B, and G. Gibson, *Disk failures in the real world: What does an MTTF of 1,000,000 hours mean to you?*, FAST '07: 5th USENIX Conference on File and USENIX Association Storage Technologies (2007)

[130] Selby, R., V. Basili, and F.T. Baker, Cleanroom Software Development: An Empirical Evaluation, *IEEE Transactions on Software Engineering*, Vol. 13, No. 12 (1987)

[131] Siewiorek, D. and R. Swarz, *Reliable Computer Systems: Design and Evaluation*, Digital Press, Newton, MA (1998)

[132] Software Rejuvenation
http://srejuv.ee.duke.edu/

[133] Spin model checker
http://spinroot.com

[134] Spivey, J.M., *The Z Notation: A Reference Manual*
http://spivey.oriel.ox.ac.uk/mike/zrm/

[135] Splint — Secure Programming Lint
http://www.splint.org/

[136] SRI International, PVS Specification and Verification System
http://pvs.csl.sri.com/

[137] Sutton, J. and B. Carré, (eds.), *Achieving High Integrity at Low Cost: A Constructive Approach*, Elsevier (1997)

[138] The System Safety Society
http://www.system-safety.org/

[139] Toulmin, S., *The Uses of Argument*, Cambridge University Press (1958)

[140] U.K. Minstry of Defence, *Safety Management Requirements for Defence Systems*, Defence Standard 00-56 (2007)

[141] U.K. Civil Aviation Authority, *CAP 670 Air Traffic Services Safety Requirements* (2009)

[142] University of York, Department of Computer Science, GSN Editing Add-on for Microsoft Visio
http://www.cs.york.ac.uk/~tpk/gsn/gsnaddoninstaller.zip

[143] U.S. Department of Energy, *Advisory Notice, L-117: The Code Red Worm*
http://www.ciac.org/ciac/bulletins/l-117.shtml

[144] von Neumann, J., *First Draft of a Report on the EDVAC, Contract No. W-670-ORD-492*, Moore School of Electrical Engineering, Univ. of Penn., Philadelphia (1945)

[145] Vouk, M.A., *On Back-To-Back Testing*, Computer Assurance, 1988, Gaithersburg, MD (1988)

[146] Weaver, R.A., The Safety of Software – Constructing and Assuring Arguments, D. Phil. Thesis, Department of Computer Science, University of York, U.K. (September 2003)

[147] Weimer, W., T. Nguyen, C. Le Goues, and S. Forrest, *Automatically Finding Patches Using Genetic Programming*, International Conference on Software Engineering (ICSE), Vancouver, BC (2009)

[148] Wika, K., *Safety Kernel Enforcement of Software Safety Policies*, Ph.D. dissertation, Department of Computer Science, University of Virginia (May 1995)
http://www.cs.virginia.edu/dissertations/9504.pdf

[149] Wika, K. and J. Knight, *On the Enforcement of Software Safety Policies*, 10th Annual IEEE Conference on Computer Assurance (COMPASS '95), Gaithersburg, MD (June 1995)

[150] Wikipedia, *As Low As Reasonably Practicable*
http://en.wikipedia.org/wiki/ALARP#Carrot_diagrams

[151] Wikipedia, *List of tools for static code analysis*
http://en.wikipedia.org/wiki/
List_of_tools_for_static_code_analysis

[152] Wikipedia, *The Pentium FDIV Bug*
http://en.wikipedia.org/wiki/Pentium_FDIV_bug

[153] Wikipedia, *U.S.S. Yorktown (CG-48)*
http://en.wikipedia.org/wiki/USS_Yorktown_(CG-48)

[154] Wordsworth, J., *Software Development With Z*, Addison Wesley (1994)

[155] Yeh, Y.C., *Safety Critical Avionics for the 777 Primary Flight Controls System*, 20th Digital Avionics Systems Conference, Daytona Beach, FL (2001)

[156] Yu, W., A Software Fault Prevention Approach in Coding and Root Cause Analysis, *Bell Labs Technical Journal* (April-June, 1998)

Index

Printed in the United States
by Baker & Taylor Publisher Services